VISUAL QUICKSTART GUIDE

MAC OS X 10.3 PANTHER

Maria Langer

 Peachpit Press

Visual QuickStart Guide
Mac OS X 10.3 Panther
Maria Langer

Peachpit Press
1249 Eighth Street
Berkeley, CA 94710
510-524-2178 • 800-283-9444
510-524-2221 (fax)

Find us on the World Wide Web at: www.peachpit.com

Peachpit Press is a division of Pearson Education

Editors: Clifford Colby, Karen Reichstein
Technical Editor: Clifford Colby, Victor Gavenda
Indexer: Emily Glossbrenner
Cover Design: The Visual Group
Cover Production: Nathalie Valette
Production: Maria Langer, Connie Jeung-Mills

Colophon

This book was produced with Adobe InDesign 2.0 and Adobe Photoshop 7.0 on a Power Macintosh G4. The fonts used were Utopia, Meta Plus, and PIXymbols Command. Screenshots were created using Snapz Pro X on an eMac. Screenshots reprinted by permission of Apple Computer, Inc.

Notice of Rights

Notice of Liability

Trademarks

ISBN 0-321-21351-3

9 8 7 6 5 4 3 2

Printed and bound in the United States of America.

Dedication

To Connie Jeung-Mills

(Aren't you glad you didn't
have to lay this one out?)

Thanks!

To Cliff Colby, for his guidance in preparing the outline and helping with the editing for this book. Cliff helped me take two books and merge them into one—not as easy a task as we originally thought. (We won't discuss the commas.) Also, a big thanks for Cliff for telling me that he wasn't panicking—even though I knew he was.

To Karen Reichstein, for more editing. Karen caught the kinds of things that neither Cliff nor I ever could, helping to make the grammar and typing in the final manuscript pretty darn close to perfect. (I'm sure we'll find a few boo-boos that slipped through the cracks after the book is in print.)

To Victor Gavenda, for his assistance with a few technical questions I had during the writing process. Victor got me quick answers when I needed them.

To Connie Jeung-Mills, for yet another smooth project. I think I'm getting the hang of the re-ragging thing now...I catch lots of problems before Connie ever sees them.

To the rest of the folks at Peachpit Press, for doing what they do so well.

To Mike Shebanek at Apple Computer, Inc., for getting me the software I needed to write this book. Without his help, it would be impossible for me to finish this book in time for Panther's release.

To the developers at Apple, for continuing to refine the world's best operating system. In my opinion, this is the best version of Mac OS so far!

To the folks at Ambrosia Software, for developing and continuing to update Snapz Pro X. I could not have taken the 2,000+ screen shots in this book without this great software program.

To Alta Waddell and Gary Smith, for taking some of my hours at the airport during crunch week. You'll never know how much I appreciate your help.

And to Mike, for the usual reasons.

www.marialanger.com

Table of Contents

TABLE OF CONTENTS

Introduction
to Mac OS X

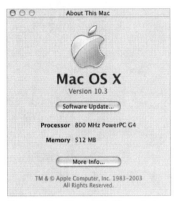

Figure 1 The About This Mac window for Mac OS X 10.3.

✔ Tips

- The "X" in "Mac OS X" is pronounced "ten."

- This book combines revised material from *Mac OS X 10.2: Visual QuickStart Guide* and *Mac OS X 10.2 Advanced: Visual QuickPro Guide*. You can find additional material that didn't make it into this book on the book's companion Web site, www.marialanger.com/booksites/macosx/.

Introduction

Mac OS X 10.3 (**Figure 1**) is the latest version of the computer operating system that put the phrase *graphic user interface* in everyone's vocabulary. With Mac OS, you can point, click, and drag to work with files, applications, and utilities. Because the same intuitive interface is utilized throughout the system, you'll find that a procedure that works in one program works in virtually all the others.

This Visual QuickStart Guide will help you learn Mac OS X 10.3 by providing step-by-step instructions, plenty of illustrations, and a generous helping of tips. On these pages, you'll find everything you need to know to get up and running quickly with Mac OS X—and a lot more!

This book was designed for page flipping. Use the thumb tabs, index, or table of contents to find the topics for which you need help. If you're brand new to Mac OS, however, I recommend that you begin by reading at least the first two chapters. In them, you'll find basic information about techniques you'll use every day with your computer.

If you're interested in information about new Mac OS X features, be sure to browse through this **Introduction**. It'll give you a good idea of what you can expect to see on your computer.

New Features in Mac OS X 10.3

Mac OS X 10.3 (Panther) is a major revision to Mac OS X. Here's a look at some of the new and revised features you can expect to find.

✔ Tip

- Many of these features are covered in this book.

Finder

- The new Sidebar, which appears in Finder windows (**Figure 2**), Open dialogs (**Figure 3**), and Save dialogs (**Figure 4**), makes it easy to access the volumes, files, and folders you use most. This feature, which replaces the Favorites feature in previous versions of Mac OS X, is fully customizable.

- In the Open and Save dialogs (**Figures 3** and **4**), you can now view files in list or column view and sort files by name or the date they were modified.

- The Finder now includes a fully integrated Network browser, which makes it possible to access networked volumes from within Finder windows (**Figure 5**).

Figure 2 The new Sidebar makes it easy to access the volumes, files, and folders you use most.

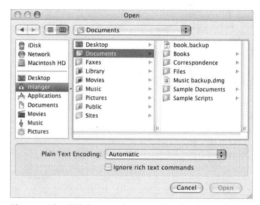

Figure 3 The Sidebar can be found in the Open dialog, which has been revised.

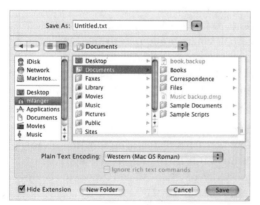

Figure 4 The Save dialog was revised to include the Sidebar and other features.

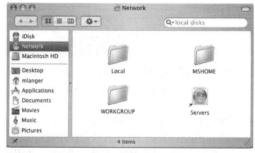

Figure 5 The Finder's Network browser makes it possible to access network volumes from within Finder windows.

Figure 6 The Search field in Finder windows now finds files more quickly.

Figure 7 The new Action pop-up menu offers commands for selected items in Finder windows.

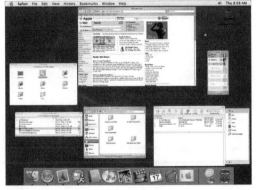

Figure 8 Exposé makes it possible to see into all windows, no matter how cluttered your screen is.

◆ The Search field in Finder windows makes finding files faster than ever. Choose where you want to search, enter part of the file name, and you'll immediately see a list of files that match your search criteria (**Figure 6**).

◆ The new Action pop-up menu in the Finder window toolbar offers commands for working with selected items within the window (**Figure 7**).

◆ The brand new Exposé feature makes it possible to see all open windows at once (**Figure 8**)—no matter how cluttered your screen is. It can also instantly display all windows in the current application or the items on your desktop.

◆ The Finder's new Archive command enables you to create .zip format compressed archive files.

iDisk & .Mac

◆ iDisk is now fully integrated with the Finder.

◆ Synchronizing your iDisk makes it possible to access iDisk items, even when you are not connected to the Internet. Your computer will automatically update your iDisk when you connect.

◆ .Mac includes new features for synchronizing your Address Book entries and Safari bookmarks, so you can access this information from any computer with an Internet connection.

NEW FEATURES IN MAC OS X 10.3

Printing & Faxing

◆ Printing improvements include the ability to schedule print jobs from within the Print dialog (**Figure 9**), the ability to print cover pages, and the return of Desktop Printing, which was available in Mac OS 9.2 and earlier.

◆ You can now fax documents from within the Print dialog (**Figure 10**). The fax feature is fully integrated with Address Book for sending faxes.

◆ You can also receive faxes on your computer and have them automatically saved, e-mailed, and/or printed when received.

Multiple Users

◆ The new Fast User Switching feature (**Figure 11**) makes it possible for a user to log in to his account on the computer without another user logging out. This means you don't have to close documents and quit applications when someone else needs to use the computer.

Security

◆ The Finder's new Secure Empty Trash command completely erases files, making them virtually impossible to unerase, even with powerful third-party software.

◆ The new FileVault feature makes it possible to encrypt your Home folder.

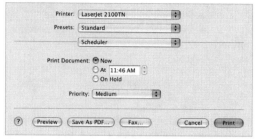

Figure 9 You can now schedule print jobs when you print them.

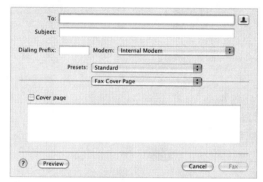

Figure 10 You can fax documents from within the Print dialog.

Figure 11
The Fast User Switching feature makes it quick and easy to log in to your account without logging out someone else.

Figure 12 The new Safari Web browser.

Figure 13 iChat AV makes video conferencing easy!

Figure 14 Font Book's main window.

Applications

◆ The new Safari Web browser (**Figure 12**) offers a variety of features to make surfing the Net quicker and easier.

◆ Mail has been improved to include better message threading, drag-and-drop addressing, safe addressing, and response history.

◆ iChat AV (**Figure 13**) makes it possible to conduct audio and video conferences, as well as plain old textual chats.

◆ iTunes now gives you access to the iTunes Music Store, where you can buy music to play on your computer, iPod, or MP3 player.

◆ Preview's PDF-viewing features have been improved to make it faster and more powerful. Preview now supports indexed text searching, URLs, text copying, and the ability to view PostScript and EPS files.

◆ Disk Utility now includes the features of Disk Copy, which is no longer part of Mac OS X.

◆ Font Book makes it easier to install, preview, organize, and activate the fonts you need. Its Character Palette feature enables you to preview and select just the right variation of a character.

Working with Windows

◆ The Finder's Network browser can display SMB servers on a Windows network.

◆ Mac OS users can easily share files and printers with Windows users.

Setting Up Mac OS X 10.3

Setting Up Mac OS X 10.3

Before you can use Mac OS X, you must install it on your computer and configure it to work the way you need it to. The steps you need to complete to do this depend on the software currently installed on your computer.

Use the Mac OS X 10.3 installer to do one of the following:

▲ Update an existing Mac OS X installation to Mac OS X 10.3.

▲ Install Mac OS X 10.3 to replace an existing Mac OS X installation.

▲ Install Mac OS X 10.3 on a computer with a Mac OS 9.2 or earlier installation and no version of Mac OS X.

Then restart your computer and use the Mac OS Setup Assistant to configure Mac OS X.

This chapter explains how to properly install and configure Mac OS X 10.3 on your computer.

✔ Tips

■ Not sure which version of Mac OS is installed on your computer? I explain how to find out on the next page.

■ To run Mac OS 9-compatible applications in the Classic environment, Mac OS 9.1 or later must also be installed on your computer. The Classic environment is discussed in **Chapter 16**.

Determining Which Mac OS Versions Are Installed

In order to know which installation and configuration steps you need to perform, you must first learn which versions of Mac OS are installed. There are several ways to do this; the easiest is to consult the Startup Disk control panel (on Mac OS 9.2.2 or earlier) or the Startup Disk pane of System Preferences (on Mac OS X or later).

✔ Tips

- If your computer is brand new and you haven't started it yet, chances are you have Mac OS X 10.3 and Mac OS 9.2 (or later versions of each) installed. When you start your computer, it'll display the Mac OS Setup assistant. Skip ahead to the section titled "Configuring Mac OS X 10.3" later in this chapter.

- A quick way to tell whether your computer is currently running Mac OS 9.2 or earlier or Mac OS X or later is to consult the Apple menu icon on the far left end of the menu bar. A six-color apple appears on Mac OS 9.2 or earlier; a blue 3-D-looking apple appears on Mac OS X or later.

To check the Startup Disk control panel on Mac OS 9.2 or earlier

1. Choose Apple > Control Panels > Startup Disk (**Figure 1**) to display the Startup Disk control panel.

2. If necessary, click the triangle beside the name of your hard disk to display the System folders installed on your computer (**Figures 2** and **3**). The Version column indicates which versions of Mac OS are installed.

3. Click the Startup Disk control panel's close box to dismiss it.

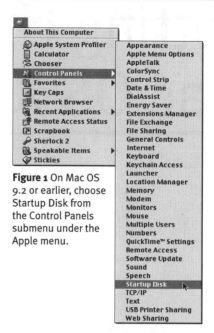

Figure 1 On Mac OS 9.2 or earlier, choose Startup Disk from the Control Panels submenu under the Apple menu.

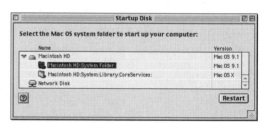

Figure 2 Here's what the Startup Disk control panel might look like with Mac OS 9.1 and Mac OS X installed...

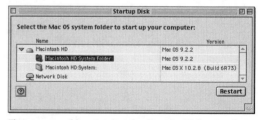

Figure 3 ... and here's what the Startup Disk control panel might look like with Mac OS 9.2.2 and Mac OS X 10.2.8 installed.

Figure 4
Choose System Preferences from the Apple menu to display System Preferences.

Figure 5 The System Preferences window looks like this in Mac OS X 10.0....

Figure 6 ... and like this in Mac OS X 10.2.8.

Figure 7 Here's what the Startup Disk pane might look like with Mac OS 9.1 and Mac OS X 10.0 installed ...

To check the Startup Disk preferences pane on Mac OS X or later

1. Choose Apple > System Preferences (**Figure 4**) to display the System Preferences window (**Figures 5** and **6**).

2. Click the Startup Disk icon to display the Startup Disk preferences pane (**Figures 7** and **8**). The installed versions of Mac OS appear beneath each System folder icon.

3. Choose System Preferences > Quit System Preferences (**Figure 9**), or press ⌃⌘Q to dismiss System Preferences.

Figure 8 ... and here's what it might look like with Mac OS 9.2.2 and Mac OS X 10.2.8 installed.

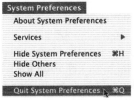

Figure 9
Choose Quit System Preferences from the System Preferences menu to dismiss System Preferences.

Installing Mac OS X 10.3

Mac OS X's installer application handles all aspects of a Mac OS X installation. It restarts your computer from the Mac OS Installer CD-ROM, then displays step-by-step instructions to install Mac OS X 10.3 from its two install discs. When the installation process is finished, the installer automatically restarts your computer from your hard disk and displays the Mac OS Setup Assistant so you can configure Mac OS X 10.3 for your use.

This part of the chapter explains how to install and configure Mac OS X. Unfortunately, since there does not appear to be a way to take screen shots of the Mac OS X installation and configuration procedure, this part of the chapter won't be very "visual." Follow along closely and you'll get all the information you need to complete the installation and configuration process without any problems.

✔ Tips

- The installation instructions in this chapter assume you know basic Mac OS techniques, such as pointing, clicking, double-clicking, dragging, and selecting items from a menu. If you're brand new to the Mac and don't know any of these techniques, skip ahead to **Chapter 2,** which discusses Mac OS basics.

- You can click the Go Back button in an installer window at any time during installation to change options in a previous window.

- Remember, you can skip using the Mac OS X 10.3 installer if Mac OS X 10.3 or later is already installed on your computer. Consult the section titled "Determining Which Mac OS Versions Are Installed" earlier in this chapter to see what is installed on your computer.

Figure 10
When you insert the first Mac OS X User Install disc, its icon appears on the desktop...

Figure 11 ...and a Welcome to Mac OS X window opens.

Figure 12 The Mac OS X installer prompts you to restart your computer.

Figure 13 If you're upgrading an existing installation of Mac OS X, you'll have to enter an administrator name and password to complete the installation.

Figure 14 The installer comes with a file full of important information about Mac OS X 10.3 compatibility and other issues.

To launch the Mac OS X installer & select an installation language

1. Insert the Mac OS X User Install 1 disc in your CD-ROM drive. A Mac OS X Install Disc 1 icon should appear on your desktop (**Figure 10**), along with a Welcome to Mac OS window (**Figure 11**).

2. Double-click the Install Mac OS X icon.

3. An Install Mac OS X dialog appears (**Figure 12**). Click Restart.

4. If you're using any version of Mac OS X, an authenticate dialog like the one in **Figure 13** may appear. Enter the Name and password for an administrator and click OK.

5. Wait while Mac OS X and the installer load from the CD-ROM disc.

6. In the Select Language window that appears, select the primary language you want to use with the installer and Mac OS X.

7. Click Continue.

✔ Tips

- It's a good idea to open and read the file named Read Before You Install.pdf that's included on Mac OS X Install Disc 1 (**Figure 11**). This document (**Figure 14**) contains important information about compatibility and other installation issues.

- The Authenticate dialog (**Figure 13**) prevents someone without administrator privileges from installing system software. This is especially important on a computer used by more than one person.

- These instructions assume you're installing in English. Obviously, the onscreen instructions will be different if you're installing in another language!

LAUNCHING THE MAC OS X INSTALLER

To read important information about the installer & Mac OS X

1. Read the information in the Introduction ("Welcome to the Mac OS X Installer") window.

2. Click Continue.

3. Read the information in the Read Me ("Important Information") window.

4. Click Continue.

5. Read the information in the License ("Software License Agreement") window.

6. Click Continue.

7. Click the Agree button in the dialog sheet that appears.

✔ Tips

- Read the information in the "Important Information" window carefully! It provides important, late-breaking news about installing Mac OS, including compatibility information and special instructions not included in this book.

- If necessary, in step 5 you can use the pop-up menu to select a different language for the license agreement.

- In step 7, if you click the Disagree button, you will not be able to install Mac OS X.

To select a destination disk

1. In the Select Destination ("Select a Destination") window, click to select the icon for the disk on which you want to install Mac OS X. A green arrow appears on the disk icon. The installer automatically knows if it has to upgrade an existing Mac OS X installation or install Mac OS X 10.3 from scratch.

2. To set advanced installation options, click the Options button. A dialog sheet offers up to three options, depending on what is already installed on the destination disk:

    ▲ **Upgrade Mac OS X** upgrades an existing Mac OS X installation to Mac OS X 10.3.

    ▲ **Archive and Install** moves existing Mac OS X System files to a folder named Previous System and installs Mac OS X 10.3 from scratch. You might want to use this option if you suspect there's something wrong with your Mac OS X installation and you want to force the installer to start fresh. If you select this option, you can turn on the Preserve Users and Networks Settings check box to automatically move all existing Mac OS X settings to the new installation. This also skips the Setup Assistant.

    ▲ **Erase and Install** completely erases the destination disk and installs Mac OS X 10.3 from scratch. Use this option only after backing up your data, since all data on the disk will be lost. If you select this option, choose a disk format from the "Format disk as" pop-up menu; your options are Mac OS Extended and Unix File System.

3. Click Continue.

✔ Tips

■ A note beneath the disk icons indicates how much space is available on each disk. You can see how much space a Mac OS X installation takes by looking at the bottom of the window. Make sure the disk you select has enough space for the installation.

■ Step 2 is optional. If you follow step 2 and don't know what to select, click Cancel to use the default installation option.

■ In step 2, if you select the Erase and Install option and don't know what disk format to choose from the pop-up menu, choose Mac OS Extended (Journaled). (If you wanted the UNIX File System option, you'd know it.)

SELECTING A DESTINATION DISK

To complete the installation

1. In the Installation Type ("Easy Install")
   window, you have two options:

   ▲ To perform a standard Mac OS X 10.3
     installation, click the Install button.

   ▲ To perform a custom Mac OS X 10.3
     installation, click the Customize
     button. In the Custom Install window
     that appears, toggle check marks to
     specify which Mac OS X components
     should be installed. Then click Install.

2. Wait while software from the first install
   disc is installed. A status area in the
   Installing ("Install Software") window
   tells you what the installer is doing and
   may indicate how much longer the
   installation will take.

3. When the installer is finished with the
   first install disc, it displays a message
   telling you that the software was successfully installed. Click the Restart button or
   wait until the computer restarts automatically.

4. When the computer has finished restarting, it ejects the disc and prompts you to
   insert the second disc. Insert the disc in
   the drive and close the drive.

5. Wait while software from the second
   install disc is installed.

6. When the installer is finished, it ejects the
   disc, restarts the computer, and displays
   the first screen of the setup application.

✔ Tip

■ The Customize option is provided for
  Mac OS X "Power Users" and should only
  be utilized if you have a complete understanding of Mac OS X components and
  features.

COMPLETING THE INSTALLATION

Configuring Mac OS X 10.3

When your computer restarts after a Mac OS X installation, the Mac OS X Setup Assistant automatically appears. This program uses a simple question-and-answer process to get information about you and the way you use your computer. The information you provide is automatically entered in the various System Preferences panes of Mac OS X to configure your computer for Mac OS X.

✔ Tips

- If you just bought your Macintosh and Mac OS X is installed, the first time you start your computer, you'll see the Mac OS X Setup Assistant described here. Follow these instructions to configure your computer.

- If the Mac OS X Setup Assistant does not appear, Mac OS X is already configured. You can skip this section.

To set basic configuration options

1. In the Welcome window that appears after installing Mac OS X and restarting, select the name of the country you're in. Click Continue.

2. In the Personalize Your Settings window, select a keyboard layout. Click Continue.

3. In the Your Apple ID window, select one of the three options:

   ▲ **My Apple ID is** enables you to enter your Apple User Name and Password, which you were assigned if you have registered to use Apple's Internet-based support features or if you have a .Mac account. If you select this option, be sure to fill in the boxes with your Apple ID information.

   ▲ **Create an Apple ID for me** tells Mac OS X to create an Apple ID for you as part of the registration process. An Apple ID enables you to make one-click purchases with iTunes, iPhoto, and the Apple Store. It also gives you a 60-day trial membership to .Mac.

   ▲ **Don't create an Apple ID for me** skips the Apple ID process.

4. In the Registration Information window, fill in the form. You can press (Tab) to move from one field to another. Click Continue.

5. In the A Few More Questions window, use the pop-up menus and radio buttons to answer a few marketing questions. Click Continue.

5. Read the information in the Thank You window, and click Continue.

6. In the Create Your Account window, fill in the form to enter information to set up your Mac OS X account. Click Continue.

7. Continue following the instructions in one of the following sections:

   ▲ "To set up Mac OS X to use a new EarthLink Internet account"

   ▲ "To set up Mac OS X to use your existing Internet service"

   ▲ "To skip Internet setup"

✔ Tips

■ If your country is not listed in step 1, turn on the Show All check box to display more options.

■ In step 2, you can turn on the Show All check box to show additional keyboard layouts.

■ In step 3, you can learn about Apple's privacy policy by clicking the Privacy button. When you're finished reading the information in the dialog sheet that appears, click OK to dismiss it and return to the Registration Information window.

■ I tell you about iTunes and iPhoto in **Chapter 8** and about .Mac in **Chapter 12**.

To set up Mac OS X to use a new EarthLink Internet account

1. In the Get Internet Ready window, select one of the following radio buttons:

   ▲ **I'd like a free trial account with EarthLink** enables you to set up a free trial account with EarthLink.

   ▲ **I have a code for a special offer from EarthLink** enables you to set up an account with EarthLink using a special offer code you already have.

2. Click Continue.

3. In the EarthLink As Your Provider window, enter your name, address, and billing information. If you have a special offer code, be sure to enter it in the appropriate box.

4. Click Continue.

5. Skip ahead to the section titled "To get an Apple ID" to continue.

✔ Tip

■ EarthLink is an Internet Service Provider (ISP). I tell you more about ISPs in **Chapter 11**, which covers Internet features and software.

To set up Mac OS X to use your existing Internet service

1. In the Get Internet Ready window, select the radio button for I'll use my existing Internet service, and click Continue.

2. In the How Do You Connect window, select the radio button for your connection method. Your options are Telephone modem, Cable modem, DSL modem, Local network (Ethernet), or Local network (AirPort Wireless).

3. Click Continue.

4. Follow the instructions in one of the next four sections for your connection method.

✔ Tips

- You can only select the AirPort Wireless option if you have an AirPort card installed in your computer.

- You can get all of the information you need for setup from your ISP or network administrator.

To set up a telephone modem connection

1. In the Set Up Existing Service window, enter information about your ISP connection, including your user name, password, ISP phone number, and any dialog prefix required to get an outside line.

2. Click Continue.

3. In the Set Up Your Modem window, select your modem connection port and make and model.

4. Click Continue.

5. Skip ahead to the section titled "To get an Apple ID" to continue.

To set up a cable or DSL modem connection

1. In the Your Internet Connection window, select an option from the TCP/IP Connection Type pop-up menu. The option you select will determine what fields appear beneath it.

2. Enter IP address, subnet mask, router address, DNS hosts, domain name, and proxy server information as required.

3. Click Continue.

4. Skip ahead to the section titled "To get an Apple ID" to continue.

To set up a local area network connection

1. The Your Local Area Network window may appear to tell you that your network configuration has been obtained from a DHCP server.

   ▲ If you want to use this information, select Yes and click Continue. You can then skip ahead to the section titled "To get an Apple ID or set .Mac options" to continue.

   ▲ If this window does not appear or you don't want to use this information, select No, change the configuration, and click Continue.

2. In the Your Internet Connection window, select an option from the TCP/IP Connection Type pop-up menu. The option you select will determine what fields appear beneath it.

3. Enter IP address, subnet mask, router address, DNS hosts, domain name, and proxy server information as required.

4. Click Continue.

5. Skip ahead to the section titled "To get an Apple ID" to continue.

SETTING UP AN EXISTING INTERNET SERVICE

To skip Internet setup

1. In the Get Internet Ready window, select the radio button for "I'm not ready to connect to the Internet."

2. Click Continue.

3. In the dialog sheet that appears, click OK to confirm that you don't want to set up an Internet connection.

4. In the Register With Apple window, select one of the options:

   ▲ **Register Now** enables you to use your Internet connection to send registration information to Apple. Click Continue.

   ▲ **Register Later** enables you to skip registration for now. Click Continue and skip ahead to the section titled "To set the time zone."

5. In the Your Phone Service window, provide telephone information as requested.

6. Click Continue.

7. In the Set Up Your Modem window, provide modem information.

8. Click Continue.

9. Continue following instructions in the section titled "To get an Apple ID."

SKIPPING INTERNET SETUP

To get an Apple ID

1. If the Your Apple ID window does not appear, skip to step 3.

   or

   In the Your Apple ID window, select one of the options:

   ▲ **Use my .Mac membership** enables you to enter your .Mac user name and password. Click Continue and skip ahead to step 3.

   ▲ **Create my Apple ID** enables you to create a new trial .Mac account. Click Continue.

2. In the Your .Mac Membership window, enter a desired user name, password, password hint, and birthdate information and click Continue.

3. If you indicated earlier in the setup process that you want to set up a new EarthLink account, the Your EarthLink Account window appears. Enter user name, password, and birthdate information to set up a new EarthLink account and click Continue.

4. If you indicated that you want to use an existing Internet service, continue following instructions in the section titled "To set up an e-mail account."

   or

   If you indicated that you wanted to set up an EarthLink account or not set up an Internet connection at all, continue following instructions in the section titled "To send registration information."

✔ Tips

- You can click the Learn More button in the Get .Mac window to display a dialog with more information about .Mac. When you're finished reading about it, click the OK button to dismiss the dialog.

- **Chapter 12** provides more information about .Mac.

To send registration information

1. In the Your Phone Service window, enter your telephone number and provide other information as requested.

2. Click Continue.

3. In the Set Up Your Modem window, modem information.

4. Click Continue.

5. If the You're Ready to Connect window appears, read its contents and click Connect. Then wait while your computer uses its modem to connect to the Internet and exchange registration information with Apple and, if necessary, EarthLink.

6. If you indicated that you want to set up an EarthLink account earlier in the setup process, continue following the instructions in the section titled "To complete EarthLink Setup."

   or

   If you indicated that you want to set up an Apple ID, continue following the instructions in the section titled "To confirm account information."

   or

   If you're using an existing Internet account and existing .Mac membership, continue following instructions in the section titled "To set up an e-mail account."

   or

   If you indicated that you want to skip both the Internet and Apple ID setup, continue following instructions in the section titled "To set the time zone, date, & time."

SENDING REGISTRATION INFORMATION

To complete an EarthLink setup

1. Read the Internet Service Plan window that appears.

2. Click Accept.

3. Read the License Agreement window that appears.

4. Click Accept.

5. In the Choose a Local Number window that appears, select a phone number.

6. Click Continue.

7. In the Choose a Number Format window that appears, choose the dialing format you want to use for the number.

8. Click Continue.

9. Continue following instructions in the section titled "To confirm account information."

To confirm account information

1. In the Account Information dialog that appears, make a note of the information it provides:

   ▲ **Your email address** is the address that's set up with your trial .Mac membership.

   ▲ **Your EarthLink email address** is the address that's set up with your trial EarthLink account.

2. Click Continue.

3. Continue following instructions in the section titled "To set the time zone, date, & time."

COMPLETING EARTHLINK SETUP

To set up an e-mail account

1. If the Set Up Mail window appears, use it to enter information about your e-mail account.

2. Click Continue.

✔ Tip

■ If the Set Up Mail window identifies your .Mac e-mail account and you want to add another account, select the "Add my existing e-mail account" radio button. Then enter information for your account.

To set the time zone, date, & time

1. In the Select Time Zone window, click the map to indicate your time zone.

2. If necessary, choose an option from the pop-up menu to specify the exact time zone by name.

3. Click Continue.

4. If the Set Your Date and Time window appears, use it to set your computer's date and time:

   ▲ To set the date, click today's date on the calendar. (You may have to use the arrow keys beside the name of the month and the year number to set the appropriate month and year first.)

   ▲ To set the time, click the time digits you want to change and type a new entry. Repeat this process to enter the current time, then click Save.

5. Click Continue.

6. Continue following instructions in the section titled "To finish the installation."

✔ Tip

■ In step 4, you can also change the time by dragging the clock's hands and clicking Save when the time is correct.

Figure 15 At the end of the installation, the Mac OS X 10.3 desktop and your Home folder window appear.

Figure 16 Software Update tells you if you need to update any Mac OS X software.

Figure 17 A Previous Systems folder appears on your hard disk if you performed a "clean" installation of Mac OS X 10.3.

To finish the installation

1. In the Thank You window that appears, click Go.

2. The Mac OS X desktop appears with your Home folder window open (**Figure 15**).

✔ Tips

- I explain how to work with the Mac OS Desktop and Finder in **Chapters 2 through 4**.

- The Software Update utility may run right after installing Mac OS X 10.3. If any software updates are available for your computer, a dialog like the one in **Figure 16** appears. I explain how to use Software Update in **Chapter 18**.

- If you chose the Install and Archive option when you installed Mac OS X 10.3, a folder named Previous Systems appears on your hard disk (**Figure 17**). You can move items you need out of that folder and into appropriate locations on your hard disk. Delete this folder if it is no longer needed.

Finder Basics

The Finder & Desktop

The *Finder* is a program that is part of Mac OS. It launches automatically when you start your computer.

The Finder provides a graphic user interface called the *desktop* (**Figure 1**) that you can use to open, copy, delete, list, organize, and perform other operations on computer files.

This chapter provides important instructions for using the Finder and items that appear on the Mac OS X desktop. It's important that you understand how to use these basic Finder techniques, since you'll use them again and again every time you work with your computer.

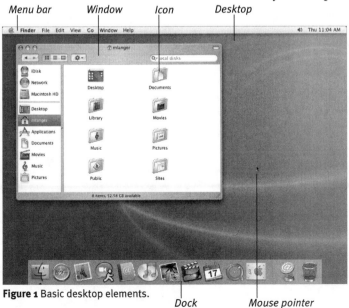

Menu bar   Window   Icon   Desktop

Figure 1 Basic desktop elements.

Dock   Mouse pointer

✔ Tips

- You never have to manually launch the Finder; it always starts automatically.

- Under normal circumstances, you cannot quit the Finder.

- If you're new to Mac OS, don't skip this chapter. It provides the basic information you'll need to use your computer successfully.

The Mouse

Mac OS, like most graphic user interface systems, uses the mouse as an input device. There are several basic mouse techniques you must know to use your computer:

- **Point** to a specific item onscreen.

- **Click** an item to select it.

- **Double-click** an item to open it.

- **Press** an item to activate it.

- **Drag** to move an item or select multiple items.

✔ Tip

- Some computers use either a trackball or a trackpad instead of a mouse.

To point

1. Move the mouse on the work surface or mouse pad.

   or

   Use your fingertips to move the ball of the trackball.

   or

   Move the tip of one finger (usually your forefinger) on the surface of the trackpad.

   The mouse pointer, which usually looks like an arrow (**Figure 2**), moves on your computer screen.

2. When the tip of the mouse pointer's arrow is on the item you want to point to (**Figure 3**), stop moving it.

✔ Tip

- The tip of the mouse pointer is its "business end."

Figure 2 The mouse pointer usually looks like an arrow pointer when you are working in the Finder.

Applications

Figure 3 Move the mouse pointer so the arrow's tip is on the item to which you want to point.

Figure 4
Click to select
an icon...

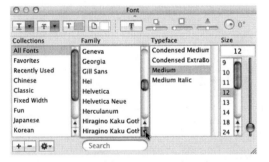

Figure 5 ...or an item in a list.

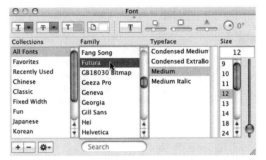

Figure 6 Press a scroll bar arrow to activate it.

Figure 7 Drag to move items
such as folders.

To click

1. Point to the item you want to click.

2. Press (and release) the mouse button once. The item you clicked becomes selected (**Figures 4** and **5**).

To double-click

1. Point to the item you want to double-click.

2. Press (and release) the mouse button twice quickly. The item you double-clicked opens.

✔ Tip

■ Keep the mouse pointer still while double-clicking. If you move the mouse pointer during the double-click process, you may move the item instead of double-clicking it.

To press

1. Point to the item you want to press.

2. Press and hold the mouse button without moving the mouse. The item you are pressing is activated (**Figure 6**).

✔ Tip

■ The press technique is often used when working with scroll bars, as shown in **Figure 6**, where pressing is the same as clicking repeatedly.

To drag

1. Point to the item you want to drag.

2. Press the mouse button down.

3. While holding the mouse button down, move the mouse pointer. The item you are dragging moves (**Figure 7**).

USING THE MOUSE

Menus

The Finder—and most other Mac OS pro-grams—offers menus full of options. There are four types of menus in Mac OS X:

◆ A **pull-down menu** appears on the menu bar at the top of the screen (**Figure 8**).

◆ A **submenu** appears when a menu option with a right-pointing triangle is selected (**Figure 9**).

◆ A **pop-up menu**, which displays a triangle (or arrow), appears within a window (**Figures 10** and **11**).

◆ A **contextual menu** appears when you hold down [Control] while clicking an item (**Figure 12**).

✔ Tips

■ A menu option followed by an ellipsis (…) (**Figure 8**) will display a dialog when chosen. Dialogs are discussed in detail in **Chapter 5**.

■ A menu option that is dimmed or gray cannot be chosen. The commands that are available vary depending on what is selected on the desktop or in a window.

■ A menu option preceded by a check mark (**Figure 8**) is enabled, or "turned on."

■ A menu option followed by a series of keyboard characters (**Figure 8**) has a keyboard shortcut. Keyboard shortcuts are discussed later in this chapter.

■ Contextual menus only display options that apply to the item you are pointing to.

■ In Mac OS X, menus are slightly translu-cent. Although this makes them look cool on screen, it doesn't always look good when illustrated on paper.

Figure 8
The menu bar offers pull-down menus.

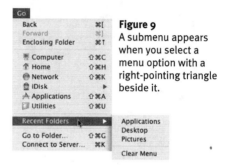

Figure 9
A submenu appears when you select a menu option with a right-pointing triangle beside it.

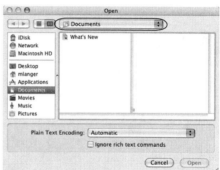

Figure 10 Pop-up menus can appear within dialogs.

Figure 11 To display a pop-up menu, click it.

Figure 12
A contextual menu appears when you hold down [Control] while clicking.

MENUS

Figure 13 Point to the menu name.

Figure 14 Click (or press) to display the menu.

Figure 15 Click (or drag) to choose the menu option you want.

Users

Figure 16 Hold down Control while pointing to an item.

Figure 17 A contextual menu appears when you click.

Figure 18 Click (or drag) to choose the option you want.

To use a menu

1. Point to the name of the menu (**Figure 13**).

2. Click. The menu opens, displaying its options (**Figure 14**).

3. Point to the menu option you want (**Figure 15**).

4. Click to choose the option. The menu disappears.

✔ Tips

- Mac OS X's menus are "sticky menus"— each menu opens and stays open when you click its name.

- To close a menu without choosing an option, click outside the menu.

- This book uses the following notation to indicate menu commands: *Menu Name > Submenu Name* (if necessary) > *Command Name*. For example, the instructions for choosing the Documents command from the Favorites submenu under the Go menu (**Figure 9**) would be: "choose Go > Favorites > Documents."

To use a contextual menu

1. Point to the item on which you want to act.

2. Press and hold down Control. A tiny contextual menu icon appears beside the mouse pointer (**Figure 16**).

3. Click. A contextual menu appears at the item (**Figure 17**).

4. Click the menu option you want (**Figure 18**).

✔ Tip

- Contextual menus are similar to the Action pop-up menu. I tell you about this new Mac OS X 10.3 feature later in this chapter.

The Keyboard

The keyboard offers another way to communicate with your computer. In addition to typing text and numbers, you can also use it to choose menu commands.

There are three types of keys on a Mac OS keyboard:

◆ **Character keys**, such as letters, numbers, and symbols, are for typing information. Some character keys have special functions, as listed in **Table 1**.

◆ **Modifier keys** alter the meaning of a character key being pressed or the meaning of a mouse action. Modifier keys are listed in **Table 2**.

◆ **Function keys** perform specific functions in Mac OS or an application. Dedicated function keys, which always do the same thing, are listed in **Table 3**. Function keys labeled [F1] through [F12] or [F1] through [F15] on the keyboard can be assigned specific functions by applications.

✔ Tips

■ [⌘] is called the *Command key* (not the Apple key).

■ Contextual menus are discussed on the previous page.

Table 1

Special Character Keys	
Key	**Function**
[Enter]	Enters information or "clicks" a default button.
[Return]	Begins a new paragraph or line or "clicks" a default button.
[Tab]	Advances to the next tab stop or the next item in a sequence.
[Delete]	Deletes a selection or the character to the left of the insertion point.
[Del]	Deletes a selection or the character to the right of the insertion point.
[Esc]	"Clicks" a Cancel button or ends the operation that is currently in progress.

Table 2

Modifier Keys	
Key	**Function**
[Shift]	Produces uppercase characters or symbols. Also works with the mouse to extend selections and to restrain movement in graphic applications.
[Option]	Produces special symbols.
[⌘]	Accesses menu commands via keyboard shortcuts.
[Control]	Modifies the functions of other keys and displays contextual menus.

Table 3

Dedicated Function Keys	
Key	**Function**
[Help]	Displays onscreen help.
[Home]	Scrolls to the beginning.
[End]	Scrolls to the end.
[Page Up]	Scrolls up one page.
[Page Down]	Scrolls down one page.
[←][→][↑][↓]	Moves the insertion point or changes the selection.

To use a keyboard shortcut

1. Hold down the modifier key(s) in the sequence. This is usually (⌃ ⌘), but can be (Option), (Control), or (Shift).

2. Press the letter, number, or symbol key in the sequence.

For example, to choose the Open command, which can be found under the File menu (**Figure 15**), hold down (⌃ ⌘) and press (O).

✔ Tips

■ You can learn keyboard shortcuts by observing the key sequences that appear to the right of some menu commands (**Figures 8, 9**, and **14**).

■ Some commands include more than one modifier key. You must hold all modifier keys down while pressing the letter, number, or symbol key for the keyboard shortcut.

■ You can find a list of all Finder keyboard shortcuts in **Appendix A**.

■ Some applications refer to keyboard shortcuts as *keyboard equivalents* or *shortcut keys*.

USING KEYBOARD SHORTCUTS

Icons

Mac OS uses icons to graphically represent files and other items on the desktop, in the Dock, or within Finder windows:

◆ **Applications** (**Figure 19**) are programs you use to get work done. **Chapters 5** through **7** discuss working with applications.

◆ **Documents** (**Figure 20**) are the files created by applications. **Chapter 5** covers working with documents.

◆ **Folders** (**Figure 21**) are used to organize files. **Chapters 3** and **4** discuss using folders.

◆ **Volumes** (**Figure 22**), including hard disks, CDs, DVDs, iPods, and network disks, are used to store data. **Chapter 3** covers working with volumes.

◆ The **Trash** (**Figure 23**), which is in the Dock, is for discarding items you no longer want and for ejecting removable media. The Trash is covered in **Chapter 3**.

✔ Tip

■ Icons can appear a number of different ways, depending on the view and view options chosen for a window. Windows are discussed later in this chapter; views are discussed in **Chapter 3**.

TextEdit   Preview   Microsoft Word

Figure 19 Application icons.

Letter   Picture.gif   Note

Figure 20 Document icons, including a TextEdit document, a Preview document, and a Word document.

Applications   System   My Stuff

Figure 21 Folder icons.

Macintosh HD   iDisk   Network

Figure 22 Three different volume icons: hard disk, iDisk, and Network.

Figure 23 The three faces of the Trash icon in the Dock: empty, full, and while dragging removable media.

ICONS

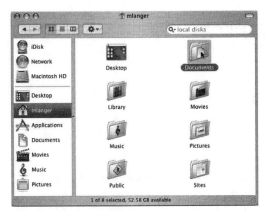

Figure 24 To select an icon, click it.

Figure 25 Hold down ⌘ while clicking other icons to add them to a multiple selection.

To select an icon

Click the icon that you want to select. The icon darkens, and its name becomes highlighted (**Figure 24**).

✔ Tip

■ You can also select an icon in an active window by pressing the keyboard key for the first letter of the icon's name or by pressing Tab, Shift Tab, ←, →, ↑, or ↓ until the icon is selected.

To deselect an icon

Click anywhere in the window or on the Desktop other than on the selected icon.

✔ Tips

■ If you select one icon and then click another icon, the originally selected icon is deselected and the icon you clicked becomes selected instead.

■ Windows are discussed later in this chapter.

To select multiple icons by clicking

1. Click the first icon that you want to select.

2. Hold down ⌘ and click another icon that you want to select (**Figure 25**).

3. Repeat step 2 until all icons that you want to select have been selected.

✔ Tip

■ Icons that are part of a multiple selection must be in the same window.

SELECTING & DESELECTING ICONS

To select multiple icons by dragging

1. Position the mouse pointer slightly above and to the left of the first icon in the group that you want to select (**Figure 26**).

2. Press the mouse button, and drag diagonally across the icons you want to select. A shaded box appears to indicate the selection area, and the items within it become selected (**Figure 27**).

3. When all the icons that you want to select are included in the selection area, release the mouse button (**Figure 28**).

✔ Tip

- To select multiple icons by dragging, the icons must be adjacent.

To select all icons in a window

Choose Edit > Select All (**Figure 29**), or press ⌃⌘A.

All icons in the active window are selected.

✔ Tip

- Activating windows is covered later in this chapter.

To deselect one icon in a multiple selection

Hold down ⌃⌘ while clicking the icon that you want to deselect. That icon is deselected while the others remain selected.

Figure 26 Position the mouse pointer above and to the left of the first icon that you want to select.

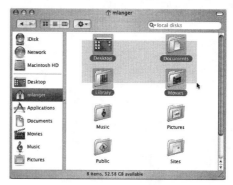

Figure 27 Drag to draw a shaded selection box around the icons that you want to select.

Figure 28 Release the mouse button to complete the selection.

Figure 29 Choose Select All from the Edit menu to select all items.

Figure 30 Point to the icon that you want to move.

Figure 31 Drag the icon to the new location.

Figure 32 Release the mouse button to complete the move.

To move an icon

1. Position the mouse pointer on the icon that you want to move (**Figure 30**).

2. Press the mouse button, and drag the icon to the new location. As you drag, a shadowy image of the icon moves with the mouse pointer (**Figure 31**).

3. Release the mouse button when the icon is in the desired position (**Figure 32**).

✔ Tips

■ You cannot drag to reposition icons within windows set to list or column view. Views are discussed in **Chapter 3**.

■ You move icons to rearrange them in a window or on the desktop, or to copy or move the items they represent to another folder or disk. Copying and moving items is discussed in **Chapter 3**.

■ You can also move multiple icons at once. Simply select the icons first, then position the mouse pointer on one of the selected icons and follow steps 2 and 3 above. All selected icons move together.

■ To force an icon to snap to a window's invisible grid, hold down ⌘ while dragging it. The grid, which I tell you more about in **Chapter 4**, ensures consistent spacing between icons, so your window looks neat.

MOVING ICONS

To open an icon

1. Select the icon you want to open (**Figure 33**).

2. Choose File > Open (**Figure 34**), or press ⌃ ⌘ O.

or

Double-click the icon that you want to open.

✔ Tips

- Only one click is necessary when opening an item in a Finder window toolbar or the Dock. The toolbar and Dock are covered in detail later in this chapter.

- What happens when you open an icon depends on the type of icon you open. For example:

  - ▲ Opening a disk or folder icon displays the contents of the disk or folder in the same Finder window (**Figure 35**). Windows are discussed next.

  - ▲ Opening an application icon launches the application so that you can work with it. Working with applications is covered in **Chapter 5** and elsewhere in this book.

  - ▲ Opening a document icon launches the application that created that document and displays the document so you can view or edit it. Working with documents is covered in **Chapter 5**.

  - ▲ Opening the Trash displays items that will be deleted when you empty the Trash. Using and emptying the Trash is discussed in **Chapter 3**.

- To open a folder or disk in a new Finder window, hold down ⌃ ⌘ while opening it.

- The File menu's Open With submenu, which is discussed in **Chapter 5**, enables you to open a document with a specific application.

Figure 33 Select the icon.

Figure 34 Choose Open from the File menu.

Figure 35 Here's the window from **Figure 33** with the Applications folder's contents displayed.

Close   Minimize button
button   Zoom   Search Toolbar
         button   Toolbar Title bar   box   control

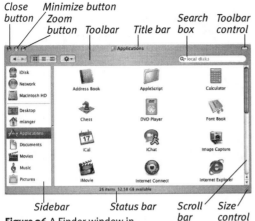

Sidebar   Status bar   Scroll   Size
                                 bar   control

Figure 36 A Finder window in icon view.

Close   Minimize button   Column heading
button   Zoom   Title   Search Toolbar
         button   Toolbar bar   box   control

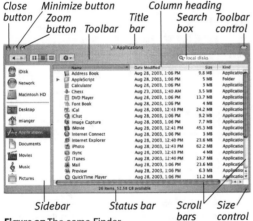

Sidebar   Status bar   Scroll   Size
                                 bars   control

Figure 37 The same Finder window in list view.

✔ Tips

- By default, when you open a folder or disk icon, its contents appear in the active window. As discussed in **Chapter 4**, you can use Finder Preferences to tell Mac OS X to open folders in new windows.

- I cover the Finder's three window views in **Chapter 3**, the toolbar and Sidebar later in this chapter, and the status bar and Search box in **Chapter 4**.

Windows

Mac OS makes extensive use of windows for displaying icons and other information in the Finder and documents in other applications. **Figures 36** and **37** show two different views of a Finder window.

Each window includes a variety of controls you can use to manipulate it:

- ◆ The **close button** closes the window.

- ◆ The **minimize button** collapses the window to an icon in the Dock.

- ◆ The **zoom button** toggles the window's size between full size and a custom size.

- ◆ The **toolbar** displays buttons and controls for working with Finder windows.

- ◆ The **title bar** displays the window's icon and name.

- ◆ The **Search box** enables you to search for files based on file name.

- ◆ The **toolbar hide control** toggles the display of the toolbar.

- ◆ The **Sidebar**, which is new in Mac OS X 10.3, shows commonly accessed volumes and folders, including the default folders in your Home folder.

- ◆ The **status bar** provides information about items in a window and space available on disk.

- ◆ The **size control** enables you to set a custom size for the window.

- ◆ **Scroll bars** scroll the contents of the window.

- ◆ **Column headings** (in list view only) display the names of the columns and let you quickly sort by a column. (The selected column heading is the column by which the list is sorted.)

WINDOWS

To open a new Finder window

Choose File > New Finder Window (**Figure 38**), or press ⌃⌘N. A new Home folder window for your account appears (**Figure 39**).

✔ Tip

- The Home folder is discussed in **Chapter 3**.

To open a folder or disk in a new Finder window

Hold down ⌃⌘ while opening a folder or disk icon. A new window containing the contents of the folder or disk appears.

✔ Tip

- Opening folders and disks is explained earlier in this chapter.

To close a window

Click the window's close button (**Figures 36** and **37**).

or

Choose File > Close Window (**Figure 40**), or press ⌃⌘W.

To close all open windows

Hold down Option while clicking the active window's close button (**Figures 36** and **37**).

or

Hold down Option while choosing File > Close All (**Figure 41**), or press ⌃⌘Option W.

✔ Tip

- The Close Window/Close All commands (**Figures 40** and **41**) are examples of *dynamic menu items*—pressing a modifier key (in this case, Option) changes the menu command from Close Window (**Figure 40**) to Close All (**Figure 41**).

Figure 38
Choose New Finder Window from the File menu.

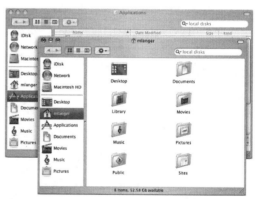

Figure 39 The active window appears atop all other windows and the buttons on the left end of its title bar appear in color.

Figure 40 Choose Close Window from the File menu...

Figure 41 ...or hold down Option and choose Close All from the File menu.

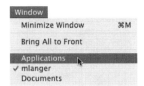

Figure 42 The Window menu lists all open Finder windows.

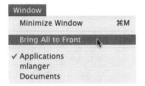

Figure 43 The Bring All to Front command brings all Finder windows to the top.

To activate a window

Click anywhere in or on the window.

or

Choose the name of the window you want to activate from the Window menu (**Figure 42**).

✔ Tips

- It's important to make sure that the window you want to work with is open and active *before* using commands that work on the active window—such as Close Window, Select All, and View menu options.

- You can distinguish between active and inactive windows by the appearance of their title bars; the buttons on the left end of an active window's title bar are in color (**Figure 39**). In addition, a check mark appears beside the active window's name in the Window menu (**Figure 42**).

- When two or more windows overlap, the active window will always be on top of the stack (**Figure 39**).

To bring all Finder windows to the top

Choose Window > Bring All to Front (**Figure 43**). All open Finder windows that are not minimized are moved in front of any windows opened by other applications.

✔ Tip

- Finder windows can be intermingled with other applications' windows. The Bring All to Front command gathers the windows together in the top layers. You may find this command useful when working with many windows from several different applications.

ACTIVATING WINDOWS

To move a window

1. Position the mouse pointer on the window's title bar (**Figure 44**) or border.

2. Press the mouse button and drag the window to a new location. As you drag, the window moves along with your mouse pointer (**Figure 45**).

3. When the outline of the window is in the desired position, release the mouse button.

✔ Tip

■ As discussed later in this chapter, hiding the toolbar and Sidebar removes window borders. If window borders are not showing, the only way to move a window is to drag its title bar.

To resize a window

1. Position the mouse pointer on the size control in the lower-right corner of the window (**Figure 46**).

2. Press the mouse button and drag. As you drag, the size control moves with the mouse pointer, changing the size and shape of the window (**Figure 47**).

3. When the window is the desired size, release the mouse button.

✔ Tips

■ The larger a window is, the more you can see inside it.

■ By resizing and repositioning windows, you can see inside more than one window at a time. This comes in handy when moving or copying the icons for files and folders from one window to another. Moving and copying files and folders is covered in **Chapter 3**.

Figure 44 Position the mouse pointer on the title bar.

Figure 45 As you drag, the window moves.

Figure 46 Position the mouse pointer on the size control.

Figure 47 As you drag, the window's size and shape changes.

Figure 48
The Minimize Window command minimizes the active window.

Figure 49 Minimized windows shrink down into icons in the Dock.

Figure 50
A diamond beside a window name indicates that the window has been minimized.

To minimize a window

Click the window's minimize button (**Figures 36** and **37**).

or

Choose Window > Minimize Window (**Figure 48**), or press ⌃ ⌘ M.

or

Double-click the window's title bar.

The window shrinks into an icon and slips into the Dock at the bottom of the screen (**Figure 49**).

✔ Tip

■ To minimize all windows, hold down Option and choose Windows > Minimize All Windows, or press Option ⌃ ⌘ M.

To redisplay a minimized window

Click the window's icon in the Dock (**Figure 49**).

or

Choose the window's name from the Window menu (**Figure 50**).

To zoom a window

Click the window's zoom button (**Figures 36** and **37**).

Each time you click the zoom button, the window's size toggles between two sizes:

◆ **Standard state** size is the smallest possible size that would accommodate the window's contents and still fit on your screen (**Figure 36**).

◆ **User state** size, which is the size you specify with the size control (**Figure 47**).

To scroll a window's contents

Click one of the scroll bar arrows (**Figure 51**) as follows:

◆ To scroll the window's contents up, click the down arrow on the vertical scroll bar.

◆ To scroll the window's contents down, click the up arrow on the vertical scroll bar.

◆ To scroll the window's contents to the left, click the right arrow on the horizontal scroll bar.

◆ To scroll the window's contents to the right, click the left arrow on the horizontal scroll bar.

✔ Tips

■ If you have trouble remembering which scroll arrow to click, think of it this way:

▲ Click down to see down.

▲ Click up to see up.

▲ Click right to see right.

▲ Click left to see left.

■ You can also scroll a window's contents by either clicking in the scroll track on either side of the scroller or by dragging the scroller to a new position on the scroll bar. Both of these techniques enable you to scroll a window's contents more quickly.

■ Scroll bars only appear when necessary—when part of a window's contents are hidden. In **Figure 36**, for example, it isn't necessary to scroll from side to side so the horizontal scroll bar does not appear. In **Figure 46**, all of the window's contents are displayed so no scroll bars appear.

■ The scrollers in Mac OS X are proportional—this means that the more of a window's contents you see, the more space the scroller will take up in its scroll bar.

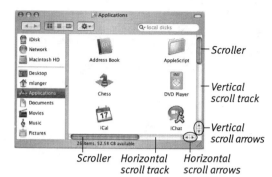

Figure 51 Scroll bar components.

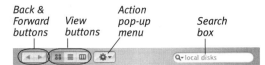

Figure 52 The toolbar.

Figure 53 The Action pop-up menu offers commands for working with selected items in a window.

Figure 54 When the window is narrow, some toolbar items may be hidden.

Figure 55 Click the double arrow to display a menu of hidden items.

The Toolbar

The toolbar (**Figure 52**) offers navigation tools and view buttons within Finder windows:

◆ The **Back button** displays the previous window's contents.

◆ The **Forward button** displays the window that was showing before you clicked the Back button.

◆ **View buttons** enable you to change the window's view.

◆ The **Action pop-up menu** (**Figure 53**) offers commands for working with an open window or selected object(s) within the window. This is new in Mac OS X 10.3.

◆ **Search box** enables you to quickly search the window for a file by name.

✔ Tips

■ The toolbar can be customized to show the items you use most; **Chapter 4** explains how.

■ Does the Action pop-up menu in **Figure 53** look familiar? It should! It's very similar to the contextual menu shown in **Figure 17**.

■ Views and using the Search box are covered in detail in **Chapter 4**; file management and navigation is discussed in **Chapter 3**.

■ If the window is not wide enough to show all toolbar buttons, a double arrow appears on the right side of the toolbar (**Figure 54**). Click the arrow to display a menu of missing buttons (**Figure 55**), and select the button you want.

THE TOOLBAR

To hide or display the toolbar

Click the toolbar control button (**Figure 56**).

One of two things happens:

◆ If the toolbar is displayed, it disappears (**Figure 56**).

◆ If the toolbar is not displayed, it appears (**Figure 57**).

✔ Tips

■ As shown in **Figure 56**, hiding the toolbar also hides the Sidebar (which is discussed on the next page) and window borders and moves the status bar so it appears right beneath the title bar. This makes the window smaller and more like the windows in Mac OS 9 and earlier.

To use a toolbar button

Click the button once.

To use the Action pop-up menu

1. If necessary, select the icon(s) for the items you want to work with.

2. Click the Action pop-up menu to display a menu of commands (**Figure 53**).

3. Choose the command you want to use.

Toolbar control

Figure 56 The toolbar control button can hide the toolbar...

Figure 57 ...or display it.

Sidebar

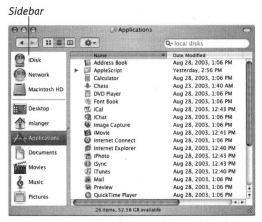

Figure 58 The Sidebar appears on the left side of a Finder window when toolbars are displayed.

Figure 59 If the Sidebar is too short to display its contents, a scroll bar appears within it.

Figure 60 Dragging the border between the Sidebar and window contents ...

Figure 61 ... enables you to change its width.

The Sidebar

The *Sidebar*, which is new in Mac OS X 10.3, appears on the left side of Finder windows when toolbars are displayed (**Figure 58**). It offers quick access to the items you use most.

The Sidebar has two parts:

◆ The upper part of the Sidebar displays icons for volumes that are accessible by your computer, such as your hard disk, iDisk, network disks, and CD-ROM discs.

◆ The lower part of the Sidebar displays icons for the Desktop, your Home folder, and several commonly-accessed folders within your Home folder.

✔ Tips

■ You can customize the lower part of the Sidebar to display whatever items you want. I explain how in **Chapter 4**.

■ I tell you about your Home folder and volumes in **Chapter 3**.

■ When a window is resized, the size of the Sidebar may also change. If the Sidebar is too short to display its contents, a vertical scroll bar appears within it (**Figure 59**).

■ You can change the width of the Sidebar by dragging the divider between it and the window contents (**Figures 60** and **61**).

To use the Sidebar

Click the icon for the item you want.

One of two things happens:

◆ If the item was a volume or folder, the window's contents change to display the contents of the item you clicked.

◆ If the item was an application or document, the item opens in its own application window.

THE SIDEBAR

The Dock

The Dock (**Figure 62**) offers easy access to often-used applications and documents, as well as minimized windows.

✔ Tip

■ The Dock can be customized; **Chapter 4** explains how.

To identify items in the Dock

Point to the item. The name of the item appears above the Dock (**Figure 63**).

To identify items in the Dock that are running

Look at the Dock. A triangle appears beneath each item that is running, such as the Finder in **Figures 62**, **63**, and **64**.

To open an item in the Dock

Click the icon for the item you want to open. One of four things happens:

◆ If the icon is for an application that is running, the application becomes the active application.

◆ If the icon is for an application that is not running, the application launches. While the application launches, the icon in the Dock bounces (**Figure 64**) so you know something is happening.

◆ If the icon is for a minimized window, the window is displayed.

◆ If the icon is for a document that is not open, the application that created the document launches (if necessary) and the document opens.

Figure 62 The Dock displays often-used applications and documents.

Figure 63 Point to an icon to see what it represents.

Figure 64 An item's icon bounces while it is being opened.

✔ Tip

■ Using applications and opening documents is discussed in greater detail in **Chapter 5**; minimizing and displaying windows is discussed earlier in this chapter.

THE DOCK

Figure 65
Four commands under the Apple menu let you change the work state of your computer.

Sleeping, Restarting, & Shutting Down

The Apple menu (**Figure 65**) offers several options that change the work state of your computer:

◆ **Sleep** puts the computer into a state where it uses very little power. The screen goes blank and the hard disk may stop spinning.

◆ **Restart** instructs the computer to shut down and immediately start back up.

◆ **Shut Down** closes all open documents and programs, clears memory, and cuts power to the computer.

◆ **Log Out** *User Name* closes all open documents and programs and clears memory. Your computer remains running until you or someone else logs in.

I discuss all of these commands on the following pages.

✔ Tips

■ If your computer's keyboard includes a power key, pressing it displays a dialog with buttons for the Restart, Sleep, and Shut Down commands. This feature, however, does not work with all Mac OS–computer models.

■ Do *not* restart or shut down a computer by simply flicking off the power switch. Doing so prevents the computer from properly closing files, which may result in file corruption and related problems.

■ Mac OS X also includes a screen saver, which automatically starts up when your computer is inactive for five minutes. Don't confuse the screen saver with System or display sleep—it's different. To display the screen again, simply move the mouse or press any key. You can customize screen saver settings with the Desktop & Screen Saver preferences pane, which is covered in **Chapter 19**.

To put your computer to sleep

Choose Apple > Sleep (**Figure 65**).

✔ Tips

- When you put your computer to sleep, everything in memory is preserved. When you wake the computer, you can quickly continue working where you left off.

- Sleep mode is an effective way to conserve the battery life of a PowerBook or iBook without turning it off.

- By default, Mac OS X automatically puts a computer to sleep when it is inactive for 20 minutes. You can change this setting in the Energy Saver preferences pane, which is discussed in **Chapter 18**.

To wake a sleeping computer

Press any keyboard key. You may have to wait several seconds for the computer to fully wake.

✔ Tips

- It's much quicker to wake a sleeping computer than to restart a computer that has been shut down.

- On some computer models, pressing [Caps Lock] or certain other keys may not wake the computer. When in doubt, press a letter key—they always work.

Figure 66 This dialog appears when you choose the Restart command from the Apple menu.

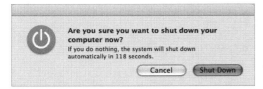

Figure 67 This dialog appears when you choose the Shut Down command from the Apple menu.

To restart your computer

1. Choose Apple > Restart (**Figure 65**).

2. In the dialog that appears (**Figure 66**), click Restart or press Return or Enter.

   or

   Do nothing. Your computer will automatically restart in 2 minutes.

✔ Tip

■ Restarting the computer clears memory and reloads all system files.

To shut down your computer

1. Choose Apple > Shut Down (**Figure 65**).

2. In the dialog that appears (**Figure 67**), click Shut Down or press Return or Enter.

   or

   Do nothing. Your computer will automatically shut down in 2 minutes.

✔ Tip

■ On most computers, the Shut Down command will cut power to the computer as part of the shut down process. If it doesn't, a dialog will appear onscreen, telling you it's safe to turn off your computer. You can then use the power switch to cut power to the computer.

RESTARTING & SHUTTING DOWN

Logging Out & In

If your computer is shared by multiple users, you may find it more convenient to log out when you're finished working. The Log Out command under the Apple menu (**Figure 65**) closes all applications and documents and closes your account on the computer. The computer remains running, making it quick and easy for the next person to log in and get right to work.

✔ Tips

- If you are your computer's only user, you'll probably never use the Log Out command. (I hardly ever do.)

- Mac OS X 10.3 introduces *fast user switching*, a feature that makes it quicker and easier to switch from one user account to another. I explain how this feature works in **Chapter 15**.

To log out

1. Choose Apple > Log Out *User Name* (**Figure 65**), or press (Shift)(⌃)(⌘)(Q).

2. A confirmation dialog like the one in **Figure 68** appears. Click Log Out or press (Return) or (Enter).

   or

   Do nothing. Your computer will automatically log you out in 2 minutes.

   Your computer closes all applications and documents, then displays the Login Screen.

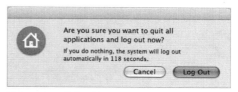

Figure 68 A dialog like this one confirms that you really do want to log out.

To log in

1. If the Login Screen displays icons for user accounts, click the icon for your account.

2. Enter your password in the Password box that appears.

3. Click Log In.

or

1. If the Login Screen displays only Name and Password boxes, enter your full or short account name in the Name box and your password in the Password box.

2. Click Log In.

Your Mac OS desktop appears, looking the same as it did when you logged out or shut down your computer.

✔ Tips

■ The appearance of the Login Screen varies depending on how the Accounts preference pane has been configured by the system administrator. (Unfortunately, Mac OS X 10.3 does not allow me to take screen shots of these screens, so I can't show them to you.) Account options are discussed in **Chapter 15**.

■ Your user name and short name are created when you use the Mac OS Setup Assistant to configure Mac OS X, as discussed in **Chapter 1**. You can use either name to log in.

LOGGING IN

File Management

File Management

In Mac OS, you use the Finder to organize and manage your files. You can:

- ◆ View the contents of your disks in windows in a variety of ways.

- ◆ Automatically sort items by name, kind, creation date, or other criteria in ascending or descending order.

- ◆ Rename items.

- ◆ Create folders to store related items.

- ◆ Move items stored on disk to organize them so they're easy to find and back up.

- ◆ Copy items to other disks to back them up or share them with others.

- ◆ Delete items you no longer need.

- ◆ Mount and eject disks.

- ◆ Write to, or "burn," CD-ROMs.

✔ Tip

- ■ If you're brand new to Mac OS, be sure to read the information in **Chapter 2** before working with this chapter. That chapter contains information and instructions about techniques that are used throughout this chapter.

Mac OS X Disk Organization

Like previous versions of Mac OS and most other computer operating systems, Mac OS X uses a hierarchical filing system (HFS) to organize and store files, including system files, applications, and documents.

The top level of the filing system is the computer level, which corresponds to the top section of the Sidebar (**Figure 1**). This level shows the computer's internal hard disk, any other disks the computer has access to (including iDisk, if you are a .Mac member), and the Network icon.

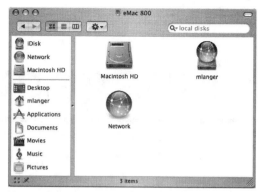

Figure 1 The top level of your computer shows all mounted disks and a Network icon.

The next level down is the computer's hard disk level. You can view this level by clicking the name of your hard disk in the Sidebar (**Figure 1**) or on the desktop. While the contents of your hard disk may differ from what's shown in **Figure 2**, some elements should be the same:

Figure 2 A typical hard disk window might look like this.

◆ **Applications** contains Mac OS X applications.

◆ **Applications (Mac OS 9)** contains applications that run under the Classic environment.

◆ **System** and **Library** contain the Mac OS X system files.

◆ **Users** (**Figure 3**) contains individual folders for each of the computer's users, as well as a Shared folder.

◆ **System Folder** contains the Mac OS 9.x system files for running the Classic environment.

◆ **Documents** contains documents you saved on your hard disk before upgrading to Mac OS X.

◆ **Desktop (Mac OS 9)** contains items that appear on the desktop when you start your computer with Mac OS 9.x.

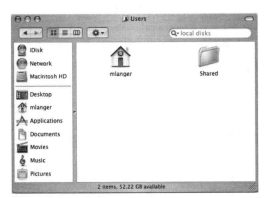

Figure 3 The Users folder contains a home folder for each user, as well as a Shared folder.

Figure 4 Your home folder is preconfigured with folders for storing a variety of item types.

By default, a Mac OS X hard disk is organized for multiple users. Each user has his or her own "home" folder, which is stored in the Users folder (**Figure 3**). You can view the items inside your home folder by opening the house icon with your name on it inside the Users folder (**Figure 3**) or by clicking the Home icon in the toolbar of any Finder window. Your home folder is preconfigured with folders for all kinds of items you may want to store on disk (**Figure 4**).

✔ Tips

- When you install new applications on your computer, you should install Mac OS X–compatible applications in the Applications folder and Mac OS 9.x– compatible applications in the Applications (Mac OS 9) folder.

- If you upgraded from a previous version of Mac OS to Mac OS X, you may want to move the contents of the Documents folder on your hard disk (**Figure 2**) to the Documents folder inside your home folder (**Figure 4**) to keep your documents together and easier to find. As you can see, these are different Documents folders.

- Unless you are an administrator, you cannot access the files in any other user's home folder except those in the user's Public and Sites folders.

- If you place an item in the Shared folder inside the Users folder (**Figure 3**), it can be opened by anyone who uses the computer.

- I discuss applications in **Chapter 5**, the Classic environment in **Chapter 16**, sharing computers in **Chapter 15**, and networking in **Chapter 14**.

MAC OS X DISK ORGANIZATION

Pathnames

A *path* or *pathname* is a kind of address for a file on disk. It includes the name of the disk on which the file resides, the names of the folders the file is stored within, and the name of the file itself. For example, the pathname for a file named *Letter.rtf* in the Documents folder of the mlanger folder shown in **Figure 4** would be: Macintosh HD/Users/mlanger/Documents/Letter.rtf

When entering a pathname from a specific folder, you don't have to enter the entire pathname. Instead, enter the path as it relates to the current folder. For example, the path to the above-mentioned file from the mlanger folder would be: Documents/Letter.rtf

To indicate a specific user folder, use the tilde (~) character followed by the name of the user account. So the path to the mlanger folder (**Figure 4**) would be: ~mlanger. (You can omit the user name if you want to open your own user folder.)

To indicate the top level of your computer, use a slash (/) character. So the path to Super iMac (**Figure 1**) would be: /

When used as part of a longer pathname, the slash character indicates the *root level* of your hard disk. So /Applications/AppleScript would indicate the AppleScript folder inside the Applications folder on your hard disk.

Don't worry if this sounds confusing to you. Fortunately, you don't really need to know it to use Mac OS X. It's just a good idea to be familiar with the concept of pathnames in case you run across it while working with your computer.

Figure 5
The Go menu.

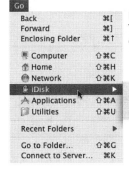

Figure 6
The iDisk submenu
on the Go menu.

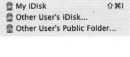

Figure 7
The Recent Folders
submenu lists recently
opened folders.

✔ Tip

■ I discuss iDisk in **Chapter 12** and connecting to network servers in **Chapter 14**.

The Go Menu

The Go menu (**Figure 5**) offers a quick way to
open specific locations on your computer:

◆ **Back** ([⌘[]) displays the contents of the
folder or disk you were looking in before
you viewed the current folder or disk.
This command is only active if the current window has displayed the contents
of more than one folder or disk.

◆ **Forward** ([⌘]]) displays the contents of
the window you were viewing before you
clicked the Back button. This command
is only available if a window is active and
if the Back button has been clicked.

◆ **Enclosing Folder** ([⌘↑]) opens the
parent folder for the active window's
folder. This command is only available if
a window is active and if the window was
used to display the contents of a folder.

◆ **Computer** ([Shift][⌘C]) opens the top
level window for your computer (**Figure 1**).

◆ **Home** ([Shift][⌘H]) opens your home
folder (**Figure 4**).

◆ **iDisk** displays a submenu of options for
accessing iDisk accounts and folders on
Apple's .Mac server via the Internet
(**Figure 6**).

◆ **Applications** ([Shift][⌘A]) opens the
Applications folder.

◆ **Utilities** ([Shift][⌘U]) opens the Utilities
folder inside the Applications folder.

◆ **Recent Folders** displays a submenu of
recently opened folders (**Figure 7**).

◆ **Go to Folder** ([Shift][⌘G]) lets you open
any folder your computer has access to.

◆ **Connect to Server** ([⌘K]) enables you
to open a server accessible via a network.

THE GO MENU

To open a Go menu item

Choose the item's name from the Go menu (**Figure 5**) or one of its submenus (**Figures 6** and **7**).

To go to a folder

1. Choose Go > Go to Folder (**Figure 5**), or press ⌈Shift⌉⌈⌘⌉⌈G⌉.

2. In the Go To Folder dialog that appears (**Figure 8**), enter the pathname for the folder you want to open.

3. Click Go.

   If you entered a valid pathname, the folder opens in a Finder window.

   or

   If you did not enter a valid pathname, an error message appears in the Go To Folder dialog (**Figure 9**). Repeat steps 2 and 3 to try again, or click Cancel to dismiss the dialog.

✔ Tip

■ If a window is open when you use the Go to Folder command, the Go To Folder dialog will appear as a dialog *sheet* attached to the window (**Figure 10**). The pathname you enter must be from that window's folder location on your hard disk.

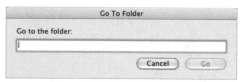

Figure 8 Use the Go To Folder dialog to enter the pathname of the folder you want to open.

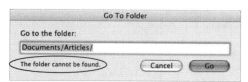

Figure 9 An error message appears in the Go To Folder window if you enter an invalid pathname.

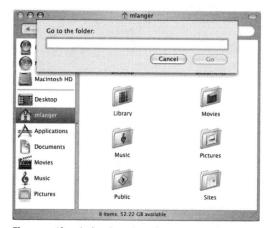

Figure 10 If a window is active when you use the Go to Folder command, the dialog appears as a sheet attached to the window.

Figure 11 You can display a window's contents as icons,...

Figure 12 ...as a list,...

Figure 13 ...or as columns.

Figure 14
The View menu offers a variety of options for changing a window's view, along with three new command key equivalents for switching from one view to another.

Figure 15 The view buttons in the toolbar.

Views

A Finder window's contents can be displayed using three different views:

- ◆ **Icons** displays the window's contents as small or large icons (**Figure 11**).

- ◆ **List** displays the window's contents as a sorted list (**Figure 12**).

- ◆ **Columns** displays the window's contents with a multiple-column format that shows the currently selected disk or folder and the items within it (**Figure 13**).

✔ Tip

- ■ You can customize views by setting view options globally or for individual windows. I explain how in **Chapter 4**.

To change a window's view

1. If necessary, activate the window whose view you want to change.

2. Choose the view option you want from the View menu (**Figure 14**) or press the corresponding shortcut key.

   or

   Click the toolbar's view button for the view you want (**Figure 15**).

The view of the window changes.

✔ Tips

- ■ Commands on the View menu (**Figure 14**) work on the active window only.

- ■ A check mark appears on the View menu beside the name of the view applied to the active window (**Figure 14**).

- ■ You can set the view for each window individually.

To neatly arrange icons in icon view

1. Activate the window that you want to clean up (**Figure 16**).

2. Choose View > Clean Up (**Figure 14**). The icons are arranged in the window's invisible grid (**Figure 17**).

   or

   Choose one of the commands from the Arrange submenu under the View menu (**Figure 18**):

   ▲ **by Name** arranges the icons alphabetically by name (**Figure 11**).

   ▲ **by Date Modified** arranges the icons chronologically by the date they were last modified, with the most recently modified item last.

   ▲ **by Date Created** arranges the icons by the date they were created, with the most recently created item last.

   ▲ **by Size** arranges the icons in size order, with the largest item last. (Folders have a size of 0 for this option.)

   ▲ **by Kind** arranges the icons alphabetically by the kind of file.

   ▲ **by Label** arranges the icons by color-coded label (if applied).

   The icons are arranged in the window's invisible grid in the order you specified (**Figure 11**).

✔ Tips

■ A window's invisible grid ensures consistent spacing between icons.

■ You can manually position an icon in the window's invisible grid by holding down ⌃⌘ while dragging it within the window.

Figure 16 Start with a messy window like this one...

Figure 17 ...and use the Clean Up command to put the icons in place.

Figure 18 The Arrange submenu offers several options for neatly arranging icons.

■ When one or more icons are selected, the Clean Up command becomes the Clean Up Selection command. Choosing it arranges just the selected icons.

■ I tell you how to apply and customize labels in **Chapter 4.**

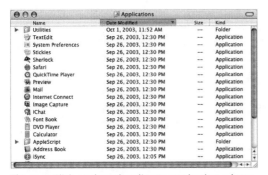

Figure 19 Click a column heading to sort by that column.

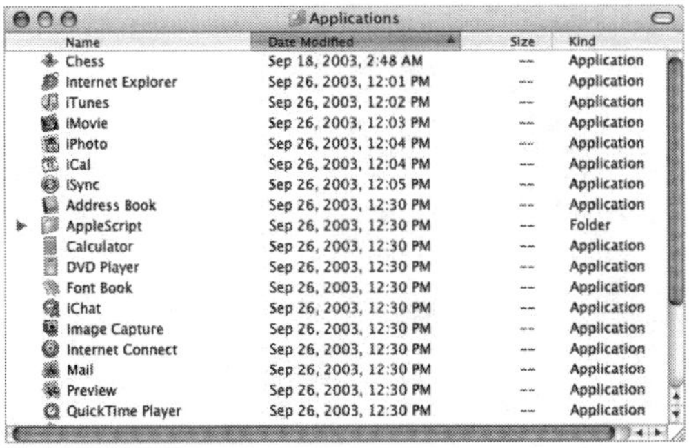

Figure 20 Click the same column heading to reverse that column's sort order.

To sort a window's contents in list view

Click the column heading for the column you want to sort by. The list is sorted by that column (**Figure 19**).

✔ Tips

- You can identify the column by which a list is sorted by its colored column heading (**Figures 12, 19**, and **20**).

- You can reverse a window's sort order by clicking the sort column's heading a second time (**Figure 20**).

- You can determine the sort direction by looking at the arrow in the sort column. When it points up, the items are sorted in ascending order (**Figure 20**); when it points down, the items are sorted in descending order (**Figure 19**).

- To properly sort by size, you must turn on the Calculate all sizes option for the window. I explain how in **Chapter 4**.

- You can specify which columns should appear in a window by setting View Options. I explain how to do that in **Chapter 4**, too.

Icon Names

Mac OS X is very flexible when it comes to names for files, folders, and disks.

- ◆ A file or folder name can be up to 255 characters long. A disk name can be up to 27 characters long.

- ◆ A name can contain any character except a colon (:).

This makes it easy to give your files, folders, and disks names that make sense to you.

✔ Tips

- ■ Normally, you name documents when you save them. Saving documents is covered in **Chapter 5**.

- ■ A lengthy file name may appear truncated (or shortened) when displayed in windows and lists.

- ■ Since Mac OS 9.x and earlier cannot recognize very long file names, it's not a good idea to use them to name files you may work with in Mac OS 9. Instead, stick to file names of 31 characters or less.

- ■ No two documents in the same folder can have the same name.

- ■ Because slash characters (/) are used in pathnames, it's not a good idea to use them in names. In fact, some programs (such as Microsoft Word X) won't allow you to include a slash in a file name.

- ■ Working with and naming disks is covered later in this chapter.

Figure 21
Start by selecting the icon.

Figure 22
When you click, an edit box appears around the name.

Figure 23
Type a new name for the icon.

Figure 24
When you press Return, the name changes.

To rename an icon

1. Click the icon to select it (**Figure 21**).

2. Point to the name of the icon, and click. After a brief pause, a box appears around the name and the name becomes selected (**Figure 22**).

3. Type the new name. The text you type automatically overwrites the selected text (**Figure 23**).

4. Press Return or Enter, or click anywhere else. The icon is renamed (**Figure 24**).

✔ Tips

- Not all icons can be renamed. If the edit box does not appear around an icon name (as shown in **Figure 22**), that icon cannot be renamed.

- You can also rename an icon in the Info window, which is covered in **Chapter 4**.

RENAMING ICONS

Folders

Mac OS uses folders to organize files and other folders on disk. You can create a folder, give it a name that makes sense to you, and move files and other folders into it. It's a lot like organizing paper files and folders in a file cabinet.

✔ Tips

- A folder can contain any number of files and other folders.

- It's a good idea to use folders to organize the files on your hard disk. Imagine a file cabinet without file folders—that's how your hard disk would appear if you never used folders to keep your files tidy.

- As discussed earlier in this chapter, your home folder includes folders set up for organizing files by type. You'll find that these folders often appear as default file locations when saving specific types of files from within software programs. Saving files from within applications is covered in **Chapter 5**.

To create a folder

1. Choose File > New Folder (**Figure 25**), or press Shift ⌘ N. A new untitled folder (**Figure 26**) appears in the active window.

2. While the edit box appears around the new folder's name (**Figure 26**), type a name for it (**Figure 27**) and press Return.

✔ Tips

- You can rename a folder the same way you rename any other icon. Renaming icons is discussed on the previous page.

- Working with windows is discussed in **Chapter 2**.

Figure 25
Choose New Folder from the File menu.

Figure 26
A new folder appears.

Figure 27
Enter a name for the folder while the edit box appears around it.

Moving & Copying Items

In addition to moving icons around within a window or on the desktop (see **Chapter 2**), you can move or copy items to other locations on the same disk or to other disks by dragging them:

◆ When you drag an item to a location on the same disk, the item is moved to that location.

◆ When you drag an item to a location on another disk, the item is copied to that location.

◆ When you hold down Option while dragging an item to a location on the same disk, the item is copied to that location.

The next few pages provide instructions for all of these techniques, as well as instructions for duplicating items.

✔ Tips

■ You can move or copy more than one item at a time. Begin by selecting all of the items that you want to move or copy, then drag any one of them to the destination. All items will be moved or copied.

■ You can continue working with the Finder or any other application—even start more copy jobs—while a copy job is in progress.

■ In Mac OS X, you can also copy Finder items using the Copy and Paste commands under the Finder's Edit menu. I explain how to use Copy and Paste in **Chapter 7**.

MOVING & COPYING ITEMS

To move an item to another location on the same disk

1. Drag the icon for the item that you want to move as follows:

   ▲ To move the item into a specific folder on the disk, drag the icon onto the icon for the folder. The destination folder icon becomes selected when the mouse pointer moves over it (**Figure 28**).

   ▲ To move the item into a specific window on the disk, drag the icon into the window. A border appears around the inside of the destination window (**Figure 29**).

2. Release the mouse button. The item moves.

✔ Tip

■ If the destination location is on another disk, the item you drag will be copied rather than moved. To move (rather than copy) an item to another disk, hold down ⌘ while dragging it to the disk.

Figure 28 Drag the icon onto the icon for the folder to which you want to move it...

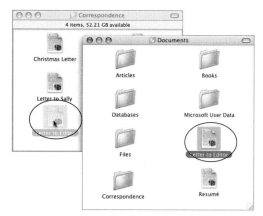

Figure 29 ...or drag the icon into the window in which you want to move it.

Figure 30 Drag the icon to the destination disk's icon...

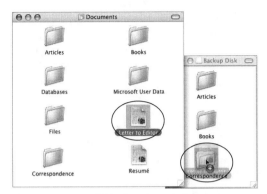

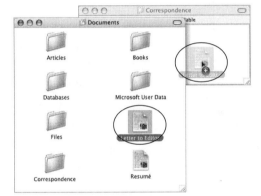

Figure 31 ...or to a folder icon in a window on the destination disk, ...

Figure 32 ...or to an open window on the destination disk.

Figure 33 A window like this indicates copy progress.

Figure 34 If a file with the same name already exists in the destination, Mac OS tells you.

To copy an item to another disk

1. Drag the icon for the item that you want to copy as follows:

   ▲ To copy the item to the top (or *root*) level of a disk, drag the icon to the icon for the destination disk (**Figure 30**).

   ▲ To copy the item into a folder on the disk, drag the icon to the icon for the folder on the destination disk (**Figure 31**).

   ▲ To copy the item into a specific window on the disk, drag the icon into the window (**Figure 32**).

   When the item you are dragging moves on top of the destination location, a plus sign in a green circle appears beneath the mouse pointer. If the destination is an icon, the icon becomes selected.

2. Release the mouse button. A Copy window like the one in **Figure 33** appears. When it disappears, the copy is complete.

✔ Tips

■ You cannot copy items to a disk that is write protected or to a folder for which you don't have write privileges. When you try, the green plus sign changes to a circle with a line through it. I tell you about write-protected disks later in this chapter.

■ If a file with the same file name already exists in the destination location, an error message appears in the Copy window (**Figure 34**). Click Stop to dismiss the window without making the copy, or click Replace to replace the existing file with the one you are copying.

■ Because copying small files happens so quickly in Mac OS X, you probably won't see the Copy window (**Figure 33**) very often. It doesn't have time to appear!

To copy an item to another location on the same disk

1. Hold down (Option) while dragging the icon for the item that you want to copy onto a folder icon (**Figure 35**) or into a window (**Figure 36**).

   When the mouse pointer on the item you are dragging moves on top of the destination location, a plus sign in a green circle appears beneath it. If the destination is an icon, the icon becomes highlighted.

2. Release the mouse button. A Copy window like the one in **Figure 33** appears. When it disappears, the copy is complete.

✔ Tips

■ When copying an item to a new location on the same disk, you *must* hold down (Option). If you don't, the item will be moved rather than copied.

■ If a file with the same file name already exists in the destination location, an error message appears in the Copy window (**Figure 34**). Click Stop to dismiss the window without making the copy, or click Replace to replace the existing file with the one you are copying.

To duplicate an item

1. Select the item that you want to duplicate.

2. Choose File > Duplicate (**Figure 37**), or press (⌃ ⌘ D).

   or

   Hold down (Option) while dragging the item that you want to duplicate to a different location in the same window.

A copy of the item you duplicated appears beside the original. The word *copy* is appended to the file name (**Figure 38**).

Figure 35
Hold down (Option) while dragging the item onto a folder...

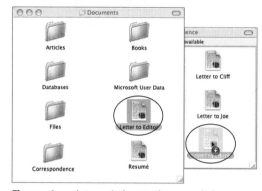

Figure 36 ...or into a window on the same disk.

Figure 37
Choose Duplicate from the File menu.

Letter to Editor copy

Figure 38
A duplicate appears beneath the original.

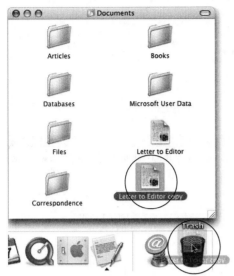

Figure 39 To move an item to the Trash, drag it there...

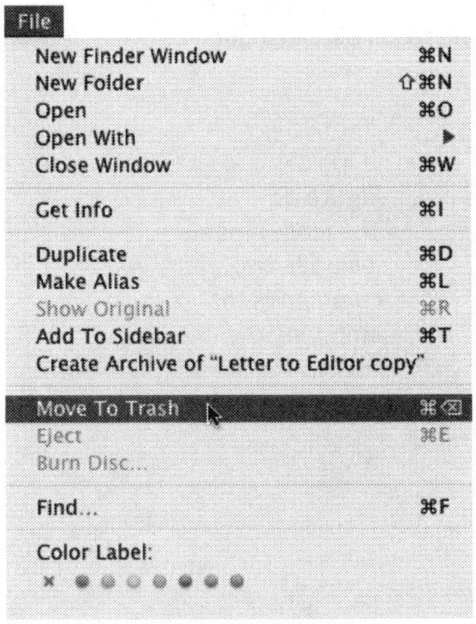

Figure 41
When an item has been moved to the Trash, the Trash icon looks full.

Figure 40
...or select the item and choose Move To Trash from the File menu.

The Trash & Deleting Items

The Trash is a special place on your hard disk where you place items you want to delete. Items in the Trash remain there until you empty the Trash, which removes them from your disk. In Mac OS X, the Trash appears as an icon in the Dock.

To move an item to the Trash

1. Drag the icon for the item you want to delete to the Trash icon in the Dock.

2. When the mouse pointer moves over the Trash icon, the Trash icon becomes selected (**Figure 39**). Release the mouse button.

or

1. Select the item that you want to delete.

2. Choose File > Move To Trash (**Figure 40**), or press ⌃ ⌘ Delete.

✔ Tips

■ The Trash icon's appearance indicates its status:

▲ If the Trash is empty, the Trash icon looks like an empty wire basket.

▲ If the Trash is not empty, the Trash icon looks like a wire basket with crumpled papers in it (**Figure 41**).

■ You can delete more than one item at a time. Begin by selecting all the items you want to delete, then drag any one of them to the Trash. All items will be moved to the Trash.

■ Moving a disk icon to the Trash does not delete or erase it. Instead, it *unmounts* it. Working with disks is covered a little later in this chapter.

■ You cannot drag an item to the Trash if the item is locked. I tell you about locking and unlocking items in **Chapter 4**.

To move an item out of the Trash

1. Click the Trash icon in the Dock to open the Trash window (**Figure 42**).

2. Drag the item from the Trash window to the Desktop or to another window on your hard disk.

   The item is moved from the Trash to the window you dragged it to.

or

Choose Edit > Undo Move of "*Item Name*" (**Figure 43**), or press ⌃ ⌘ Z. The item is moved back to where it was before you moved it to the Trash.

✔ Tip

■ The Undo command (**Figure 43**) will only take an item out of the Trash if the last thing you did was put it in the Trash.

To empty the Trash

1. Choose Finder > Empty Trash (**Figure 44**), or press Shift ⌃ ⌘ Delete.

2. A Trash warning dialog like the one in **Figure 45** appears. Click OK to delete all items that are in the Trash.

or

1. Point to the Trash icon, press the mouse button, and hold it down until a menu appears (**Figure 46**).

2. Choose Empty Trash. The contents of the Trash are deleted. No warning appears.

✔ Tip

■ You can disable the Trash warning dialog (**Figure 45**) in the Finder Preferences window. I explain how in **Chapter 4**.

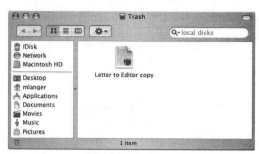

Figure 42 Opening the Trash displays the Trash window.

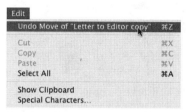

Figure 43 If the last thing you did was to put an item in the Trash, you can use the Undo command to take it back out.

Figure 44
The Finder menu includes two commands for emptying the Trash.

Figure 45 The Trash warning dialog asks you to confirm that you really do want to delete the items in the Trash.

MOVING ITEMS FROM & EMPTYING THE TRASH

Figure 46 When you point to the Trash icon in the Dock and hold the mouse button down, a menu with an Empty Trash option appears.

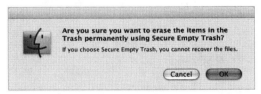

Figure 47 Using the Secure Empty Trash command displays a warning dialog like this.

To permanently remove items in the Trash from your disk

1. Choose Finder > Secure Empty Trash (**Figure 44**).

2. A Trash warning dialog like the one in **Figure 47** appears. Click OK to permanently remove all items that are in the Trash.

✔ Tips

- The Secure Empty Trash command, which is new in Mac OS X 10.3, makes it impossible to use special data recovery software to unerase deleted files.

- You may want to use the Secure Empty Trash command to erase personal files on a shared computer or a computer you plan to give away or sell.

- Deleting files from disk with the Secure Empty Trash command may take longer than using the Empty Trash command, especially when deleting large files.

- You can disable the Trash warning dialog (**Figure 47**) in the Finder Preferences window. I explain how in **Chapter 4**.

Storage Media

A Macintosh computer can read data from, or write data to, a wide range of storage media, including:

◆ **Hard disks**—high capacity magnetic media.

◆ **CD-ROM, CD-R, DVD, and DVD-R discs**—high capacity, removable optical media.

◆ **Zip, or other disks or cartridges**—high capacity, removable magnetic media.

◆ **Floppy disks or diskettes**—low capacity, removable magnetic media.

To use storage media, it must be:

◆ **Mounted**—inserted, attached, or otherwise accessible to your computer.

◆ **Formatted** or **initialized**—specially prepared for use with your computer.

All of these things are covered in this section.

✔ Tips

■ Don't confuse storage media with memory. The term *memory* usually refers to the amount of RAM in your computer, not disk space. RAM is discussed in **Chapter 5**.

■ At a minimum, all new Macintosh computers include a hard disk and CD-ROM drives.

■ Storage devices can be internal (inside your computer) or external (attached to your computer by a cable).

■ Some external storage devices must be properly connected and turned on *before* you start your computer or your computer may not recognize the device.

Table 1

Terminology for Storage Media Capacity		
Term	Abbreviation	Size
byte	byte	1 character
kilobyte	KB	1,024 bytes
megabyte	MB	1,024 KB
gigabyte	GB	1,024 MB

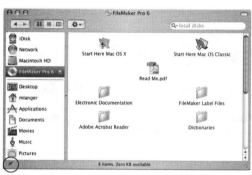

Figure 48 A write-protected icon appears in the status bar of CD-ROM discs and other write-protected media.

■ Disk storage media capacity is specified in terms of bytes, kilobytes, megabytes, and gigabytes (**Table 1**).

■ If a disk is *write-protected* or *locked*, files cannot be saved or copied to it. A pencil with a line through it appears in the status bar of write-protected or locked disks (**Figure 48**). I tell you more about the status bar in **Chapter 4**.

■ You cannot write data to a CD-ROM. But if your Mac has a CD-Recordable (CD-R) drive or SuperDrive, you can use special software to create or *burn* your own CDs.

Figure 49 Here's a desktop with an internal hard disk, CD-ROM disc, floppy disk, and network volume mounted.

Mounting Disks

You *mount* a disk by inserting it in the disk drive so it appears in the top level computer window (**Figure 49**). When a disk is mounted, your computer "sees" it and can access the information it contains.

✔ Tips

- You must mount a disk to use it.

- To learn how to mount disks that are not specifically covered in this book, consult the documentation that came with the disk drive.

- Mounted disks appear in the top-level window for your computer (**Figure 49**). You can display this window by choosing Go > Computer (**Figure 5**), as discussed earlier in this chapter.

- Mounted disks may also appear on the desktop, as shown in **Figure 49**, depending on how Finder preferences are set for the display of items on the desktop. I explain how to set Finder preferences in **Chapter 4**.

- You mount a network volume by using the Connect to Server command under the Go menu (**Figure 5**) or by browsing the network and opening the disk you want to mount. I explain how to access network volumes in **Chapter 14**.

To mount a CD or DVD disc

Insert the CD or DVD disc into the CD or
DVD slot.

or

1. Follow the manufacturer's instructions to
   open the CD or DVD disc tray or eject the
   CD or DVD caddy.

2. Place the CD or DVD disc in the tray or
   caddy, label side up.

3. Gently push the tray or caddy into the
   drive. After a moment, the disc icon
   appears in the top-level computer window. **Figure 49** shows a mounted
   CD-ROM (FileMaker Pro 6).

✔ Tip

■ If your CD or DVD drive does not use a
  disc tray or caddy, consult its documentation for specific instructions.

To mount a Zip disk

Insert the disk in the Zip drive, label side up,
metal side in. After a moment, the disk icon
appears in the top-level computer window.

To mount a floppy disk

Insert the disk in the floppy disk drive, label
side up, metal side in. The disk's icon appears
in the top-level computer window. **Figure 49**
shows a mounted floppy disk (Untitled).

Figure 50 Select the disk, and then choose Eject "Disk Name" from the File menu to eject the disk.

Figure 51 Or click the Eject button beside the item's name in the Sidebar.

Figure 52 Or drag the disk icon to the Trash.

Figure 53 When you drag a disk icon, the Trash icon changes into an icon like this.

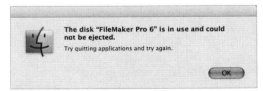

Figure 54 A dialog like this appears if you try to eject a disk that contains open files.

Ejecting Disks

When you eject a disk, the disk is physically removed from the disk drive and its icon disappears from the top-level computer window.

✔ Tip

- When the disk's icon disappears from the top-level computer window, it is said to be *unmounted*.

To eject a disk

1. Click the disk's icon once to select it.

2. Choose File > Eject "*Disk Name*" (**Figure 50**), or press ⌥⌘E.

or

1. Select the name of the disk in the Sidebar.

2. Click the eject button to the right of the disk name (**Figure 51**).

or

1. Drag the disk's icon to the Trash (**Figure 52**). As you drag, the Trash icon turns into a rectangle with a triangle on top (**Figure 53**).

2. When the mouse pointer moves over the Trash icon, it becomes selected (**Figure 52**). Release the mouse button.

or

Press the Media Eject key on the keyboard.

✔ Tips

- If you try to eject a disk that contains a file that is in use by your computer, a dialog like the one in **Figure 54** appears. Click OK to dismiss the dialog, then quit the open application. You should then be able to eject the disk. Working with applications is covered in **Chapter 5**.

- Not all keyboards include a Media Eject key. On some keyboards, F12 may act as a Media Eject key.

EJECTING DISKS

71

Burning CDs

If your Macintosh includes a CD-R drive or SuperDrive, you can write, or *burn*, files onto blank CD-R media. This is a great way to archive important files that you don't need on your computer's hard disk and to share files with other computer users.

✔ Tip

■ This part of the chapter provides one technique for burning a CD with the Finder's Burn Disc command. You can also burn CDs or DVDs from within iTunes, iDVD, or other third-party utilities, such as Roxio Toast. iTunes is discussed in **Chapter 8**.

To burn a CD

1. Insert a blank CD-R disc into your computer's CD-R drive or SuperDrive.

2. A dialog like the one in **Figure 55** appears. Make sure Open Finder is chosen from the Action pop-up menu (**Figure 56**). Then enter a suitable name for the disc in the edit box and click OK.

3. Wait while your computer prepares the disc. When it is finished, a CD disc icon appears on the desktop (**Figure 57**).

4. Drag the files you want to write on the disc onto the disc icon or into the open disc window (**Figure 58**).

5. Wait while your computer copies the files.

6. Repeat steps 4 and 5 until all files you want on the disc have been copied.

7. Arrange the icons in the disc's window or change the window's view as desired. (The window's view is also written to disc.)

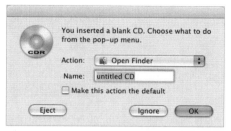

Figure 55 When you insert a blank CD-R disc, your Mac asks what you want to do.

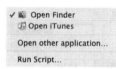

Figure 56
The Action pop-up menu enables you to choose the application you want to use to burn the CD.

Figure 57
An icon for the disc appears on the desktop.

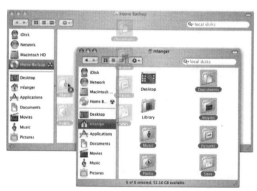

Figure 58 Copy the items you want to include on the disc to the disc's window.

Figure 59 Choose Burn Disc from the File menu...

Figure 60 ... or click the Burn Disc button beside the disc name in the Sidebar.

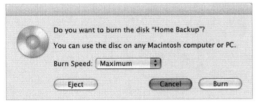

Figure 61 Your computer confirms that you want to burn the disc and enables you to choose the burn speed.

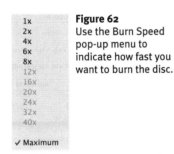

Figure 62 Use the Burn Speed pop-up menu to indicate how fast you want to burn the disc.

Figure 63 The Burn window appears while the disc is being prepared, burned, and verified.

8. Choose File > Burn Disc (**Figure 59**).

    or

    Click the Burn Disc button beside the name of the disc in the Sidebar (**Figure 60**).

9. A confirmation dialog like the one in **Figure 61** appears. If desired, choose a speed from the Burn Speed pop-up menu (**Figure 62**) and then click Burn.

10. Wait while your computer prepares, burns, and verifies the disc. A Burn Disc window (**Figure 63**) reports its progress. When it disappears, the disk is ready.

✔ Tips

■ If you choose a different application from the Action pop-up menu (**Figure 56**) in step 2, Mac OS X will open that application so you can use it to burn the disc. The remaining steps do not apply.

■ In step 9, the options that appear in the Burn Speed pop-up menu (**Figure 62**) vary depending on the speed of your CD-R or DVD-R drive.

■ If you're not sure which speed to choose in step 9, choose Maximum.

BURNING CDS

Advanced Finder Techniques

4

Advanced Finder Techniques

In addition to the basic Finder and file management techniques covered in **Chapters 2** and **3**, Mac OS X offers more advanced techniques you can use to customize the Finder, work with windows, and manage files:

- ◆ Customize the way the Finder looks and works.

- ◆ Customize the toolbar, Sidebar, and Dock to add the items you use most.

- ◆ Customize icon and list view windows to change the way contents are displayed.

- ◆ Use hierarchical outlines in list view.

- ◆ Use spring-loaded folders to access folders while copying or moving items.

- ◆ Use Exposé to quickly view open applications or documents.

- ◆ Apply color-coded labels to Finder items.

- ◆ Use aliases to make frequently used files easier to access without moving them.

- ◆ Create archives to save space on disk or minimize data transfer time.

- ◆ Quickly reopen recently used items.

- ◆ Find files and folders on any mounted disk.

- ◆ Use the Info window to learn more about an item or set options for it.

- ◆ Undo actions you performed while working with the Finder.

✔ Tips

- ■ If you're brand new to Mac OS, be sure to read the information in **Chapters 2** and **3** before working with this chapter. Those chapters contain information and instructions about techniques that are used throughout this chapter.

- ■ This chapter is especially useful for experienced Mac OS users since it goes beyond the basics with new or advanced Mac OS features.

Finder Preferences

Finder preferences enables you to customize several aspects of the desktop and Finder. In Mac OS X 10.3, the Finder's preferences window is organized into four different panes of options:

◆ **General** lets you set options for the desktop and Finder windows.

◆ **Labels** enables you to set colors and label names for the Finder's label feature, which is discussed later in this chapter.

◆ **Sidebar** lets you set options for the Sidebar.

◆ **Advanced** enables you to set options for the display of file extensions, the Trash warning, and file searching.

✔ Tip

■ Customizing Finder labels and the Sidebar are covered later in this chapter.

To set General Finder Preferences

1. Choose Finder > Preferences (**Figure 1**) or press ⌘, to display the Finder Preferences window.

2. If necessary, click the General button to display General options (**Figure 2**).

3. Toggle check boxes to specify what items should appear on the desktop:

   ▲ **Hard disks** displays icons for mounted hard disks.

   ▲ **CDs, DVDs, and iPods** displays icons for removable media, including CDs, DVDs, Zip, Jaz, and floppy disks, as well as iPods.

   ▲ **Connected servers** displays icons for mounted server volumes.

Figure 2
The default settings for General Finder preferences.

Figure 3
Use this pop-up menu to specify what should appear in a new Finder window.

Figures 4, 5, 6, & 7 A new Finder window can display the top-level computer window, your hard disk contents, your Home folder contents, or your Documents folder contents.

Figure 8
Use a dialog like this to display a specific folder when you open a new Finder window.

4. Choose an option from the pop-up menu (**Figure 3**) to determine what should appear in a new Finder window (the window that appears when you choose File > New Finder Window):

▲ **Computer** displays the icons for the network and all mounted volumes (**Figure 4**).

▲ *Hard Disk name* displays the root level of your hard disk (**Figure 5**).

▲ **iDisk** displays the top level of your iDisk. (This option only appears if you are a .Mac subscriber and have an iDisk.)

▲ **Home** displays the contents of your Home folder (**Figure 6**).

▲ **Documents** displays the contents of the Documents folder inside your Home folder (**Figure 7**).

▲ **Other** displays the Choose a Folder dialog (**Figure 8**), which you can use to select a different folder to display.

5. Toggle check boxes to set other options:

▲ **Always open folders in a new window** opens a new window to display the contents of the folder you open. This makes Mac OS X work more like Mac OS 9.2 and earlier.

▲ **Open new windows in column view** opens all new windows in column view, regardless of which view was last used to view the window.

▲ **Spring-loaded folders and windows** enables the spring-loaded folders feature. You can use the slider to set the delay time for this feature.

✔ Tip

■ I discuss the spring-loaded folders feature later in this chapter, disks and mounting disks in **Chapter 3**, and views in **Chapter 3** and later in this chapter.

To set Advanced Finder Preferences

1. Choose Finder > Preferences (**Figure 1**) or press ⌘ , to display the Finder Preferences window.

2. If necessary, click the Advanced button to display Advanced options (**Figure 9**).

3. Toggle check boxes to set options:

   ▲ **Show all file extensions** displays file extensions in Finder windows (**Figure 10**).

   ▲ **Show warning before emptying the Trash** displays a confirmation dialog like the one in **Figure 11** each time you choose Finder > Empty Trash or Finder > Secure Empty Trash. Turning off this check box prevents the dialog from appearing.

4. To specify the languages you want to use when finding files by content, click the Select button. In the Languages dialog that appears (**Figure 12**), toggle check marks to indicate which languages are in your documents. Then click OK.

✔ Tips

■ In step 4, choose as few languages as possible. This makes the index file used for finding files smaller and faster.

■ I discuss finding files later in this chapter and the Trash in **Chapter 3**.

Figure 9
The default settings for Advanced Finder preferences.

Figure 10 You can set up the Finder so it always displays file extensions as part of an item's name.

Figure 11 The Trash warning dialog.

Figure 12 Use the Languages dialog to indicate which languages you will use with the find by content feature.

Figure 13
The View menu.

Figure 14 The Customize Toolbar window.

Figure 15 To add an item, drag it from the center part of
the dialog sheet to the toolbar.

Figure 16 When you release the mouse button, the
item is added.

Customizing the Toolbar

The toolbar, which is discussed in **Chapter 2**,
can be customized to include buttons and
icons for a variety of commands and items.

✔ Tips

- When you customize the toolbar, your
  changes affect the toolbar in all windows
  in which the toolbar is displayed.

- To display the toolbar, click the Toolbar
  control button in the upper-right corner
  of a Finder window, choose View > Show
  Toolbar, or press Option ⌘ T.

To customize the toolbar

1. With any Finder window open and the
   toolbar displayed, choose View > Customize Toolbar (**Figure 13**). The Customize
   Toolbar dialog sheet appears (**Figure 14**).

2. To add an item to the toolbar, drag it from
   the dialog sheet to the position you want
   it to occupy in the toolbar (**Figure 15**).
   When you release the mouse button, the
   item appears on the toolbar (**Figure 16**).

3. To remove an item from the toolbar, drag
   it from the toolbar into the center part of
   the window (**Figure 17**). When you release
   the mouse button, the item disappears
   (**Figure 18**).

4. To rearrange the order of items on the
   toolbar, drag them into the desired
   position (**Figure 19**). When you release
   the mouse button, the items are rearranged (**Figure 20**).

Continued on next page...

CUSTOMIZING THE TOOLBAR

Continued from previous page.

5. To specify how items should appear on the toolbar, choose an option from the Show pop-up menu at the bottom of the window (**Figure 21**):

   ▲ **Icon & Text** displays both the icon and the icon's name (**Figure 22**).

   ▲ **Icon Only** displays only the icon (**Figure 20**).

   ▲ **Text Only** displays only the name of the icon (**Figure 23**).

6. To display smaller size toolbar buttons, turn on the Use Small Size check box.

7. When you are finished making changes, click Done.

✔ Tip

■ In past versions of Mac OS X, you could add any icon, such as one for your favorite application, to the toolbar. Although this is no longer true, you can add any icon to the Sidebar, which is new in Mac OS X 10.3. I explain how a little later in this chapter.

To restore the toolbar to its default settings

1. With any Finder window displaying the toolbar open, choose View > Customize Toolbar (**Figure 13**). The Customize Toolbar dialog sheet appears (**Figure 14**).

2. Drag the group of items in a box near the bottom of the window to the toolbar (**Figure 24**). When you release the mouse button, the toolbar's default items appear (**Figure 13**).

3. Click Done.

Figure 17
To remove an item, drag it off the toolbar.

Figure 18 When you release the mouse button, the item is removed.

Figure 19 To rearrange toolbar items, drag them around the toolbar.

Figure 20 When you release the mouse button, the items are rearranged.

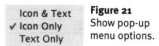
Figure 21 Show pop-up menu options.

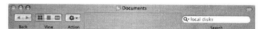
Figures 22 & 23 You can also display the toolbar as icons and text (above) or as text only (below).

Figure 24 Drag the default set of icons to the toolbar.

Figure 25 Position the mouse pointer on the border between the Sidebar and the rest of the window...

Figure 26 ...and drag to move the border, thus changing the Sidebar's width.

Customizing the Sidebar

The Sidebar, which is discussed in **Chapter 2**, can be customized a number of ways:

◆ Change the width of the Sidebar to better display long item names or just show icons.

◆ Use Finder preferences to specify which standard Mac OS X items should automatically appear in the Sidebar.

◆ Manually add or remove folders, files, and other items in the bottom half of the Sidebar.

✔ Tips

■ The Sidebar is new in Mac OS X 10.3.

■ The Sidebar only appears if the toolbar is displayed.

To change the width of the Sidebar

1. Position the mouse pointer on the divider between the Sidebar and the rest of the Finder window. The mouse pointer turns into a line with two arrows coming out of it (**Figure 25**).

2. Press the mouse button down and drag. As you drag, the Sidebar's width changes (**Figure 26**).

3. When the Sidebar is the desired width, release the mouse button.

✔ Tip

■ The Sidebar's border may "snap" to a certain width as you drag. This width will be wide enough to fully display all Sidebar item names. You can continue to drag to change this width if desired.

CHANGING THE SIDEBAR WIDTH

To specify which standard items should appear in the Sidebar

1. Choose Finder > Preferences (**Figure 1**) or press ⌃ ⌘, to display the Finder Preferences window.

2. If necessary, click the Sidebar button to display Sidebar options (**Figure 27**).

3. Toggle check boxes to specify what items should appear in the Sidebar.

4. Click the Sidebar preferences window's close button to save your settings.

To add an item to the Sidebar

1. Drag the icon for the item you want to add onto the Sidebar. A blue line indicates where it will appear (**Figure 28**).

2. Release the mouse button. The item appears on the Sidebar (**Figure 29**).

✔ Tip

- Adding an item to the Sidebar does not move it from where it resides on disk. Instead, it creates and adds a pointer to the original item to the Sidebar.

To remove an item from the Sidebar

1. Drag the item off the Sidebar (**Figure 30**).

2. Release the mouse button. The item disappears (**Figure 31**).

✔ Tip

- Removing an item from the Sidebar does not delete it from disk. Instead, it removes the pointer to the original item from the Sidebar.

Figure 27
The default settings in the Sidebar preferences window of Finder preferences.

Figure 28 To add an item to the Sidebar, drag it on.

Figure 29
The item appears where you positioned it.

Figure 30 To remove an item from the Sidebar, drag it off.

Figure 31 The item is removed.

Figure 32 Pressing the mouse button on a Dock item often displays a menu. In this example, pressing the open iChat application icon displays a menu of options for iChat.

Figure 33 Creative use of folders in the Dock can put all your frequently used files at your fingertips—without turning the Dock into a cluttered mess. (As this real-life example shows, however, the menus themselves can become cluttered messes!)

Customizing the Dock

The Dock, which is discussed in **Chapter 2**, can be customized to include icons for specific documents and applications that you use often. This makes them quick and easy to open any time you need them.

✔ Tips

- The Dock was designed to take the place of the customizable Apple menu in Mac OS 9.2 and earlier.

- When you press the mouse button down on a Dock icon, a menu with commands or other options that apply to that icon appears (**Figure 32**). You can select a command like any other menu command.

- When you press the mouse button down on a folder in the Dock, it appears as a menu. Choose an item to open it or point to a folder within the menu to display a submenu of items within it. **Figure 33** shows an example of how you can use this feature.

To add an icon to the Dock

1. Open the window containing the icon you want to add to the Dock.

2. Drag the icon from the window to the Dock. Items on the Dock shift to make room for the new item (**Figure 34**).

3. Release the mouse button. The icon appears (**Figure 35**).

✔ Tips

- Dragging an icon to the Dock does not remove it from its original location.

- When dragging items to the Dock, drag applications to the left of the divider and documents, folders, Web sites, and servers to the right of the divider.

To remove an icon from the Dock

1. Drag the item from the Dock to the desktop (**Figure 36**).

2. Release the mouse button. The icon disappears.

✔ Tips

- Removing an icon from the Dock does not delete it from disk.

- If you try to remove an icon for an application that is running, the icon will not disappear from the Dock until you quit the application.

Figure 34 Drag an icon from the window to the Dock.

Figure 35 The icon appears in the Dock.

Figure 36 Drag an icon off the Dock.

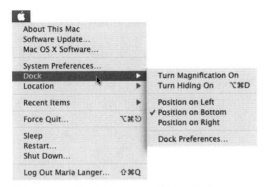

Figure 37 The Dock submenu under the Apple menu offers options for customizing the way the Dock looks and works.

Figure 38 When magnification is turned on, pointing to an icon enlarges it.

Figure 39 You can position the Dock on the side of the screen instead of the bottom.

Figure 40 You can resize the Dock by pointing to the divider line and dragging.

To set basic Dock options

Choose options from the Dock submenu under the Apple menu (**Figure 37**):

◆ **Turn Magnification On** magnifies a Dock icon when you point to it (**Figure 38**). With this option enabled, the command changes to **Turn Magnification Off**, which disables magnification.

◆ **Turn Hiding On** (Option ⌃ ⌘ D) automatically hides the Dock until you point to where it should appear. This is a great way to regain screen real estate normally occupied by the Dock. With this option enabled, the command changes to **Turn Hiding Off**, which displays the Dock all the time.

◆ **Position on Left**, **Position on Bottom**, and **Position on Right** move the Dock to the left side, bottom, or right side of the screen. The option that is not available (Position on Bottom in **Figure 37**) is the one that is currently selected. When positioned on the left or right, the Dock fits vertically down the screen (**Figure 39**).

◆ **Dock Preferences** displays the Dock preferences pane, which includes a few additional options for customizing the Dock. I cover the Dock preferences pane in **Chapter 18**.

✔ Tip

■ To change the size of the Dock, point to the divider line. When the mouse pointer turns into a line with two arrows (**Figure 40**), press the mouse button down and drag to make the Dock bigger or smaller.

Customizing Window & Desktop Views

As discussed in **Chapter 3**, a window's view determines how icons and other information appear within it. Mac OS X remembers a window's view settings and uses them whenever you display the window.

You can customize views a number of ways:

◆ Change the settings for the default view for icon, list, and column views.

◆ Change the settings for an individual window's icon or list view.

◆ Change the view for the desktop.

View settings offer a number of options:

◆ Icon view settings include icon size, label text size and position, display options, arrangement, and background.

◆ List view settings include icon size, text size, columns, date format, and item size calculation, as well as column width and the order in which columns appear.

◆ Column view settings include text size, icon appearance, and preview column.

◆ Desktop view settings include icon size, label text size and position, display options, and arrangement.

You can also display a status bar with disk information in any Finder window.

✔ Tip

■ The only time the Finder does not use a window's custom view is when you have the "Open new windows in Column View" option set in the Finder preferences' General window (**Figure 2**). I tell you about this option earlier in this chapter.

CUSTOMIZING WINDOW & DESKTOP VIEWS

Figure 41
The view options for a Finder window in icon view.

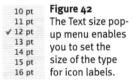

Figure 42
The Text size pop-up menu enables you to set the size of the type for icon labels.

Figures 43 & 44 You can place icon labels beneath the icons (above), which is the default setting or to the right of icons (below).

To set icon view options

1. To set icon view options for a specific window, activate that window and make sure it is displayed in icon view.

   or

   To set default icon view options, activate any window that is displayed in icon view.

2. Choose View > Show View Options (**Figure 13**), or press ⌃ ⌘ J to display the view options window (**Figure 41**).

3. Select the radio button for the type of option you want to set:

   ▲ **This window only** customizes the settings for the active window.

   ▲ **All windows** sets options for all icon view windows that do not have custom settings.

4. Use the Icon size slider to set the size of icons:

   ▲ Drag the slider to the left to make the icon size smaller.

   ▲ Drag the slider to the right to make the icon size larger.

5. Choose a type size from the Text size pop-up menu (**Figure 42**).

6. Select a Label position radio button to specify where icon labels should appear:

   ▲ **Bottom** displays labels below the icons (**Figure 43**).

   ▲ **Right** displays labels to the right of the icons (**Figure 44**).

Continued on next page...

SETTING ICON VIEW OPTIONS

Continued from previous page.

7. Toggle check boxes to specify how icons should appear:

▲ **Snap to grid** forces icons to snap to the window's invisible grid, thus ensuring consistent spacing between icons.

▲ **Show item info** displays information about the item beneath its name. **Figure 45** shows an example with graphic file size, in pixels, displayed.

▲ **Show icon preview** displays a document's preview, if available, in place of its standard icon. **Figures 43 through 45** show preview icons for two graphic files.

▲ **Keep arranged by** automatically arranges icons in a certain order. If you select this option, choose a sort order from the pop-up menu beneath it (**Figure 46**).

8. Select a Background option:

▲ **White** makes the background white.

▲ **Color** enables you to select a background color for the window. If you select this option, click the color well that appears beside it (**Figure 47**), use the Colors palette (**Figure 48**) to select a color, and click OK.

▲ **Picture** enables you to set a background picture for the window. If you select this option, click the Select button that appears beside it (**Figure 49**), use the Select a Picture dialog to locate and select a background picture (**Figure 50**), and click Select.

9. When you're finished setting options, click the view option window's close button to dismiss it.

Figure 45 You can display information about an item beneath its label.

Figure 46
Use this pop-up menu to specify an automatic arrangement order.

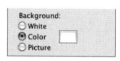

Figure 47
When you select the Color radio button, a color well appears.

Figure 48
Use the Colors palette to select a new background color.

Figure 49
When you select the Picture radio button, a Select button appears.

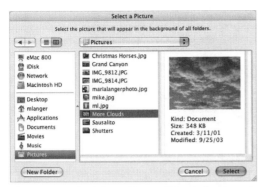

Figure 50 Use the Select a Picture dialog to locate and select a background picture.

Figure 51 A background picture appears behind icons.

✔ Tips

- To restore the current window's options to the default settings for all icon view windows, select the All windows radio button in step 3.

- I explain how to select a color with the Colors palette in **Chapter 9**.

- Working with dialogs is discussed in **Chapter 5**.

- A background picture fills the window's background behind the icons (**Figure 51**).

To set list view options

1. To set list view options for a specific window, activate that window and make sure it is displayed in list view.

   or

   To set default list view options, activate any window that is displayed in list view.

2. Choose View > Show View Options (**Figure 13**) or press ⌃⌘J to display the view options window (**Figure 52**).

3. Select the radio button for the type of option you want to set:

   ▲ **This window only** customizes the settings for the active window.

   ▲ **All windows** sets options for all list view windows that do not have custom settings.

4. Select an Icon size option by clicking the radio button beneath the size you want.

5. Choose a type size from the Text size pop-up menu (**Figure 42**).

6. Select the columns you want to appear in list view by turning Show columns check boxes on or off:

   ▲ **Date Modified** is the date and time an item was last changed.

   ▲ **Date Created** is the date and time an item was first created.

   ▲ **Size** is the amount of disk space the item occupies.

   ▲ **Kind** is the type of item. I tell you about types of items in **Chapter 2**.

   ▲ **Version** is the item's version number.

   ▲ **Comments** is the information you entered in the Comments field of the Info window. I tell you about the Info window later in this chapter.

   ▲ **Label** is the label assigned to the item.

Figure 52
The view options for list view.

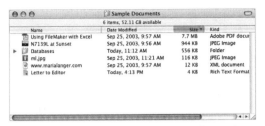

Figure 53 When you turn on the Calculate all sizes in the list view options for a window, you can sort the window's contents by size. This example also shows the Use relative dates option enabled.

Figure 54
The view options for column view.

Figure 55 With the Show preview column option enabled, selecting an item that includes a preview displays the preview in the far right column.

7. To display the date in relative terms (that is, using the words "today" and "yesterday"), turn on the Use relative dates check box.

8. To display the disk space occupied by items and the contents of folders in the list, turn on the Calculate all sizes check box.

9. When you're finished setting options, click the view option window's close button to dismiss it.

✔ Tips

■ Turning on the Calculate all sizes check box in step 8 makes it possible to sort all of a window's contents by size, including folders (**Figure 53**). Sorting window contents is covered in **Chapter 3**.

■ The Label option is new in Mac OS X 10.3.

To set column view options

1. Activate any window that is displayed in column view.

2. Choose View > Show View Options (**Figure 13**) or press ⌃⌘J to display the view options window (**Figure 54**).

3. Choose a type size from the Text size popup menu (**Figure 42**).

4. To display icons beside item names, turn on the Show icons check box.

5. To display previews (when available) for selected items (**Figure 55**), turn on the Show preview column check box.

6. When you're finished setting options, click the view option window's close button to dismiss it.

To set desktop view options

1. Click anywhere on the desktop to activate it.

2. Choose View > Show View Options (**Figure 13**) or press ⌃⌘J to display the Desktop view options window (**Figure 56**).

3. Use the Icon size slider to set the size of icons:

   ▲ Drag the slider to the left to make the icon size smaller.

   ▲ Drag the slider to the right to make the icon size larger.

4. Choose a type size from the Text size pop-up menu (**Figure 42**).

5. Select a radio button to specify where icon labels should appear:

   ▲ **Bottom** displays labels below the icons.

   ▲ **Right** displays labels to the right of the icon.

6. Toggle check boxes to specify how icons should appear:

   ▲ **Snap to grid** forces icons to snap to the desktop's invisible grid, thus ensuring consistent spacing between icons.

   ▲ **Show item info** displays information about the item beneath its name.

   ▲ **Show icon preview** displays a document's preview, if available, in place of its standard icon.

   ▲ **Keep arranged by** automatically arranges icons in a certain order. If you select this option, choose a sort order from the pop-up menu beneath it (**Figure 47**).

7. When you're finished setting options, click the view option window's close button to dismiss it.

Figure 56
View options for the desktop.

✔ Tip

■ You can set the desktop color or picture in the Desktop & Screen Saver preferences pane, which I cover in **Chapter 18**.

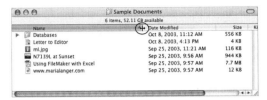

Figure 57 Position the mouse pointer on the column border.

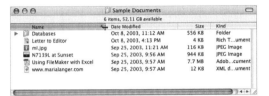

Figure 58 When you press the mouse button down and drag, the column's width changes.

Figure 59 Drag a column heading...

Figure 60 ...to change the column's position.

To change a column's width

1. Position the mouse pointer on the line between the heading for the column whose width you want to change and the column to its right. The mouse pointer turns into a vertical bar with two arrows (**Figure 57**).

2. Press the mouse button down and drag:
   ▲ To make the column narrower, drag to the left (**Figure 58**).
   ▲ To make the column wider, drag to the right.

3. When the column is displayed at the desired width, release the mouse button.

✔ Tip

■ If you make a column too narrow to display all of its contents, information may be truncated or condensed.

To change a column's position

1. Position the mouse pointer on the heading for the column you want to move.

2. Press the mouse button down and drag:
   ▲ To move the column to the left, drag to the left (**Figure 59**).
   ▲ To move the column to the right, drag to the right.

   As you drag, the other columns shift to make room for the column you're dragging.

3. When the column is in the desired position, release the mouse button. The column changes its position (**Figure 60**).

✔ Tip

■ You cannot change the position of the Name column.

To display the status bar

Choose View > Show Status Bar (**Figure 61**).

The status bar appears above the window's contents (**Figure 62**).

✔ Tips

- The status bar always appears when the toolbar and Sidebar are displayed (**Figure 63**).

- As shown in **Figures 62** and **63**, the status bar shows the number of items in the window and the total amount of space available on the disk.

- If one or more items are selected in a window, the status bar reports how many items are selected (**Figure 64**).

- When the status bar is displayed, it appears in all Finder windows.

To hide the status bar

Choose View > Hide Status Bar (**Figure 65**).

The status bar disappears.

✔ Tip

- The status bar cannot be hidden when the toolbar and Sidebar are displayed.

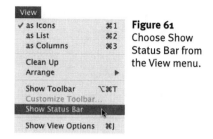

Figure 61
Choose Show Status Bar from the View menu.

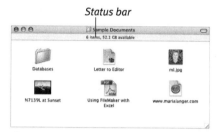

Figure 62 When the toolbar is not displayed, the status bar appears above the window's contents.

Figure 63 When the toolbar is displayed, the status bar appears at the bottom of the window.

Figure 64 The status bar can also report how many items are selected in a window.

Figure 65
When the status bar is displayed, the Hide Status Bar command appears on the View menu.

Figure 66 Position the mouse pointer in front of the first icon you want to select.

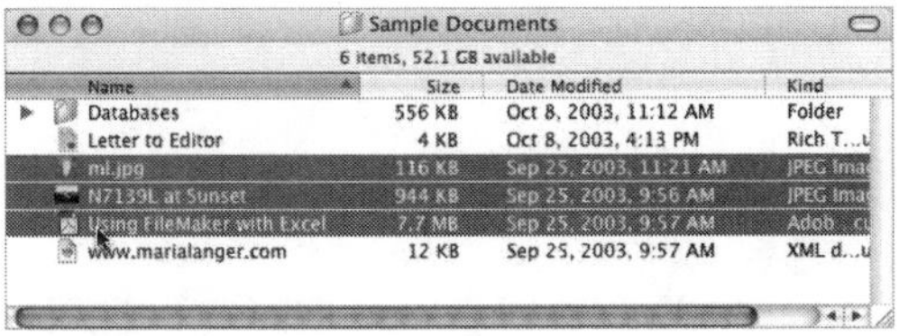

Figure 67 Drag over the other icons you want to select.

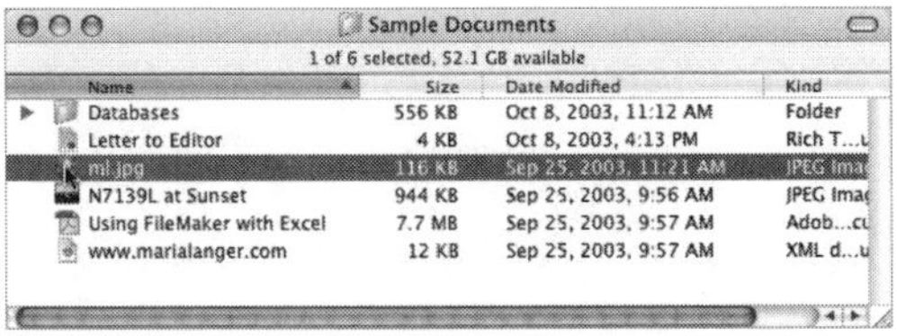

Figure 68 Select the first icon.

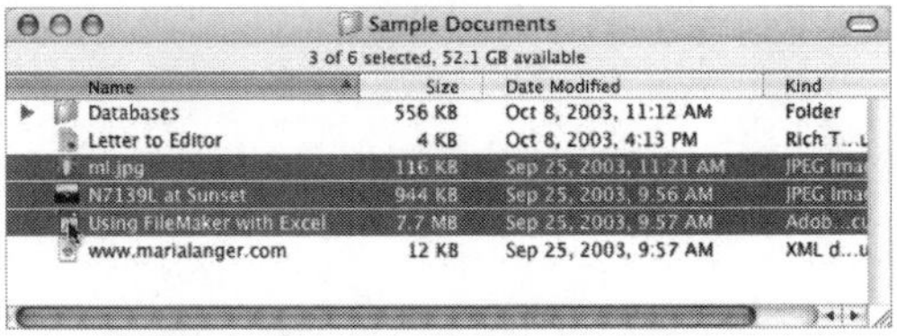

Figure 69 Hold down Shift and click the last icon.

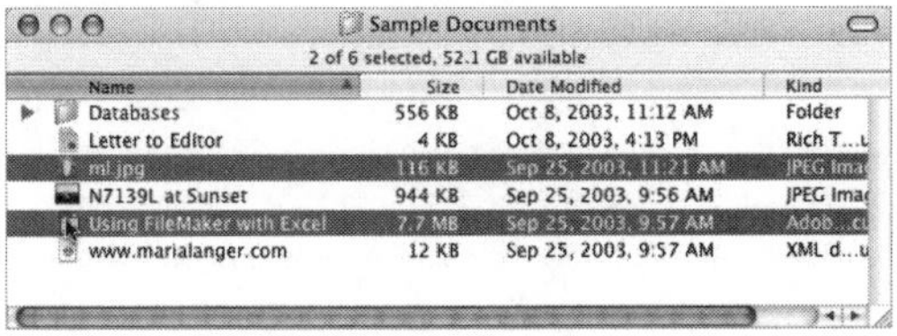

Figure 70 Hold down ⌃⌘ and click another icon.

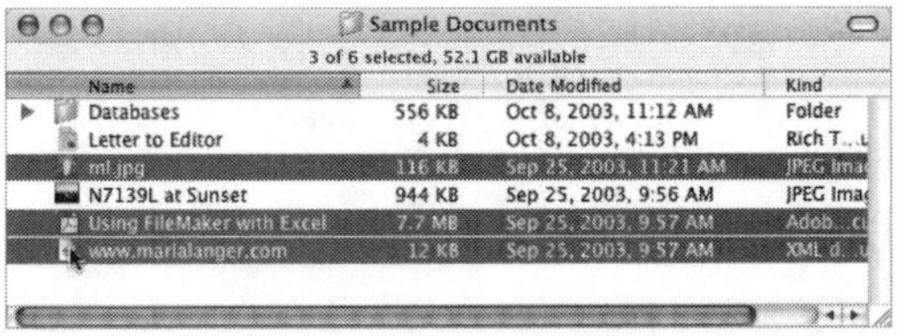

Figure 71 Continue holding down ⌃⌘ and clicking icons until you're finished selecting the icons you want.

Selecting Icons in List View

In Mac OS X 10.3, Apple made subtle changes to the way icons are selected in list view. Rather than just the icon and its name being selected when you click it, now the entire line for the icon is selected (**Figures 67** through **71**). In addition, there are a few "tricks" for making multiple icon selections.

To select multiple contiguous icons

1. Position the mouse pointer in front of the first icon you want to select (**Figure 66**).

2. Hold the mouse button down and drag over the other icons you want to select (**Figure 67**).

or

1. Click to select the first icon you want to select (**Figure 68**).

2. Hold down Shift and click the last icon in the group you want to select (**Figure 69**).

To select multiple noncontiguous icons

1. Click to select the first icon you want to select (**Figure 68**).

2. Hold down ⌃⌘ and click the next icon you want to select (**Figure 70**).

3. Repeat step 2 until all icons have been selected (**Figure 71**).

To deselect icons

Click anywhere in the window other than on an icon's line of information.

Working with Outlines in List View

Windows displayed in list view have a feature not found in icon or column views: They can display the contents of folders within the window as an outline (**Figures** 73 and 74).

✔ Tip

■ Views are discussed in detail in **Chapter 3** and earlier in this chapter.

To display a folder's contents

Click the right-pointing triangle beside the folder (**Figure** 72).

or

Click the folder once to select it, and press ⌃⌘→.

The items within that folder are listed below it, slightly indented (**Figure** 73).

✔ Tip

■ As shown in **Figure** 74, you can use this technique to display multiple levels of folders in the same window.

To hide a folder's contents

Click the down-pointing triangle beside the folder (**Figure** 73).

or

Click the folder once to select it, and press ⌃⌘←.

The outline collapses to hide the items in the folder (**Figure** 72).

Click a right-pointing triangle to expand the outline.

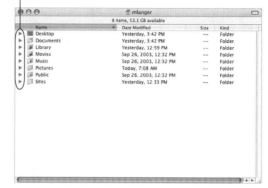

Figure 72 Right-pointing triangles indicate collapsed outlines.

Click a down-pointing triangle to collapse an outline.

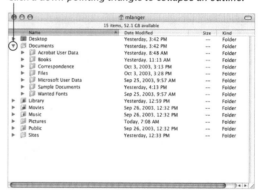

Figure 73 Folder contents can be displayed as an outline...

Figure 74 ...that can show several levels.

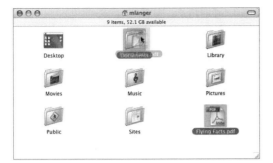

Figure 75 Drag an icon onto a folder and wait...

Figure 76 ...until the folder opens.

Spring-Loaded Folders

The spring-loaded folders feature lets you move or copy items into folders deep within the file structure of a disk—without manually opening a single folder. Instead, you simply drag icons onto folders (**Figures 75** and **77**) and wait as they're automatically opened (**Figures 76** and **78**). When you drop the icon into the final window, all windows except the source and destination windows automatically close (**Figure 79**).

✔ Tips

- The spring-loaded folders feature is sometimes referred to as *spring-open folders*.

- Using the spring-loaded folders feature requires a steady hand, good mouse skills, and knowledge of the location of folders on your disk.

- To use the spring-loaded folders feature, the Spring-loaded folders and windows check box must be turned on in the General window of Finder preferences (**Figure 2**). You can also set the spring-loaded folder delay length in this window. I tell you about General Finder Preferences at the beginning of this chapter.

- To use the spring-loaded folders feature to move or copy more than one item at a time, select the items first, then drag any one of them.

To move an item using spring-loaded folders

1. Drag the item you want to move onto the folder to which you want to move it (**Figure 75**), but do not release the mouse button. After a moment, the folder blinks and opens (**Figure 76**).

2. Without releasing the mouse button, repeat step 1. The destination folder becomes selected (**Figure 77**), then blinks and opens (**Figure 78**). Do this until you reach the final destination.

3. Release the mouse button to place the item into the destination window. All windows other than the source and destination windows close; the source window remains active (**Figure 79**).

✔ Tips

- In steps 1 and 2, to open a folder immediately, press Spacebar while dragging an item onto it.

- To close a folder's window so you can open a different folder in the same window, drag the item away from the open window. The window closes so you can drag the item onto a different folder and open it.

To copy an item using spring-loaded folders

Hold down Option while following the above steps.

✔ Tip

- If the destination folder is on another disk, it is not necessary to hold down Option to copy items; they're automatically copied.

Figure 77 Continue to drag the icon onto a folder in that window and wait...

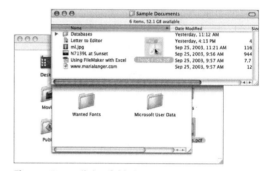

Figure 78 ...until that folder opens.

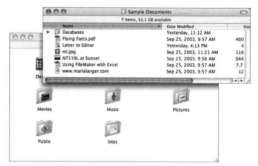

Figure 79 When you're finished, only the source window (which is active) and the destination window remain open.

Table 1

Standard Shortcut Keys for Exposé	
Key	**Description**
F9	Displays all open windows at once.
F10	Displays all open windows for the current application at once.
F11	Displays the desktop.

Figure 80 Pressing F9 displays all open windows.

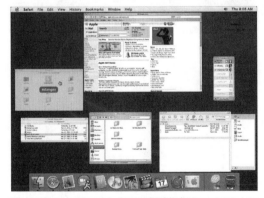

Figure 81 Point to a window to highlight its name.

Exposé

If you're like most Mac OS X users, you probably have multiple applications and windows open at the same time while you work. The result can be a cluttered screen, with many layers of windows hiding other windows and the desktop.

Exposé, which is new in Mac OS X 10.3, helps solve the problem of screen clutter by making it easy to see all open windows in all applications (**Figure 80**), all open windows in a single application (**Figure 82**), or the entire desktop (**Figure 83**) at once. Simply press one of Exposé's shortcut keys (**Table 1**) to see what you need to see.

✔ Tips

- You can customize Exposé's shortcut keys or add additional Exposé triggers. I explain how later in this section.

- You can use Exposé while copying or moving items. Use the appropriate Exposé keystroke for the view you need, then drag or drop while Exposé is active.

To see all open windows at once

1. Press F9.

   All open windows resize so you can see into each one (**Figure 80**).

2. To activate a window, point to it to highlight its name (**Figure 81**) and click it or press F9 again. Exposé is released and the window comes to the front.

   or

   To release Exposé without activating a specific window, press F9 again.

To see all open windows in the current application

1. Press F10.

   All open windows in the current application resize so you can see into each one and other application windows are dimmed (**Figure 82**).

2. To activate a window, point to it to highlight its name and click it or press F10 again. Exposé is released and the window comes to the front.

   or

   To release Exposé without activating a specific window, press F10 again.

To see the desktop

1. Press F11.

   All open windows shift to the edges of the screen so you can see the desktop (**Figure 83**).

2. To release Exposé, press F11 again.

To switch from one Exposé view to another

Press the shortcut key for the other view.

Figure 82 Pressing F10 displays all of the windows in the currently active application—in this case, Finder.

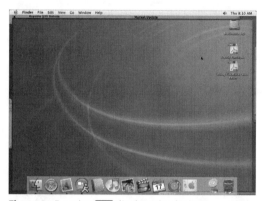

Figure 83 Pressing F11 displays the desktop.

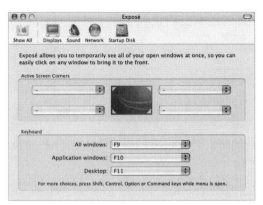

Figure 84 The default settings in the Exposé preferences pane.

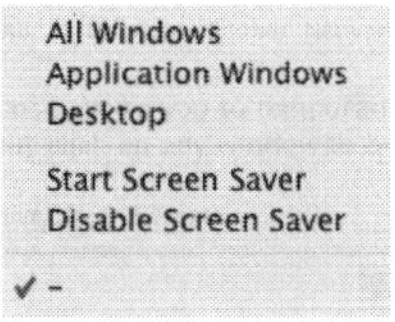

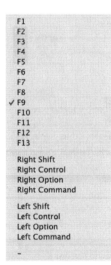

Figure 85
Use a pop-up menu like this one to set active screen corners for invoking Exposé.

Figure 86 Pop-up menus in the Keyboard area enable you to choose different shortcut keys for invoking Exposé.

Figure 87 Holding down (Shift) displays more shortcut key choices.

To customize the way Exposé works

1. Choose Apple > System Preferences or click the System Preferences icon in the Dock.

2. In the System Preferences window that appears, click the Exposé icon to display its options (**Figure 84**).

3. To add Exposé triggers based on mouse position, choose an option from any combination of the four pop-up menus in the Active Screen Corners area (**Figure 85**). For example, if you choose All Windows from the top-left Active Screen Corner pop-up menu, moving the mouse pointer to the top-left corner of the screen will automatically display all open windows—just as if you'd pressed (F9).

4. To change an Exposé shortcut key, choose an option from the appropriate pop-up menu in the Keyboard area (**Figure 86**). Choosing - disables keyboard access for that Exposé feature.

5. When you are finished making changes, click the Exposé window's close button or choose System Preferences > Quit System Preferences.

✔ Tips

■ As shown in **Figure 85**, you can use the Active Screen Corners pop-up menus to set screen saver options. I tell you how to use Apple's built-in screen saver in **Chapter 18**.

■ You can see more keyboard options by pressing (Shift), (Control), or (⌃ ⌘) while a Keyboard area pop-up menu is displayed (**Figure 87**).

Labels

Labels, a feature of Mac OS 9.2 and earlier, was added back to Mac OS X in version 10.3. This feature enables you to assign color-coded labels to Finder icons. You can then sort list view windows by label or search for items based on label. With a little imagination, labels can be a useful file management tool.

✔ Tip

- You can only sort a window by labels if the Label column is displayed in that window (**Figure 97**). I explain how to customize a list view window earlier in this chapter.

To assign a label to an item

1. In a Finder window, select the icon(s) you want to apply a label to (**Figure 88**).

2. From the File menu, choose the color of the label you want to apply (**Figure 89**).

   The name of the icon is enclosed in an oval in the color you choose (**Figure 90**).

To remove a label from an item

1. In a Finder window, select the icon you want to remove a label from (**Figure 91**).

2. From the File menu, choose the X beneath Color Label (**Figure 92**).

   The label is removed.

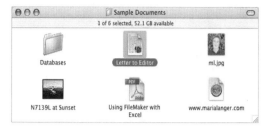

Figure 88 Select the icon you want to apply a label to.

Figure 89 Choose a label color from the bottom of the File menu.

Figure 90 The color you chose is applied to the icon's name. (I know it doesn't look red here, but it is.)

Figure 92 Choosing the X under Color Label removes the label from selected icons.

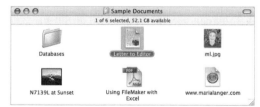

Figure 91 Select the icon you want to remove the label from.

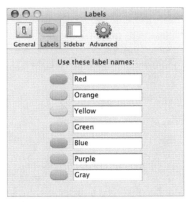

Figure 93 The default settings in the Labels window of Finder preferences.

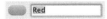

Figure 94 To change a label, select it ...

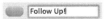

Figure 95 ... and enter a new label.

Figure 96
The new label appears on the File menu.

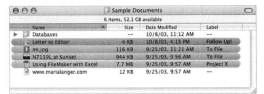

Figure 97 Here's what labels look like in list view. Three different customized labels have been applied and the Label column is displayed. (Someday Peachpit will let me do a color book. For now, just trust me: there are three different colors here.)

To customize labels

1. Choose Finder > Preferences (**Figure** 1) or press ⌃ ⌘ to display the Finder Preferences window.

2. If necessary, click the Labels button to display Labels options (**Figure 93**).

3. To change the name of a label, select the text for the label you want to change (**Figure 94**) and enter new text (**Figure 95**).

4. Repeat step 3 for each label you want to change.

5. Click the window's close button to save your settings.

✔ Tip

■ The names of labels appear on the File menu when you point to a label (**Figures 89** and **96**) and in a list view window when the Label column is displayed (**Figure 97**).

CUSTOMIZING LABELS

Aliases

An *alias* (**Figure 98**) is a pointer to an item.
You can make an alias of an item and place it
anywhere on your computer. Then, when you
need to open the item, just open its alias.

✔ Tips

- It's important to remember that an alias
  is not a copy of the item—it's a pointer.
  If you delete the original item, the alias
  will not open.

- You can use the Select New Original dialog
  (**Figure 135**) to reassign an original to an
  alias, as explained later in this chapter.

- By putting aliases of frequently used items
  together where you can quickly access
  them—such as on the desktop—you
  make the items more accessible without
  actually moving them.

- The Favorites and Recent Items features
  work with aliases. These features are
  discussed a little later in this chapter.

- You can name an alias anything you like,
  as long as you follow the file naming
  guidelines discussed in **Chapter 3**. An
  alias's name does not need to include the
  word *alias*.

- The icon for an alias looks very much like
  the icon for the original item but includes
  a tiny arrow in the bottom-left corner
  (**Figure 98**).

- You can move, copy, rename, open, and
  delete an alias just like any other file.

iTunes

iTunes alias

Figure 98
The icon for an
alias looks like
the original item's
icon but includes
a tiny arrow.

ALIASES

Figure 99
To create an alias, begin by selecting the item for which you want to make an alias.

Figure 100
Choose Make Alias from the File menu.

Figure 101 The alias appears with the original.

Figure 102
Choose Show Original from the File menu.

To create an alias

1. Select the item you want to make an alias for (**Figure 99**).

2. Choose File > Make Alias (**Figure 100**), or press ⌃⌘L.

   The alias appears right beneath the original item (**Figure 101**).

or

Hold down ⌃⌘Option and drag the item for which you want to make an alias to a new location. The alias appears in the destination location.

✔ Tip

- An alias's name is selected right after it is created (**Figure 101**). If desired, you can immediately type a new name to replace the default name.

To find an alias's original file

1. Select the alias's icon.

2. Choose File > Show Original (**Figure 102**), or press ⌃⌘R.

   A window for the folder in which the original resides opens with the original item selected (**Figure 103**).

Figure 103 The original item appears selected in its window.

WORKING WITH ALIASES

Favorites

The Favorites feature, which was introduced in the first release of Mac OS X, enabled you to add frequently accessed items to a Favorites submenu under the Go menu, in Open and Save As dialogs, and in a Favorites folder in Finder window toolbars. In Mac OS X 10.3, Apple removed access to Favorite items and is phasing out the Favorites feature, encouraging users to take advantage of the Sidebar instead.

If you're already using the Favorites feature and don't want to give it up, here are a few things you can do to keep using it.

✔ Tips

- If you're brand new to Mac OS X or you are not already using Favorites, my advice is to skip this section. It's never a good idea to start using a feature that's being phased out.

- The Favorites feature works with aliases, which are discussed on the previous two pages.

To add a favorite item

1. In the Finder, select the icon for the item that you want to add as a favorite item (**Figure 104**).

2. Hold down ⇧Shift and choose File > Add To Favorites (**Figure 105**), or press ⇧Shift ⌘ T.

   The item is added to your Favorites folder (**Figure 106**).

✔ Tip

- Favorite items are stored in the Favorites folder in the Library folder inside your home folder (**Figure 106**). You can learn more about your home folder in **Chapter 3**.

Figure 104
Select the item that you want to add as a favorite item.

Figure 105 Hold down ⇧Shift and choose Add to Favorites from the File menu.

Figure 106 The item is added as an alias to the Favorites folder inside the Library folder in your Home folder.

Figure 107 The Favorites folder can include aliases for folders, applications, or other items.

Figure 108 Adding the Favorites folder to the Sidebar is one good way to make Favorite items easily accessible.

Figure 109 The Dock is another good place for the Favorites folder.

To make Favorites more accessible

1. Locate the Favorites folder in the Library folder inside your Home folder (**Figure 107**).

2. Following instructions provided earlier in this chapter, do one or both of the following:
   ▲ Add the Favorites folder to the Sidebar (**Figure 108**).
   ▲ Add the Favorites folder to the Dock (**Figure 109**).

To remove a favorite

1. Open the Favorites folder in the Library folder inside your Home folder (**Figure 108**).

2. Drag the item that you want to remove out of the window.

3. Close the Favorites folder window.

USING & REMOVING FAVORITES

Recent Items

Mac OS automatically tracks the things you open. It creates submenus of the most recently opened items in three categories—applications, documents, and folders—making it quick and easy to open them again.

✔ Tip

■ You can specify how many recent applications and documents Mac OS X should track in the Recent Items submenu (**Figure 110**) by setting options in the Appearance preferences pane. I explain how in **Chapter 18**.

To open recent items

To open a recently used application or document, choose its name from the Recent Items submenu under the Apple menu (**Figure 110**).

or

To open a recently used folder, choose its name from the Recent Folders submenu under the Go menu (**Figure 111**).

✔ Tips

■ Recent items works with aliases, which are discussed earlier in this chapter.

■ Working with applications and documents is discussed in **Chapter 5**.

To clear the Recent Items submenu

Choose Apple > Recent Items > Clear Menu (**Figure 110**).

✔ Tip

■ Clearing the Recent Items submenu does not delete any application or document files.

Figure 110
Mac OS tracks the most recently used applications, documents ...

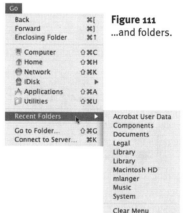

Figure 111
...and folders.

To clear the Recent Folders submenu

Choose Go > Recent Folders > Clear Menu (**Figure 111**).

✔ Tip

■ Clearing the Recent Folders submenu does not delete any folders.

Search field

Figure 112 The Search field appears in the toolbar of Finder windows.

Figure 113
Choose a search location from a pop-up menu.

Figure 114 When you enter search criteria in the Search field, your computer instantly displays matches.

Searching for Items

Mac OS X offers two ways to search for items on disk:

◆ The Search field in a Finder window's toolbar (**Figure 112**) offers a quick way to search for items based on the name.

◆ The File menu's Find command (**Figure 115**) enables you to search disks or specific disk locations for items based on name, content, or other criteria.

✔ Tip

■ Search criteria is not case-sensitive. That means *Letter* is the same as *letter* or *leTTer*.

To search for items by name

1. If necessary, open a Finder window and display the toolbar (**Figure 112**).

2. To search a specific location, click the triangle beside the magnifying glass to display a menu (**Figure 113**) and choose the appropriate location:

 ▲ **Local disks** searches only volumes that are directly connected to your computer, including internal hard disks and inserted media such as CD-ROMs. This is the default choice.

 ▲ **Home** searches your Home folder.

 ▲ **Selection** searches a selected disk or folder. If you choose this option, select the item you want to search.

 ▲ **Everywhere** searches all mounted volumes.

3. Enter all or part of the item name in the Search field. As you type, your computer begins to search for matches. When you finish typing, the matches appear in the window (**Figure 114**)

To search for items based name, content, or other criteria

1. Choose File > Find (**Figure 115**) or press ⌃⌘F to display the Find dialog (**Figure 116**).

2. Choose the location you want to search from the Search in pop-up menu (**Figure 117**):

   ▲ **Everywhere** searches all mounted volumes.

   ▲ **Local disks** searches only volumes that are directly connected to your computer, including internal hard disks and inserted media such as CD-ROMs.

   ▲ **Home** searches your Home folder.

   ▲ **Specific places** expands the Find window so you can toggle check marks for specific volumes you want to search (**Figure 118**).

3. To search by file name, choose an option from the pop-up menu in the file name line (**Figure 119**) and enter all or part of the file name in the edit box beside it (**Figure 120**).

   or

   To search by file content, enter text you expect to appear within the document in the content line (**Figure 121**).

   or

   To search by some other criteria, choose an option from the first pop-up menu in either criteria line (**Figure 122**). Then set search criteria on that line.

4. To add more criteria for the search, click a + button to add another criteria line. Then set options in that line. You can repeat this process for as many search criteria items as you like. **Figure 123** shows an example with all kinds of search criteria added.

Figure 115 Choose Find from the File menu.

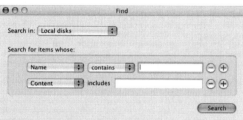

Figure 116 The Find window.

Figure 117 Use the Search in pop-up menu to indicate where you want to look for the file.

Figure 118 If you choose Specific places from the Search in pop-up menu, the Find window expands to show all mounted volumes.

Figure 119 Use the pop-up menu in the file name line to indicate how you want to match your search criteria...

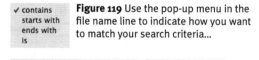

Figure 120 ...and then enter the search criteria in the box beside it.

Figure 121 To search by content, simply enter the search criteria in the edit box on the content line.

Figure 122
To enter other types of search criteria, choose an option from the first pop-up menu on a criteria line.

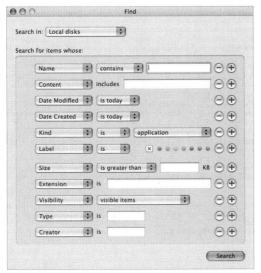

Figure 123 Here's what the Find window looks like with all kinds of criteria added. This is for illustrational purposes only—you'll never have to use all these options to find a file!

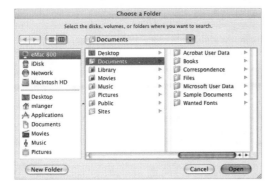

Figure 124 Use the Choose a Folder dialog to add more specific places to search.

5. When you are finished setting search criteria, click Search. Mac OS X displays the Search Results window (**Figures 125 and 126** on the next page) with all files it found that match your search criteria.

✔ Tips

- In step 2, if you chose Specific places from the Search in pop-up menu, you can click the Add button in the Find window (**Figure 118**) to display the Choose a Folder dialog (**Figure 124**). Use that dialog to locate and select specific folders to search. Each folder you add remains in the dialog until you remove it by selecting it and clicking the Remove button. The Choose a Folder dialog works much like the Open dialog, which I cover in **Chapter 5**.

- To remove search criteria you don't want to use, click the – button beside its line. The line disappears.

- The find feature attempts to find files that match *all* search criteria. For example, the search criteria in **Figures 120** and **121**, when used together, will find all files with names that contain the word *Letter* and content that contain the word *Joe*. The more criteria you enter, the narrower the search and the fewer items will be found.

- Finding by content takes significantly longer than finding by any other criteria.

- Finding by content works with an index file that is created and maintained by Mac OS X. You can manually update a disk or folder's index in the Info window; I explain how later in this chapter.

- The Relevance column in the Search Results window for finding files by content (**Figure 126**) indicates how often the search criteria was found in each file. The larger the Relevance bar, the more occurrences of the search criteria.

To work with found items

You can use commands on the File menu to perform a number of tasks with selected items in the Search Results window (**Figures 125** and **126**):

◆ **Open** (⌘⌥O) opens the selected item.

◆ **Open With** enables you to select an application to open the item with. This option, which I discuss in **Chapter 5**, only applies to document files.

◆ **Get Info** opens the Info window for the selected item. I tell you about the Info window on the next page.

◆ **Open Enclosing Folder** (⌘⌥R) opens the folder in which the selected item resides.

◆ **Add to Sidebar** (⌘⌥T) adds the selected item as an alias to the Sidebar. I tell you about the Sidebar in **Chapter 2** and earlier in this chapter.

◆ **Move to Trash** (⌘⌥Delete) moves the selected item to the Trash.

✔ Tip

■ You can also use the search results window to move or copy an item. Drag the item from the top half of the window to a destination disk or folder. The item remains in the Search Results window but, if it is moved, its path changes.

To learn where a found item resides on disk

Select the name of the item in the top half of the Search Results window. The path to the file appears in the bottom half of the window (**Figure 127**).

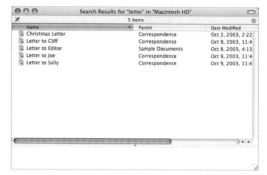

Figure 125 Here are the results for the search criteria in Figure 120 ...

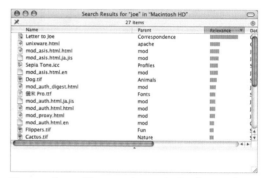

Figure 126 ... and here are the results for the search criteria in **Figure 121**.

Figure 127 When you select a found item, the path to the item appears in the bottom pane of the Search Results window.

Figure 128
The Info window
for a hard disk.

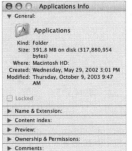

Figure 129
The Info window
for a folder.

Figure 130
The Info window for
an application.

Figure 131
The Info window
for a document.

The Info Window

You can learn more about an item by opening its Info window (**Figures 128** through **131**). Depending on the type of icon (disk, folder, application, document, alias, etc.), the General information in the Info window will provide some or all of the following:

◆ **Icon** that appears in the Finder.

◆ **Name** of the item.

◆ **Kind** or type of item.

◆ **Size** of item or contents (folders and files only).

◆ **Where** item is on disk.

◆ **Created** date and time.

◆ **Modified** date and time.

◆ **Format** of item (disks only).

◆ **Capacity** of item (disks only).

◆ **Available** space on item (disks only).

◆ **Used** space on item (disks only).

◆ **Version** number or copyright date (files only).

◆ **Original** location on disk (aliases only).

◆ **Stationery Pad** check box (documents only) to convert the file into a stationery format file, which is like a document template.

◆ **Locked** check box to prevent the file from being deleted or overwritten (folders and files only).

✔ Tip

■ Other types of information available for a disk, folder, or file can be displayed by clicking triangles at the bottom of the info window (**Figures 128** through **131**).

THE INFO WINDOW

To open the Info window

1. Select the item for which you want to open the Info window (**Figure 99**).

2. Choose File > Get Info (**Figure 132**), or press ⌃ ⌘ ⓘ.

   The Info window for that item appears (**Figure 130**).

To enter comments in the Info window

1. Open the Info window for the item for which you want to enter comments (**Figure 131**).

2. Click the triangle beside Comments in the bottom of the window. The window expands to show the Comments box.

3. Type your comments into the Comments box (**Figure 133**). They are automatically saved.

✔ Tip

■ As discussed earlier in this chapter, you can set a window's list view to display comments entered in the Info window.

To lock an application or document

1. Open the Info window for the item you want to lock (**Figures 128** through **131**).

2. Turn on the Locked check box.

✔ Tip

■ Locked items cannot be deleted or over-written. They can, however, be moved.

Figure 132
Choose Get Info from the File menu.

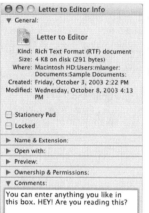

Figure 133
You can enter information about the item in the Comments box.

Figure 134
You can click the Select New Original button in the Info window for an alias to assign a new original to the alias.

Figure 135 Use the Select New Original dialog to locate and choose a new original for an alias.

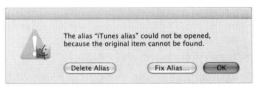

Figure 136 This dialog appears when you attempt to open an alias for which the original cannot be found.

Figure 137
The Content Index area shows you the index status and enables you to delete or recreate an index.

To select a new original item for an alias

1. In the Info window for the alias (**Figure 134**), click the Select New Original button.

2. Use the Select New Original dialog that appears (**Figure 135**) to locate and select the item that you want to use as the original for the alias.

3. Click Choose. The item you selected is assigned to the alias.

✔ Tips

- The Select New Original dialog is similar to an Open dialog, which is covered in **Chapter 5**.

- If you try to open an alias for which the original cannot be found, a dialog like the one in **Figure 136** appears. Click Fix Alias to display the Select New Original dialog (**Figure 135**), and select a new original.

- I discuss aliases earlier in this chapter.

To reindex a folder or disk

1. Open the Info window for the item you want to reindex (**Figure 137**).

2. Click the triangle beside Content Index. The window expands to show the index information.

3. Click Index now. The Content Index area changes to show index status. You can continue to work on other things while the index is being created.

✔ Tips

- The content index is used by the find by content feature, which I discuss earlier in this chapter.

- Be advised: indexing an entire hard disk can take a very long time!

WORKING WITH THE INFO WINDOW

115

Working with Archives

Mac OS X 10.3's new archive feature enables you to create compressed copies of items called *archived files* or *archives*. Archives take up less space on disk than regular files. You may find them useful for backing up files or sending files to others over a network or via e-mail.

✔ Tip

■ The archive feature uses ZIP format compression, which was originally developed as a DOS and Windows PC format. As a result, document archives created with this feature are fully compatible with DOS and Windows PCs.

To archive a file or folder

1. Select the item you want to archive (**Figure 138**).

2. Choose File > Create Archive of "*Item Name*" (**Figure 139**).

3. Wait while your computer creates the archive. While it works, a Copy status dialog appears (**Figure 140**). When the dialog disappears, the archive file appears in the same location as the original as a .zip file (**Figure 141**).

✔ Tip

■ You can archive multiple items at once. Select the items, then choose File > Create Archive of *n* items (where *n* is the number of selected items). When the archive appears, it will be named *Archive.zip*.

To open an archive

Double-click the archive file. The archive's contents are uncompressed and appear on disk.

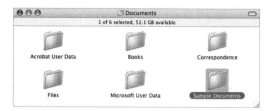

Figure 138 Select the item you want to archive.

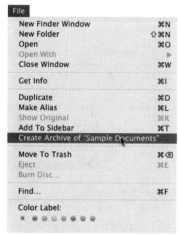

Figure 139 Choose Create Archive from the File menu.

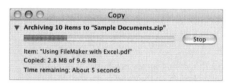

Figure 140 A Copy progress dialog appears while the file is being compressed.

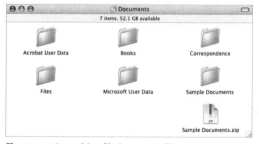

Figure 141 An archive file has a .zip file extension.

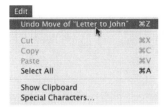

Figure 142
The Undo command enables you to undo the last action you performed.

Figure 143
If an action cannot be undone, the words *Can't Undo* will appear at the top of the Edit menu in gray.

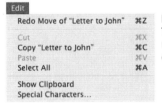

Figure 144
The Redo command undoes the Undo command.

Undoing Finder Actions

The Mac OS X Finder includes limited support for the Undo command, which can reverse the most recently completed action. Say, for example, that you move a file from one folder to another folder. If you immediately change your mind, you can choose Edit > Undo Move (**Figure 142**) to put the file back where it was.

✔ Tips

- Don't depend on the Undo command. Unfortunately, it isn't available for all actions (**Figure 143**).

- The exact wording of the Undo command varies depending on the action and the item it was performed on. In **Figure 142**, for example, the command is Undo Move of "Letter to John" because the last action was to move a document icon named *Letter to John*.

- The Undo command is also available (and generally more reliable) in most Mac OS applications. You'll usually find it at the top of the Edit menu.

To undo an action

Immediately after performing an action, choose Edit > Undo *action description* (**Figure 142**), or press ⌃⌘Z. The action is reversed.

To redo an action

Immediately after undoing an action, choose Edit > Redo *action description* (**Figure 144**). The action is redone—as if you never used the Undo command.

✔ Tip

- Think of the Redo command as the Undo-Undo command since it undoes the Undo command.

Application Basics

Applications

Applications, which are also known as *programs*, are software packages you use to get work done. Here are some examples:

◆ **Word processors**, such as TextEdit and Microsoft Word, are used to write letters, reports, and other text-based documents.

◆ **Spreadsheets**, such as Microsoft Excel, have built-in calculation features that are useful for creating number-based documents such as worksheets and charts.

◆ **Databases**, such as FileMaker Pro, are used to organize information, such as the names and addresses of customers or the artists and titles in a record collection.

◆ **Graphics** and **presentation** programs, such as Adobe Photoshop and Microsoft PowerPoint, are used to create illustrations, animations, and presentations.

◆ **Communications** programs, such as Internet Connect and Safari, are used to connect to other computers via modem or to the Internet.

◆ **Integrated** software, such as AppleWorks, combines "lite" versions of several types of software into one application.

◆ **Utility** software, such as Disk Utility and StuffIt Expander, performs tasks to manage computer files or keep your computer in good working order.

✔ Tips

■ Your Macintosh comes with some application software, some of which is discussed throughout this book.

■ Make sure the software you buy is Mac OS-compatible, and if possible, labeled "Built for Mac OS X." You may see Mac OS X applications referred to as *Carbon* or *Cocoa* applications. (Carbon and Cocoa are two methods for writing Mac OS X software.)

■ If Mac OS 9.x is installed on your computer, your computer can also run *Classic applications*—those applications written for Mac OS 9.x or earlier. This chapter discusses Mac OS X applications only; to learn about using Classic applications, consult **Chapter 16**.

Multitasking & the Dock

Mac OS uses a form of *multitasking*, which makes it possible for more than one application to be open at the same time. Only one application, however, can be *active*. You must make an application active to work with it. Other open applications continue running in the background.

Mac OS X uses *preemptive multitasking*, a type of multitasking in which the operating system can interrupt a currently running task in order to run another task, as needed.

✔ Tips

- Mac OS 8 and 9 use *cooperative multi- tasking*, a type of multitasking in which a running program can receive processing time only if other programs allow it. Each application must "cooperate" by giving up control of the processor in order to allow others to run.

- Mac OS X also features *protected memory*, a memory management system in which each program is prevented from modify- ing or corrupting the memory partition of another program. This means that if one application freezes up or bombs, your computer won't freeze up. You can continue using the other applications that are running.

- One application that is always open is Finder, which I cover in detail in **Chap- ters 2** through **4**.

- The active application is the one whose name appears at the top of the applica- tion menu—the menu to the right of the Apple menu—on the menu bar (**Figure 3**). The application menu is covered a little later in this chapter.

To learn what applications are running

Look at the Dock. A tiny triangle appears beneath each application that is running (**Figure 1**).

Figure 1 A tiny triangle appears beneath each open application. Click an icon to make its application active.

Figure 2 When you hold down ⌃ ⌘ Tab, icons for each open application appear onscreen.

🍎　**iTunes**　**File**　**Edit**

Figure 3 The name of the active application appears at the top of the application menu.

To switch from one open application to another

In the Dock (**Figure 1**), click the icon for the application you want to activate.

or

1. Hold down ⌃ ⌘ Tab. A large icon for each open application appears onscreen (**Figure 2**).

2. Use the ← or → key to select the icon for the application you want to activate and press Return.

   or

   Click the icon for the application you want to activate.

The windows for the application you selected come to the front and the application name appears on the Application menu (**Figure 3**).

✔ Tips

- Another way to activate an application is to click any of its windows. This brings the window to the foreground onscreen and makes the application active.

- You can also use Exposé to activate an application's windows. I explain how to use Exposé in **Chapter 4**.

SWITCHING APPLICATIONS

Using Applications & Creating Documents

You use an application by opening, or *launching*, it. It loads into the computer's memory. Its menu bar replaces the Finder's menu bar and offers commands that can be used only with that application. It may also display a document window and tools specific to that program.

Most applications create *documents*—files written in a format understood by the application. When you save documents, they remain on disk so you can open, edit, print, or just view them at a later date.

For example, you may use Microsoft Word to write a letter. When you save the letter, it becomes a Word document file that includes all the text and formatting you put into the letter, written in a format that Microsoft Word can understand.

Your computer keeps track of applications and documents. It automatically associates documents with the applications that created them. That's how your computer is able to open a document with the correct application when you open the document from the Finder.

✔ Tips

- You can launch an application by opening a document that it created.

- A document created by an application that is not installed on your computer is sometimes referred to as an *orphan* document since no *parent* application is available. An orphan document usually has a generic document icon (**Figure 4**).

Chapter 5

Figure 4
An orphan document often has a generic document icon like this one. This example shows an Adobe InDesign document copied to a computer that does not have InDesign installed.

Figure 5
Select the icon for the application that you want to open.

Figure 6
Choose Open from the File menu.

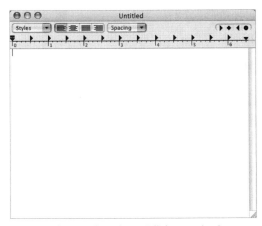

Figure 7 When you launch TextEdit by opening its application icon, it displays an empty document window.

Figure 8
Select the icon for the document you want to open.

Letter to John

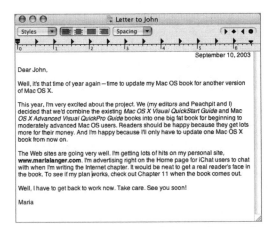

Figure 9 When you launch TextEdit by opening one of its documents, it displays the document.

To launch an application

Double-click the application's icon.

or

1. Select the application's icon (**Figure 5**).

2. Choose File > Open (**Figure 6**), or press
    Ⓒ⌘Ⓞ.

or

If an icon for the application is in the toolbar or the Dock, click that icon once.

The application opens (**Figure 7**).

To open a document & launch the application that created it at the same time

Double-click the icon for the document that you want to open.

or

1. Select the icon for the document that you want to open (**Figure 8**).

2. Choose File > Open (**Figure 6**), or press
    Ⓒ⌘Ⓞ.

or

If an icon for the document is in the toolbar or the Dock, click that icon once.

If the application that created the document is not already running, it launches. The document appears in an active window (**Figure 9**).

To open a document with drag & drop

1. Drag the icon for the document that you want to open onto the icon for the application with which you want to open it.

2. When the application icon becomes selected (**Figure 10**), release the mouse button. The application launches and displays the document (**Figure 9**).

✔ Tips

- Drag and drop is a good way to open a document with an application other than the one that created it.

- Not all applications can read all documents. Dragging a document icon onto the icon for an application that can't open it either won't launch the application, with open the document but display only gibberish, or will display an error message.

- In step 1, the application icon can be in a Finder window (or the desktop), in the Sidebar, or on the Dock.

To open a document with the Open With command

1. Select the icon for the document that you want to open (**Figure 8**).

2. Choose File > Open With to display the Open with Submenu (**Figure 11**) and choose the application you want to use to open the file. The application you chose opens and displays the document.

✔ Tip

- The Open With submenu (**Figure 11**) will only list applications that are installed on your computer and are capable of opening the selected document.

Figure 10 Drag the icon for the document you want to open onto the icon for the application you want to open it with.

Figure 11 The Open With submenu lists installed applications that can open a selected document. The options that appear depend on what type of document is selected and what applications are installed on your computer.

Standard Application Menus

Apple's Human Interface Guidelines provide basic recommendations to software developers to ensure consistency from one application to another. Nowhere is this more obvious than in the standard menus that appear in most applications: the application, File, Edit, Window, and Help menus. You'll see these menus with the same kinds of commands over and over in most of the applications you use. This consistency makes it easier to learn Mac OS applications.

The next few pages provide a closer look at the standard menus you'll find in most applications.

✔ Tips

- The Finder, which is covered in **Chapters 2** through **4**, has standard menus similar to the ones discussed here.

- The Finder rules regarding the ellipsis character (…) and keyboard shortcuts displayed on menus also apply to applications. **Chapter 2** explains these rules.

The Application Menu

The application menu takes the name of the currently active application—for example, the TextEdit application menu (**Figure 12**) or the iTunes application menu (**Figure 13**). It includes commands for working with the entire application.

To learn about an application

1. From the application menu, choose About *application name* (**Figures 12** and **13**).

2. A window with version and other information appears (**Figure 14**). Read the information it contains.

3. When you're finished reading about the application, click the window's close button.

To set application preferences

1. From the application menu, choose Preferences (**Figures 12** and **13**).

2. The application's Preferences window (**Figure 15**) or dialog appears. Set options as desired.

3. Click the window's close button.

   or

   Click the dialog's OK or Save button.

✔ Tip

■ Preference options vary greatly from one application to another. To learn more about an application's preferences, check its documentation or onscreen help.

Figures 12 & 13
The TextEdit application menu (left), and the iTunes application menu (right).

Figure 14 The About window for TextEdit provides its version number and other information.

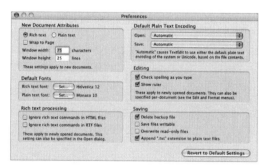

Figure 15 TextEdit's Preferences window offers a number of options you can set to customize the way TextEdit works.

To hide an application

From the application menu, choose Hide *application name* (**Figures 12** and **13**) or press ⌃ ⌘ H. All of the application's windows, as well as its menu bar, are hidden from view.

✔ Tip

■ You cannot hide the active application if it is the only application that is open (the Finder) or if all the other open applications are already hidden.

To hide all applications except the active one

From the application menu, choose Hide Others (**Figures 12** and **13**) or press Option ⌃ ⌘ H.

To hide the active application and display another application

Hold down Option while switching to another application.

To display a hidden application

Click the application's icon (or any of its document icons) in the Dock (**Figure 1**).

To unhide all applications

From the application menu, choose Show All (**Figures 12** and **13**).

To quit an application

1. From the application menu, choose Quit *application name* (**Figures 12** and **13**), or press ⌃ ⌘ Q.

2. If unsaved documents are open, a dialog appears, asking whether you want to save changes to documents. The appearance of this dialog varies depending on the application that displays it. **Figure 16** shows an example from TextEdit when multiple unsaved documents are open. Click the appropriate button to save the document(s) or quit without saving (Cancel).

   The application closes all windows, saves preference files (if applicable), and quits.

✔ Tips

- Closing all of an application's open windows is not the same as quitting. An application normally remains running until you quit it.

- I tell you more about saving documents later in this chapter.

- If an application is unresponsive and you cannot access its menus or commands, you can use the Force Quit command to make it stop running. I explain how near the end of this chapter.

Figure 16 This dialog appears when you close a TextEdit document that contains unsaved changes.

Figures 17, 18, & 19
The File menu in QuickTime Player (top left), Safari (bottom left), and TextEdit (above).

Figure 20 Internet Explorer's New Window command opens a new Web browser window displaying the default Home page.

The File Menu

The File menu (**Figures 17**, **18**, and **19**) includes commands for working with files or documents. This section discusses the commands most often found under the File menu: New, Open, Close, and Save.

✔ Tip

- The Page Setup and Print commands are also found on the File menu. These commands are discussed in detail in **Chapter 10**.

To create a new document or window

Choose File > New (**Figure 19**).

or

Choose File > New Window (**Figure 18**).

or

Press ⌘N.

A new untitled document (**Figure 7**) or window (**Figure 20**) appears.

✔ Tip

- As shown in **Figures 17**, **18**, and **19**, the exact wording of the command for creating a new document or window varies depending on the application and what the command does. This command, however, is usually the first one on the File menu.

To open a file

1. Choose File > Open (**Figures 17, 18,** or **19**), or press ⌘O to display the Open dialog (**Figure 21**).

2. Use any combination of the following techniques to locate the document you want to open:

   ▲ Use the From pop-up menu (**Figure 22**) to backtrack from the currently displayed location to one of its enclosing folders.

   ▲ Click one of the items in the Sidebar list on the left side of the dialog to view the contents of that item.

   ▲ Press ⇧⌘H to view the contents of your Home folder.

   ▲ Click one of the items in either list to view its contents in the list on the right side of the window. (The list containing the item you clicked shifts to the left if necessary.)

   ▲ Use the scroll bar at the bottom of the two lists to shift lists. Shifting lists to the right enables you to see your path from the item selected in the Sidebar list.

3. When the name of the file you want to open appears in the list on the right side of the window, use one of the following techniques to open it:

   ▲ Select the file name and then click Open or press Return or Enter.

   ▲ Double-click the file name.

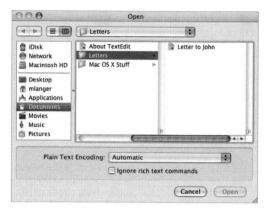

Figure 21 TextEdit's Open dialog includes all of the elements found in a standard Open dialog.

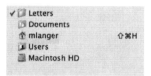

Figure 22 The From (and Where) pop-up menu enables you to backtrack from the currently displayed location to the folders in which it resides.

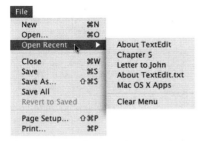

Figure 23 TextEdit's Open Recent submenu makes it easy to reopen a recently opened document.

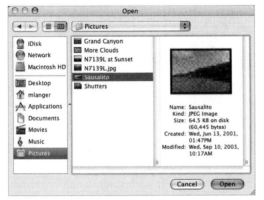

Figure 24 When you select a file in the Open dialog, the file's icon or a preview and other information for the file appears. This example shows Preview's Open dialog with a JPEG format file selected. The image in the right side of the dialog is the file's custom icon, which was created automatically by Photoshop when the image was saved.

✔ Tips

- The exact wording of the Open command varies depending on the application and what you want to open. For example, the Open command on QuickTime Player's File menu (**Figure 17**) is Open Movie in New Player and the Open command on Safari's File menu (**Figure 18**) is Open File.

- The Open Recent command, which is available on the File menu of some applications (**Figures 17** and **19**), displays a submenu of recently opened items (**Figure 23**). Choose the item you want to open it again.

- As illustrated in **Figures 21** and **24**, the Open dialog has many standard elements that appear in all Open dialogs.

- In step 3, you can only select the files that the application can open; other files will either not appear in the list or will appear in gray. Some applications, such as Microsoft Word, include a pop-up menu that enables you to specify the types of files that appear in the Open dialog.

- In step 3, selecting a file's name in the Open dialog displays its icon or a preview and other information for the file on the right side of the dialog (**Figure 23**).

- The From pop-up menu (**Figure 22**) has been modified for Mac OS X 10.3. In previous versions of Mac OS X, it listed several standard locations, which now appear in the Sidebar list. The From pop-up menu now works as it did in Mac OS 9.x and earlier.

- The Sidebar is covered in **Chapter 2**, file paths are discussed in **Chapter 3**, and iDisk is covered in **Chapter 12**.

OPENING FILES

131

To close a window

1. Choose File > Close (**Figures 17, 18, and 19**), or press ⌃ ⌘ W.

   or

   Click the window's close button.

2. If the window contains a document with changes that have not been saved, a dialog sheet similar to the one in **Figure 25** appears.

   ▲ Click Don't Save to close the window without saving the document.

   ▲ Click Cancel or press Esc to keep the window open.

   ▲ Click Save or press Return or Enter to save the document.

✔ Tip

■ The exact appearance of the dialog sheet that appears when you close a document with unsaved changes varies depending on the application. All versions of the dialog should offer the same three options, although they may be worded differently. **Figure 25** shows the dialog that appears in TextEdit.

Figure 25 A dialog like this one appears if you close a document with unsaved changes. This is the TextEdit version of the dialog.

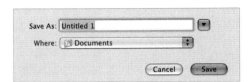

Figure 26 The Save dialog sheet can be collapsed to offer fewer options...

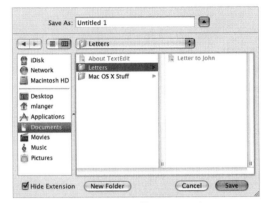

Figure 27 ...or expanded to offer more options.

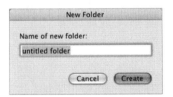

Figure 28 Use the New Folder dialog to enter a name for a new folder.

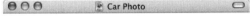

Figure 29 The name of the newly saved file appears in the window's title bar.

To save a document for the first time

1. Choose File > Save (**Figure 19**) or press ⌃⌘S to display the Save dialog (**Figure 26** or **27**).

2. Use the Where pop-up menu (**Figure 22**) to select a location in which to save the document.

   or

   If necessary, click the triangle beside the Where pop-up menu (**Figure 26**) to expand the dialog (**Figure 27**). Then use any combination of the following techniques to select a location in which to save the document:

   ▲ Use the Where pop-up menu (**Figure 22**) to backtrack from the currently displayed location to one of its enclosing folders.

   ▲ Click one of the items in the Sidebar list on the left side of the dialog to view the contents of that item.

   ▲ Press Shift ⌃⌘H to view the contents of your Home folder.

   ▲ Click one of the items in either list to view its contents on the right side of the dialog. (The list containing the item you clicked shifts to the left if necessary.)

   ▲ Use the scroll bar at the bottom of the two lists to shift lists. Shifting lists to the right enables you to see your path from the item selected in the Sidebar.

   ▲ Click the New Folder button to create a new folder inside the currently selected folder. Enter a name for the folder in the New Folder dialog that appears (**Figure 28**), and click Create.

Continued on next page...

SAVING DOCUMENTS

Continued from previous page.

3. When the name of the folder in which you want to save the document appears on the Where pop-up menu, enter a name for the document in the Save As box and click Save.

   The document is saved in the location you specified. The name of the file appears in the document window's title bar (**Figure 29**).

✔ Tips

- Not all applications enable you to save documents. The standard version of QuickTime Player, for example, does not include a Save command on its File menu (**Figures 17**).

- The Save dialog (**Figures 26** and **27**) is also known as the Save Location dialog because it enables you to select a location in which to save a file.

- In step 1, you can also use the Save As command. The first time you save a document, the Save and Save As commands do the same thing: display the Save dialog.

- Some applications automatically append a period and a three-character *extension* to a file's name when you save it. Extensions are used by Mac OS X and Windows applications to identify the file type. You can toggle the display of file name extensions in Finder preferences, which I discuss in **Chapter 4**.

- The Sidebar is covered in **Chapter 2**, file paths are discussed in **Chapter 3**, and iDisk is covered in **Chapter 12**.

SAVING DOCUMENTS

Close button

Figure 30 A bullet in the close button of a document window indicates that the document has unsaved changes.

To save changes to a document

Choose File > Save (**Figure 19**), or press ⌃⌘S.

The document is saved in the same location with the same name, thus overwriting the existing version of the document with the new version.

✔ Tip

- Mac OS X includes three ways to indicate whether a window contains unsaved changes:
  - ▲ A bullet character appears in the close button on the title bar of the window for a document with unsaved changes (**Figure 30**).
  - ▲ The document icon appears faded on the title bar of the window for a document with unsaved changes (**Figure 30**).
  - ▲ A bullet character appears in the Window menu beside the name of the window for a document with unsaved changes (**Figure 34**). The Window menu is discussed a little later in this chapter.

SAVING CHANGES TO DOCUMENTS

To save a document with a new name or in a new location

1. Choose File > Save As (**Figures 18** and **19**) to display the Save dialog sheet (**Figure 26** or **27**).

2. Follow steps 2 and 3 in the section titled "To save a document for the first time" to select a location, enter a name, and save the document.

✔ Tips

■ Saving a document with a new name or in a new location creates a copy of the existing document. The open document is the copy, not the original. Any further changes you make and save for the open document are saved to the copy rather than the original.

■ If you use the Save dialog to save a document with the same name as a document in the selected location, a confirmation dialog like the one in **Figure 29** appears. You have two options:

  ▲ Click Cancel or press (Esc) to return to the Save dialog and either change the document's name or the save location.

  ▲ Click Replace or press (Return) or (Enter) to replace the document on disk with the current document.

Figure 31 This dialog appears when you try to save a file with the same name as another file in a folder. This is what the dialog looks like in TextEdit.

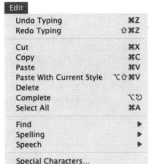

Figures 32 & 33
The Edit menus for TextEdit (left) and Address Book (bottom).

The Edit Menu

The Edit menu (**Figures 32** and **33**) includes commands for modifying the contents of a document. Here's a quick list of the commands you're likely to find, along with their standard keyboard equivalents:

- ◆ **Undo** (⌘Z) reverses the last editing action you made.

- ◆ **Redo** (Shift ⌘Z) reverses the last undo.

- ◆ **Cut** (⌘X) removes a selection from the document and puts a copy of it in the Clipboard.

- ◆ **Copy** (⌘C) puts a copy of a selection in the Clipboard.

- ◆ **Paste** (⌘V) inserts the contents of the Clipboard into the document at the insertion point or replaces selected text in the document with the contents of the Clipboard.

- ◆ **Clear** or **Delete** removes a selection from the document. This is the same as pressing (Delete) when document contents are selected.

- ◆ **Select All** (⌘A) selects all text or objects in the document.

✔ Tips

- ■ Not all Edit menu commands are available in all applications at all times.

- ■ Edit menu commands usually work with selected text or graphic objects in a document.

- ■ Most Edit menu commands are discussed in greater detail in **Chapter 7**, which covers TextEdit.

The Window Menu

The Window menu (**Figures 34** and **35**) includes commands for working with open document windows as well as a list of the open windows.

✔ Tips

- The windows within applications have the same basic parts and controls as Finder windows, which are discussed in detail in **Chapter 2**.

- A bullet character beside the name of a window in the Window menu (**Figure 34**) indicates that the window contains a document with unsaved changes.

To zoom a window

Choose Window > Zoom (**Figures 34** and **35**).

The window toggles between its full size and a custom size you create with the window's size control.

✔ Tip

- I explain how to resize a window with the size control in **Chapter 2**.

To minimize a window

Choose Window > Minimize (**Figures 34** and **35**), or press ⌘M.

or

Click the Minimize button on the window's title bar.

The window shrinks down to the size of an icon and slips into the Dock (**Figure 36**).

Figures 34 & 35
The Window menus for TextEdit (left) and iTunes (right).

Figure 36 The icon for a minimized window appears in the Dock. If you look closely, you can see a tiny icon for the application in which it is open.

To display a minimized window

With the application active, choose the window's name from the Window menu (**Figures 34** and **35**).

or

Click the window's icon in the Dock (**Figure 36**).

The window expands out of the Dock and appears onscreen.

To bring all of an application's windows to the front

Choose Window > Bring All to Front (**Figures 34** and **35**).

All of the application's open windows are displayed on top of open windows for other applications.

✔ Tip

■ Mac OS X allows an application's windows to be mingled in layers with other applications' windows.

To activate a window

Choose the window's name from the bottom of the Window menu (**Figures 34** and **35**).

DISPLAYING WINDOWS

The Help Menu

The Help menu (**Figures 37** and **38**) includes commands for viewing onscreen help information specific to the application. Choosing the primary Help command (or pressing ⌘?) launches the Help Viewer application with help information and links (**Figure 39**).

✔ Tips

- Onscreen help is covered in **Chapter 20**.

- Although the Help menu may only have one command for a simple application (**Figures 37** and **38**), it can have multiple commands to access different kinds of help for more complex applications.

Figures 37 & 38 The Help menu for Sherlock (left) and TextEdit (right).

Figure 39 Choosing iChat Help from iChat's Help menu displays this Help Viewer window.

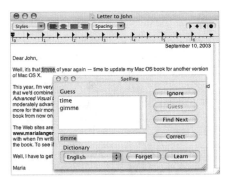

Figure 40 This Spelling dialog in TextEdit is an example of a modeless dialog—you can interact with the document while the dialog is displayed.

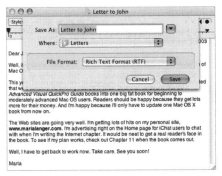

Figure 41 A standard Save Location dialog sheet is an example of a document modal dialog—you must address and dismiss it before you can continue working with the document it is attached to.

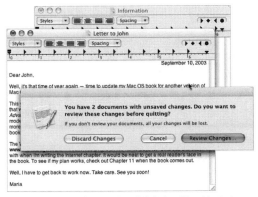

Figure 42 An application modal dialog like this Quit dialog requires your attention before you can continue working with the application.

Dialogs

Mac OS applications use *dialogs* to tell you things and get information from you. Think of them as the way your computer has a conversation—or dialog—with you.

Mac OS X has three main types of dialogs:

- ◆ *Modeless* dialogs enable you to work with the dialog while interacting with document windows. These dialogs usually have their own window controls to close and move them (**Figure 40**).

- ◆ *Document modal* dialogs usually appear as dialog *sheets* attached to a document window (**Figure 41**). You must address and dismiss these dialogs before you can continue working with the window, although you can switch to another window or application while the dialog is displayed.

- ◆ *Application modal* dialogs appear as movable dialogs (**Figure 42**). These dialogs must be addressed and dismissed before you can continue working with the application, although you can switch to another application while the dialog is displayed.

✔ Tips

- ■ You don't need to remember *modeless* vs. *modal* terminology to work with Mac OS X. Just understand how the dialogs differ and what the differences mean.

- ■ Some dialogs are very similar from one application to another. This chapter covers some of these standard dialogs , including Open (**Figure 21**), Save Location (**Figures 25, 26,** and **41**), Save Changes (**Figures 16** and **25**), and Replace Confirmation (**Figure 31**). Two more standard dialogs—Page Setup and Print—are covered in **Chapter 10.**

To use dialog parts

◆ Click a *tab control* to view a *pane* full of related options (**Figure 43**).

◆ Use *scroll bars* to view the contents of *scrolling lists* (**Figure 44**). Click a list item once to select it or to enter it in a *combination box* (**Figure 44**).

◆ Enter text or numbers into *entry fields* (**Figure 45**), including those that are part of combination boxes (**Figure 44**).

◆ Click a *pop-up menu* (**Figures 44** and **45**) to display its options. Click a menu option to choose it.

◆ Click a *check box* (**Figure 46**) to toggle it on or off. (A check box is turned on when a check mark or X appears inside it.)

◆ Click a *radio button* (**Figure 46**) to choose its option. (A radio button is chosen when a bullet appears inside it.)

◆ Drag a *slider* control (**Figures 44** and **46**) to change a setting.

◆ Consult a preview area (**Figure 43**) to see the effects of your changes.

◆ Drag an image file into an *image well* (**Figure 45**).

◆ Click a *push button* (**Figures 43** and **45**) to activate it.

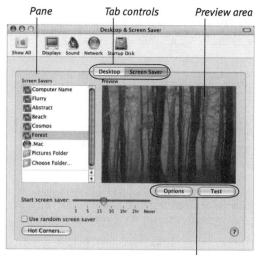

Figure 43 The Screen Saver pane of Desktop & Screen Saver preferences.

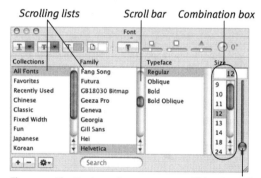

Figure 44 The Font panel.

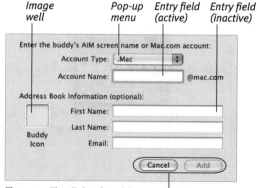

Figure 45 The dialog for adding buddy information to iChat.

Check box   *Slider control*   *Radio button*

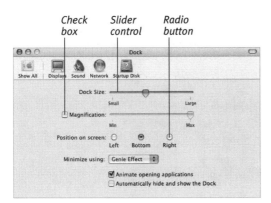

Figure 46 Dock preferences.

✔ Tips

- An entry field with a dark border around it is the active field (**Figure 45**). Typing automatically enters text in this field. You can advance from one entry field to the next by pressing (Tab).

- If an entry field has a pair of arrows or triangles beside it you can click the triangles to increase or decrease a value already in the field.

- The default push button is the one that pulsates. You can always select a default button by pressing (Enter) and often by pressing (Return).

- You can usually select a Cancel button (**Figure 45**) by pressing (Esc).

- You can select as many check boxes (**Figure 46**) in a group as you like.

- One and only one radio button in a group can be selected (**Figure 46**). If you try to select a second radio button, the first button becomes deselected.

- If you click the Cancel button in a dialog (**Figure 45**), any options you set are lost.

- To select multiple items in a scrolling list, hold down (⌘) while clicking each one. Be aware that not all dialogs support multiple selections in scrolling lists.

- There are other standard controls in Mac OS X dialogs. These are the ones you'll encounter most often.

USING DIALOGS

Force Quitting Applications

Occasionally, an application may freeze, lock up, or otherwise become unresponsive. When this happens, you can no longer work with that application or its documents. Sometimes, you can't access any application at all!

The Force Quit command (**Figure 47**) enables you to force an unresponsive application to quit. Then you can either restart it or continue working with other applications.

✖ Warning!

- When you use the Force Quit command to quit an application, any unsaved changes in that application's open documents may be lost. Use the Force Quit command only as a last resort, when the application's Quit command cannot be used.

✔ Tips

- Mac OS X's protected memory, which is discussed at the beginning of this chapter, makes it possible for applications to continue running properly on your computer when one application locks up.

- If more than one application experiences problems during a work session, you might find it helpful to restart your computer. This clears out RAM and forces your computer to reload all applications and documents into memory. You can learn more about troubleshooting Mac OS X in **Chapter 20**.

Figure 47
Choose Force Quit from the Apple menu.

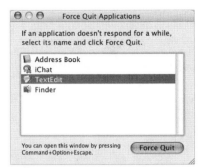

Figure 48 Select the application you want to force to quit.

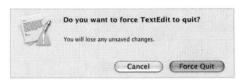

Figure 49 Use this dialog to confirm that you really do want to force quit the application.

To force quit an application

1. Choose Apple > Force Quit (**Figure 47**), or press Option ⌃ ⌘ Esc.

2. In the Force Quit Applications window that appears (**Figure 48**), select the application you want to force to quit.

3. Click Force Quit.

4. A confirmation dialog like the one in **Figure 49** appears. Click Force Quit.

   The application immediately quits.

✔ Tip

■ If you selected Finder in step 2, the button to click in step 3 is labeled Relaunch.

Using Mac OS X Applications

Figure 1 The contents of the Applications folder.

Mac OS Applications

Mac OS X includes a variety of software applications that you can use to perform tasks on your computer.

This chapter covers the following Apple programs in the Applications folder (**Figure 1**):

◆ **Address Book,** which enables you to keep track of contact information for friends, family members, and business associates.

◆ **Calculator**, which enables you to perform calculations and conversions.

◆ **Chess,** which is a computerized version of the game of chess.

◆ **DVD Player,** which enables you to play movies on DVD discs.

◆ **Image Capture**, which enables you to download image files from a digital camera or import images from a scanner and save them on disk.

◆ **Preview**, which enables you to view images and PDF files.

◆ **QuickTime Player**, which enables you to view QuickTime movies, sounds, and streaming video.

◆ **Stickies**, which enables you to place colorful notes on your computer screen.

◆ **AppleScript** enables you to automate tasks and create applications.

Continued on next page...

Figure 2 By default, the Dock is configured with icons for several Mac OS X applications.

Continued from previous page.

✔ Tips

- The Mac OS X 10.3 installer places icons for some Mac OS X applications in the Dock (**Figure 2**).

- The Clock application that appeared in previous versions of Mac OS X is not included with Mac OS X 10.3. Instead, its functionality is included in the Date & Time preferences pane, which I discuss in **Chapter 18**.

- Mac OS X includes a number of other applications that are discussed elsewhere in this book:
  - ▲ TextEdit is covered in **Chapter 7**.
  - ▲ iCal, iMovie, iPhoto, iSync, and iTunes are covered in **Chapter 8**.
  - ▲ Font Book is covered in **Chapter 9**.
  - ▲ iChat, Internet Connect, Internet Explorer, Mail, and Safari are covered in **Chapter 11**.
  - ▲ Sherlock is covered in **Chapter 13**.
  - ▲ System Preferences are covered in **Chapter 18**.
  - ▲ The applications in the Utilities folder are covered in **Chapter 19**.

MAC OS APPLICATIONS

Figure 3 The main Address Book window, with several records already created.

View Card and Column
View Card Only

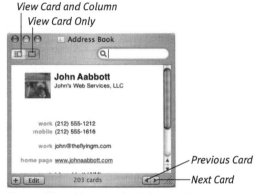

Previous Card
Next Card

Figure 4 The Address Book window can be collapsed to display just one record's card.

Address Book

Address Book, which has been updated for Mac OS X 10.3, enables you to keep track of the names, addresses, phone numbers, e-mail addresses, and Web URLs of people you know. The information you store in Address Book's database can be used by Mail to send e-mail messages and iChat to send instant messages.

In this chapter, I provide enough information to get you started using Address Book for your contact management needs. You can explore the rest of Address Book's features on your own.

✔ Tips

- You must have an Internet connection to send e-mail or use iChat.

- Mail and iChat are covered in **Chapter 11**.

To launch Address Book

Double-click the Address Book icon in the Applications folder (**Figure 1**) to select it.

or

1. Click the Address Book icon in the Applications folder (**Figure 1**).

2. Choose File > Open, or press ⌘ O.

or

Click the Address Book icon in the Dock (**Figure 2**).

Address Book's main window appears (**Figure 3**).

✔ Tip

- If the Address Book window looks more like what's shown in **Figure 4**, you can click the View Card and Column button in its upper-left corner to expand the view to show all three columns (**Figure 3**).

To add a new card

1. Click the Add New Person button (a plus sign) beneath the Name column in the main Address Book window (**Figure 3**).

   or

   Choose File > New Card (**Figure 5**), or press ⌘N.

   A *No Name* record is created in the Name column and a blank address card appears beside it, with the *First* field active (**Figure 6**).

2. Enter information about the contact into appropriate fields. When a field is active, text appears within it to prompt you for information (**Figure 7**). Press Tab or click on a field to move from field to field.

3. To change the label that appears beside a field, click the tiny triangles beside it (**Figure 8**) to display a menu (**Figure 9**), then choose the label you prefer.

4. To add more fields, click the green plus sign button beside a similar field (**Figure 8**). For example, to add another phone number field, click the plus sign beside a phone number. Then enter information and choose a field label as discussed in steps 2 and 3.

5. To remove a field, click the red minus sign button beside it.

6. When you are finished entering information, click the Edit button to view the completed card (**Figure 10**).

Figure 5
Address Book's File menu.

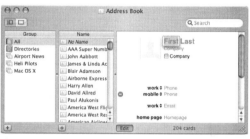

Figure 6 When you click the Add New Person button, Address Book creates an unnamed card record and selects the first field for entry.

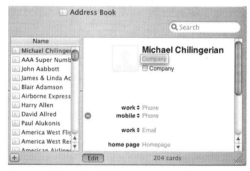

Figure 7 Each active field prompts you for entry information.

Figure 8
Once you have entered some contact information, button and menu icons appear beside field names.

ADDING A NEW CARD

Figure 9
Click the triangles to display a menu of applicable field labels.

Figure 10 The completed contact record appears in the column on the right side of the window.

Figure 11 You can choose to list a contact by its company name rather than the person's name.

Figure 12 Address Book's Phone preferences pane lets you set up phone number formatting options.

Figure 13
You can use this dialog to create a custom label for a record's card.

✔ Tips

- You can enter information into any combination of fields; if you do not have information for a specific field, skip it and it will not appear in the completed card.

- To list the entry by company name, rather than the person's name, as shown in **Figure 11**, turn on the Company check box beneath the Company field (**Figure 7**) when entering contact information. A contact that does not include a person's name is automatically listed by the company name.

- By default, Address Book automatically formats telephone numbers to enclose the area code in parentheses. It doesn't matter how you enter a phone number; Address Book will change it to this format. You can turn off automatic phone number formatting in the Phone preferences pane (**Figure 12**); choose Address Book > Preferences and click the Phone button to display it.

- In step 3, if you choose Custom from the pop-up menu, use the Adding new custom label dialog that appears (**Figure 13**) to enter a custom label and click OK.

To delete a contact record

1. In the Name column of the Address Book window, select the contact you want to delete.

2. Press ⟨Delete⟩.

3. In the confirmation dialog that appears, click Yes. The contact disappears.

ADDING & REMOVING CARDS

151

To edit a contact card

1. In the Name column of the Address Book window, select the contact you want to edit.

2. Click the Edit button.

3. Make changes as desired in the record's address card.

4. When you are finished making changes, click Edit again to save your changes and view the modified card.

✔ Tip

- The Card menu (**Figure 14**) includes commands you can use to modify the currently selected card.

To add an image to a contact card

1. In the Name column of the Address Book window, select the contact for which you want to add a picture or logo to display the contact card.

2. Drag the icon for the file containing the photo or logo you want to add from a Finder window to the image well in the address card window (**Figure 15**).

3. When you release the mouse button, the image appears a dialog like the one in **Figure 16**. Click Set.

   The image appears in the card (**Figure 17**).

✔ Tips

- Another way to add an image to a card is to choose Card > Choose Custom Image to display a dialog like the one in **Figure 16**. Then either drag the image into that dialog or click the Choose button to use another dialog to locate and select the image you want to use.

- To remove a photo or logo from a contact record, select the contact and choose Card > Clear Custom Image (**Figure 14**).

Figure 14
The Card menu.

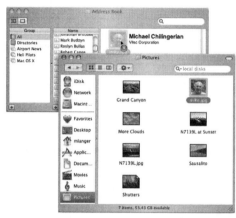

Figure 15 To add a picture for a record, simply drag its icon into the image well.

Figure 16
The image appears in a dialog like this one. (Yes, that's Mike, my significant other for the past 20 years.)

Figure 17
The picture is added to the record's card.

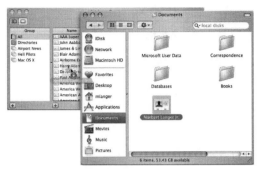

Figure 18 Drag a vCard file's icon into the Address Book window's Name column.

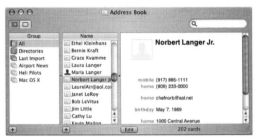

Figure 19 The vCard information is added to your Address Book as a contact card.

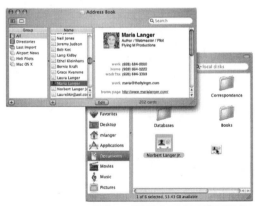

Figure 20 Drag the name of a contact from the Name column of the Address Book window to a Finder window.

Figure 21
A saved vCard file's icon looks like this.

To add information from a vCard

Drag the icon for the vCard from a Finder window to the Name column in the Address Book window (**Figure 18**).

or

Double-click the icon for a vCard file.

An Address Book contact card is created based on the vCard information (**Figure 19**).

✔ Tips

- *vCard*, or *virtual address card*, files are commonly used to share contact information electronically.

- When you import a vCard, Address Book creates (or modifies) a Last Import group. I tell you about groups on the next page.

To save information as a vCard

Drag the name of a contact from the Name column of the Address Book window to a Finder window (**Figure 20**).

The vCard file's icon (**Figure 21**) appears where you dragged it.

✔ Tips

- You can save multiple vCards at once. Simply hold down ⌘ while clicking contact names to select multiple contacts and then drag any of them to a Finder window as discussed above.

- You can send your vCard via e-mail to anyone you like. This makes it easy for people to add your contact information to their contact database.

- The vCard format is recognized by most Mac OS and Windows contact management software.

To organize contact cards into groups

1. Click the Add New Group button (a plus sign) under the Group column of the Address Book window (**Figure 3**).

   or

   Choose File > New Group (**Figure 5**) or press Shift ⌘ N.

2. A new entry appears in the Group column. Its name, *Group Name,* is selected (**Figure 22**). Enter a new name for the Group and press Return to save it (**Figure 23**).

3. Repeat steps 1 and 2 to add as many groups as you need to organize your contacts.

4. Select All in the Group column.

5. Drag a contact name from the Name column onto the name of the group you want to associate it with in the Group column. When a box appears around the group name (**Figure 24**), release the mouse button to add the contact to that group.

6. Repeat step 5 to organize contact cards as desired.

✔ Tips

- To see which contact cards are in a group, click the name of the group in the Group column. The Name column changes to display only those contacts in the selected group (**Figure 25**).

- A contact can be included in more than one group.

- The Directories entry in the Group field enables you to use an LDAP server to search for an e-mail address. This is an advanced feature that is beyond the scope of this book.

Figure 22
When you click the Add New Group button, a new group appears in the Group column, with its default name selected.

Figure 23
Enter a new name for the group and press Return to save it.

Figure 24
To add a contact to a group, simply drag its name to the group name.

Figure 25
To see which contacts are in a group, select the name of the group.

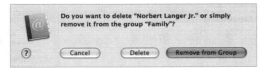

Figure 26 This dialog confirms that you want to delete a record from a group...

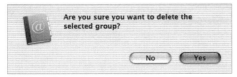

Figure 27 ...and this dialog confirms that you want to delete a group.

To remove a contact from a group

1. In the Group column, select the group you want to remove the contact from (**Figure 25**).

2. In the Name column, select the contact you want to remove.

3. Press Delete.

4. Click the appropriate button in the confirmation dialog that appears (**Figure 26**):

   ▲ **Cancel** does not delete the contact.

   ▲ **Delete** deletes the contact from the Address Book database.

   ▲ **Remove from Group** removes the contact from the group. The contact remains in the Address Book database.

✖ Warning

■ If you delete a contact from the All group, you will remove the contact from the Address Book database.

To remove a group

1. In the Group column, select the group you want to remove (**Figure 25**).

2. Press Delete.

3. In the confirmation dialog that appears (**Figure 27**), click Yes. The group is removed but all contacts within it remain in the Address Book database.

✔ Tip

■ You cannot remove the All group.

To search for a contact card

1. In the Group column, select the name of the group in which you expect to find the contact.

2. Enter all or part of the contact name in the Search box at the top of the Address Book window (**Figure 28**).

   The names of contacts that match what you typed appear in the Name column (**Figure 28**).

✔ Tips

- In step 1, if you're not sure which group a contact is in, select All.

- Search results begin appearing in the Name column as soon as you begin entering search characters in the Search box. The more you enter, the fewer results are displayed.

- If no contact cards match your search criteria, the Name column will be empty.

Figure 28 Enter all or part of a contact name in the Search box to find that contact.

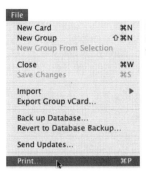

Figure 29
Choose Print from the File menu.

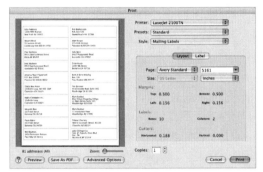

Figure 30 The Mailing Labels Layout options.

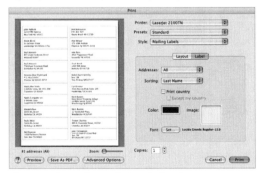

Figure 31 The Mailing Labels Label options.

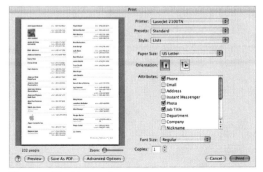

Figure 32 The Lists options.

To print Address Book records

1. In the Group column, select the group containing the records you want to print.

2. To print information for only some records in the group, hold down ⌘ and click in the Name column to select each record you want to print.

3. Choose File > Print (**Figure 29**) or press ⌘P. A Print dialog like the one in **Figure 30** appears.

4. Choose the name of the printer you want to use from the Printer pop-up menu.

5. Choose an option from the Style pop-up menu:

   ▲ **Mailing Labels** (**Figures 30** and **31**) enables you to print mailing labels.

   ▲ **Lists** (**Figure 32**) enables you to print contact lists.

6. Set options in the dialog as desired:

   ▲ For mailing labels, click the Layout button (**Figure 30**) and set label options with the Page pop-up menu and the drop-down list beside it. Then click the Label button (**Figure 31**) and set options for label content, sort order, color, and font.

   ▲ For lists (**Figure 32**), set Paper Size, Orientation, and Font Size options. Then turn on check boxes in the Attributes area to specify what information you want to print for each record.

7. Click Print. Address Book sends the information to your printer and it prints.

✔ Tip

■ I discuss printing in greater detail in **Chapter 10**.

Calculator

Calculator displays a simple calculator that can perform addition, subtraction, multiplication, and division, as well as complex mathematical calculations and conversions.

✔ Tip

■ The Calculator, which has been around since the early days of the Mac, received a minor upgrade for Mac OS X 10.3.

To launch Calculator

Double-click the Calculator icon in the Applications folder (**Figure 1**).

or

1. Click the Calculator icon in the Applications folder (**Figure 1**) to select it.

2. Choose File > Open, or press ⌃ ⌘ O.

The Calculator window appears (**Figure 33**).

To perform basic calculations

Use your mouse to click buttons for numbers and operators.

or

Press keyboard keys corresponding to numbers and operators.

The numbers you enter and the results of your calculations appear at the top of the Calculator window.

✔ Tip

■ You can use the Cut, Copy, and Paste commands to copy the results of calculations into documents. **Chapter 7** covers the Cut, Copy, and Paste commands.

Figure 33
The Calculator looks and works like a $10 pocket calculator.

Figure 34
Calculator's
View menu.

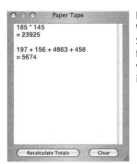

Figure 35
When you choose
Show Paper Tape
from the View menu,
your entries appear
in a separate window.

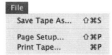

Figure 36 The File menu
includes commands for saving
and printing the paper tape.

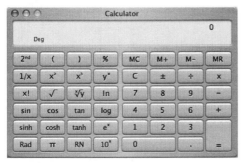

Figure 37 Clicking the Advanced button expands
the Calculator to display mathematical functions.

To keep track of your entries

Choose View > Show Paper Tape (**Figure 34**).
The Paper Tape window appears. It displays
your entries as you make them (**Figure 35**).

✔ Tips

- To hide the Paper Tape window, choose
  View > Hide Paper Tape or click the Paper
  Tape window's close button.

- To start with a fresh tape, click the Clear
  button.

- You can use commands under the File
  menu (**Figure 36**) to save or print the
  paper tape.

To perform advanced calculations

1. Choose View > Advanced (**Figure 34**) or
   press ⌃⌘2. The window expands to
   show a variety of complex mathematical
   functions (**Figure 37**).

2. Click buttons for the functions, values, and
   operators to perform your calculations.

✔ Tips

- To hide advanced functions, choose
  View > Basic (**Figure 34**) or press ⌃⌘1.

To perform conversions

1. Enter the value you want to convert.

2. Choose the conversion you want from the Convert menu (**Figure 38**).

3. In the dialog that appears, set options for the conversion you want to perform. **Figure 39** shows an example that converts speed from miles per hour to knots.

4. Click OK. The original value you entered is converted and appears at the top of the Calculator window.

✔ Tips

■ The Convert menu's Recent Conversions submenu makes it easy to repeat conversions you have done recently.

■ If you have an Internet connection, you should choose Convert > Update Currency Exchange Rates before using the Convert menu to perform currency conversions.

Figure 38 The Convert menu lists a variety of common conversions.

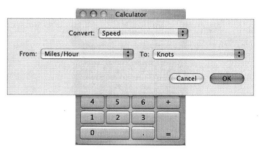

Figure 39 Set conversion options in a dialog sheet like this.

Figure 40 The Chess window displays a three-dimensional chess board.

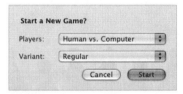

Figure 41 A dialog sheet like this one appears when you choose New from the File menu.

Human vs. Human
✓ Human vs. Computer
Computer vs. Human
Computer vs. Computer

✓ Regular
Crazyhouse
Suicide
Losers

Figures 42 & 43
The Players (top) and Variants (bottom) pop-up menus enable you to set options for a new game.

Chess

Chess is a computerized version of the classic strategy game of chess. Your pieces are white and you go first; the computer's pieces are black.

To launch Chess

Double-click the Chess icon in the Applications folder (**Figure 1**).

or

1. Click the Chess icon in the Applications folder (**Figure 1**) to select it.

2. Choose File > Open, or press ⌃⌘O.

The Chess window appears (**Figure 40**).

To move a chess piece

Drag the piece onto any valid square on the playing board.

✔ Tips

■ The computer moves automatically after each of your moves.

■ If you attempt to make an invalid move, an alert sounds and the piece returns to where it was.

■ If Speakable Items is enabled, you can use spoken commands to move chess pieces. I tell you about Speakable Items in **Chapter 18**.

To start a new game

1. Choose Game > New. A dialog sheet like the one in **Figure 41** appears.

2. Choose an option from the Players pop-up menu (**Figure 42**).

3. If desired, choose an option from the Variant pop-up menu (**Figure 43**).

4. Click Start.

CHESS

DVD Player

DVD Player enables you to play DVD-Video on your Macintosh.

✔ Tip

■ To use DVD Player, your Macintosh must have a DVD-ROM drive or SuperDrive. For that reason, the Mac OS X installer only installs DVD Player on computers that have one of these drives. If you can't find DVD Player in your Applications folder, chances are that your computer can't play DVD-Video anyway.

To launch DVD Player

Insert a DVD-Video into your computer. DVD Player should launch and do one of two things:

◆ Display a black Viewer window with a floating Controller palette (**Figure 44**).

◆ Immediately begin DVD play (**Figure 45**).

If DVD Player does not launch at all, then:

Double-click the DVD Player icon in the Applications folder (**Figure 1**).

or

1. Click the DVD Player icon in the Applications folder (**Figure 1**) to select it.

2. Choose File > Open or press ⌘ ⌘ O.

✔ Tip

■ If a Drive Region Code dialog like the one in **Figure 46** appears the first time you play a DVD-Video, click the Set Drive Region button to set DVD Player's region to match that of the disc you inserted. Then click OK to dismiss the confirmation dialog that appears.

LAUNCHING DVD PLAYER

Figure 44 DVD Player either starts with a blank Viewer window and Controller palette...

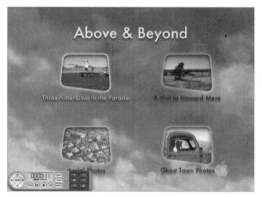

Figure 45 ...or begins playing the DVD-Video. (This is the first DVD I created with iDVD. It didn't get any awards.)

Figure 46 This dialog may appear the first time you insert a DVD-Video.

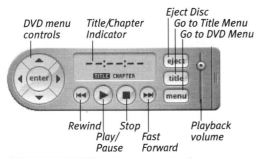

DVD menu controls — Title/Chapter Indicator — Eject Disc — Go to Title Menu — Go to DVD Menu

Rewind — Play/Pause — Stop — Fast Forward — Playback volume

Figures 47a & 47b
The Controller comes in two styles: horizontal (above) and vertical (left). Both have the same controls.

Figure 48
The Controls menu includes commands for controlling DVD play.

Controls	
Use Vertical Controller	⌥⌘C
Open Control Drawer	⌘]
Use Standard Info Window	⌥⌘I
Add Bookmark...	⌘=
Edit Bookmarks...	⌥⌘B
Play	space
Stop	⌘.
Scan Forward	⇧⌘→
Scan Backwards	⇧⌘←
Scan Rate	▶
Volume Up	⌘↑
Volume Down	⌘↓
Mute	⌥⌘↓
Closed Captioning	▶
Eject	⌘E

Figure 49 A horizontal Controller, expanded to show additional control buttons. Point to a button to learn its name.

Video	
Half Size	⌘1
Normal Size	⌘2
Maximum Size	⌘3
Enter Full Screen	⌘0

Figure 50
The Video menu enables you to set the size of the Viewer window.

To display the Controller

Move the mouse while the DVD is playing.

or

Choose Window > Show Viewer (the menu appears, if necessary, when you point to it), or press [Control][C].

The Controller appears (**Figure 47a** or **47b**).

✔ Tips

■ You can change the appearance of the Controller from horizontal (**Figure 47a**) to vertical (**Figure 47b**) by choosing an option from the Controller Type submenu under the Controls menu (**Figure 48**).

■ To display additional DVD controls on the Controller, double-click the pair of tiny lines on the right (**Figure 47a**) or bottom (**Figure 47b**) of the Controller. **Figure 49** shows a horizontal Controller expanded to show these controls.

To control DVD play

Click buttons on the Controller (**Figure 47a**, **47b**, or **49**).

or

Choose a command from the Controls menu (**Figure 48**).

✔ Tip

■ The Pause button on the Controller (**Figures 47a** and **47b**) and the Pause command on the Controls menu (**Figure 48**) change into a Play button and a Play command when a DVD is not playing.

To resize the Viewer window

Choose an option from the Video window (**Figure 50**) or press the corresponding short-cut key.

Image Capture

Image Capture is an application that performs two functions:

◆ Download image files from a digital camera to your computer's hard disk.

◆ Operate your scanner to scan and save images.

In this part of the chapter, I explain how to download images from a digital camera with Image Capture.

✔ Tips

■ Some digital cameras and scanners require that driver software be installed on Mac OS X before the camera or scanner can be used. Consult the documentation that came with your scanner or camera or check the device manufacturer's Web site for Mac OS X compatibility and driver information.

■ Not all digital cameras or scanners are compatible with Image Capture. Generally speaking, if Image Capture does not "see" your camera or scanner when it is connected and turned on, the camera or scanner is probably not compatible with Image Capture and Image Capture cannot be used.

■ You can also download images from a digital camera using iPhoto, which offers additional features for managing photos saved to disk. I tell you about iPhoto in **Chapter 8**.

Figure 51 Image Capture's main window is named for the camera you have attached and turned on.

Figure 52 Use this window to select the images you want to download.

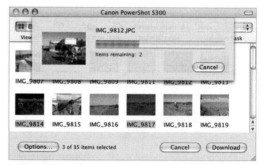

Figure 53 A progress window appears as the pictures are downloaded.

IMAGE CAPTURE

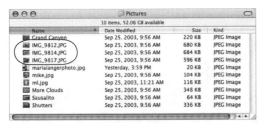

Figure 54 Image Capture switches to the Finder and opens the folders where it downloaded the images and/or movies. In this example, it has downloaded four images from my Canon PowerShot 300 to the Pictures folder in my Home folder.

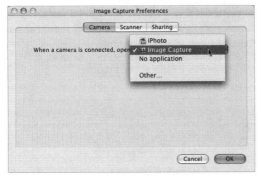

Figure 55 You can set options in the Image Capture Preferences window to choose applications for working with your digital camera and scanner.

✔ Tips

- If Image Capture doesn't launch automatically after step 2, you can open it by double-clicking its icon in the Applications folder (**Figure 1**).

- If iPhoto is installed on your computer, it may launch instead of Image Capture when you connect a digital camera. If so, you must manually launch Image Capture by opening its application icon (**Figure 1**) to use it.

To download images from a digital camera

1. Attach your digital camera to your computer's USB or FireWire port, using the applicable cable.

2. Turn the camera on and, if necessary, set it to review mode. The main Image Capture window should appear (**Figure 51**).

3. To download all images on the camera, click the Download All button in the main Image Capture window (**Figure 51**).

   or

   To download some of the images on the camera, click the Download Some button in the main Image Capture window (**Figure 51**). A window full of thumbnail images appears (**Figure 52**). Select the images you want to download. To select more than one image, hold down ⌘ while clicking each image. Then click the Download button.

   A dialog sheet appears, showing the progress of the download (**Figure 53**). When it disappears, the download is complete and Image Capture displays the window(s) for the folder(s) in which it downloaded the pictures (**Figure 54**).

- To specify which application should open when you attach a camera, choose Image Capture > Preferences to display the Image Capture Preferences dialog. Click the Camera button to display camera preferences, use the pop-up menu to choose an application (**Figure 55**), and click OK.

- You can also use the thumbnail window (**Figure 52**) to delete images on the camera. Select the images you want to delete, click the Delete button, and click Delete in the confirmation dialog that appears.

Preview

Preview, which was revised and improved for Mac OS X 10.3, is a program that enables you to open and view two kinds of files:

◆ **Image files** (**Figure 56**), including files in JPEG, TIFF, PICT, GIF, PS (PostScript), and EPS formats.

◆ **PDF,** or **Portable Document Format, files** (**Figure 57**) created with Mac OS X's Print command, Adobe Acrobat software, or other software capable of creating PDFs.

✔ Tips

■ I explain how to create PDF files with the Print command in **Chapter 10**.

■ You can also open PDF files with Adobe Acrobat Reader software. You can learn more about Acrobat Reader—and download a free copy of the software—on the Adobe Systems Web site, www.adobe.com/products/acrobat/readstep.html.

Figure 56 Here's an image file opened with Preview. (Cherokee and Jake, wearing their Christmas hats. And yes, Cherokee is sticking out his tongue.)

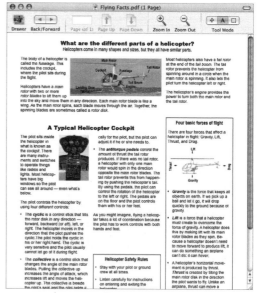

Figure 57 Here's a PDF file opened with Preview. (Want to learn how helicopters fly? You can download this PDF from www.marialanger.com/articles/FlyingFacts.pdf.)

Figure 58 One way to open a file with Preview is to drag the file's icon onto the Preview icon.

Figure 59
You can also double-click a Preview document's file icon.

Flying Facts.pdf

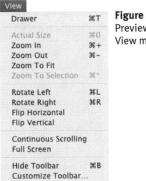

Figure 60
Preview's View menu.

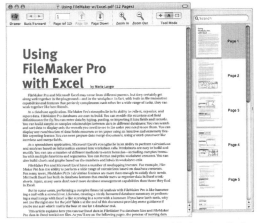

Figure 61 You can display a Drawer with thumbnails for a multi-page document.

To open a file with Preview

Drag the document file's icon onto the Preview icon in the Applications folder (**Figure 58**).

or

Double-click the icon for a Preview document (**Figure 59**).

Preview launches and displays the file in its window (**Figures 56** and **57**).

✔ Tips

- You can also use Preview's Open command to open any compatible file on disk. I explain how to use an application's Open command in **Chapter 5**.

- To open multiple files at once, select all of their icons and drag any one of them onto the Preview icon.

- You can use options on a Preview window's toolbar (**Figures 56** and **57**) or Preview's View menu (**Figure 60**) to zoom in or out, rotate the window's contents, or view a specific page.

- If a document has multiple pages or if you opened multiple image files at once, you can click the Drawer button in the window's toolbar to display or hide a drawer with thumbnail images of each page (**Figure 61**) or image. Click a thumbnail to move quickly to that page or image.

OPENING FILES WITH PREVIEW

To search for text in a PDF file

1. Open the PDF file you want to search.

2. If necessary, click the Drawer button to display the drawer.

3. Enter a search word or phrase in the Search box at the top of the drawer.

   As you type, Preview searches the document for the text you entered. It displays a list of sentences containing that text in the drawer, along with corresponding page numbers. It also highlights the first occurrence of the search text in the main document window. You can see all this in **Figure 62**.

✔ Tips

- To display a specific occurrence of the search text, click its reference in the drawer (**Figure 62**).

- To view thumbnails rather than search results in the drawer (**Figure 61**), clear the search text by clicking the tiny X icon on the right side of the Search box at the top of the drawer (**Figure 62**).

- The more text you enter in the Search box, the fewer matches Preview finds.

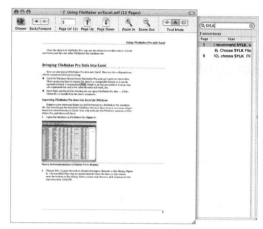

Figure 62 When you enter search text in the Search box, Preview quickly displays matches.

Figure 63
Preview's tool buttons for a PDF file. (The Text tool button does not appear for image files.)

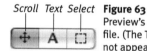

Figure 64
The Tools menu, with a PDF file open. (The Text tool is not available for image files.)

Figure 65 With the Scroll tool selected, the mouse pointer turns into a hand when over the document window. Drag to reposition the contents of the window.

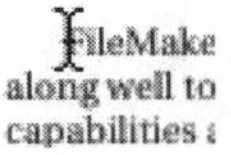

FileMaker
along well to
capabilities ε

Figure 66
The mouse pointer turns into an I-beam pointer.

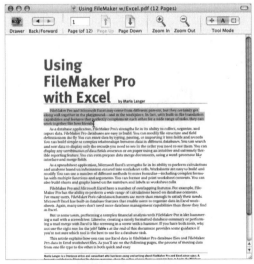

Figure 67 Drag to select

To shift the document view

1. In Preview's toolbar, click the Scroll tool button (**Figure 63**), choose Tools > Scroll Tool (**Figure 64**), or press ⌃ ⌘ 1.

2. Position the mouse pointer over the document window. It turns into a hand pointer (**Figure 65**).

3. Press the mouse button down and drag to shift the contents of the document window.

✔ Tip

■ To use the Scroll tool, the document must be too large to fit into the window.

To select text in a PDF file

1. In Preview's toolbar, click the Text tool button (**Figure 63**), choose Tools > Text Tool (**Figure 64**), or press ⌃ ⌘ 2.

2. Position the mouse pointer over text in the document window. It turns into an I-beam pointer (**Figure 66**).

3. Press the mouse button down and drag to select text (**Figure 67**).

✔ Tip

■ Once text is selected, you can use the Copy command to copy it to the clipboard. I tell you about the Copy and Paste commands in **Chapter 7**.

To select document contents

1. In Preview's toolbar, click the Select tool button (**Figure 63**), choose Tools > Select Tool (**Figure 64**), or press ⌘⌘3.

2. Position the mouse pointer over text in the document window. It turns into a crosshairs pointer (**Figure 68**).

3. Press the mouse button down and drag to select document contents (**Figure 69**).

✔ Tips

- To deselect document contents, click in the document window anywhere other than on the selection.

- You can use the Select tool to crop an image. Simply select the part of the image you want to keep and choose Tools > Crop Image or press ⌘⌘K. The document is cropped (**Figure 70**). Be sure to choose File > Save or File > Save As to save your changes.

Figure 68
The mouse pointer turns into a crosshairs pointer.

Figure 69 Drag to select document contents.

Figure 70 The Crop Image command removes everything except the selection.

Figure 71 When you launch QuickTime, it uses your Internet connection to obtain content from Apple's QuickTime Web site—in this case, an image for the White Stripes' "Hardest Button to Button" video. Clicking the button in this window takes you to the What's On page on Apple's QuickTime site.

Figure 72 When you launch QuickTime Player, Apple tries to sell you QuickTime Pro.

Figure 73 The What's On page of Apple's QuickTime Web site changes regularly.

QuickTime Player

QuickTime is a video and audio technology developed by Apple Computer, Inc. It is widely used for digital movies as well as streaming audio and video available via the Internet. QuickTime Player is an application you can use to view QuickTime movies and streaming Internet content.

✔ Tips

- There are two versions of QuickTime Player: the standard version, which is included with Mac OS X, and the Pro version, which enables you to edit and save QuickTime files. You can learn about QuickTime Pro on Apple's QuickTime Web site, www.apple.com/quicktime/, and in *QuickTime 6: Visual QuickStart Guide*.

- Internet access is covered in **Chapter 11**.

To launch QuickTime Player

Click the QuickTime Player icon in the Dock (**Figure 2**).

or

Open the QuickTime Player icon in the Applications folder (**Figure 1**).

A QuickTime Player window appears (**Figure 71**).

✔ Tips

- When you launch QuickTime Player, a dialog like the one in **Figure 72** may appear. Click Later to dismiss it.

- Clicking contents in a QuickTime Player window may display the What's On page of Apple's QuickTime Web site (**Figure 73**).

To open a QuickTime movie file

Double-click the QuickTime movie file icon (**Figure 74**).

If QuickTime Player is not already running, it launches. The movie's first frame appears in a window (**Figure 75**).

✔ Tip

■ You can also open a QuickTime movie file by using the Open Movie in New Player command on QuickTime Player's File menu (**Figure 76**). The Open dialog is covered in **Chapter 5**.

To control movie play

You can click buttons and use controls in the QuickTime Player window (**Figure 75**) to control movie play:

◆ **Go To Start** displays the first movie frame.

◆ **Fast Rewind** plays the movie backward quickly, with sound.

◆ **Play** starts playing the movie. When the movie is playing, the Play button turns to a **Pause** button, which pauses movie play.

◆ **Fast Forward** plays the movie forward quickly, with sound.

◆ **Go To End** displays the last movie frame.

◆ **Time line** tracks movie progress. By dragging the slider, you can scroll through the movie without sound.

◆ **Volume** changes movie volume; drag the slider left or right.

To specify movie size

Select a size option from the Movie menu (**Figure 77**). The size of the movie's window changes accordingly.

Figure 74
A QuickTime
The Medallion.mov movie file icon.

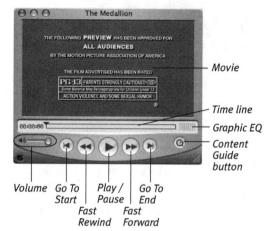

Figure 75 The first frame of the movie appears in a QuickTime Player window.

Figure 76
QuickTime Player's
File menu. There
are more menu
commands in
QuickTime Pro.

Figure 77
Use the Movie menu
to change the size of
the movie's window.

Figure 78 QuickTime's Content Guide, with the Movie Trailers button selected.

Figure 79 Clicking the More link in the Content Guide for Movie Trailers displays this page.

Figure 80 QuickTime content can appear in a Web browser window, like this.

To open QuickTime content on the Internet

1. If necessary, connect to the Internet.

2. Click the Content Guide button in a QuickTime window to display the QuickTime Content Guide (**Figure 78**).

3. Click one of the Content Guide buttons.

4. A graphic for the featured content appears in the right side of the window (**Figure 78**). Click the More link below it.

5. QuickTime launches your Web browser and opens the Web page for the content category you selected in step 3 (**Figure 79**). Use the Web browser to locate and display content that interests you. QuickTime movies appear within the browser window (**Figure 80**) or within a QuickTime Player window.

✔ Tips

- QuickTime content available on the Web includes *streaming* audio or video *channels*. This requires a constant connection to the Internet while content is downloaded to your computer. Streaming content continues downloading until you close its window.

- I tell you more about the Internet and using Web browser software in **Chapter 11**.

Stickies

Stickies is an application that displays computerized "sticky notes" that you can use to place reminders on your screen.

To launch Stickies

Double-click the Stickies icon in the Applications folder (**Figure 1**).

or

1. Click the Stickies icon in the Applications folder (**Figure 1**) to select it.

2. Choose File > Open, or press ⌃⌘O.

The default Stickies windows appear (**Figure 81**).

✔ Tips

■ Read the text in the default Stickies windows (**Figure 81**) to learn more about Stickies and how the Mac OS X version differs from previous versions.

■ Sticky notes remain on the desktop until you quit Stickies.

■ When you quit Stickies, all notes are automatically saved to disk and will reappear the next time you launch Stickies.

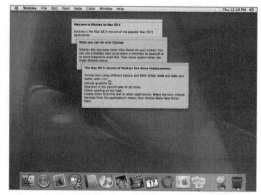

Figure 81 The default windows that appear when you first launch Stickies tell you a little about the program.

Figure 82
Stickies' File
menu.

Figure 83
Here's a blank
new sticky note...

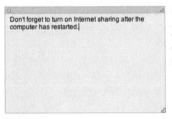

Figure 84
...and here's
the same note
with a reminder
typed in.

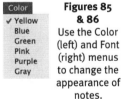

**Figures 85
& 86**
Use the Color
(left) and Font
(right) menus
to change the
appearance of
notes.

Figure 87 The Print dialog.

To create a sticky note

1. Choose File > New Note (**Figure 82**) or press ⌃ ⌘ N to display a blank new note (**Figure 83**).

2. Type the text that you want to include in the note (**Figure 84**).

✔ Tip

■ You can use options under the Color and Font menus (**Figures 85** and **86**) to change the appearance of notes or note text. Common text formatting options are covered in **Chapters 7** and **9**.

To print sticky notes

1. To print just one sticky note, click it to activate it and then choose File > Print Active Note (**Figure 82**) or press ⌃ ⌘ P.

   or

   To print all sticky notes, choose File > Print All Notes (**Figure 82**).

2. Use the Print dialog that appears to set options for printing and click the Print button (**Figure 87**).

✔ Tip

■ **Chapter 10** covers the Print dialog and printing.

To close a sticky note

1. Click the close box for the sticky note you want to close.

   or

   Activate the sticky note you want to close and choose File > Close (**Figure 82**) or press ⌘⌘W.

2. A Close dialog like the one in **Figure 88** may appear.

   ▲ **Don't Save** closes the note without saving its contents.

   ▲ **Cancel** leaves the note open.

   ▲ **Save** displays the Export dialog (**Figure 89**), which you can use to save the note as plain or formatted text in a file on disk. Enter a name and select a disk location for the note's contents, then choose a file format and click Save.

✔ Tip

■ Once a sticky note has been saved to disk, it can be opened and edited with TextEdit or any other program capable of opening text files.

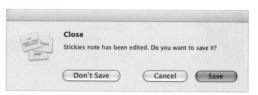

Figure 88 The Close dialog asks if you want to save note contents.

Figure 89 Use the Export dialog to save a note as plain or formatted text in a file on disk.

CLOSING STICKY NOTES

Figure 90 The contents of the AppleScript folder inside the Applications folder.

AppleScript Basics

AppleScript (**Figure 90**) is the scripting language that comes with Mac OS. It enables you to automate tasks and extend the functionality of Mac OS X.

You use AppleScript's Script Editor application to write small programs or *scripts* that include specially worded *statements*. AppleScript statements are converted by Mac OS into *Apple events*—messages that can be understood by the operating system and applications. When you run a script, the script can send instructions to the operating system or applications and receive messages in return.

For example, say that at the end of each working day, you back up the contents of a specific folder to a network disk before you shut down your computer. The folder is large and the network is slow, so you often have to wait ten minutes or more to shut down the computer when the backup is finished. You can write a script that mounts the network drive, backs up the folder, and shuts down your computer automatically. You simply run the script, turn out the lights, and go home. AppleScript does the rest.

In this part of the chapter, I introduce AppleScript's components to give you an idea of how it works and what you can do with it.

✔ Tip

■ You can find a lot more information about AppleScript, including tutorials, sample scripts, and a reference manual, at Apple's AppleScript Web site, www.apple.com/applescript/.

AppleScript Files

There are three main types of AppleScript files (**Figure 91**):

- ◆ **Scripts** (formerly *compiled scripts*) are completed scripts that can be launched from an application's script menu or the Script Menu. Double-clicking a compiled script icon launches Script Editor.

- ◆ **Applications** (or *applets*) are full-fledged applications that can be launched by double-clicking their icons.

- ◆ **Text files** are plain text files containing AppleScript statements. They can be opened with Script Editor or any text editor and can be run from within Script Editor. Double-clicking a script text file icon launches the application in which it was written.

Script Editor

Script Editor, which has been completely rewritten for Mac OS X 10.3, is an application you can use to write AppleScript scripts. It has a number of features that make it an extremely useful tool for script writing:

- ◆ The Script Editor window (**Figure 92**) can automatically format script statements so they're easy to read.

- ◆ The syntax checker can examine your script statements and identify any syntax errors that would prevent the script from running or compiling.

- ◆ The Open Dictionary command makes it possible to view an application's dictionary of AppleScript commands and classes (**Figure 93**).

- ◆ The record script feature can record actions as script steps.

- ◆ The Save and Save As commands enable you to save scripts in a variety of formats.

Figure 91 The three basic file formats for an Apple-Script: a script (left), an application (middle), and a text file (right). Note the file name extensions for these formats.

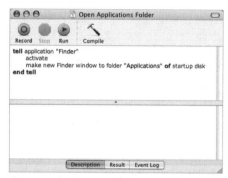

Figure 92 The Script Editor window with a very simple script. Note how Script Editor formats the script for easy reading.

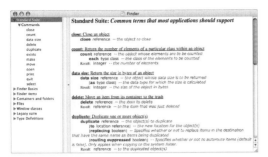

Figure 93 The Standard Suite of Finder's AppleScript dictionary.

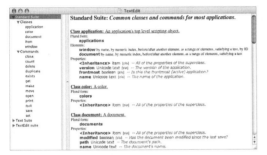

Figure 94 The Standard Suite of TextEdit's AppleScript dictionary.

AppleScript Dictionaries

Scriptable applications include *AppleScript dictionaries,* which list and provide syntax information for valid AppleScript commands and classes. These dictionaries are a valuable reference for anyone who wants to write scripts.

An AppleScript dictionary is organized into *suites.* Each suite includes a number of related *commands* and *classes.* Commands are like verbs—they tell an application to do something. Classes are types of *objects* that a command can be performed on. For example, in TextEdit's Standard Suite, *close* is a command that can be performed on an object such as *window.*

Figures 93 and **94** show examples of Apple-Script Dictionaries for two applications: Finder and TextEdit. In each illustration, the first suite is selected to display all commands and classes in that suite. On the left side of the window, suite names appear in bold text, commands appear in normal text, and classes appear in italic text.

✔ Tip

- Although dictionaries are helpful for learning valid AppleScript commands, they are not sufficient for teaching a beginner how to write scripts.

Script Menu

Script Menu is a utility that enables you to access AppleScripts from the Finder's menu bar. When installed, it adds a script menu full of example scripts to the menu bar. You can modify this menu by removing scripts you don't use or adding your own custom scripts.

Folder Actions

Folder Actions is a feature of Mac OS X that works with AppleScript. You create a script that performs a specific task, then attach that script to a folder. When the folder is modified in a predefined way—for example, when it is opened or a file is added to it—the script activates and performs its task.

How can Folder Actions help you? Here's an example. Suppose you're writing a book and every time you finish a chapter, you need to upload a copy of it to an FTP site so your editors can download and review it. You can write a script that uploads any new file added to a folder to the FTP site. Attach that script to a folder and *voilà*! Every time you save a copy of a chapter to the folder, it is automatically sent for review.

✔ Tip

■ To learn more about writing scripts for Folder Actions, visit www.apple.com/applescript/folder_actions/.

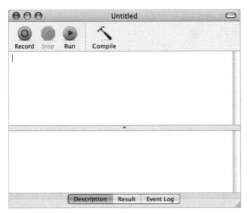

Figure 95 A new untitled Script Editor window.

Figure 96
Script Editor's
File menu.

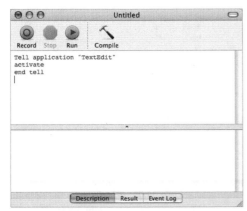

Figure 97 A painfully simple script.

Using AppleScript

As with most programming languages, AppleScript can be extremely complex—far too complex to fully cover in this book. On the following pages, I explain how you can get started using AppleScript. This introduction should be enough to help you decide whether you want to fully explore the world of AppleScript programming.

✔ Tip

■ When you're ready for more how-to information for using AppleScript, I highly recommend Ethan Wilde's excellent book, *AppleScript for Applications: Visual QuickStart Guide*, published by Peachpit Press.

To launch Script Editor

Open the Script Editor icon in the Apple-Script folder in your Applications folder (**Figure 90**). An untitled Script Editor window appears (**Figure 95**).

or

Open the icon for a script (**Figure 91**, left). The script appears in a Script Editor window (**Figure 92**).

To write a script

1. If necessary, choose File > New (**Figure 96**) or press ⌘N to open an empty Script Editor window (**Figure 95**).

2. If desired, type a description for the script in the bottom half of the window.

3. Type the script steps in the top half of the window. Be sure to press Return after each line. **Figure 97** shows an example of another simple script.

To check the syntax for a script

Click the Compile button in the script window (**Figure 97**).

If your script's syntax is error-free, Script Editor formats and color-codes your statements (**Figure 98**).

or

If Script Editor finds a problem with your script, it displays a dialog that describes the problem (**Figure 99**) and indicates where it is in the script by selecting it (**Figure 100**). Click OK to dismiss the dialog and fix the problem.

✔ Tips

- The syntax checker uses AppleScript's *compiler* to translates the script into *code* that can be read and understood by your computer. (Compiled code does not appear on screen.) If the script cannot be compiled, a syntax error results.

- Unfortunately, even if you write a script without any syntax errors, the script is not guaranteed to work. The only way to make sure a script works is to run it.

Figure 98 The script from **Figure 97** after it has been compiled.

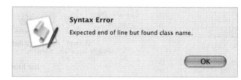

Figure 99 If the script contains an error, you'll see a dialog sheet like this one when you attempt to compile it.

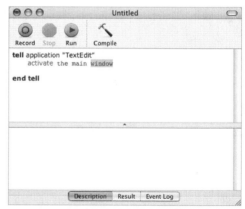

Figure 100 Script Editor helps you debug a script by highlighting problems.

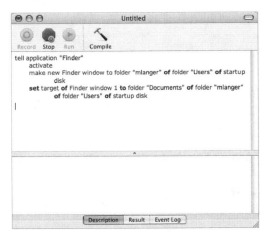

Figure 101 Script Editor records the steps as you complete them.

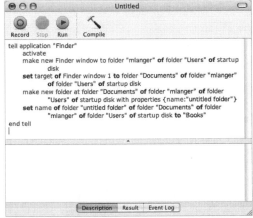

Figure 102 When you click the Stop button, Script Editor writes the last step.

To record a script

1. If necessary, choose File > New Script (**Figure 96**) or press ⌃ ⌘ N to open an empty Script Editor window (**Figure 95**).

2. If desired, type a description for the script in the bottom half of the window.

3. Click the Record button.

4. Perform the steps you want Script Editor to record. As you work, Script Editor writes AppleScript instructions in the Script Editor window (**Figure 101**).

5. When you are finished recording steps, switch to the Script Editor window and click the Stop button. Script Editor writes the last instruction for the script (**Figure 102**).

✔ Tips

- Unfortunately, Script Editor's recorder does not work with all applications. If you attempt to record a task and Script Editor does not write any instructions, the application you are using is not recordable.

- Before you record a script, it's a good idea to know exactly what you want to do. This will prevent errors—which will also be recorded by Script Editor's recorder!

- Once you have a script recorded by Script Editor, you can edit it as necessary to customize it.

RECORDING SCRIPTS

183

To save a script

1. Choose File > Save (**Figure 96**) or press ⌃ ⌘ S to display the Save Location dialog (**Figure 103**).

2. Enter a script name in the Save As box.

3. Choose a file format from the File Format pop-up menu (**Figure 104**).

4. Use the Where part of the dialog to select a location in which to save the file.

5. Click Save.

    The file is saved on disk. The script name appears in the title bar of the Script Editor window (**Figure 92**).

Figure 103 Script Editor's Save Location dialog.

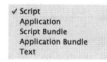

Figure 104
The File Format pop-up menu.

✔ Tips

- You cannot save a script if it will not compile. Check the script syntax before attempting to save the file; I explain how earlier in this section.

- If you're not sure what to choose in step 3, choose Script.

- It's a good idea to save a script before trying to run it for the first time.

- Using the Save Location dialog is covered in **Chapter 5**.

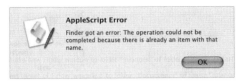

Figure 105 When you run a script that contains an error, AppleScript displays an error message like this one.

Figure 106 Use the Open Dictionary dialog to open the AppleScript dictionary for a scriptable application.

To run a script

Do one of the following:

◆ To run a compiled script from within Script Editor, click the Run button in the Script Editor window (**Figure 100**).

◆ To run an application from the Finder, double-click the icon for the applet (**Figure 91**, middle).

If the script is valid, it performs all script commands.

or

If the script is not valid, an error message appears (**Figure 105**). Click OK.

To open an application's AppleScript dictionary

1. Choose File > Open Dictionary (**Figure 96**) or press [Shift] [⌘] [O].

2. In the Open Dictionary dialog that appears (**Figure 106**), select a dictionary and click Open. The dictionary opens in its own window (**Figures 93** and **94**).

3. Click the name of a suite, command, or class to display its information in the right side of the window.

To examine an example script

1. Double-click the Example Scripts alias icon in the AppleScript folder (**Figure 90**) to open the Scripts folder (**Figure 107**).

2. Open the folder containing the script you want to examine.

3. Double-click the example script file's icon to open it in Script Editor (**Figures 108** and **109**).

✔ Tips

- You can modify and experiment with these example scripts as desired.

- If you make changes to an example script, I highly recommend that you use the Save As command to save the revised script with a different name or in a different location. Doing so will keep the original example intact, in case you want to consult it again.

- You can download additional sample scripts from Apple's AppleScript Web site, www.apple.com/applescript/.

Figure 108
Some scripts can be simple, like this one to open AppleScript Help ...

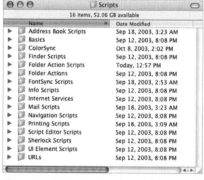

Figure 107 AppleScript comes with dozens of sample scripts to perform a wide variety of tasks.

Figure 109 ... while others can be complex, like this one, which accesses the Internet to get the current temperature at your location. (A thermometer outside your window would be simpler.)

EXAMINING EXAMPLE SCRIPTS

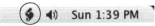

Figure 110 The Script menu icon appears near the far right end of the menu bar.

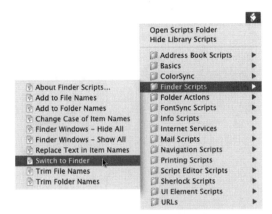

Figure 111 Script Menu's submenus correspond to the folders in the Scripts folder shown in Figure 107.

To enable Script Menu

Double-click the Install Script Menu icon in the AppleScript folder (**Figure 90**). The Script Menu installer runs. A tiny Script menu icon appears near the right end of the Menu bar (**Figure 110**).

To run a script with Script Menu

Choose the script you want to run from one of the submenus under the Script menu (**Figure 111**).

To remove a Script Menu script

1. Double-click the Example Scripts alias icon in the AppleScript folder (**Figure 90**) to open the Scripts folder (**Figure 107**).

2. Open the folder that contains the script you want to remove.

3. Drag the script out of the folder.

✔ Tip

■ To move a script from one Script menu submenu to another, drag it from the folder in which it is stored to the folder corresponding to the submenu you want it to appear on.

To add a Script Menu script

1. Write or record an AppleScript and save it as a script.

2. Double-click the Example Scripts alias icon in the AppleScript folder (**Figure 90**) to open the Scripts folder (**Figure 107**).

3. Drag the icon for the script you want to add into the folder corresponding to the submenu you want the script to appear on.

To disable Script Menu

Double-click the Remove Script Menu icon in the AppleScript folder (**Figure 90**). The Script Menu uninstaller runs. The Script menu disappears from the menu bar.

Using TextEdit

Figure 1
The TextEdit application icon.

TextEdit

Figure 2
A TextEdit document's icon.

Letter

TextEdit

TextEdit (**Figure 1**), which was updated for Mac OS X 10.3, is a text editing application that comes with Mac OS. As its name implies, TextEdit lets you create, open, edit, and print text documents (**Figure 2**), including the "Read Me" files that come with many applications.

This chapter explains how to use TextEdit to create, edit, format, open, and save documents.

✔ Tips

- TextEdit 1.3, which comes with Mac OS X 10.3, can open and save Microsoft Word format files. This makes it possible to work with and create Microsoft Word documents, even if you don't have Microsoft Word.

- Although TextEdit offers many of the features found in a word processing application, it falls far short of the feature list of word processors such as Microsoft Word and the word processing components of integrated software such as AppleWorks.

- If you're new to computers, don't skip this chapter. It not only explains how to use TextEdit but provides instructions for basic text editing skills—like text entry and the Copy, Cut, and Paste commands —that you'll use in all Mac OS-compatible applications.

Launching & Quitting TextEdit

Like any other application, you must launch TextEdit before you can use it. This loads it into your computer's memory so your computer can work with it.

To launch TextEdit

Double-click the TextEdit application icon in the Applications folder window (**Figure 3**).

or

1. Select the TextEdit application icon in the Applications folder window (**Figure 3**).

2. Choose File > Open, or press ⌃ ⌘ O.

   TextEdit launches. An untitled document window appears (**Figure 4**).

✔ Tip

■ As illustrated in **Figure 4**, the TextEdit document window has the same standard window parts found in Finder windows. I tell you how to use Finder windows in **Chapter 2**; TextEdit and other application windows work the same way.

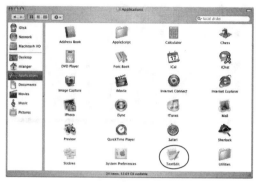

Figure 3 You can find TextEdit in the Applications folder.

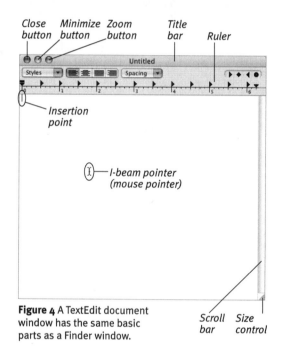

Figure 4 A TextEdit document window has the same basic parts as a Finder window.

Figure 5
Choose Quit
TextEdit from the
TextEdit menu.

Figure 6 A dialog sheet like this appears when you quit TextEdit with an unsaved document open.

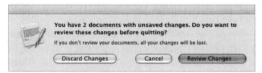

Figure 7 A dialog like this appears when you quit TextEdit with multiple unsaved documents open.

To quit TextEdit

1. Choose TextEdit > Quit TextEdit (**Figure 5**), or press ⌃ ⌘ Q.

2. If a single unsaved document is open, a dialog sheet like the one in **Figure 6** appears, attached to the document window.

   ▲ Click Don't Save to quit without saving the document.

   ▲ Click Cancel or press Esc to return to the application without quitting.

   ▲ Click Save or press Return or Enter to save the document.

   or

   If multiple unsaved documents are open, a dialog like the one in **Figure 7** appears:

   ▲ Click Discard Changes to quit TextEdit without saving any of the documents.

   ▲ Click Cancel or press Esc to return to the application without quitting.

   ▲ Click Review Changes or press Return or Enter to view each unsaved document with a dialog like the one in **Figure 6** to decide whether you want to save it.

   TextEdit closes all windows and quits.

✔ Tip

■ You learn more about saving TextEdit documents later in this chapter.

Entering & Editing Text

You enter text into a TextEdit document by typing it in. Don't worry about making mistakes; you can fix them as you type or when you're finished. This section tells you how.

✔ Tip

■ The text entry and editing techniques covered in this section work exactly the same in most word processors, as well as many other Mac OS applications.

To enter text

Type the text you want to enter. It appears at the blinking insertion point (**Figure 8**).

✔ Tips

■ It is not necessary to press Return at the end of a line. When the text you type reaches the end of the line, it automatically begins a new line. This is called *word wrap* and is a feature of all word processors. By default, in TextEdit, word wrap is determined by the width of the document window.

■ The insertion point moves as you type.

■ To correct an error as you type, press Delete. This key deletes the character to the left of the insertion point.

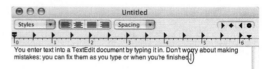

Figure 8 The text you type appears at the blinking insertion point.

ENTERING TEXT

Figure 9
Position the mouse pointer...

Figure 10
...and click to move the insertion point.

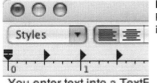
Figure 11
Position the insertion point...

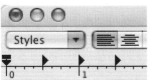
Figure 12
...and type the text that you want to appear.

To move the insertion point

Press ←, →, ↑, or ↓ to move the insertion point left, right, up, or down one character or line at a time.

or

1. Position the mouse pointer, which looks like an I-beam pointer, where you want the insertion point to appear (**Figure 9**).

2. Click the mouse button once. The insertion point appears at the mouse pointer (**Figure 10**).

✔ Tips

- Since the text you type appears at the insertion point, it's a good idea to know where the insertion point is *before* you start typing.

- When moving the insertion point with the mouse, you must click to complete the move. If you simply point with the I-beam pointer, the insertion point will stay right where it is (**Figure 9**).

To insert text

1. Position the insertion point where you want the text to appear (**Figure 11**).

2. Type the text that you want to insert. The text is inserted at the insertion point (**Figure 12**).

✔ Tip

- Word wrap changes automatically to accommodate inserted text.

To select text by dragging

Drag the I-beam pointer over the text you want to select (**Figure 13**).

To select text with Shift-click

1. Position the insertion point at the beginning of the text you want to select (**Figure 14**).

2. Hold down (Shift) and click at the end of the text you want to select. All text between the insertion point's original position and where you clicked becomes selected (**Figure 15**).

✔ Tip

■ This is a good way to select large blocks of text. After positioning the insertion point as instructed in step 1, use the scroll bars to scroll to the end of the text you want to select. Then Shift-click as instructed in step 2 to make the selection.

To select a single word

Double-click the word (**Figure 16**).

✔ Tip

■ In some applications, such as Microsoft Word, double-clicking a word also selects the space after the word.

To select all document contents

Choose Edit > Select All (**Figure 17**), or press (⌃ ⌘ A).

✔ Tip

■ There are other selection techniques in TextEdit and other applications. The techniques on this page work in every application.

You enter text into a TextEdit document
typing mistakes; you can fix them as you

Figure 13 Drag the I-beam pointer over the text that you want to select.

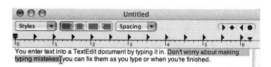
You enter text into a TextEdit document by typing it in. Don't worry about making typing mistakes; you can fix them as you type or when you're finished.

Figure 14 Position the insertion point at the beginning of the text you want to select.

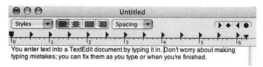
You enter text into a TextEdit document by typing it in. Don't worry about making typing mistakes; you can fix them as you type or when you're finished.

Figure 15 Hold down (Shift) and click at the end of the text you want to select.

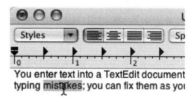
You enter text into a TextEdit document
typing mistakes; you can fix them as you

Figure 16 Double-click the word that you want to select.

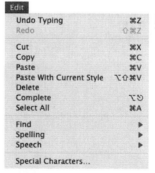

Figure 17
The Edit menu.

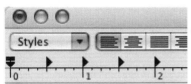

You enter text into a TextEdit doc
typing mistakes; you can fix them

Figure 18 Select the text that you want to delete.

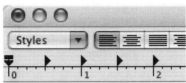

You enter text into a TextEdit doc
mistakes; you can fix them as you

Figure 19 When you press ⌈Delete⌉, the selected text disappears.

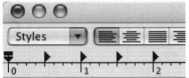

You enter text into a TextEdit doc
mistakes; you can fix them as you

Figure 20 Select the text that you want to replace.

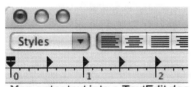

You enter text into a TextEdit doc
errors; you can fix them as you ty

Figure 21 The text you type replaces the selected text.

To delete text

1. Select the text that you want to delete (**Figure 18**).

2. Press ⌈Delete⌉ or ⌈Del⌉. The selected text disappears (**Figure 19**).

✔ Tip

■ You can delete a character to the left of the insertion point by pressing ⌈Delete⌉. You can delete a character to the right of the insertion point by pressing ⌈Del⌉.

To replace text

1. Select the text that you want to replace (**Figure 20**).

2. Type the new text. The selected text is replaced by what you type (**Figure 21**).

Basic Text Formatting

TextEdit also offers formatting features that you can use to change the appearance of text.

◆ **Font formatting** enables you to change the appearance of text characters. This includes the font typeface and family, character style, character size, and character color.

◆ **Text formatting** enables you to change the appearance of entire paragraphs of text. This includes the alignment, line spacing, and ruler settings such as tabs and indentation.

✔ Tips

■ This chapter introduces the most commonly used formatting options in TextEdit. You can further explore these and other options on your own.

■ Some text formatting options are on the ruler. If the ruler is not showing, you can display it by choosing Format > Text > Show Ruler or by pressing ⌘ R.

To apply font formatting

1. Select the text you want to apply font formatting to (**Figure 22**).

2. Use any combination of the following techniques to apply font formatting:

   ▲ Choose Format > Font > Show Fonts (**Figure 23**), or press ⌘ T to display the Font panel (**Figure 24**). Set options in the Font panel as desired. You can immediately see the results of your changes in the document window behind the Font panel (**Figure 25**); make changes if you don't like what you see. You can also select different text to format it without closing the Font panel window.

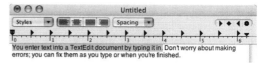

Figure 22 Select the text you want to format.

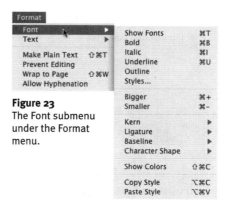

Figure 23 The Font submenu under the Format menu.

Figure 24 The Font panel.

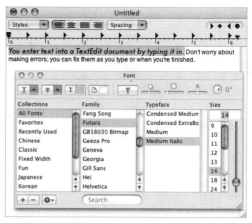

Figure 25 The changes you make in the Font panel are immediately applied to the selected text.

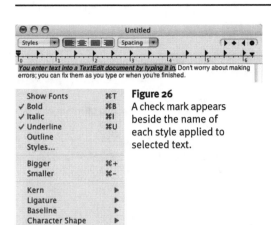

Figure 26
A check mark appears beside the name of each style applied to selected text.

Figure 27
You can use the Styles pop-up to apply certain font styles to selected text.

Table 1

Shortcut Keys for TextEdit Font Formatting	
Keystroke	**Formatting Applied**
⌃ ⌘ B	Bold
⌃ ⌘ I	Italic
⌃ ⌘ U	Underline
⌃ ⌘ +	Bigger
⌃ ⌘ −	Smaller

▲ Choose options from the Format menu's Font submenu (**Figure 23**) to apply formatting. You can choose any combination of options. A check mark appears beside the type of formatting applied to selected text (**Figure 26**).

▲ Choose an option from the Styles pop-up menu on the ruler (**Figure 27**). The Default option removes formatting applied with the Styles pop-up menu.

▲ Press the shortcut key for the type of formatting you want to apply. Consult **Table 1** for a list.

✔ Tips

■ Generally speaking, a *font* is a style of typeface.

■ You can apply more than one style to text (**Figure 26**).

■ A check mark appears on the Font submenu beside each style applied to a selection (**Figure 26**).

■ To remove an applied style, choose it from the Font submenu again.

■ Some styles are automatically applied when you select a specific typeface for a font family in the Font panel (**Figure 25**). Similarly, if you select a typeface in the Font panel, certain style options become unavailable for characters with that typeface applied. For example, if you apply Futura Medium Italic font, as shown in **Figure 25**, the Bold option on the Font submenu cannot be applied to that text.

■ I tell you more about fonts and explain how to use the Font panel in **Chapter 9**.

To apply text formatting

1. Select the paragraph(s) you want to format.

2. Use any combination of the following techniques to apply font formatting:

   ▲ Choose an option from the Format menu's Text submenu (**Figure 28**) to apply formatting.

   ▲ Click one of the alignment buttons on the ruler (**Figure 29**).

   ▲ Choose an option from the Spacing pop-up menu on the ruler (**Figure 30**).

   ▲ Press the shortcut key for the type of formatting you want to apply. Consult **Table 2** for a list.

✔ Tip

■ Alignment and spacing options affect all lines in a paragraph.

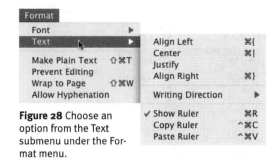

Figure 28 Choose an option from the Text submenu under the Format menu.

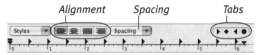

Figure 29 You can use buttons and a pop-up menu on the ruler to set alignment, line spacing, and tabs.

Figure 30 Use the Spacing pop-up menu to set line spacing for selected paragraphs.

Table 2

Shortcut Keys for TextEdit Text Formatting	
Keystroke	**Formatting Applied**
⌥ ⌘ {	Align Left
⌥ ⌘ I	Center
⌥ ⌘ }	Align Right

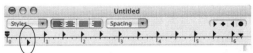

Figure 31 Drag the tab off the ruler. (The mouse pointer disappears as you do this, so it isn't easy to illustrate!)

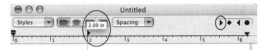

Figure 32 Drag one of the tab icons from the top half of the ruler into position on the ruler. Although the mouse pointer disappears as you drag, a tiny box with the tab location in it appears as you drag.

Figure 33 Start by setting tabs and positioning the insertion point at the beginning of the line.

First Name

Figure 34 If desired, enter text at the beginning of the line.

First Name   Last Name

Figure 35 Press Tab and enter text at the first tab stop.

First Name   Last Name   Title   Rate

Figure 36 The first line of a table created with tabs.

First Name	Last Name	Title	Rate
John	Aabbott	Webmaster	12.5
Maria	Langer	Pilot	15.25
Michael	Chilingerian	Manufacturer's Rep	18
Lucky Jack	The Dog	Wonder Dog	30.759
Alex	The Bird	Chatterbox	1.9

Figure 37 A completed table. Note how the text lines up with each type of tab stop.

To set tab stops

Add and remove tab stops from the bottom half of the ruler as follows:

◆ To remove a tab stop, drag it from the ruler into the document window (**Figure 31**). When you release the mouse button, the tab is removed.

◆ To add a tab stop, drag one of the tab icons on the ruler—left, center, right, or decimal—into position on the ruler (**Figure 32**). When you release the mouse button, the tab is placed.

✔ Tips

■ A tab stop is the position the insertion point moves to when you press Tab.

■ Tab settings affect entire paragraphs. When you press Return to begin a new paragraph, the tab stops you set for the current paragraph are carried forward.

To use tab stops

1. Add and remove tab stops as instructed above.

2. Position the insertion point at the beginning of the paragraph for which tab stops are set (**Figure 33**).

3. If desired, enter text at the beginning of the line (**Figure 34**).

4. Press Tab.

5. Enter text at the tab stop (**Figure 35**).

6. Repeat steps 4 and 5 until you have entered text as desired at all tab stops. **Figure 36** shows an example.

7. Press Return.

8. Repeat steps 2 through 7 for each paragraph you want to use the tab stops for. **Figure 37** shows a completed table using tab stops.

To set indentation

1. Select the paragraph(s) for which you want to set indentation (**Figure 38**).

2. Drag one of the icons on the end of the ruler (**Figure 39**) to the left or right:

   ▲ To set the first line indentation for a paragraph, drag the horizontal rectangle icon.

   ▲ To set the left indent, drag the downward-facing triangle on the left end of the ruler.

   ▲ To set the right indent, drag the downward-facing triangle on the right end of the ruler.

   As you drag, a yellow box with a measurement inside it indicates the exact position of the indent. When you release a marker, the text shifts accordingly (**Figure 40**).

✔ Tip

■ TextEdit Help refers to the left and right indents as *margins*. Technically speaking, this is incorrect terminology, since margins normally refer to the area between the printable area and edge of the paper.

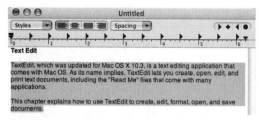

Figure 38 Select the paragraphs you want to format.

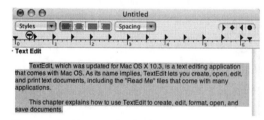

Figure 39 The indent markers on TextEdit's ruler.

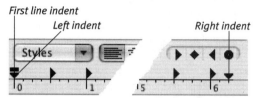

Figure 40 In this example, the first line indent marker was shifted to the right, thus indenting just the first line of each paragraph.

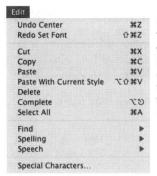

Figure 41
The Edit menu with Undo and Redo commands displayed. If one of these commands were not available, it would be gray.

Undoing & Redoing Actions

The Undo command enables you to reverse your last action, thus offering an easy way to fix errors immediately after you make them. The Redo command, which is available only when your last action was to use the Undo command, reverses the undo action.

✔ Tips

- The Undo and Redo commands are available in most applications and can be found at the top of the Edit menu.

- TextEdit supports multiple levels of undo (and redo). That means you can undo (or redo) several actions, in the reverse order that they were performed (or undone).

- The exact wording of the Undo (and Redo) command depends on what was last done (or undone). For example, if the last thing you did was center text in a paragraph, the Undo command will be Undo Center (**Figure 41**).

To undo the last action

Choose Edit > Undo (**Figure 41**), or press ⌃ ⌘ Z. The last thing you did is undone.

✔ Tip

- To undo multiple actions, choose Edit > Undo repeatedly.

To redo an action

After using the Undo command, choose Edit > Redo (**Figure 41**), or press Shift ⌃ ⌘ Z. The last thing you undid is redone.

✔ Tip

- To redo multiple actions, choose Edit > Redo repeatedly.

Copy, Cut, & Paste

The Copy, Cut, and Paste commands enable you to duplicate or move document contents. Text that is copied or cut is placed on the Clipboard, where it can be viewed if desired and pasted into a document.

✔ Tip

■ Almost all Mac OS-compatible applications include the Copy, Cut, and Paste commands on the Edit menu. These commands work very much the same in all applications.

To copy text

1. Select the text that you want to copy (**Figure 42**).

2. Choose Edit > Copy (**Figure 43**), or press ⌃⌘C.

   The text is copied to the Clipboard so it can be pasted elsewhere. The original remains in the document.

To cut text

1. Select the text that you want to cut (**Figure 42**).

2. Choose Edit > Cut (**Figure 43**), or press ⌃⌘X.

   The text is copied to the Clipboard so it can be pasted elsewhere. The original is removed from the document.

To paste Clipboard contents

1. Position the insertion point where you want the Clipboard contents to appear (**Figure 44**).

2. Choose Edit > Paste (**Figure 43**), or press ⌃⌘V.

   The Clipboard's contents are pasted into the document (**Figure 45**).

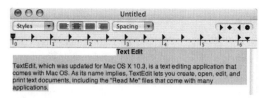

Figure 42 Select the text you want to copy or cut.

Figure 43 The Copy, Cut, and Paste commands are all on the Edit menu.

Figure 44 Position the insertion point where you want the contents of the Clipboard to appear.

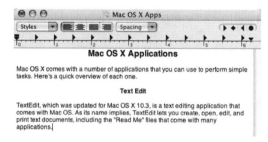

Figure 45 The contents of the Clipboard are pasted into the document.

✔ Tip

■ The Clipboard contains only the last item that was copied or cut. Using the Paste command, therefore, pastes in the most recently cut or copied selection.

COPYING, CUTTING, & PASTING TEXT

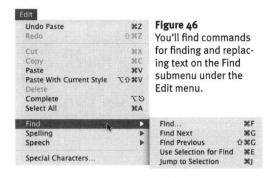

Figure 46
You'll find commands for finding and replacing text on the Find submenu under the Edit menu.

Figure 47 The Find panel.

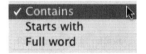

Figure 48 Use this pop-up menu to indicate how TextEdit should match the Find text.

Find & Replace

TextEdit's find and replace features enable you to quickly locate or replace occurrences of text strings in your document.

✔ Tip

■ Most word processing and page layout applications include find and replace features. Although these features are somewhat limited in TextEdit, full-featured applications such as Microsoft Word and Adobe InDesign enable you to search for text, formatting, and other document elements as well as plain text.

To find text

1. Choose Edit > Find > Find (**Figure 46**), or press ⌘F. The Find panel appears (**Figure 47**).

2. Enter the text that you want to find in the Find field.

3. To find text from the insertion point forward (rather than the entire document), turn off the Wrap Around check box.

4. To perform a case-sensitive search, turn off the Ignore Case check box.

5. To indicate how TextEdit should match the Find text, select the appropriate option from the pop-up menu (**Figure 48**).

6. Click Next, or press Return or Enter. If the text you entered in the Find field is found, it is highlighted in the document.

✔ Tip

■ To find subsequent or previous occurrences of the Find field entry, choose Edit > Find > Find Next or Edit > Find > Find Previous (**Figure 47**) or press ⌘G or Shift ⌘G.

To replace text

1. Choose Edit > Find > Find (**Figure 46**), or press ⌃⌘F. The Find panel appears (**Figure 47**).

2. Enter the text that you want to replace in the Find field.

3. Enter the replacement text in the Replace with field (**Figure 49**).

4. To replace text from the insertion point forward (rather than the entire document), turn off the Wrap Around check box.

5. To perform a case-sensitive search, turn off the Ignore Case check box.

6. To indicate how TextEdit should match the Find text, select the appropriate option from the pop-up menu (**Figure 48**).

7. Click the buttons at the bottom of the Find panel to find and replace text:

   ▲ **Replace All** replaces all occurrences of the Find word with the Replace word.

   ▲ **Replace** replaces the currently selected occurrence of the Find word with the Replace word.

   ▲ **Replace & Find** replaces the currently selected occurrence of the Find word with the Replace word and then selects the next occurrence of the Find word.

   ▲ **Previous** selects the previous occurrence of the Find word.

   ▲ **Next** selects the next occurrence of the Find word.

8. When you're finished replacing text, click the Find panel's close button to dismiss it.

✖ Warning!

■ Use the Replace All button with care! It will not give you an opportunity to preview and approve any of the replacements it makes.

Figure 49 You can set up the Find panel to find and replace text.

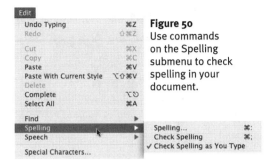

Figure 50
Use commands on the Spelling submenu to check spelling in your document.

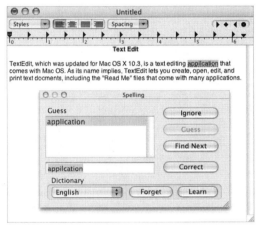

Figure 51 Use the Spelling panel to resolve possible misspelled words.

Checking Spelling

TextEdit includes a spelling checker that you can use to manually or automatically check spelling in your document.

To manually check spelling

1. Choose Edit > Spelling > Spelling (**Figure 50**) or press Shift ⌘ ; to display the Spelling panel and start the spelling check.

    TextEdit selects and underlines the first possible misspelled word it finds. The word appears in a field in the Spelling panel and any suggested corrections appear in the Guess list (**Figure 51**).

2. You have several options:
    ▲ To replace the word with a guess, select the replacement word and click Correct.
    ▲ To enter a new spelling for the word, enter it in the box where the incorrect spelling appears and click Correct.
    ▲ To ignore the word, click Ignore.
    ▲ To skip the word and continue checking, click Find Next.
    ▲ To add the word to TextEdit's dictionary, click Learn. TextEdit will never stop at that word again in any document.

3. Repeat step 2 for each word that TextEdit identifies as a possible misspelling.

4. When you're finished checking spelling, click the Spelling panel's close button to dismiss it.

✔ Tip

■ You can use the Forget button in the Spelling dialog (**Figure 51**) to remove a word that you previously added to the dictionary. Select the Word in the Guess list, then click the Forget button. The word is removed.

To check spelling as you type

1. Choose Edit > Spelling > Check Spelling As You Type (**Figure 50**).

   As you enter text into the document, TextEdit checks the spelling of each word. It places a dashed red underline under each word that isn't in its dictionary. (**Figure 52**).

2. Manually correct a misspelled word using standard text editing techniques covered near the beginning of this chapter.

   or

   Hold down (Control) and click on a misspelled word. Then choose a correct spelling from the contextual menu that appears (**Figure 53**). The misspelled word is replaced with the word you chose.

✔ Tips

- The Check Spelling As You Type option in TextEdit may automatically be enabled. To disable it, choose Edit > Spelling > Check Spelling As You Type.

- If you display a contextual menu as instructed in step 2 (**Figure 53**), you can also use the Ignore Spelling or Learn Spelling commands to ignore the underlined word or add it to the dictionary.

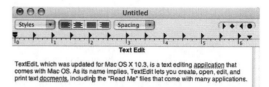

Figure 52 With automatic spelling check enabled, Text-Edit underlines possible misspelled words as you type.

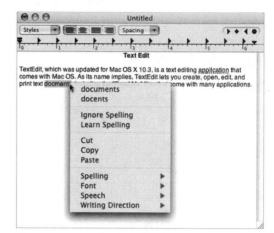

Figure 53 You can display a contextual menu that lists corrections and other options for an unknown word.

Figure 54
The File menu includes commands for working with files.

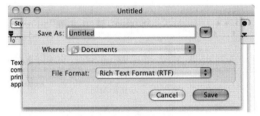

Figure 55 Use the Save As dialog to enter a name and select a location for saving a file.

Figure 56 The name of a saved document appears in its title bar.

Saving & Opening Files

When you're finished working with a Text-Edit document, you may want to save it. You can then open it another time to review, edit, or print it.

To save a document for the first time

1. Choose File > Save (**Figure 54**), or press ⌃ ⌘ S.

   or

   Choose File > Save As (**Figure 54**), or press Shift ⌃ ⌘ S.

   The Save As dialog sheet appears (**Figure 55**).

2. Enter a name and select a location for the file.

3. Choose an option from the File Format pop-up menu:

   ▲ **Rich Text Format (RTF)** is a standard format that can be read by most word processing and page layout applications.

   ▲ **Word Format** is Microsoft Word format, which can be opened and read by Microsoft Word and any other application capable of reading Word files.

4. Click Save, or press Return or Enter.

   The document is saved with the name you entered in the location you specified. The name of the document appears on the document's title bar (**Figure 56**).

Continued on next page...

SAVING DOCUMENTS

Continued from previous page.

✔ Tips

■ I explain how to use the Save As dialog in **Chapter 5**.

■ There's only one difference between the File menu's Save and Save As commands (**Figure 54**):

   ▲ The Save command opens the Save As dialog only if the document has never been saved.

   ▲ The Save As command *always* opens the Save As dialog.

■ By default, TextEdit creates Rich Text Format (RTF) files and appends the *.rtf* extension to the files it saves. This extension does not appear unless the Show all file extensions option is enabled in Finder Preferences. I discuss Finder preferences in **Chapter 4**.

■ To save a TextEdit document as a plain text document (with a *.txt* extension), choose Format > Make Plain Text (**Figure 57**) and click OK in the confirmation dialog that may appear. Then follow the steps on the previous page to save the document. As shown in **Figure 58**, the pop-up menu in the Save As dialog offers a variety of Plain Text Encoding options rather than Rich Text Format and Word Format. Keep in mind that if you save a document as a plain text document, any formatting applied to document text will be lost.

■ Generally speaking, plain text documents are more compatible than RTF or Word documents and RTF documents are more compatible than Word documents.

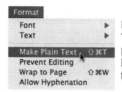

Figure 57
To save a document as a plain text document, begin by choosing Make Plain Text from the Format menu.

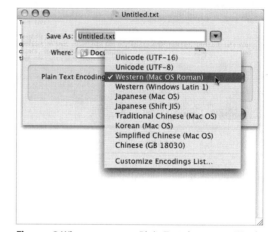

Figure 58 When you save a Plain Text document, Word offers other formatting options. If you're not sure what to pick here, leave it set to the default setting.

Figure 59 A bullet in the document window's close button...

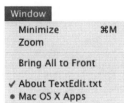

Figure 60
...or beside its name in the Window menu indicates that the document has unsaved changes.

To save changes to an existing document

Choose File > Save (**Figure 54**), or press ⌘ S.

The document is saved. No dialog appears.

✔ Tips

- TextEdit identifies a document with changes that have not been saved by displaying a bullet in the document window's close button (**Figure 59**) and to the left of the document's name in the Window menu (**Figure 60**).

- It's a good idea to save changes to a document frequently as you work with it. This helps prevent loss of data in the event of a system crash or power outage.

To save an existing document with a new name or in a new location

1. Choose File > Save As (**Figure 54**).

2. Use the Save As dialog that appears (**Figure 55**) to enter a different name or select a different location (or both) for the file.

3. Click Save, or press Return or Enter.

   A copy of the document is saved with the name you entered in the location you specified. The new document name appears in the document's title bar. The original document remains untouched.

✔ Tip

- You can use the Save As command to create a new document based on an existing document—without overwriting the original document with your changes.

SAVING DOCUMENTS

To open a document

1. Choose File > Open (**Figure 54**), or press
   ⌃ ⌘ O.

2. Use the Open dialog that appears (**Figure 61**) to locate and select the document that you want to open.

3. Click Open, or press Return or Enter.

✔ Tip

■ I explain how to use the Open dialog in **Chapter 5**.

To close a document

1. Choose File > Close (**Figure 54**), or press
   ⌃ ⌘ W.

2. If the document contains unsaved changes, a Close dialog like the one in **Figure 6** appears.

   ▲ Click Don't Save to close the document without saving it.

   ▲ Click Cancel or press Esc to return to the document without closing it.

   ▲ Click Save or press Return or Enter to save the document.

   The document closes.

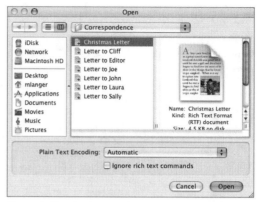

Figure 61 Use the Open dialog to locate and open a file.

Using Mac OS i-Applications

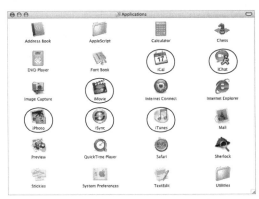

Figure 1 You can find all of Apple's i-Apps in the Applications folder.

✔ Tips

- iChat, another one of Mac OS X's i-Apps, is covered in **Chapter 11** as part of my discussion of the Internet.

- iDVD, which works on computers with a SuperDrive, enables you to create your own DVDs with content from iPhoto, iMovie, and other applications. iDVD is not covered in this book.

- Peachpit Press offers a number of titles in its *Visual QuickStart Guide* series that cover each of these programs. To get the most out of a specific application, I highly recommend that you obtain one of these books. You can learn more on the Peachpit Press Web site, www.peachpit.com.

Using Mac OS X i-Applications

Mac OS X comes with a number of useful applications that help you get the most out of your computer. Commonly known as *i-Applications* (or just *i-Apps*), these applications, which can be found in the Applications folder (**Figure 1**), include:

- ◆ **iCal** lets you keep track of appointments, events, and to-do lists. You can publish your calendars on the Web or share them with other iCal users.

- ◆ **iMovie** enables you to create your own movies, complete with transitional effects, subtitles, and voiceovers, from digital video clips.

- ◆ **iPhoto** lets you store, organize, and share digital photos.

- ◆ **iSync** enables you to synchronize your iCal calendar, Address Book data, and Safari bookmarks with another computer or computing device.

- ◆ **iTunes** lets you play CDs, record music from a CD to your hard disk, burn music CDs, or download music to an iPod or other MP3 player.

This chapter covers the basics of each of these applications—just enough information to help you explore them on your own.

iCal

iCal is a personal calendar application that enables you to keep track of appointments and other events. With iCal, you can:

◆ Create multiple color-coded calendars for different categories of events—for example, home, business, or school. You can view your calendars individually or together.

◆ View calendars by day, week, or month.

◆ Share calendars on the Web with family, friends, and business associates.

◆ Send e-mail invitations for events to people in your Mac OS X Address Book.

◆ Get notification of upcoming events on screen or by e-mail.

◆ Create and manage a priorities-based to-do list.

This part of the chapter provides basic instructions for setting up and using iCal.

✔ Tip

■ You can learn more about iCal's features and public calendars you can subscribe to at Apple's iCal Web site, www.apple.com/ical/.

To launch iCal

Double-click the iCal icon in your Applications folder (**Figure 1**). Its main window appears (**Figure 2**).

Calendar list
Mini-month calendar

Figure 2 iCal's main window, showing a week at a glance view.

iCAL

Figure 3 Use these buttons to switch between Day, Week, and Month view or to go back or forward in the calendar.

Figure 4 Day view shows one day at a time.

Figure 5 Month view shows a month at a time.

Figure 6 The navigation buttons above the mini-month calendar.

To change the calendar view

Click one of the view buttons at the bottom of the calendar window (**Figure 3**).

◆ **Day** shows a day at a glance (**Figure 4**).

◆ **Week** shows a week at a glance (**Figure 2**).

◆ **Month** shows a month at a glance (**Figure 5**).

To view a specific day, week, or month

1. Follow the instructions in the previous section to change the view.

2. Click the Next or Previous button (**Figure 6**) above the mini-month calendar until the date's month appears as one of the mini-month calendars. For example, to view June 30, 2004, you'd click the Next or Previous button until June 2004 appeared.

3. In the mini-month calendar, click the day, week, or month you want to view. It appears in the main calendar window.

✔ Tips

■ This is just one way to view a day, week, or month. As you work with iCal, you'll find other ways.

■ To view today's date, click the Today button above the mini-month calendar or press ⌃ ⌘ T.

VIEWING SPECIFIC DAYS, WEEKS, OR MONTHS

To create an event by dragging

1. In the Calendar list on the upper-left corner of the calendar window, click the name of the calendar you want to add the event to.

2. In Day or Week view, drag from the event's start time to end time (**Figure 7**). When you release the mouse button, a box for the event appears in the calendar window with its default name (New Event) selected (**Figure 8**).

3. Enter a new name for the event, and press Return.

✔ Tip

■ Another way to create an event is to double-click anywhere in the date box. This is almost the same as using the New Event command discussed next; it creates a new event with default settings and displays the Event Info window (**Figure 10**).

To create an event with the New Event command

1. In any calendar view window, select the day you want to add the event to.

2. Choose File > New Event (**Figure 9**), or press ⌘N. A box for the event appears in the calendar window with its default name (New Event) selected (**Figure 10**).

3. Enter a new name for the event and press Return.

✔ Tip

■ The Info drawer automatically appears when you insert an event with the New Event command (**Figure 10**). I explain how to use the Info drawer to enter event details next.

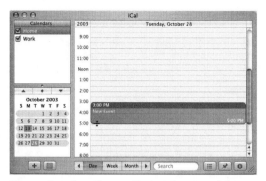

Figure 7 Drag from the event's start time to end time.

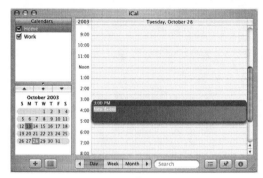

Figure 8 When you release the mouse button, the event box appears with its default name selected.

Figure 9 iCal's File menu.

Info drawer

Figure 10 A new event inserted in month view, using the New Event command.

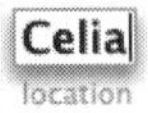

location

Figure 11 To enter an event name or location, click the field and enter the information you want to appear.

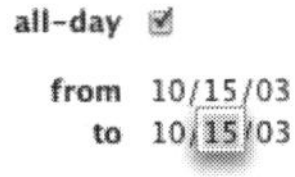

Figure 12 When you turn on the all-day check box, you can enter starting and ending dates.

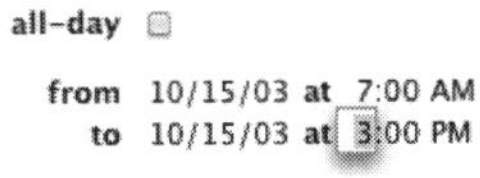

Figure 13 With the all-day check box turned off, you can enter starting and ending times.

Figure 14 As you enter a name in the attendees field, iCal attempts to match it to an Address Book entry.

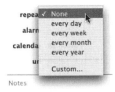

Figure 15 You can assign a status to an event.

Figure 16 Use the repeat pop-up menu to set an event to repeat regularly.

Figure 17 Choosing Custom from the repeat pop-up menu displays this dialog.

repeat Custom... ⇕
         every 2 weeks
end   on date ⇕   12/31/04

Figure 18 An example of a custom repeating option with an end date.

To set event details

1. In the calendar window, select the event you want to modify.

2. If necessary, click the Show Info button in the lower-right corner of the window or press ⌃⌘I to display the Info drawer.

3. To enter an event name and location, click in the appropriate field at the top of the Info drawer and type what you want to appear (**Figure 11**).

4. To indicate that the event last all day (or more than one day), turn on the all-day check box. You can then enter an ending date in the to date box (**Figure 12**).

   or

   To specify starting and ending times for the event, make sure the all-day check box is turned off and then enter the starting and ending times in the two time boxes (**Figure 13**).

5. To identify one or more people involved with the event, enter each person's name in the Attendees field. As you type, iCal attempts to match names to those in your Address Book database (**Figure 14**), but you can enter any name.

6. To assign a status to the event, choose an option from the status pop-up menu (**Figure 15**).

7. To set the event to repeat on a regular basis, choose an option from the repeat pop-up menu (**Figure 16**). If none of the standard options apply, you can choose Custom and use the dialog that appears (**Figure 17**) to set a custom repeating schedule. Then, if necessary, set an ending option in the end field that appears (**Figure 18**).

Continued on next page...

Continued from previous page.

8. To be reminded about the event, choose an option from the Alarm pop-up menu (**Figure 19**). Then set other alarm options as necessary (**Figure 20**).

9. To specify a calendar to add the event to, choose a calendar from the calendar pop-up menu (**Figure 21**). The menu lists all calendars you have created.

10. To associate a Web page with the event, enter a URL in the url field (**Figure 22**).

11. To add notes about the event, click the Notes field and type what you want to appear (**Figure 23**).

Figure 24 shows an example of an event with detailed information in the Info drawer.

✔ Tips

- You can use these steps to add settings for a new event or make changes to an existing event.

- The All-day event check box is handy for entering information about vacations and other events that span multiple days.

- In step 4, the ending date must be after the starting date. It may be necessary to change AM to PM *before* entering the second time.

- A quick way to change an event's date is to drag its event box from one date to another in the main calendar window. This automatically changes the date info in the Info drawer for the event.

- A quick way to change an event's time is to drag its top or bottom border in Day or Week view of the main calendar window. This automatically changes the time info in the Info drawer for the event.

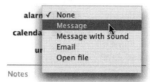

Figure 19 Choosing an option from the alarm pop-up menu sets a reminder for the event.

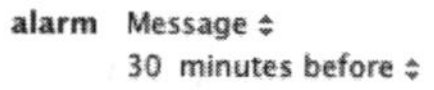

Figure 20 If you choose an alarm, you must set how far in advance it should activate.

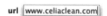

Figure 21 You can add an event to any calendar.

url [www.celiaclean.com]

Figure 22 You can associate a Web page's URL with an event.

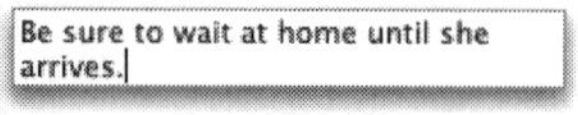

Be sure to wait at home until she arrives.

Figure 23 Enter notes about the event in the notes field.

Figure 24 Here's an example of a completed event with its details in Week view.

Figure 25 When you click an attendee's name, iCal displays a menu of options for working with that attendee.

Figure 26 Clicking the attendees label displays a menu of options for all event attendees.

Changing a recurring event

You're changing the end date of a recurring event. Do you want to change only the end date of this occurrence or change this and all future events?

Cancel   All Future Events   Only This Event

Figure 27 A dialog like this appears when you make a change to a repeating event.

- If an event has attendees, you can click an attendee's name to access a menu of options for that attendee. **Figure 25** shows an example for an attendee from my Address Book database; note that iCal has automatically looked up the person's e-mail address.

- Clicking attendees displays a menu of options for inviting attendees to an event or opening Address Book (**Figure 26**).

- If you set an event to repeat, any time you change that event's details, a dialog like the one in **Figure 27** appears. Click the appropriate button for the change.

- Icons for some settings appear in the upper-right corner of the event box when viewed in Day or Week view (**Figure 24**).

- I tell you more about individual calendars later in this section.

To delete an event

1. In the calendar window, select the event you want to delete.

2. Press ⌈Delete⌋. The event disappears.

To create a to do item

1. Choose File > New To Do (**Figure 9**), or press ⌃⌘K. If the To Do items list was not already showing, it appears. An untitled To Do item appears in the list with its default name (New To Do) selected (**Figure 28**).

2. Enter a name for the To Do item and press Return.

To set To Do item details

1. If necessary, click the Show To Do list button in the lower-right corner of the window or press Option⌃⌘T to display the To Do items list.

2. In the To Do items list, select the item you want to modify.

3. If necessary, click the Show Info button in the lower-right corner of the window or press ⌃⌘I to display the Info drawer (**Figure 29**).

4. To enter an item name, click in the field at the top of the Info drawer and type what you want to appear.

5. To mark the item as completed, turn on the completed check box.

6. To set a priority for the item, choose an option from the priority pop-up menu (**Figure 30**).

7. To set a due date for the item, turn on the due date check box and enter a date in the field beside it (**Figure 31**). You can then use the Alarm pop-up menu (**Figure 19**) and associated options (**Figure 20**) to set a reminder for the item.

8. To specify a calendar to add the event to, choose a calendar from the calendar pop-up menu (**Figure 21**). The menu lists all calendars you have created.

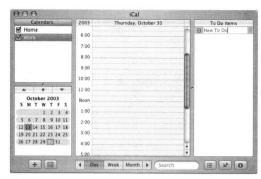

Figure 28 The To Do items list with a new To Do item added.

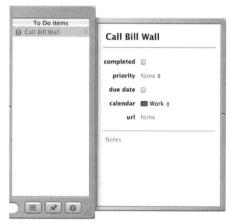

Figure 29 You can use the Info drawer to set options for a To Do item.

Figure 30 Use the priority pop-up menu to prioritize To Do items.

Figure 31 When you turn on the due date check box, you can enter a deadline for the item.

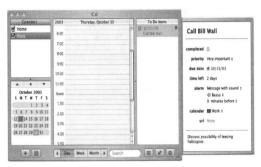

Figure 32 A completed To Do item.

9. To associate a Web page with the event, enter a URL in the url field (**Figure 22**).

10. To add notes about the event, click the Notes field and type what you want to appear (**Figure 23**).

Figure 32 shows an example of a To Do item with several options set.

✔ Tips

■ You can mark a To Do item as complete by clicking its check box in the To Do items list (**Figure 32**).

■ The stack of lines to the left of a To Do item's name in the To Do items list (**Figure 32**) indicates its priority: the more lines, the more important the item is. If you have good eyes and a steady hand, you can click this stack of icons to change the priority.

To delete a To Do item

1. If necessary, click the Show To Do list button in the lower-right corner of the window or press Option ⌃ ⌘ T to display the To Do items list.

2. In the To Do items list, select the item you want to delete.

3. Press Delete. The item disappears.

To create a calendar

1. Choose File > New Calendar (**Figure 9**) or press (Option)(⌃)(⌘)(N). An untitled calendar appears in the Calendars list with its default name selected (**Figure 33**).

2. Enter a name for the Calendar and press (Return).

To set calendar options

1. In the Calendars list, select the calendar you want to set options for.

2. If necessary, click the Show Info button in the lower-right corner of the window or press (⌃)(⌘)(I) to display the Info drawer (**Figure 34**).

3. Click the Name or Description field or use the color pop-up menu (**Figure 35**) to modify calendar settings.

✔ Tips

- Choosing Custom from the colors pop-up menu (**Figure 35**) displays the Colors palette, which you can use to select a custom color. I tell you how to use the Colors palette in **Chapter 9**.

- To display events from only certain calendars, in the Calendars list, turn off the check boxes for the calendars you don't want to view.

To delete a calendar

1. In the Calendars list, select the calendar you want to delete.

2. Press (Delete).

3. In the confirmation dialog that appears (**Figure 36**), click Delete. The calendar and all of its events are removed.

Figure 33
A new calendar in the Calendars list.

Figure 34 Use the Info drawer for a calendar to change its name, add a description, or set its color.

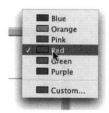

Figure 35
You can change the color assigned to a calendar.

Figure 36 A dialog like this confirms that you really do want to delete a calendar and all of its events.

Figure 37
The Calendar menu before a selected calendar has been published.

Figure 38
Use this dialog to set options for publishing a calendar.

Figure 39
The dialog expands to offer additional options when you indicate that you want to publish on a WebDAV server.

Figure 40 A dialog like this confirms that the calendar has been published and provides information about accessing it.

To publish a calendar

1. In the Calendars list, select the calendar you want to publish.

2. Choose Calendar > Publish (**Figure 37**).

3. A dialog sheet like the one in **Figure 38** appears. Set options as desired:
   - ▲ **Publish name** is the name of the calendar as it will be published.
   - ▲ **Publish changes automatically** updates the calendar online whenever you make changes to it in iCal.
   - ▲ **Publish subjects and notes** includes event or item names and notes in the published calendar.
   - ▲ **Publish alarms** includes event or item alarms in the published calendar.
   - ▲ **Publish To Do items** includes To Do items in the published calendar.
   - ▲ **Publish calendar** enables you to select a location for the calendar to be published: on .Mac or on a WebDAV server. If you choose WebDAV server, the dialog expands so you can enter details about the server (**Figure 39**).

4. Click Publish.

5. Wait while your computer connects to the Internet and uploads the calendar.

6. When the upload is complete, a dialog like the one in **Figure 40** appears. You have three options:
   - ▲ **Visit page** launches your Web browser, connects to the Internet, and displays the calendar page (**Figure 41**).
   - ▲ **Send Mail** launches your e-mail application and creates a message with the calendar's access information (**Figure 42**). You can address the

Continued on next page...

PUBLISHING A CALENDAR

Continued from previous page.

message and send it to people you want to inform about the calendar.

▲ **OK** simply dismisses the dialog.

✔ Tips

■ You must have a connection to the Internet to publish a calendar.

■ You must have a .Mac account to publish a calendar on .Mac. I tell you more about .Mac in **Chapter 12**.

■ In step 3, if you choose not to automatically update the calendar, you can do so manually. Select the calendar in the Calendars list and choose Calendar > Refresh (**Figure 43**) or press ⌃⌘R.

■ To create a new e-mail message with information about accessing a calendar (**Figure 42**), select the calendar in the Calendars list and choose Calendar > Send publish email (**Figure 43**).

■ In the Calendars list, a curves icon appears beside the name of a calendar that has been published (**Figure 45**).

To unpublish a calendar

1. In the Calendars list, select the calendar you want to remove from the Web.

2. Choose Calendar > Unpublish (**Figure 43**).

3. In the confirmation dialog that appears, click Unpublish.

Figure 41 Here's a calendar published on .Mac. (I wish I had that many tours scheduled this week!)

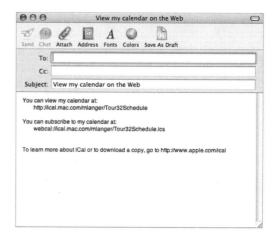

Figure 42 If you click the Send Mail button, an e-mail message with access information is prepared automatically.

Figure 43 When you select a calendar that has been published, the Calendar menu changes to offer additional options.

PUBLISHING & UNPUBLISHING CALENDARS

Figure 44
Use this dialog to subscribe to a calendar.

Figure 45 This example shows four calendars, including one that is published (Tour Schedule) and one that is subscribed to (Airport Events). (Yes, we do have coffee and donuts at Wickenburg Airport every Sunday morning. Why not stop by and say hello?)

To subscribe to a calendar

1. Choose Calendar > Subscribe (**Figure 37** or **43**).

2. A dialog sheet like the one in **Figure 44** appears. Set options as desired:

   ▲ **Calendar URL** is the URL for subscribing to the calendar. This normally begins with webcal://.

   ▲ **Refresh** instructs iCal to refresh the calendar periodically. You might want to use this option if you expect the calendar to changed often.

   ▲ **Remove alarms** disables any alarms that have been set for and published with the calendar.

   ▲ **Remove To Do items** removes any To Do items that may have been published with the calendar.

3. Click Subscribe.

4. Wait while iCal downloads the calendar. When it is finished, the calendar's events appear in the calendar window (**Figure 45**).

✔ Tips

■ In the Calendars list, an arrow icon appears beside the name of a calendar that has been subscribed to (**Figure 45**).

■ You cannot add, modify, or delete events on a calendar that you subscribe to.

■ To update the contents of a calendar you have subscribed to, choose Calendar > Refresh (**Figure 43**) or press ⌃ ⌘ R.

■ To unsubscribe from a calendar, delete it from the Calendars list. I explain how to delete calendars earlier in this chapter.

■ To find more calendars you can subscribe to, check out www.apple.com/ical/library. You can find everything from Apple Store events to Blue Angels appearances.

SUBSCRIBING TO CALENDARS

iMovie

iMovie is like a director's editing studio right inside your Mac. You can use it to do several things:

◆ Import movie clips from a digital video camera into your computer.

◆ Edit clips for length and content.

◆ Add titles, special transitional effects, music, and voiceovers.

◆ Combine the clips to make a movie.

◆ Export the completed movie to a file on disk or to a video camera.

The next few pages provide some basic information about using iMovie to import, edit, and combine movie clips, as well as how to save a finished movie as a QuickTime movie.

✔ Tip

■ To import movie clips from a digital video camera, you must have a video camera that can be connected to your computer via FireWire cable and is compatible with iMovie. You can learn more about camera compatibility at Apple's iMovie Web site, www.apple.com/imovie/.

Figure 46 This iMovie welcome screen appears when you first launch iMovie.

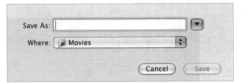

Figure 47 Use this dialog to enter a name and select a disk location for your movie project.

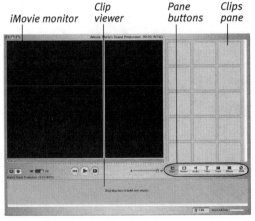

Figure 48 iMovie's interface includes three main areas.

To launch iMovie

1. Double-click the iMovie icon in your Applications folder (**Figure 1**).

   If you have already used iMovie to work with movie clips, it opens and displays its windows for the last movie you worked on. Skip the remaining steps.

2. If this is the first time you're running iMovie, a welcome dialog like the one in **Figure 46** appears. Click Create Project.

3. Use the dialog sheet that appears (**Figure 47**) to enter a name and select a location for your movie files. Then click Save.

   An empty iMovie project window appears (**Figure 48**).

✔ Tips

- iMovie documents are called *movie projects*. A movie project contains all of the information necessary to create your movie.

- When you create a movie project, iMovie creates a folder that contains all of the movie clips and other files for that project.

- If you have already created a movie project and want to start a new one, choose File > New Project or press ⌘⌥N. Then follow step 3 above to name and save your new project.

- To work with an existing movie project, either click Open Existing Project in the intro window (**Figure 46**) or choose File > Open Project. Then use the dialog that appears to locate and open your movie project file.

To import movie clips

1. Using a FireWire cable, connect your digital video camera to your Macintosh and turn the camera on. If necessary, set the camera to its VCR or Play mode and rewind to the beginning of the first clip you want to import.

2. If you haven't already done so, launch iMovie.

3. Set the mode switch at the bottom of the iMovie monitor to Camera mode. The iMovie monitor turns blue and the words *Camera Connected* appear (**Figure 49**).

4. Click the Import button. iMovie starts the camera and begins importing movie clips. The video for each clip appears in the iMovie monitor while each clip appears in the Clips pane (**Figures 50** and **51**).

5. When you're finished importing clips, click the Stop button at the bottom of the iMovie monitor. The camera stops.

✔ Tips

- If iMovie does not "see" your camera (**Figure 49**), it may not be compatible. You can learn more at www.apple.com/imovie/.

- iMovie can separate clips based on when the camera was stopped or paused during recording. It calculates the total time for each clip and displays it with the clip in the Clip pane (**Figures 50** and **51**).

- The free space indicator beneath the Clips pane shows how the video import consumes your hard disk space (**Figure 50**).

- When you're finished importing clips, you can disconnect and turn off your camera.

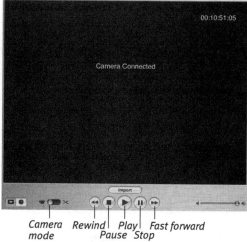

Figure 49 When iMovie "sees" your digital video camera, it tells you.

Figure 50 iMovie begins importing clips.

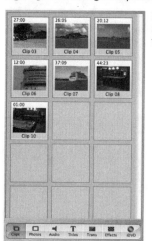

Figure 51
Each clip appears in the Clips pane.

IMPORTING MOVIE CLIPS

Figure 52 Select the clip you want to edit. (This is Mike.)

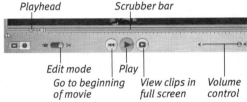

Figure 53 The controls at the bottom of the iMovie monitor when a clip is playing.

Figure 54 The scrubber bar turns yellow to indicate the portion of the clip that is selected.

Figure 55
iMovie's Edit menu when a portion of a clip is selected.

To review & edit movie clips

1. In the Clips pane, select the clip you want to review and edit. The first frame of the clip appears in the iMovie monitor and the Mode switch toggles to Edit mode (**Figure 52**).

2. To play the clip, click the Play button at the bottom of the iMovie monitor (**Figure 53**). As the movie plays, the playhead triangle moves along the blue scrubber bar to track the play progress. You can also manually drag the playhead to view a specific frame.

3. To select a portion of the movie, drag the playhead to the beginning of the portion you want to select, hold down ⟨Shift⟩, and drag the playhead to the end of the portion you want to select. The scrubber bar turns yellow between beginning and ending points (**Figure 54**).

4. Edit the clip using commands on the Edit menu (**Figure 55**):

   ▲ To cut or copy a clip selection, choose Edit > Cut (⌘X) or Edit > Copy (⌘C).

   ▲ To paste a clip selection from the clipboard into the clip at the playhead point, choose Edit > Paste (⌘V).

   ▲ To remove all of the clip except the selection, choose Edit > Crop (⌘K).

   ▲ To cut the clip into two separate clips split at the playhead, choose Edit > Split Video Clip at Playhead (⌘T).

   ▲ To create a still video frame of the image in the iMovie monitor, choose Edit > Create Still Frame (⟨Shift⟩⌘S).

To delete a clip

1. In the Clips pane, click to select the clip you want to delete.

2. Press ⌜Delete⌟. The clip is removed from the movie project.

✔ Tip

- When you delete a clip, it is moved into iMovie's trash and is no longer available for use in the movie project.

To add clips to a movie

1. Drag the clip you want to add from the Clips pane to the clip viewer (**Figure 56**). When you release the mouse button, the clip appears in the clip viewer (**Figure 57**).

2. Repeat step 1 until all clips you want to include in the movie have been added to the clip viewer (**Figure 58**).

✔ Tip

- To remove a clip from the clip viewer without deleting it from the movie project, drag it back to the Clips pane.

To remove a clip from a movie

Drag the clip from the clip viewer to an empty spot in the Clips pane.

The clip is removed from the movie but remains in the project so it can be used again.

✔ Tip

- If you select a clip in the clip viewer and press ⌜Delete⌟, the clip is removed from the movie project as well as the movie.

Figure 56 Drag a clip from the Clips pane to the clip viewer.

Figure 57 The clip you moved from the Clips pane appears in the clip viewer.

Figure 58 Multiple clips in the clip viewer.

Figure 59
The Transitions pane.

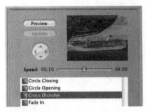

Figure 60
When you select a transition, you can watch a preview in the top of the Transitions pane.

Figure 61 Drag the transition into position in the clip viewer.

Figure 62 The transition appears as a tiny icon in the clip viewer.

Figure 63 Here's an example with several transitions added to the clip viewer. Note the progress bar for the last transition; this indicates iMovie's rendering progress.

To add transitions between clips

1. Click the Transitions button at the bottom of the Clips pane to display the Transitions pane (**Figure 59**).

2. Click to select the transition you want to use. A preview of the transition based on the currently selected clip in the clip viewer appears in the Preview area at the top of the Transitions pane (**Figure 60**).

3. Use the slider to set the speed of the transition. The Preview area shows the results of your change.

4. Drag the transition into position in the clip viewer (**Figure 61**). When you release the mouse button, it appears in the clip viewer (**Figure 62**) and iMovie *renders* it.

5. Repeat steps 2 through 4 for each transition you want to add. **Figure 63** shows what the clip viewer window might look like with several transitions added.

✔ Tips

■ Transition effects enable you to make smoother changes from one movie scene to another.

■ Some transitions will shorten your movie. For example, the Cross Dissolve transition overlaps two seconds from each clip, thus shortening the movie by about two seconds.

■ You cannot remove a clip with a transition attached to it. To move a clip with a transition, first delete the transition.

To delete a transition

1. In the clip viewer, click to select the transition you want to delete.

2. Press (Delete). The transition is removed from the movie.

To add photos

1. Click the Photos button at the bottom of the Clips pane to display the Photos pane (**Figure 64**).

2. Choose an iPhoto album from the pop-up menu. Thumbnail images for photos in that album appear beneath the pop-up menu.

3. Select the thumbnail for the photo you want to add.

4. To add a photo as a still image, turn off the Ken Burns Effect check box. Drag the Zoom slider until the preview area at the top of the pane shows the desired magnification for the image. Skip ahead to step 9.

   or

   To add a photo with zoom motion, turn on the Ken Burns Effect check box.

5. Click Start.

6. Move the Zoom slider until you see the starting point for the zoom motion in the preview area at the top of the pane (**Figure 65**).

7. Click Finish.

8. Move the Zoom slider until you see the ending point for the zoom motion in the preview area at the top of the pane (**Figure 66**).

9. Drag the duration slider to indicate the amount of time the image should appear.

10. Drag the image thumbnail from the Photos pane to the clip viewer (**Figure 67**).

    The photo is inserted in the movie. If the photo includes zoom motion, iMovie renders it.

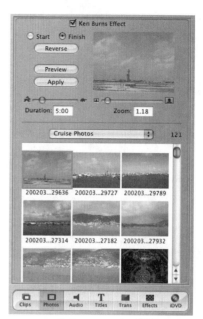

Figure 64 The Photos pane with an iPhoto album selected.

Figure 65 To add zoom motion, begin by setting the zoom magnification for the starting point. (I'm looking a bit porky here, aren't I? A cruise is a great way to gain weight fast!)

Figure 66 Set the ending point for the zoom motion. In this example, the motion will zoom out to here.

Figure 67 Drag the thumbnail to the clip viewer.

ADDING PHOTOS

✔ Tips

■ Once a photo has been added to the clip viewer, you can add transitions to it as discussed earlier in this section.

■ iMovie is a good tool for turning an iPhoto photo album into a custom slide show with zoom motion, transitions, and other features. You can export your finished show to video tape, QuickTime, or iDVD (if your computer is compatible) to create a finished product to share with others.

To remove a photo from a movie

1. In the clip viewer, click to select the photo you want to remove.

2. Press Delete. The photo is removed from the movie.

To preview a movie

1. Choose Edit > Select None (**Figure 55**), or press Shift ⌥ ⌘ A.

2. Click the Go to beginning of movie button at the bottom of the iMovie monitor (**Figure 53**).

3. Click the Play button at the bottom of the the iMovie monitor (**Figure 53**).

   The movie plays in the iMovie monitor window, from the beginning to the end, complete with transitions and other features.

✔ Tip

■ To play only part of a movie, in the clip viewer, select the clips and transitions you want to play. You can hold down ⌥ ⌘ while clicking each item to select more than one. Then click the Play button.

REMOVING PHOTOS, PREVIEWING MOVIES

To export a movie project to a camera

1. Choose File > Export, or press (Shift)(⌃)(⌘)(E).

2. In the iMovie: Export dialog that appears, choose To Camera from the Export pop-up menu (**Figure 68**) to display camera export options (**Figure 69**).

3. Enter values in each box to specify how long the computer should wait for the camera to get ready and how many seconds of black should appear before and after the movie.

4. Connect your video camera to your computer with a FireWire cable, turn it on, and set it to VTR (video tape recorder) mode.

5. Click Export.

6. Wait while iMovie prepares to export the movie, sets the camera to record, and writes the movie to tape. An export dialog like the one in **Figure 70** appears while it works. When it's done and the export is complete, the dialog disappears.

Figure 68
The Export pop-up menu offers three options.

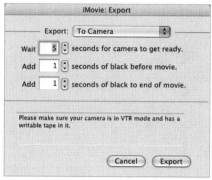

Figure 69 The iMovie: Export dialog with settings for exporting to a video camera.

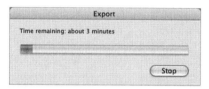

Figure 70 This dialog appears while iMovie writes the movie to a video camera.

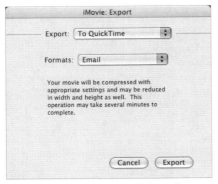

Figure 71 The iMovie: Export dialog with QuickTime export options displayed.

Figure 72
The Formats pop-up menu enables you to choose a format appropriate for how you plan to use the movie.

Figure 73 Use this dialog to save the movie.

Figure 74 A progress dialog like this one appears while the movie is being exported.

Figure 75 A movie viewed with QuickTime Player.

To export a movie project as a QuickTime movie

1. Choose File > Export, or press (Shift)(⌃)(⌘)(E).

2. In the iMovie: Export dialog that appears, choose To QuickTime from the Export pop-up menu (**Figure 68**) to display QuickTime export options (**Figure 71**).

3. Choose an appropriate option from the Formats pop-up menu (**Figure 72**).

4. Click Export.

5. Use the dialog that appears (**Figure 73**) to enter a name and select a disk location for the movie. Then click Save.

   iMovie exports the movie. As it works, a Progress dialog like the one in **Figure 74** appears. When the Progress dialog disappears, the export is finished.

✔ Tips

- In step 3, the options at the top of the menu create smaller files than those at the bottom.

- Once you have exported your movie project as a QuickTime movie, you can open and view it in QuickTime Player (**Figure 75**). Simply double-click the movie's icon. I tell you more about QuickTime Player in **Chapter 6**.

iPhoto

iPhoto is a computer-based photo storage system that enables you to do several things:

◆ Import photos from a digital camera or disk.

◆ Organize photos by name, keywords, and other criteria.

◆ Edit photos to crop them and remove red-eye.

◆ Create a book full of photos.

◆ Share photos with others by printing, exporting, or building Web pages.

The next few pages explain the basics of using iPhoto to import, organize, and share photos.

✔ Tips

■ To import photos from a digital camera, you must have a digital camera that is compatible with iPhoto. You can learn about camera compatibility on the iPhoto Web site, www.apple.com/iphoto/.

■ You can also use Image Capture to import photos from a digital camera. I tell you about Image Capture in **Chapter 6**.

■ iPhoto can only import still pictures. To import video (AVI) pictures from a digital camera, use Image Capture, which is covered in **Chapter 6**. To import movies from a digital video camera, use iMovie, which is covered earlier in this chapter.

To launch iPhoto

Double-click the iPhoto icon in your Applications folder (**Figure 1**). iPhoto's main window appears (**Figure 76**).

Figure 76 iPhoto's main window.

Figure 77 The first time you open iPhoto, it asks if you want to automatically launch it when you connect a camera.

✔ Tip

■ The first time you launch iPhoto, a dialog like the one in **Figure 77** appears. Click Use iPhoto to automatically launch iPhoto when you connect a camera.

Figure 78 iPhoto "sees" your camera and tells you how many pictures are on it.

Figure 79 iPhoto reports its progress at the bottom of the window.

Figure 80 iPhoto displays thumbnail images of the photos it has imported. (This is two months' worth from my PowerShot. I get around!)

To import photos from a camera

1. Using the USB or FireWire cable that came with your digital camera, connect the camera to your Macintosh, turn on the camera, and set the camera to review mode.

2. If iPhoto does not automatically launch, open it as discussed on the previous page. Make sure the Import button in the bottom center of the window is selected.

3. iPhoto "sees" your camera and displays information about it in the lower-left corner of the window (**Figure 78**). Click the Import button at the lower-right corner of the window.

   iPhoto imports the photos. Its progress appears in the bottom of the window (**Figure 79**). When it's finished, thumbnails of the images appear in the iPhoto window (**Figure 80**).

✔ Tips

■ If iPhoto does not "see" your camera, it may not be compatible with iPhoto. Check Apple's iPhoto Web site for more information, www.apple.com/iphoto/.

■ To have iPhoto automatically erase all photos it downloads, turn on the Erase camera contents after transfer check box.

■ When the import is complete, you can disconnect and turn off your camera.

■ iPhoto also recognizes photo CDs, including Kodak PictureCD discs, and will automatically launch when you insert a photo CD. Follow step 3 above to import the images.

To import images from disk

1. Choose File > Import.

2. Use the Import Photos dialog that appears (**Figure 81**) to locate the photo(s) you want to import.

3. To import only one photo, select the name of the photo and click Import.

    or

    To import multiple photos, hold down ⌘ while selecting the name of each photo you want to import. Then click Import.

    or

    To import all photos in a folder, select the name of the folder and click Import.

    iPhoto imports the photo(s). It displays its progress in the bottom of its window. When it's finished, the photos appear in the main window.

✔ Tip

- You may find this technique useful to add scanned photos and images to iPhoto.

To review the most recently imported files

Click Last Import in the album list. The most recently imported images appear as thumbnails in the main window (**Figure 82**).

Figure 81 The Import Photos dialog.

Figure 82 Clicking the Last Import album displays the most recently imported images.

New album   Show/Hide info

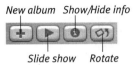

Slide show   Rotate

Figure 83 Buttons at the bottom of the album list.

Figure 84 The New Album dialog.

Figure 85
The new album is added to the album list.

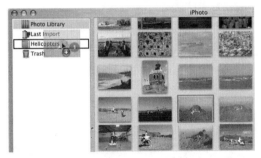

Figure 86 Drag a thumbnail image to the photo album.

To create an album

1. Click the New Album button at the bottom of the album list (**Figure 83**).

   or

   Choose File > New Album, or press ⌘N.

2. Enter a name for the album in the New Album dialog (**Figure 84**).

3. Click OK.

   The album appears in the album list (**Figure 85**).

To add a photo to an album

1. In the album list, select Photo Library or the name of the album containing the photo you want to add.

2. Drag the thumbnail image from the main window to the name of the photo album you want to add the image to (**Figure 86**). When you release the mouse button, the image is added to the album.

✔ Tip

■ You can select and drag multiple images at once. Hold down ⌘ while selecting each image, then drag any one image to the album name. All selected images are added to the album.

To remove a photo from an album

1. Select the thumbnail for the image you want to remove.

2. Press Delete. The photo disappears.

✔ Tip

■ When you remove a photo from the Photo Library (rather than an individual album), it is moved to iPhoto's Trash. You can view the contents of iPhoto's Trash by clicking its icon in the Album list.

CREATING & MODIFYING A PHOTO ALBUM

To enter information for a photo

1. If necessary, click the Organize button near the bottom of the iPhoto window.

2. Select the album containing the photo you want to enter information for.

3. Select the thumbnail for the photo.

4. Enter information as desired in the three boxes beneath the album list (**Figure 87**).

✔ Tips

- If the boxes do not appear beneath the album list, click the Show/Hide Info button (**Figure 83**) until they do.

- You can give two or more photos in the same album the same title.

- Photo titles and comments are used by some of the photo sharing features, including exporting photos and creating photo books.

- The date and time is automatically filled in when you import most photos. You can edit this information if desired.

To change the size of thumbnail images

Move the size slider to the left or right:

◆ Move the slider to the left to make the thumbnails smaller.

◆ Move the slider to the right to make the thumbnails larger (**Figure 88**).

✔ Tip

- Changes to the thumbnail size affect all albums, not just the one that is selected when you make the change.

Figure 87
Enter information for the photo in these boxes.

Figure 88 You can make the thumbnails larger—so they're easier to see!

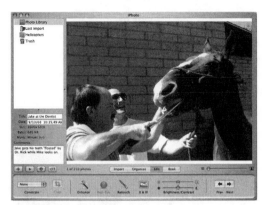

Figure 89 A photo in Edit view. (No, the horse isn't being tortured. Although he makes a funny face, getting his teeth floated doesn't hurt him.)

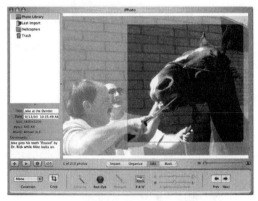

Figure 90 Select the area you want to keep.

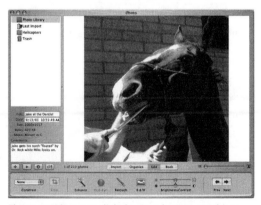

Figure 91 When you click the Crop button, anything outside the selection is removed.

To edit photos

1. Select the photo you want to edit.

2. Click the Edit button near the bottom of the iPhoto window. The view changes to show just the photo you selected, and a number of tools appears at the bottom of the window (**Figure 89**).

3. Perform any combination of the following steps to fine-tune the photo's appearance:

   ▲ To rotate a photo, click the Rotate button beneath the Albums list (**Figure 83**). You may have to click it more than once.

   ▲ To crop the photo, drag the mouse pointer to select the portion of the photo you want to retain (**Figure 90**). Then click the Crop button to cut out the unwanted part of the photo (**Figure 91**).

   ▲ To enhance photo colors, click the Enhance button.

   ▲ To reduce red-eye in a subject's eyes, drag the mouse pointer to select the subject's eye and click the Red-Eye button. Repeat for the other eye if necessary.

   ▲ To remove scratches and other blemishes from a photo, click the Retouch button and then use the mouse to drag over the blemish to blend it in with surrounding colors.

   ▲ To convert a color photo to black and white, click the B & W button.

   ▲ To change the brightness and contrast for a photo, drag the Brightness/Contrast sliders.

Continued on next page...

EDITING PHOTOS

239

Continued from previous page.

✔ Tips

- You can use the Constrain pop-up menu (**Figure 92**) to constrain a mouse selection to one of several predefined proportions. This is especially useful when cropping a photo you plan to print.

- Editing changes are automatically saved.

- To undo all editing changes to a photo, choose File > Revert to Original.

To print photos

1. If necessary, click the Organize button near the bottom of the iPhoto window.

2. Select the photos you want to print. To select more than one photo (**Figure 93**), hold down ⌘ while clicking each photo.

3. Click the Print button at the bottom of the window, choose File > Print, or press ⌘P to display the Print dialog (**Figure 94**).

4. Choose the printer you want to use from the Printer pop-up menu.

5. Choose a style from the Style pop-up menu (**Figure 95**):

   ▲ **Contact Sheet** prints multiple photos on each page. With this option chosen, the slider changes the number of photos across each page, thus changing the size of each photo (**Figure 96**).

   ▲ **Full Page** prints one photo on each page. With this option chosen, the slider adjusts the size of the page's margins (**Figure 94**).

Figure 92
Use this pop-up menu to constrain proportions when you select part of a photo.

Figure 93 Select the photos you want to print.

Figure 94 The Print dialog with the default Style option—Full Page—chosen.

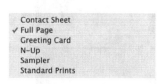

Figure 95
The Style pop-up menu.

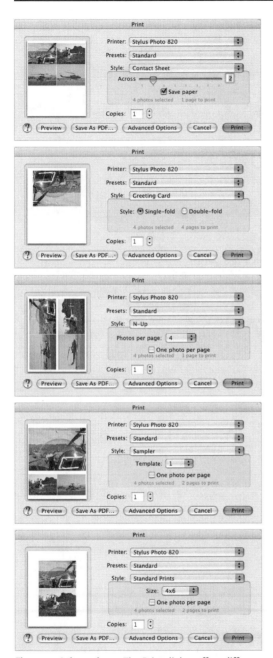

Figures 96 through 100 The Print dialog offers differ- ent options for the Contact Sheet, Greeting Card, N-Up, Sampler, and Standard Prints styles.

▲ **Greeting Card** prints one photo on each page, set up for folding as a greeting card. With this option cho- sen, you can use radio buttons to specify whether you want a single- fold (**Figure 97**) or double-fold card.

▲ **N-Up** prints the number of photos you specify per page (**Figure 98**). If you turn on the One photo per page check box, it prints duplicates of one photo on each page.

▲ **Sampler** prints different sized photos on each page (**Figure 99**). If you turn on the One photo per page check box, it prints different sizes of the same photo on each page.

▲ **Standard Prints** prints standard size prints in 2x3, 4x6, 5x7, or 8x10 sizes (**Figure 100**). If you turn on the One photo per page check box, it prints multiple copies of the same photo on each page.

6. Click Print. The photos are printed to your specifications.

✔ Tips

■ The Preview area of the Print dialog changes when you change Style settings.

■ I tell you more about printing in **Chapter 10**.

To display a slide show

1. If necessary, click the Organize button near the bottom of the iPhoto window.

2. Select the photos you want to include in the slide show. To select multiple photos, hold down ⌃⌘ while clicking each one. To select all slides in an album, simply select the name of the album.

3. Click the Slideshow button to display the Slideshow Settings dialog (**Figure 101**).

4. Enter a value in the Play each slide for box to determine how long each slide should appear onscreen.

5. Toggle check boxes as desired:

   ▲ **Display photos in random order** displays the photos in random order rather than the order in which they appear in iPhoto.

   ▲ **Repeat slideshow** repeats the slide show after all photos have been displayed once.

   ▲ **Music** plays music during the slide show. Choose an option from the pop-up menu, then click to select a specific song.

6. Click Play Slideshow.

   If you selected music for the slide show, the music begins. The first photo fades in, remains onscreen, then fades out to be replaced with the next photo.

7. To end the slide show, press [Esc].

✔ Tips

■ You can display a slide show quickly using the default settings by clicking the Slide Show button at the bottom of the album list (**Figure 83**).

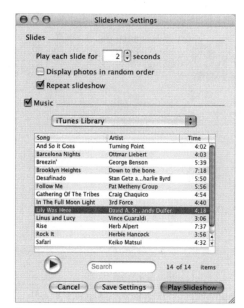

Figure 101 The Slideshow Settings dialog.

■ If any of your photos have vertical (or portrait) orientation use the Rotate button at the bottom of the album list (**Figure 83**) to correct its orientation *before* including it in a slide show. (Unless, of course, you prefer to tilt your head when that photo appears.)

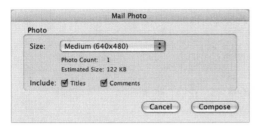

Figure 102 The Mail Photo dialog.

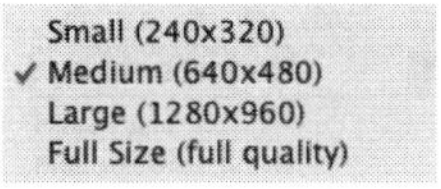

Small (240x320)
✓ Medium (640x480)
Large (1280x960)
Full Size (full quality)

Figure 103
Choose one of four sizes for the photo(s).

Figure 104 A Mail message all ready for addressing. (Looks like that train is charging out of the page, doesn't it?)

To e-mail photos

1. If necessary, click the Organize button near the bottom of the iPhoto window.

2. Select the photo(s) you want to e-mail. To select multiple photos, hold down ⌃ ⌘ while clicking each one.

3. Click the Email button to display the Mail Photo dialog (**Figure 102**).

4. Choose a size from the Size pop-up menu (**Figure 103**). The larger the size, the larger the file that will be sent with the e-mail.

5. Toggle check boxes to include photo title(s) and/or comment(s).

6. Click Compose.

7. iPhoto launches your e-mail application and creates a new message with the photo(s) inserted (**Figure 104**). Address the message and insert some message text. Then click the Send button to send the message and photo.

✔ Tips

■ Don't annoy friends, relatives, and business associates by sending large photos. If the recipient has a dial-up connection to the Internet, it could take a long time to download the photos. Instead, send smaller photos and tell the recipient that larger versions are available if they need them.

■ iPhoto photos are e-mailed as JPEG images, which can be read by any computer.

E-MAILING PHOTOS

iSync

iSync is synchronization software that keeps your iCal calendar information, Address book contact information, and Safari bookmarks up to date on your iPod, other Macs, Bluetooth-enabled mobile phone, and PDA.

This part of the chapter provides instructions for setting up and using iSync to synchronize information between your computer and an iPod or another Mac.

✔ Tips

- Although the information here does not include specific instructions for using iSync with a mobile phone or PDA, it should be enough to get you started using iSync with these devices.

- To use iSync with another Macintosh, you must have a .Mac account and each computer must have access to the Internet. I tell you about .Mac in **Chapter 12** and about connecting to the Internet in **Chapter 11**.

- To use iSync with a Bluetooth-enabled mobile phone, you must have a Bluetooth adapter connected to your Macintosh. You can learn more about Bluetooth in **Chapter 14**.

To launch iSync

Double-click the iSync icon in your Applications folder (**Figure 1**). iSync's main window appears (**Figure 105**).

✔ Tip

- By default, iSync displays a .mac device icon in its main window (**Figure 105**)—even if you do not have a .Mac account.

Figure 105 iSync's main window.

Figure 106 If your .Mac account has already been set up in the .Mac preferences pane, the .Mac configuration options may look like this.

Figure 107 If your .Mac account has not been set up in the .Mac preferences pane, the .Mac configuration options look like this.

Figure 108 Enter your .Mac member information.

Figure 109 To register a computer, you must enter a name for it.

To configure .Mac

1. In the iSync main window (**Figure 105**), click the .mac icon. The window expands to display options. If it looks like the window in **Figure 106**, skip ahead to step 3.

2. If your .Mac account settings have not been entered in the .Mac preferences pane, the window should look like **Figure 107**. Click the Configure .Mac button. Then enter your .Mac member name and password in the appropriate boxes of the .Mac preferences pane that appears (**Figure 108**) and choose System Preferences > Quit System Preferences.

3. Click the Register button.

4. In the next screen (**Figure 109**), enter the name you want to use to identify the computer on .Mac and click Continue.

5. Wait while your Mac connects to the .Mac server and gets information about any other computers already registered to your .Mac account. When it's finished, it displays configuration options (**Figure 110**).

6. Choose an option for the first synchronization from the For first sync pop-up menu. Your options are:

   ▲ **Merge data on computer and .Mac** merges the information at both locations so the newest information is at both locations.

   ▲ **Erase data on .Mac then sync** erases the information stored on .Mac and replaces it with the information on the computer you are setting up.

   ▲ **Erase data on computer then sync** erases the information on the computer you are setting up and replaces it with the information on .Mac.

Continued on next page...

CONFIGURING .MAC

Continued from previous page.

7. Toggle check boxes to set basic options:

▲ **Turn on .Mac synchronization** enables .Mac synchronization. This option cannot be toggled until after you have performed your first sync.

▲ **Automatically synchronize every hour** automatically synchronizes between the computer and .Mac every hour, as long as an Internet connection is possible.

8. Toggle check boxes in the This Computer section to specify what should be synchronized:

▲ **Safari Bookmarks** are bookmarks you create in the Safari Web browser. I tell you about Safari in **Chapter 11**.

▲ **Address Book Contacts** are entries you create in Address Book. I tell you about Address Book in **Chapter 6**.

▲ **iCal Calendars and To Do items** are events and To Do items you create in iCal. I tell you about iCal earlier in this chapter.

9. Click the .Mac icon to collapse the window and save your settings.

✔ Tips

■ If you do not have a .Mac account, you can skip these steps. You will not, however, be able to use iSync to synchronize information between two Macintosh computers, as discussed later in this section.

■ As shown in **Figure 110**, I already have two other computers registered on my .Mac account. You must register all computers you want to include in synchronizations.

Figure 110 .Mac configuration options.

CONFIGURING .MAC

Figure 111
The Devices menu.

Figure 112 The Add Device window with an iPod displayed.

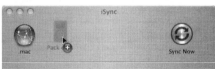

Figure 113 Drag the device's icon from the Add Device window to the iSync window.

To add another device

1. Choose Devices > Add Device (**Figure 111**), or press ⌃⌘N. The Add Device window appears and iSync begins looking for devices. When it is finished, it displays icons for all devices it found (**Figure 112**).

2. Drag the icon for the device you want to add from the Add Device window to the iSync window (**Figure 113**). An icon for the device appears in the iSync window and the window expands to show device synchronization options (**Figure 114** on next page).

✔ Tip

■ The device you are trying to add must be accessible to your Macintosh to appear in the Add Device window (**Figure 112**). If a device does not appear, make sure it is properly connected (or within range, in the case of a Bluetooth-enabled mobile phone) and turned on. Then follow steps 1 and 2 above again.

ADDING DEVICES

To configure an iPod for synchronization

1. If necessary, in the iSync window, click the iPod's device icon to show configuration options (**Figure 114**).

2. Turn on check boxes and choose other options to set synchronization preferences:

   ▲ **Turn on *iPod Name* synchronization** enables synchronization between the computer and the iPod.

   ▲ **Automatically synchronize when iPod is connected** automatically synchronizes data according to your settings each time the iPod is connected to the computer.

   ▲ **Contacts** synchronizes Address Book contacts to the Contacts extra in the iPod. With this option turned on, you can select All contacts or a specific group name from the Synchronize pop-up menu to determine which contacts should be synchronized.

   ▲ **Calendars** synchronizes iCal calendars to the Calendar extra in the iPod. With this option turned on, if you have multiple calendars you can select the Selected radio button and toggle check marks to indicate which calendars should be synchronized.

3. Click the iPod icon to collapse the window and save your settings.

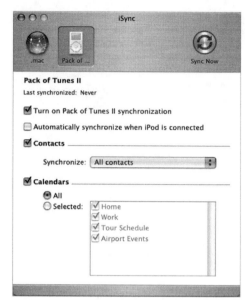

Figure 114 Configuration options for an iPod.

CONFIGURING AN iPOD

Figure 115 A progress bar and Cancel Sync button appear when a sync is in progress.

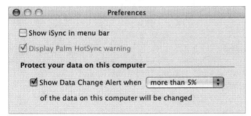

Figure 116 The Data Change Alert window appears so you can confirm the changes that need to be made.

Figure 117 The Preferences dialog enables you to change the way the Data Change Alert feature works.

To perform a synchronization

1. Click the Sync Now button in the iSync window (**Figure 105**). As shown in **Figure 115**, a status bar appears in the iSync window to indicate that a sync is in progress. In addition, the Sync Now button turns into a Cancel Sync button.

2. One or more Data Change Alert windows may appear before iSync makes any changes to your data. **Figure 116** shows an example. Click Proceed to continue the sync.

   When the progress bar disappears from the iSync window, the synchronization is complete.

✔ Tips

- You can customize the way the Data Change Alert feature works by setting options in iSync's Preferences dialog. Choose iSync > Preferences to display the Preferences dialog (**Figure 117**). To display the Data Change Alert dialog only when a certain percentage of the data is changed, choose an option from the pop-up menu. Your choices are: Any, More than 1%, More than 5%, or More than 10%. To disable the Data Change Alert feature, turn off the Show the Data Change Alert check box. This option must be disabled to perform automatic synchronizations. Close the Preferences dialog to save your settings.

- You can synchronize the data between two or more computers by performing synchronizations between each of them and your .Mac account. iSync automatically knows which data is newer and puts it on the .Mac synchronization server. When all synchronizations are complete, the data should be the same on each machine.

iTunes

iTunes is a computer-based "jukebox" that enables you to do several things:

◆ Play MP3 and AAC format audio files.

◆ Record music from audio CDs on your Macintosh as AAC and MP3 files.

◆ Create custom CDs of your favorite music.

◆ Save AAC and MP3 files to an iPod and save MP3 files to other MP3 players.

◆ Listen to Internet-based radio stations.

The next few pages explain how you can use iTunes to record and play MP3 music, copy MP3 files to an iPod, and burn audio CDs.

✔ Tips

■ MP3 and AAC are standard formats for audio files.

■ Your computer must have a CD-R drive or SuperDrive to burn CDs.

To set up iTunes

1. Double-click the iTunes icon in your Applications folder (**Figure 1**).

2. If a license agreement window appears, click Accept.

3. The iTunes Setup Assistant window appears (**Figure 118**). Read the welcome message, and click Next.

4. In the Internet Audio window (**Figure 119**), set options as desired and click Next:

   ▲ Select an Internet audio content option. **Yes, use iTunes for Internet audio content** instructs your computer to set your Web browser helper settings to use iTunes for all Internet audio playback. **No, do not modify my Internet settings** does not change your Web browser's helper settings.

Figure 118 The first screen of the iTunes Setup Assistant.

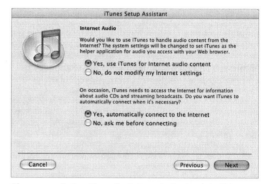

Figure 119 Set options for Internet playback in this screen.

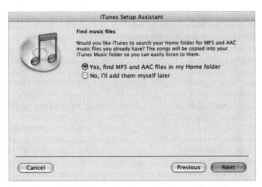

Figure 120 The Find music files window of the iTunes Setup Assistant.

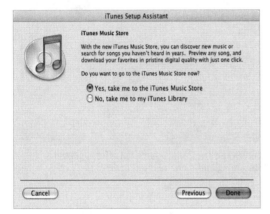

Figure 121 The iTunes Music Store window of the iTunes Setup Assistant.

Playback Source Song
controls list list

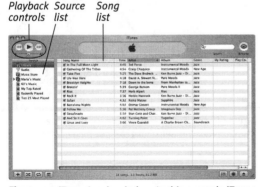

Figure 122 iTunes' main window. In this example iTunes has located some music files in my Home folder and automatically imported them.

▲ Select an Internet connection option. **Yes, automatically connect to the Internet** tells iTunes that it's okay to connect to the Internet anytime it needs to. **No, ask me before connecting** tells iTunes to display a dialog that asks your permission before connecting to the Internet.

5. In the Find music files window (**Figure 120**), select an option and click Next:

   ▲ **Yes, find MP3 and AAC files I have in my Home folder** tells iTunes to search your hard disk for music files in your Home folder (or any of its folders) and add them to you music library.

   ▲ **No, I'll add them myself later** tells iTunes not to look for music files.

6. In the iTunes Music Store window (**Figure 121**), select an option:

   ▲ **Yes, take me to the iTunes Music Store** connects to the Internet and displays the Home page of the iTunes Music Store when you click Done.

   ▲ **No, take me to my iTunes Library** displays the contents of your iTunes Music Library when you click Done.

7. Click Done.

   iTunes completes its configuration and displays the iTunes main window with either the iTunes Music Store (**Figure 125** on the next page) or your iTunes Library (**Figure 122**).

SETTING UP iTUNES

To view & listen to music by source

1. Click one of the options in the Source list (**Figure 123**) to display the contents of the source:

   ▲ **Library** displays all the music in your iTunes library (**Figure 122**).

   ▲ **Radio** connects to the Internet and displays music streams organized by category. Click a triangle to the left of a stream category in the Song list to display a list of streams (**Figure 124**).

   ▲ **Music Store** connects to the Internet and displays the iTunes Music Store (**Figure 125**).

   ▲ *Shared Music Library Name* displays all the music available via network from a shared music library (**Figure 126**). This feature, which is widely used at Peachpit Press (or so I have been told), enables you to listen to music on other network users' computers. Click the triangle to the left of the shared library name to display individual playlists within that library.

   ▲ *Smart Playlist Name* displays music in a smart playlist.

   ▲ *Playlist Name* displays music in a playlist.

2. To play music from a library or playlist (**Figures 122** and **126**), click the Play button above the Source list (**Figure 127**).

   or

   To play music from a radio stream (**Figure 124**), click the name of the stream.

   or

   To browse music in the iTunes Music Store, follow the instructions in the section titled "To shop for music online" later in this section.

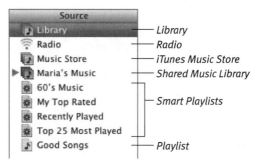

Figure 123 The Source list includes several different music sources.

Library
Radio
iTunes Music Store
Shared Music Library
Smart Playlists
Playlist

Figure 124 The Radio source list offers access to streaming audio on the Internet.

Figure 125 The iTunes Music Store is a great place to shop for music. (I think I might be its best customer.)

Figure 126 If you're on a network and others have shared their libraries, you can listen to their music.

Play *Volume*

Figure 127
Use the playback controls to play music and set the volume.

Stop
Backward | *Forward*

Figure 128
When music is playing the playback controls change.

Figure 129
The Controls menu offers options for controlling music play.

New Playlist *Shuffle*
Repeat *Song Artwork*

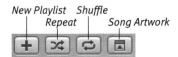

Figure 130 Use buttons at the bottom of the Source list to work with the list and control music play.

✔ Tips

- You must have access to the Internet to use the Radio and Music Store sources.

- You can listen to a specific song in a library or playlist by double-clicking the song in the Song list.

- Once you have begun playing music from a library or playlist, the Backward and Forward buttons become active and the Play button turns into a Stop button (**Figure 128**).

- The Controls menu (**Figure 129**) offers additional options for controlling music play.

- You can use buttons at the bottom of the Source list (**Figure 130**) to work with the Source list and change the way music is played.

- To sort the song list by one of its columns, click the column heading. Clicking the same heading again reverses the sort.

- Clicking the Browse button in the upper right corner of the iTunes window (**Figure 122**) splits the window so you can browse a selected source by Genre, Artist, or Album. As shown in **Figure 131**, when you click one of the browse category items, the song list changes to show only matching items.

Figure 131 Clicking the Browse button enables you to browse by genre, artist, or album.

To add songs from an audio CD to the Library

1. Insert an audio CD in your CD drive. A dialog like the one in **Figure 132** appears briefly while your computer accesses the Internet to get song names. After a moment, the CD's name appears in the Source list and a list of the tracks on it appears in the song list (**Figure 133**).

2. Turn on the check box beside each song you want to add to the Library. (They should already all be turned on.)

3. Click the Import button. iTunes begins importing the first song. The status area provides progress information (**Figure 134**). The song may play while it is imported.

✔ Tips

■ Sometime during step 1, iTunes may ask your permission to connect to the Internet. It must do this to retrieve information about the songs on the CD. If you don't connect to the Internet, song names do not appear in the Song list.

■ You can specify whether a song plays while it is imported by setting iTunes preferences. Choose iTunes > Preferences and click the Importing button to get started.

■ When iTunes is finished importing songs, it plays a sound. In most cases, iTunes will finish importing songs from a CD before it finishes playing them.

■ When you are finished importing songs from a CD, select the CD name in the Source list and click the Eject button in the lower right corner of the iTunes window (**Figure 133**) to eject the disc.

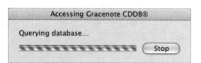

Figure 132 iTunes accesses an Internet database to get information about the songs on a CD.

Import button

Figure 133 When you insert a CD, it appears in the Source list and a list of its songs appear in the song list. (You're never too young to listen to Big Band music.)

Eject button

Figure 134 iTunes shows the import progress at the top of its window and puts an importing icon beside the song currently being imported in the song list.

Figure 135 Importing an MP3 file on disk is as easy as dragging it into the iTunes window.

Figure 136 The song you dragged in appears in the iTunes Library window.

Figure 137 Exporting a song as an AAC file is as easy as dragging it from the iTunes window to a Finder window.

Pennsylvania 6-5000.m4a

Figure 138
An icon for the exported AAC file appears where the song was dragged.

To import music files on disk to the Library

Drag the icon for the music file from the Desktop or a Finder window to the iTunes window (**Figure 135**).

After a moment, the song appears in the Library window (**Figure 136**).

✔ Tips

- You can use this technique to add a bunch of music files at once. Simply select their icons and drag any one of them into the window. I explain how to select multiple icons in the Finder in **Chapter 2**.

- You could also use the Add to Library command on the iTunes File menu, but I think this technique is quicker and easier.

To export songs from the iTunes Library as AAC files

Drag the name of the song you want to export from the iTunes Library window to the Desktop or a Finder window (**Figure 137**).

After a moment, an AAC icon for the exported song appears in the Finder (**Figure 138**).

✔ Tip

- You can use this technique to export a bunch of AAC files at once. Simply hold down ⌘ while clicking each song you want to select. Then drag any one of them into the Finder window.

IMPORTING & EXPORTING MUSIC FILES

To create a playlist

1. Click the New Playlist button (**Figure 130**), choose File > New Playlist, or press ⌃⌘N.

2. A new untitled playlist appears in the Source list (**Figure 139**). Type a name for the playlist, and press Enter (**Figure 140**).

To add songs to a playlist

1. If necessary, select Library in the source window to display all music files.

2. Drag a song you want to include in the new playlist from the Song list to the playlist name in the Source list (**Figure 141**).

3. Repeat step 2 for each song you want to add to the playlist.

4. When you're finished adding songs, click the playlist name. The songs appear in the list. You can play them by following the above instructions.

✔ Tips

- In step 2, you can select and drag multiple songs. Hold down ⌃⌘ while selecting songs to select more than one, then drag any one of them.

- You can change the order of songs in a playlist by dragging them up or down.

- You can sort songs in a playlist by clicking a column heading. Clicking once sorts in ascending order; clicking twice sorts in descending order.

To remove a song from a playlist

1. Select the song you want to remove.

2. Press Delete. The song is removed from the playlist.

✔ Tip

- Removing a song from a playlist does not remove it from the iTunes Library.

Figure 139
Clicking the New Playlist button creates a new, untitled playlist.

Figure 140
To give the playlist a name, simply type it in and press Enter.

Figure 141 To add songs to a playlist, drag them from the Song list to the playlist name.

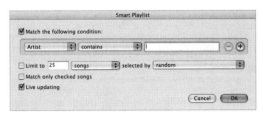

Figure 142 The Smart Playlist dialog.

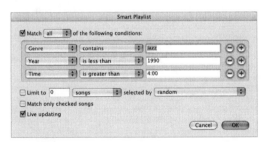

Figure 143
Use this pop-up menu to specify the type of criteria you want to match.

Figure 144 Here's an example of smart playlist settings with multiple criteria.

minutes
hours
MB
GB
✓ songs

Figure 145 Use this pop-up menu to specify how you want to limit the selection.

✓ random

album
artist
genre
song name

highest rating
lowest rating

most recently played
least recently played

most often played
least often played

most recently added
least recently added

Figure 146 Use this pop-up menu to specify how iTunes should select songs when you limit the selection.

To create a smart playlist

1. Choose File > New Smart Playlist or press Option ⌘ N to display the Smart Playlist dialog (**Figure 142**).

2. Choose an option from the first pop-up menu (**Figure 143**), and set criteria using options on that line.

3. To add additional matching criteria, click the + button. The dialog expands to offer an additional line for criteria. Set criteria as desired in this line. You can repeat this step as necessary to set all criteria. **Figure 144** shows an example with multiple criteria set.

4. If you set up multiple criteria in step 3, choose an option from the Match pop-up menu:

   ▲ **All** matches all criteria you set. This narrows down the search and produces fewer matches. Keep in mind that if criteria is mutually exclusive (for example, "Genre contains Jazz" and "Genre contains New Age") no items will be found.

   ▲ **Any** matches any criteria. This expands the search and produces more matches.

5. To limit the size of the play list by time, file size, or number of songs, turn on the Limit to check box, choose an option from the pop-up menu (**Figure 145**), and enter a value in the box beside it. You can also use the selected by pop-up menu in that line (**Figure 146**) to specify how songs should be chosen.

6. To match only songs that are checked in the song list, turn on the Match only checked songs check box.

Continued on next page...

CREATING SMART PLAYLISTS

7. To automatically update the playlist each time songs are added or removed from the Library, turn on the Live updating check box.

8. Click OK.

9. A new smart playlist appears in the Source list with a suggested name based on what you entered. When the list is selected, you can see the songs iTunes selected (**Figure 147**).

✔ Tip

- The types of criteria iTunes can use (**Figure 143**) are divided into two categories: information you can change and information you can't change. To see (and change) information for a song, select the song in the song list and choose File > Get Info or press ⌘I. **Figures 148** and **149** show examples of two panes of information for a song. Explore this feature on your own.

To delete a playlist

1. In the source window, select the playlist you want to delete (**Figure 147**).

2. Press Delete.

3. In the confirmation dialog that appears (**Figure 150**), click Yes. The playlist is removed.

✔ Tip

- Deleting a playlist does not delete the songs on the playlist from your music library.

Figure 147 iTunes selected these songs, based on the criteria shown in **Figure 144**.

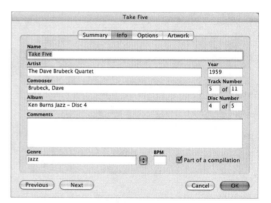

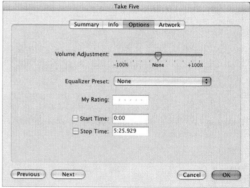

Figures 148 & 149 Two examples of the Info window for a song: Info (top) and Options (bottom).

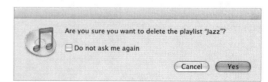

Figure 150 Confirm that you really do want to delete a playlist.

Figure 151
Your iPod or MP3 player should appear in the Source list, like my iPod, which I named "Pack of Tunes II," does.

Figure 152 Drag the song from the song list to the iPod or MP3 player.

To copy songs to an iPod or other MP3 player

1. Using the USB or FireWire cable that came with your iPod or other MP3 player, connect it to your Macintosh and, if necessary, turn it on.

2. If iTunes is not already running or does not automatically open, launch it. After a moment, the MP3 player should appear in the Source list (**Figure 151**).

3. Drag the song(s) you want to copy to the iPod or MP3 player from the Song list to the iPod or MP3 player in the Source list (**Figure 152**). The status area indicates that the song is being copied.

4. Repeat step 3 for each song you want to copy.

5. When you are finished copying songs, you can select the iPod or MP3 player in the Source list and click the Eject button to unmount it. You can then disconnect it from your Macintosh.

✔ Tips

■ If iTunes was already running when you connected your MP3 player and it did not list the MP3 player in the Source list, quit iTunes and relaunch it. If it still doesn't appear, your MP3 player may not be compatible with iTunes. Check the iTunes Web site for assistance: www.apple.com/itunes/.

■ In step 3, you can select and drag multiple songs. Hold down ⌃ ⌘ while selecting songs to select more than one, then drag any one of them.

■ The number of songs you can copy to an iPod or MP3 player is limited by the amount of storage in the player and the size of the songs.

To copy playlists to an iPod

1. Using the FireWire cable that came with your iPod, connect it to your Macintosh. If iTunes is not already running, it launches, and the iPod appears in the Source list (**Figure 151**).

2. Drag the playlist you want to copy to the iPod from the Source list to the iPod in the Source list (**Figure 153**). The playlist appears indented beneath the iPod icon (**Figure 154**).

3. Repeat step 2 for each playlist you want to copy.

4. When you are finished copying songs, you can select the iPod name in the Source disk and click the Eject button to unmount it. You can then disconnect it from your Macintosh.

✔ Tips

- You can only copy one playlist at a time.

- When you copy a playlist, any songs in the playlist that are not already on the iPod are also copied.

- You can set up your iPod to automatically update songs and playlists when you connect. Click the Display options for player button that appears at the bottom of the iTunes window when your iPod is selected in the Source list (**Figure 154**), and set options in the iPod Preferences dialog that appears (**Figure 155**).

Figure 153
You can drag a playlist to the iPod listed in the Source list to copy the playlist and its contents to the iPod.

Figure 154 This illustration shows the playlists (in the Source list) and the songs (in the Song list) copied to an iPod.

Display options for player

Figure 155 You can use the iPod Preferences dialog to set automatic update options for your iPod.

Burn Disc button

Figure 156 Select the Playlist you want to burn to CD and click the Burn CD button.

Figure 157 iTunes prompts you to click the Burn CD button again.

Figure 158 This dialog appears if you try to put too many songs on an audio CD.

To burn an audio CD

1. Create a playlist that contains the songs you want to include on the CD and select it (**Figure 156**).

2. Click the Burn CD button.

3. When prompted, insert a blank CD in your computer's CD-R drive or Super-Drive and close the drive.

4. When prompted, click the Burn CD button, which is now black and yellow (**Figure 157**).

5. Wait while iTunes prepares and burns the CD. This could take a while; the progress appears in the status window at the top of the iTunes window. You can switch to and work with other applications while you wait.

6. When iTunes is finished burning the CD, it makes a sound. The icon for the CD appears on your desktop.

✔ Tips

■ Your computer must have a compatible CD-R drive or SuperDrive to burn audio CDs. You can find a list of compatible devices on the iTunes Web site, www.apple.com/itunes/.

■ I explain how to create a playlist earlier in this section.

■ If the playlist you have selected will not fit on an audio CD, iTunes displays a dialog like the one in **Figure 158**. If you click Audio CDs, iTunes prompts you to insert a blank CD each time it needs one.

■ Do not cancel the disc burning process after it has begun. Doing so can render the CD unusable.

BURNING AN AUDIO CD

To share music with other network users

1. Choose iTunes > Preferences.

2. Click the Sharing button to display Sharing preferences (**Figure 159**).

3. To play music shared by other network users, turn on the Look for shared music check box. This displays any shared music libraries in the Source list (**Figure 123**) on your computer, so you can listen to it.

4. To share your music with other network users, turn on the Share my music check box. Then select one of the radio buttons:

   ▲ **Share entire library** shares all of your music.

   ▲ **Share selected playlists** enables you to toggle check boxes for individual playlists you want to share.

5. If you turned on the Share my music check box in step 4, enter a name for your library in the Shared name box.

6. To require other network users to enter a password to listen to your music, turn on the Require password check box and enter a password in the box beside it.

7. Click OK.

8. A dialog like the one in **Figure 160** appears. Click OK.

✔ Tips

■ Once sharing is enabled, the Status area in the Sharing preferences dialog reports whether your music is being accessed by other users on the network (**Figure 161**).

■ I tell you more about Mac OS X's networking features in **Chapter 14**.

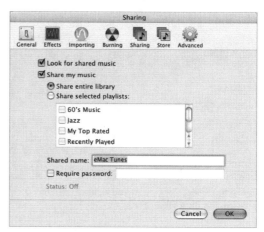

Figure 159 Sharing preferences enable you to share iTunes music.

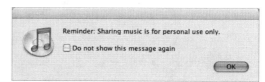

Figure 160 This dialog appears when you enable sharing. (The Apple lawyers obviously had a hand in this one.)

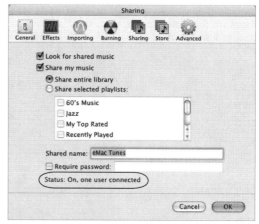

Figure 161 Sharing status appears in the bottom of the Sharing preferences dialog.

Figure 162 Search results for the phrase "Pink Floyd."

Figure 163 Clicking an artist link displays all available albums for that artist.

Figure 164 Clicking an album link displays a list of songs in that album.

Figure 165 You can monitor download progress of purchased songs at the top of the iTunes window.

To shop online for music

1. In the Source list, select Music Store.

   Your computer connects to the Internet and displays the Home page of the iTunes Music Store (**Figure 125**).

2. Use any combination of the following techniques to locate and sample songs:

   ▲ Click links in the window to browse through available albums and songs.

   ▲ To search for a specific album, song, or artist, enter a search word or phrase in the Search box at the top-right of the iTunes window and press `Return`. Search results appear in the window (**Figure 162**).

   ▲ To listen to a sample of a song, double-click its name in a search results list (**Figure 162**).

   ▲ To see matches for an artist (**Figure 163**), click an artist link or the arrow button beside the artist name in a search results list (**Figure 162**).

   ▲ To see matches for an album (**Figure 164**), click an album link or the arrow button beside the album name in a search results list (**Figure 162**).

3. To buy a song or album, click the Buy Song or Buy Album button for it. The song or album is downloaded to your computer (**Figure 165**) and appears in the Purchased Music playlist (**Figure 166**).

Continued on next page...

Figure 166 iTunes records all your music purchases in a special Purchased Music playlist.

SHOPPING FOR MUSIC ONLINE

✔ Tips

- Step 2 covers only a handful of the ways you can browse the contents of the iTunes Music Store. There are far too many other navigation tools to cover here. Explore them on your own to find your favorite ways to get around the iTunes Music Store.

- In step 3, if you are not logged into the iTunes Music Store, a dialog like the one in **Figure 167** appears. If you have an Apple ID, enter it and your password and click Buy. If you don't have an Apple ID, click the Create New Account button and follow the instructions that appear onscreen to set up an Apple ID.

- Purchased music has some limitations:

  - ▲ You can only play purchased music on up to three authorized computers—iTunes will tell you if your computer isn't authorized to play a song and give you a chance to authorize it.

  - ▲ Although you can include a purchased song on any number of CDs that you burn, you can only burn up to 10 CDs from an unchanged playlist.

- If you buy as many songs as I do at the iTunes Music Store (249 songs so far), you may want to set up a shopping cart so you can download purchased music all at once at the end of a shopping spree. Choose iTunes > Preferences and click the Store button (**Figure 168**) to get started.

Figure 167 If you are not logged in to the iTunes Music Store, a dialog like this appears when you buy music.

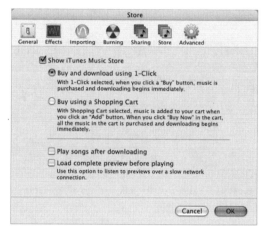

Figure 168 Use the Store preferences dialog to customize the way the iTunes Music Store works.

Fonts

Fonts & Font Formats

Fonts are typefaces that appear on screen and in printed documents. When they're properly installed, they appear on all Font menus and in font lists.

Mac OS X supports several types of fonts:

◆ **Data fork suitcase format** (.dfont) stores all information in the data fork of the file, including resources used by Mac OS drawing routines.

◆ **Microsoft Windows font formats** are Windows format font files. These include TrueType fonts (.ttf), TrueType collections (.ttc), and OpenType fonts (.otf).

◆ **PostScript fonts in Mac OS or Windows format** are used primarily for printing. These fonts must be accompanied by corresponding bitmapped font files.

◆ **Mac OS 9.x and earlier font formats** include Mac OS TrueType fonts and bitmapped fonts.

✔ Tips

■ Traditionally, Mac OS files could contain two parts, or *forks*: a *resource fork* and a *data fork*. This causes incompatibility problems with non-Mac OS systems, which do not support a file's resource fork. Data fork suitcase format fonts don't have resource forks, so they can work on a variety of computer platforms.

■ OpenType font technology was developed by Adobe Systems, Inc. and Microsoft Corporation. Designed to be cross-platform, the same font files work on both Mac OS and Windows computers.

■ PostScript font technology was developed by Adobe Systems, Inc.

Font Locations

On a typical Mac OS X system, fonts can be installed in four or more places (**Table 1**). Where a font is installed determines who can use it.

- ◆ **User fonts** are installed in a user's Fonts folder (**Figure 1**). Each user can install, control, and access his or her own fonts. Fonts installed in a user's Fonts folder are available only to that user.

- ◆ **Local fonts** are installed in the Fonts folder for the startup disk (**Figure 2**). These fonts are accessible to all local users of the computer. Only an Admin user can modify the contents of this Fonts folder.

- ◆ **System fonts** are installed in the Fonts folder for the system (**Figure 3**). These fonts are installed by the Mac OS X installer and are used by the system. The contents of this Fonts folder should not be modified.

- ◆ **Classic fonts** are installed in the Fonts folder within the Mac OS 9.x System Folder (if Mac OS 9.x is installed). These are the only fonts accessible by the Classic environment, although Mac OS X can use these fonts, even when the Classic environment is not running.

- ◆ **Network fonts** are installed in the Fonts folder for the network. These fonts are accessible to all local area network users. This feature is normally used on network file servers, not the average user's computer. Only a network administrator can modify the contents of this Fonts folder.

Table 1

Font Installation Locations	
Font Use	**Font Folder**
User	HD/Users/UserName/Library/Fonts/
Local	HD/Library/Fonts/
System	HD/System/Library/Fonts/
Classic	HD/System Folder/Fonts
Network	Network/Library/Fonts/

Figure 1 User fonts are installed in the Fonts folder within the user's Library folder.

Figure 2 Local fonts are installed in the Fonts folder within the startup disk's Library folder.

Figure 3 System fonts are installed in the Fonts folder within the System's Library folder.

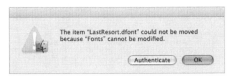

Figure 4 A dialog like this appears if you try to change a Fonts folder and do not have enough privileges.

Figure 5 If you have an Admin password, you can enter it in this dialog to complete the change.

Figure 6 To manually install a font, drag it into (or onto) the appropriate Fonts folder. This illustration shows a PostScript font file with its accompanying bitmap font file being installed.

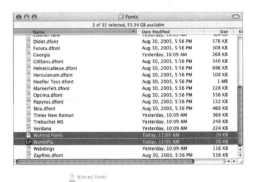

Figure 7 To manually uninstall a font, drag it out of the Fonts folder. This illustration shows the font installed in **Figure 6** being uninstalled.

✔ Tips

- Duplicate fonts are resolved based on where they are installed, in the following order: User, Local, Network, System, and Classic. For example, if the same font existed as both a User and System font, the User font would be used.

- Changes to the Fonts folder take effect when an application is opened.

- If you do not have the correct privileges to change a Fonts folder, a dialog like the one in **Figure 4** will appear. If you have an Admin password, you can click the Authenticate button and enter the password in the dialog that appears (**Figure 5**) to complete the change. Otherwise, click OK and ask a user with Admin privileges to do it for you.

- I cover Mac OS 9.x and the Classic environment in **Chapter 16**.

- You can use Font Book to easily install or uninstall a font. I tell you about this new Mac OS X utility starting on the next page.

To manually install a font

Drag all files that are part of the font into the appropriate Fonts folder (**Figure 6**).

To manually uninstall a font

Drag all files that are part of the font out of the Fonts folder they were installed in (**Figure 7**).

Font Book

Font Book is a new utility that's part of Mac OS X 10.3. It enables you to install, preview, search, activate, and deactivate fonts with an intuitive, easy-to-use interface.

Font Book organizes all of your fonts into *collections*, which are groups of fonts. Font Book comes preconfigured with several collections, but you can add, remove, or modify collections to meet your needs.

Within each collection is one or more fonts, each of which may contain one or more typefaces. Each typeface within a font is a slightly different version of the font—for example, bold, italic, or condensed.

Font Book makes it possible to turn groups of fonts or individual fonts on or off. This helps keep your applications' font menus and lists neat by letting you display only those fonts that you want to display.

✔ Tip

- The Font Book is fully integrated with the Font panel, which I discuss in detail later in this chapter.

To launch Font Book

Use one of the following techniques:

- ◆ Double-click the Font Book icon in the Applications folder (**Figure 8**).

- ◆ Choose Manage Fonts from the shortcut menu in the Font Panel (**Figure 36**).

Font Book's main window appears (**Figure 9**).

✔ Tip

- Another way to launch Font Book is to double-click a font file's icon. Doing so displays a font preview window like the one in **Figure 11**.

Figure 8 You can find Font Book in the Applications folder.

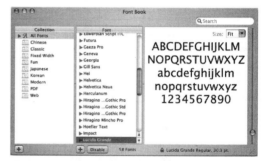

Figure 9 The main Font Book window lists collections and fonts and displays a font preview.

Figure 10 A folder containing the font files for a PostScript font, all ready to install.

Figure 11
Double-clicking a font file launches Font Book and opens a font preview window like this.

Figure 12 The font is installed and appears in the main Font Book window.

Figure 13 The Preferences window enables you to specify how certain features of Font Book should work.

Figure 14 A confirmation dialog like this one appears when you attempt to uninstall a font.

To install a font

1. Insert the disc containing the font files you want to install or copy the font files to your hard disk.

2. Launch Font Book.

3. Double-click one of the Font files (**Figure 10**). A font window like the one in **Figure 11** appears.

4. Click the Install Font button.

   The font files are copied or moved to the Fonts folder inside the Library folder for your account, thus making it available to you only. The name of the Font appears selected in the main Font Book window (**Figure 12**).

✔ Tips

■ You can change the default location for newly installed fonts. Choose Font Book > Preferences to display the Preferences window (**Figure 13**). Select one of the radio buttons in the top half of the window to specify whether fonts should be installed for you, all users, or Classic Mac OS. Close the window to save your settings.

■ You can also install a font by dragging the font's file icon(s) onto a collection name in the main Font Book window.

To uninstall a font

1. Select the name of the font in the Font column of the main Font Book window (**Figure 11**).

2. Press Delete.

3. A dialog sheet like the one in **Figure 14** appears. Click Remove.

   The font's files are moved to the Trash. Emptying the Trash removes them from your computer.

To see where fonts are installed

1. Click the triangle beside All Fonts to reveal the font locations. In **Figure 15**, there are only two locations—User and Computer—but your system can have more, depending on how it is configured.

2. Click the name of a location. A list of fonts in that location appears in the Fonts list (**Figure 16**).

✔ Tips

■ A font's location determines how it can be accessed, as discussed near the beginning of this chapter.

■ You can move a font from one location to another by dragging it from the Font list to the name of another location. For example, to make a user font available to all users, select User in the Collection list and drag the font from the Font list to Computer in the Collection list (**Figure 17**).

To view the fonts in a collection

In the Collection column of the main Font Book window, select the name of the collection you want to view.

The fonts in that collection appear in the Font column (**Figure 18**).

Figure 15
Clicking the triangle beside All Fonts displays a list of locations where fonts are installed.

Figure 16
When you select one of the locations, the Font list displays all of the fonts installed in that location.

Figure 17
You can move a font from one location to another by dragging it within the Font Book window.

Figure 18
To see the fonts in a collection, select the name of the collection in the Collection list.

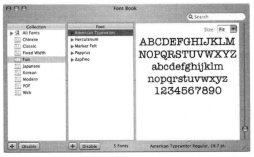

Figure 19 Select the name of a font to view the regular typeface characters of that font.

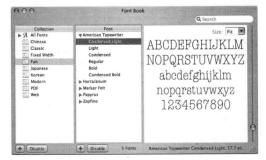

Figure 20 Select the name of a typeface to view that typeface's characters.

Figure 21 You can choose a font size from the Size drop-down list.

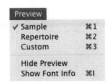

Figure 22 The Preview menu enables you to set preview area options.

To preview font or typeface characters

1. In the Collection list of the main Font Book window, select All Fonts or the name of the collection that the font is part of (**Figure 18**).

2. In the Font list, select the name of the font you want to preview. The characters for the regular typeface of the font appear on the right side of the window (**Figure 19**).

3. To see a specific typeface for the font, click the triangle to the left of the font name to display all typefaces. Then click the name of the typeface you want to see. Its characters appear on the right side of the window (**Figure 20**).

✔ Tips

- To change the size of characters in the preview part of the window, enter a value in the Size box, choose a value from the Size drop-down list (**Figure 21**), or drag the slider on the far right side of the window.

- To change the text that appears in the preview part of the window, choose one of the first three options on the Preview menu (**Figure 22**):

  ▲ **Sample** (⌘1) displays the characters shown throughout this chapter.

  ▲ **Repertoire** (⌘2) displays all characters in ASCII order.

  ▲ **Custom** (⌘3) enables you to specify your own sample text.

To add a collection

1. Click the Create a New Collection (+) button at the bottom of the Collection list in the main Font Book window.

2. A new untitled collection appears with its name selected (**Figure 23**). Enter a name for the collection, and press $\boxed{\text{Return}}$.

   The collection name appears in the list (**Figure 24**).

To add a font to a collection

1. In the Collection list of the main Font Book window, select All Fonts or the name of the collection that a font you want to add is part of (**Figure 18**).

2. Locate the font in the Font list.

3. Drag the font from the Font list onto the name of the collection you want to add it to (**Figure 25**). When you release the mouse button, the font is copied to that collection.

✔ Tip

■ Dragging a font from one collection to another does not duplicate the font's files on your computer. It just adds a reference to the font to the collection.

To remove a font from a collection

1. In the Collection list of the main Font Book window, select the name of the collection you want to modify.

2. In the Font list, select the font you want to remove from the collection.

3. Press $\boxed{\text{Delete}}$. A dialog like the one in **Figure 26** appears. Click Remove. The font is removed from the collection but remains installed on your computer.

Figure 23
An untitled collection appears in the Collection list with its name selected.

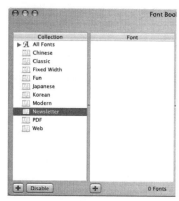

Figure 24
When you name the collection, it appears in alphabetical order in the Collection list.

Figure 25
Adding a font to a collection is a simple drag-and-drop operation.

Figure 26 Font Book confirms that you want to remove the font from the collection.

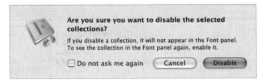

Figure 27 This dialog appears when you disable a collection ...

Figure 28 ... and this one appears when you disable a font within a collection.

To disable a collection

1. In the Collection list, select the name of the collection you want to disable.

2. Click the Disable button beneath the Collection list.

3. In the confirmation dialog that appears (**Figure 27**), click Disable.

✔ Tip

■ A disabled collection will not appear in the Font panel.

To disable a font in a collection

1. In the Collection list, select the name of the collection containing the font you want to disable.

2. In the Font list, select the font you want to disable.

3. Click the Disable button beneath the Font list.

4. In the confirmation dialog that appears (**Figure 28**), click Disable.

✔ Tip

■ When you disable a font in a collection, that font will not appear in the Font panel when the collection is selected.

To completely disable a font

1. In the Collection list, select All Fonts.

2. In the Font list, select the font you want to disable.

3. Click the Disable button beneath the Font list.

4. In the confirmation dialog that appears (**Figure 29**), click Disable.

✔ Tips

■ Using this technique to disable a font removes it from all font menus and lists in all applications—not just the Font panel.

■ If an application is running when you disable a font, you may have to restart it to see the change in its font menu or lists.

To enable a collection

1. In the Collection list, select the name of the disabled collection that you want to enable.

2. Click the Enable button beneath the Collection list (**Figure 30**). The collection is enabled.

To enable a font

1. If the font is disabled in a collection, in the Collection list, select the collection the font is part of.

   or

   If the font is disabled systemwide, in the Collection list, select All Fonts.

2. In the Font list, select the font that is disabled.

3. Click the Enable button beneath the Font list (**Figure 31**). The font is enabled.

Figure 29 Disabling a font systemwide prevents the font from appearing in any application's font menus or lists.

Figure 30 When you select a disabled collection, the Enable button appears beneath the Collection list.

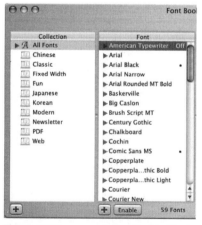

Figure 31 When you select a disabled font, the Enable button appears beneath the Font list.

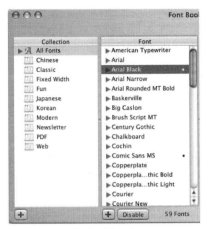

Figure 32 A bullet beside a font name indicates that the font has a conflict.

Figure 33 When you reveal the font's type-faces, you can see the problem: duplicates.

To resolve font conflicts

1. In the Collection list, select All Fonts.

2. Locate and select a font with a bullet character to the right of its name (**Figure 32**).

3. If necessary, click the triangle to the left of the font name to display its typefaces. One or more of them should have bullet characters beside them.

4. Select a typeface with a bullet character beside it (**Figure 33**).

5. Click Disable.

6. In the confirmation dialog that appears (**Figure 29**), click Disable.

✔ Tips

- Font conflicts like the one in **Figures 31, 32,** and **33** are often caused when multiple copies of a font or typeface are installed in the same computer but in different places. Disabling one of the copies stops the conflict.

- Keep in mind that if multiple users access your computer, disabling a conflicting font that is installed for the Computer (rather than for the User) may make that font unavailable for other users.

- If you prefer (and have the correct privileges), you can delete a duplicate typeface. Follow steps 1 through 4 above, then press ⎡Delete⎤. Click Remove in the confirmation dialog that appears (**Figure 14**).

The Font Panel

The Font panel (**Figure 35**), which is fully integrated with Font Book, offers a standard interface for formatting font characters in a document. In Mac OS X 10.3, the Font panel has been improved to offer more formatting options.

In this part of the chapter, I explain how to use the Font panel to format text.

✔ Tips

- This chapter looks at the Font panel as it appears in TextEdit, the text editor that comes with Mac OS X. I discuss TextEdit in detail in **Chapter 7**.

- The Font panel is only available in Carbon and Cocoa applications—those written to take advantage of Apple-created libraries of code. That's why you'll find the Font panel in only some applications.

- Although the Font panel has limited font management capabilities, the new Font Book application offers far more flexibility for managing fonts. I tell you about Font Book earlier in this chapter.

To open TextEdit's Font panel

With TextEdit active, choose Format > Font > Show Fonts (**Figure 34**) or press ⌘T. The Font panel appears (**Figure 35**).

✔ Tips

- The command to open the Font panel in other applications that support it is similar.

- You can open Font Book from within the Font panel by choosing Manage Fonts from the shortcut menu (**Figure 36**).

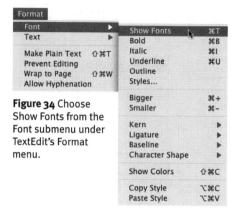

Figure 34 Choose Show Fonts from the Font submenu under TextEdit's Format menu.

Figure 35 TextEdit's Font panel.

Figure 36 The Font panel's shortcut menu.

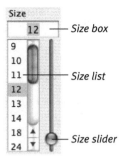

Figure 37 The Font panel offers three different ways to set the font size.

To apply basic font formatting

1. Open the Font panel (**Figure 35**).

2. Select a collection from the Collections list.

3. Select a font family from the Family list.

4. Select a style from the Typeface list.

5. Set the font size by entering a value in the Size box, selecting a size from the Size list, or dragging the Size slider up or down (**Figure 37**).

   The changes you make are applied to selected text or to text typed at the insertion point.

✔ Tips

- The styles that appear in the Typeface list vary depending on the font selected in the Family list. Some font families offer more styles than others.

- *Oblique* is similar to italic. *Light, regular, medium, bold,* and *black* refer to font weights or boldness.

APPLYING BASIC FONT FORMATTING

To apply font effects

Use the effects controls at the top of the Font Panel window (**Figure 38**) to apply other font formatting options to selected text or start formatting at the insertion point:

◆ **Text Underline** offers four underline options: None, Single, Double, and Color. If you choose Color, you can use the Colors panel that appears (**Figure 39**) to set the underline color.

◆ **Text Strikethrough** offers four strike-through options: None, Single, Double, and Color. If you choose Color, you can use the Colors panel that appears (**Figure 39**) to set the strikethrough color.

◆ **Text Color** enables you to set the color of text. When you click this button, the Colors panel appears (**Figure 39**) so you can choose a color for text.

◆ **Document Color** enables you to set the color of the document background. When you click this button, the Colors panel appears (**Figure 39**) so you can choose a color for the entire document's background.

◆ **Text Shadow** adds a shadow to text characters (**Figure 40**).

◆ **Shadow Opacity** makes an applied shadow darker or lighter. Drag the slider to the right or left.

◆ **Shadow Blur** makes the shadow sharper or more blurry. Drag the slider to the right or left.

◆ **Shadow Offset** moves the shadow closer to or farther from the text. Drag the slider to the right or left.

◆ **Shadow Angle** changes the position of the shadow in relation to the text. (It's like moving the light source.) Drag the dial around to the desired angle.

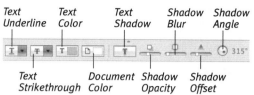

Text Underline   Text Color   Text Shadow   Shadow Blur   Shadow Angle

Text Strikethrough   Document Color   Shadow Opacity   Shadow Offset

Figure 38 Along the top of the Font panel, you'll find a collection of effects menus, buttons, and controls.

Figure 39
The Colors panel enables you to select a color.

The Shadow Knows...

Figure 40 It's easy to apply a shadow to text characters.

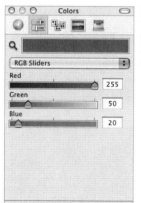

Figure 41
The Colors panel displaying the Color Sliders color model.

Figure 42
The Colors panel displaying the Color Palettes color model.

Figure 43
The Colors panel displaying the Image Palettes color model.

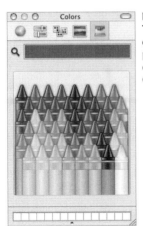

Figure 44
The Colors panel displaying my personal favorite color model: Crayons.

To use the Colors panel

1. Click the icon along the top of the Colors panel to select one of the color models.

2. How you choose a color depends on the model you selected:

   ▲ **Color Wheel** (**Figure 39**) displays a circle of color. Click inside the circle to choose a color. You can drag the vertical slider up or down to change the brightness.

   ▲ **Color Sliders** (**Figure 41**) displays several sliders you can use to change color values. Start by selecting a slider group from the pop-up menu, then move the sliders to create a color.

   ▲ **Color Palettes** (**Figure 42**) displays clickable color samples. Choose a palette from the List pop-up menu, then click the color you want.

   ▲ **Image Palettes** (**Figure 43**) displays colors from an image. Click a color to select it.

   ▲ **Crayons** (**Figure 44**) displays different colored crayons. Click a crayon to choose its color.

   The color of the selected item changes immediately.

✔ Tip

■ You can use the color wells at the bottom of the Colors panel to store frequently used colors. Then, when you open the Colors panel, simply click a stored color to apply it.

USING THE COLORS PANEL

The Character Palette

The Character Palette (**Figure 46**) enables you to type any character in any language for which a font is installed in your computer, including Asian and eastern European languages. It is especially useful for typing special characters, like mathematical symbols, arrows, and dingbats characters.

The Character Palette is available in some Mac OS X applications, including TextEdit. But it can also be displayed for any application by choosing it from the Input menu at the right side of the menu bar (**Figure 45**). Once displayed, any character you click is inserted in the current document, at the insertion point.

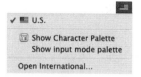

Figure 45 The Input menu.

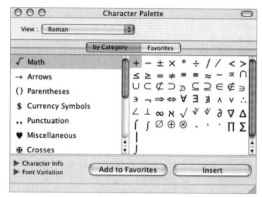

Figure 46 The Character Palette, which displays characters viewed by category.

✔ Tips

- Although you can enter foreign language characters into documents on your Macintosh, those characters may not appear properly when your documents are viewed on other computers.

- The Font panel is only available in Carbon and Cocoa applications—those written to take advantage of Apple-created libraries of code. That's why you'll find the Font panel in only some applications.

To display the Character Palette

Choose Show Character Palette from the Input menu (**Figure 45**). The Character Palette appears (**Figure 46**).

✔ Tips

- If the Input menu does not appear on your menu bar, you need to enable it in the International preferences pane. I explain how in **Chapter 18**.

Figure 47
Use this pop-up menu to choose the characters to view.

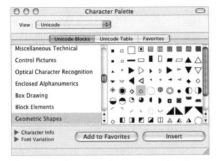

Figure 48 When you choose an option from the View pop-up menu, the options in the Character Palette change.

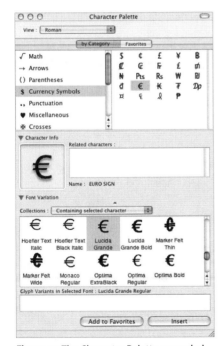

Figure 49 The Character Palette expanded to show Character Info and Font Variation.

To insert a character with the Character Palette

1. In a document window, position the insertion point where you want the character to appear.

2. Display the Character Palette (**Figure 46**).

3. Choose a character group from the View pop-up menu (**Figure 47**). The window may change to offer different options (**Figure 48**).

4. Click a button above the scrolling lists to view characters in a specific order.

5. Select one of the options in the left scrolling list.

6. Select one of the characters in the right scrolling list.

7. Click Insert. The character is inserted at the insertion point in your document.

✔ Tips

- To display information about the selected character, click the triangle beside Character Info to reveal it (**Figure 49**).

- To specify a font for the character, click the triangle beside Font Variation to display the character in multiple fonts. You can then click the character in the font you want.

USING THE CHARACTER PALETTE

Printing & Faxing

Printing & Faxing

On a Mac OS system, printing and faxing is handled by the operating system rather than individual applications. You choose the Print command in the application that created the document you want to print. Mac OS steps in, displaying the Print dialog and telling the application how to send information to the printer or faxmodem. There are two main benefits to this:

◆ If you can print documents created with one application, you can probably print documents created with any application.

◆ The Page Setup and Print dialogs look very much the same in every application.

This chapter covers most aspects of printing and faxing documents on a computer running Mac OS X.

✔ Tip

■ The ability to fax documents from within the Print dialog is brand new in Mac OS X 10.3.

To print (an overview)

1. Add your printer to the Printer List.

2. Open the document that you want to print.

3. If desired, set options in the Page Setup dialog, and click OK.

4. Set options in the Print dialog, and click Print or Fax.

Printer Drivers

A *printer driver* is software that Mac OS uses to communicate with a specific kind of printer. It contains information about the printer and instructions for using it. You can't open and read a printer driver, but your computer can.

There are basically two kinds of printers:

◆ A **PostScript** printer uses PostScript technology developed by Adobe Systems. Inside the printer is a *PostScript interpreter*, which can process PostScript language commands to print high-quality text and graphics. Examples of PostScript printers include most Apple LaserWriter printers and Hewlett-Packard LaserJet printers.

◆ A **non-PostScript** printer relies on the computer to send it all of the instructions it needs for printing text and graphics. It cannot process PostScript commands. Examples of non-PostScript printers include Apple ImageWriters and Style-Writers, Hewlett-Packard DeskJet printers, and most Epson Stylus printers. Non-PostScript printers are generally more common for home and small business use, primarily because they are less expensive than PostScript printers. Their print quality is quite acceptable for most purposes.

A standard installation of Mac OS X installs many commonly used printer drivers. When you buy a printer, it should come with a CD that includes its printer driver software; if your computer does not recognize your printer, you'll need to install this software to use it.

✔ Tips

■ If you do not have a printer driver for your printer, you may not be able to print.

■ To install a printer driver, follow the instructions that came with its installer or installation disc.

■ If you need to install printer driver software for your printer, make sure it is Mac OS X compatible. If your printer did not come with Mac OS X compatible printer software, you may be able to get it from the printer manufacturer's Web site.

Figure 1 Printer Setup Utility can be found in the Utilities folder inside the Applications folder.

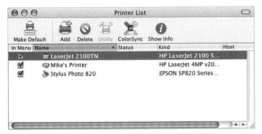

Figure 2 The Printer List window with three printers.

Printer Setup Utility

Printer Setup Utility (**Figure 1**) is an application that enables you to manage printers and print jobs. It has two main components:

◆ **Printer List** window (**Figure 2**) lists all of the printers your computer "sees." Use this window to select and configure printers.

◆ **Printer Queue** window (**Figure 68** and **69**) lists all the print jobs sent to a specific printer. Use this window to check the status of and cancel print jobs, as discussed later in this chapter.

✔ Tip

■ Printer Setup Utility is a new version of Print Center, which was introduced in the original release of Mac OS X.

To open Printer Setup Utility

1. Open the Utilities folder inside your Applications folder.

2. Double-click the Printer Setup Utility icon (**Figure 1**).

The Printer List window (**Figure 2**) should appear automatically. If it does not, follow the instructions below to display it.

✔ Tip

■ You can also open Printer Setup Utility by choosing Edit Printer List from the Printer pop-up menu (**Figure 29**) in the Print dialog.

To display the Printer List window

Choose View > Show Printer List, or press ⌃ ⌘ L.

The Printer List window appears (**Figure 2**).

To add a printer

1. Choose Printers > Add Printer (**Figure 3**).

   or

   Click the Add button in the Printer List window (**Figure 2**).

2. A dialog sheet appears. Choose an option from the top pop-up menu (**Figure 4**) to indicate the type of printer connection. The dialog sheet changes to offer appropriate options; **Figures 5** through **8** show examples.

3. If you chose AppleTalk or Epson Apple-Talk, choose a network option from the second pop-up menu. Then wait while Printer Setup Utility looks for printers and displays a list of what it finds (**Figure 5**). Select the printer you want to add, and click Add.

   or

   If you chose IP Printing, choose an option from the Printer Type pop-up menu and set other options in the dialog (**Figure 6**). Then click Add.

   or

   If you chose Open Directory, Rendezvous, USB, Epson FireWire, Epson USB, or Lexmark Inkjet Networking, Printer Setup Utility displays a list of printers connected to the computer (**Figure 7**). Select the printer you want to add, set other options if required, and click Add.

   or

   If you chose Windows Printing, choose a network option from the second pop-up menu, select a workgroup from the list, and click Choose. Select a computer in the workgroup, and click Choose again. Then log into the computer, choose a printer in the list (**Figure 8**), and click Add.

Figure 3
The Printers menu includes commands for working with the Printer List and printers.

Figure 4
Use this pop-up menu to choose the type of printer connection.

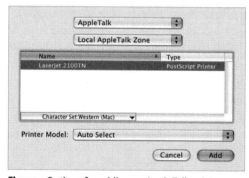

Figure 5 Options for adding an AppleTalk printer ...

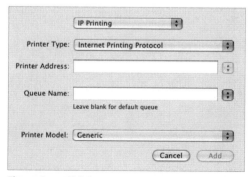

Figure 6 ...an IP Printer ...

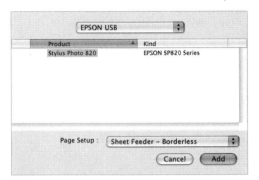

Figure 7 ... an Epson USB printer ...

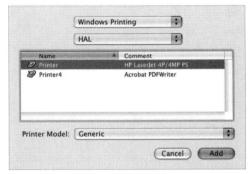

Figure 8 ... and a printer connected to a Windows computer.

or

If you chose Epson TCP/IP, enter an IP address for the printer and click Verify. Then select the printer in the list and click Add.

or

If you chose hp IP Printing you can use two different techniques to add the printer:

▲ Click the Auto button, then click Discover, select a printer in the list, and click Add.

▲ Click the Manual button, enter the IP address for the printer, click Connect, and click Add.

The printer appears in the Printer List window (**Figure 2**).

✔ Tips

■ You only have to add a printer if it does not already appear in the Printer List window (**Figure 2**). This needs to be done only once; Mac OS will remember all printers that you add.

■ In step 3, if you're not sure what options to select or enter for a network printer, ask your network administrator.

■ If your printer is properly connected but it does not appear in step 3 (**Figures 5**, **7**, and **8**), you may have to install printer driver software for it. Printer drivers are discussed earlier in this chapter.

ADDING PRINTERS

To delete a printer

1. In the Printer List window (**Figure 2**), select the printer you want to delete.

2. Choose Printers > Delete Selected Printers (**Figure 3**), or press ⌃⌘Delete.

   or

   Click the Delete button in the Printer List window (**Figure 2**).

   The printer is removed from the list.

To set the default printer

1. In the Printer list window (**Figure 2**), select the printer you want to set as the default.

2. Choose Printers > Make Default (**Figure 3**), or press ⌃⌘D.

   The name of the printer you selected becomes bold, indicating that it is the default printer.

✔ Tip

■ The default printer is the one that is automatically chosen when you open the Print dialog.

To include printers in the Printers pop-up menu

In the Printer list window, turn on the check box for each printer you want to appear in the Printer pop-up menu in the Print dialog (**Figure 29**).

✔ Tip

■ You cannot turn off the check box for the default printer.

Figure 9 Select the printer you want to configure.

Figure 10 If a list of printers appears, select the one you want to configure, and click OK.

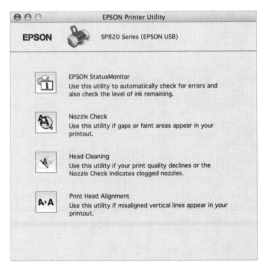

Figure 11 Here are the configuration options for an Epson Stylus Photo 820 printer. Configuration options for other printers will be different.

To configure a printer

1. Select the printer you want to configure in the Printer List window (**Figure 9**).

2. Choose Printers > Configure Printer (**Figure 3**), or click the Utility button in the Printer List window (**Figure 9**).

   Printer Setup Utility launches the configuration software for your printer. In my case, it launches Epson Printer Utility.

3. If a list of printers appears (**Figure 10**), select the printer you want to configure, and click OK.

4. Follow the instructions that appear in the configuration window to configure or maintain your printer. **Figure 11** shows an example of the options available for an Epson Stylus Photo 820 printer in the Epson Printer Utility window.

5. When you are finished configuring the printer, close the configuration window.

✔ Tips

- In step 2, if the Configure Printer command or Utility button in the Printer List window is gray or faded (**Figure 2**), the printer cannot be configured through Printer Setup Utility.

- It's not possible to show all configuration options for all printers. The instructions and illustrations here should be enough to get you started with your printer. Consult the manual that came with your printer for more information.

CONFIGURING PRINTERS

To view & change printer info

1. In the Printer List window, select the printer you want to view or change information for (**Figure 2**).

2. Choose Printers > Show Info (**Figure 3**), press ⌃⌘I, or click the Show Info button in the Printer List window (**Figure 9**). The Printer Info window for the printer appears (**Figure 12**).

3. Choose an option from the pop-up menu at the top of the dialog to view and set different options:

   ▲ **Name & Location (Figure 12)** enables you to view or change the name and location of the printer.

   ▲ **Printer Model (Figure 13)** enables you to set the brand and model for the printer.

   ▲ **Installable Options (Figure 14)** enables you to set preferences for options specific to your printer.

4. Click Apply Changes to save any changes you made.

5. Click the Printer Info window's close box to dismiss it.

✔ Tip

■ The options that appear in the Installable Options window (**Figure 14**) will vary from one printer to another.

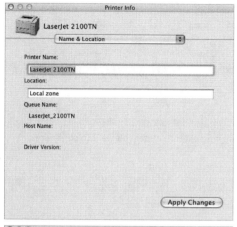

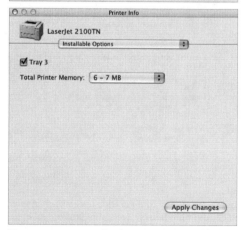

Figures 12, 13, & 14 The three panes of the Printer Info window: Name & Location (top), Printer Model (middle), and Installable Options (bottom).

Figure 15
Choose System
Preferences
from the Apple
menu.

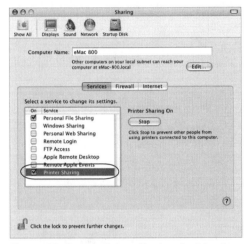

Figure 16 Turn on the Printer Sharing check box in
the Sharing preferences pane.

Figure 17 Your computer's name appears in the Host
column.

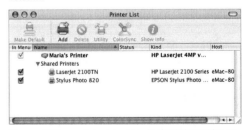

Figure 18 Your printers appear in the Printer List on
other computers.

To share a printer with other network users

1. Choose Apple > System Preferences (**Figure 15**), or click the System Preferences icon in the Dock.

2. In the System Preferences window that appears, click the Sharing icon.

3. If necessary, click the Services button to display its options (**Figure 16**).

4. Turn on the check box beside Printer Sharing in the Service list.

5. To share your printers with Windows users, turn on the Windows Sharing check box.

6. Choose System Preferences > Quit System Preferences or press ⌘Q to save your settings and dismiss System Preferences.

   Two things happen:

   ▲ The name of your computer appears in the Host column of the Printers List in Printer Setup Utility (**Figure 17**).

   ▲ The names of your shared printers appear in the Printers List in Printer Setup Utility for other computers on the network (**Figure 18**) and in Printer pop-up menu in the Print dialog (**Figure 29**).

✔ Tip

■ I tell you more about networking and the Sharing preferences pane in **Chapter** 14.

SHARING PRINTERS

The Page Setup Dialog

The Page Setup dialog (**Figures 20** and **24**) lets you set page options prior to printing, including the printer the document should be formatted for, paper size, orientation, and scale.

To open the Page Setup dialog

Choose File > Page Setup (**Figures 19a**, **19b**, and **19c**). The Page Attributes options of the Page Setup dialog appears (**Figure 20**).

To set Page Attributes

1. If necessary, choose Page Attributes from the Settings pop-up menu (**Figure 21**) in the Page Setup dialog to display Page Attributes options (**Figure 20**).

2. Set options as desired:
   ▲ To format the document for a specific printer, choose the printer from the Format For pop-up menu (**Figure 22**).
   ▲ To change the paper size, choose an option from the Paper Size pop-up menu (**Figure 23**).
   ▲ To change the page orientation, click the Orientation option you want.
   ▲ To change the print scale, enter a scaling percentage in the Scale box.

3. Click OK to save your settings and dismiss the Page Setup dialog.

✔ Tips

■ The Format for pop-up menu (**Figure 22**) should list all of the printers that appear in the Printer Setup Utility's Printer List window (**Figure 2**), with a submenu that lists any shared printers.

■ Options in step 2 vary depending on the printer selected from the Format for pop-up menu (**Figure 22**). Additional options may be available for your printer; check your printer's documentation for details.

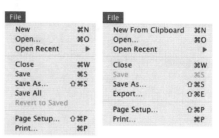

Figures 19a, 19b, & 19c
The Page Setup and Print commands appear on most File menus, including TextEdit (top left), Preview (top right), and Safari (bottom left).

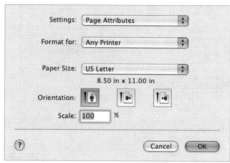

Figure 20 The Page Setup dialog sheet.

Figure 21
The Settings pop-up menu.

Figure 22
The Format for pop-up menu lists all of your printers and includes a submenu for shared printers.

Figure 23
The Paper Size pop-up menu when Any Printer is chosen from the Format for pop-up menu.

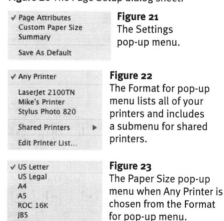

SETTING PAGE ATTRIBUTE OPTIONS

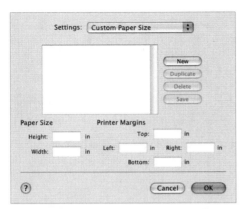

Figure 24 The Custom Paper Size options of the Page Setup dialog.

Figure 25 Click New to create an untitled paper size.

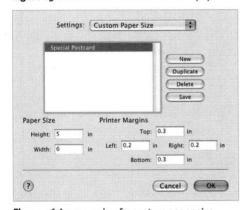

Figure 26 An example of a custom paper size.

Figure 27 Custom paper sizes appear at the bottom of the Paper Size pop-up menu.

To add a custom paper size

1. If necessary, choose Custom Paper Size from the Settings pop-up menu (**Figure 21**) in the Page Setup dialog to display Custom Paper Size options (**Figure 24**).

2. Click the New button.

3. An untitled paper size appears in the list window (**Figure 25**). Enter a name for the size and press ⌐Return⌐.

4. Enter paper size and printer margin measurements in the appropriate boxes at the bottom of the dialog. **Figure 26** shows what it might look like with sizes set for a custom postcard.

5. Click Save to save your settings.

6. Repeat Steps 2 through 5 for each custom paper size you want to create.

7. Click OK to dismiss the Page Setup dialog.

✔ Tips

- Custom paper sizes appear at the bottom of the Paper Size pop-up menu (**Figure 27**).

- To delete a custom paper size, select it in the Custom Paper Size pane of the Page Setup dialog (**Figure 26**) and click Delete.

ADDING CUSTOM PAPER SIZES

Setting Options in the Print Dialog

The Print dialog enables you to set printing options and send the print job to the printer. Like the Page Setup dialog, the Print dialog is a standard dialog, but two things can cause its appearance and options to vary:

◆ Print options vary depending on the selected printer.

◆ Additional options may be offered by specific applications.

This section explains how to set the options available for most printers and applications.

✔ Tips

■ If your Print dialog includes options that are not covered here, consult the printer's documentation.

■ For information about using Print options specific to an application, consult the application's documentation.

■ If an application offers application-specific print options, the application name will appear on the third pop-up menu (**Figures 30a** and **30b**) in the print dialog. For example, a Microsoft Word option on that menu would enable you to set Word-specific options.

To open the Print dialog

Choose File > Print (**Figures 19a**, **19b**, and **19c**), or press ⌃⌘P. The Copies & Pages pane of the Print dialog appears (**Figure 28**).

Figure 28 The Copies & Pages pane of the Print dialog.

Figure 29
The Printer
pop-up menu.

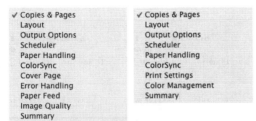

Figures 30a & 30b The pop-up menu beneath the Presets pop-up menu offers different options depending on the printer that is selected. The menu on the left is for a Hewlett-Packard LaserJet printer connected via network and the menu on the right is for an Epson Stylus Color printer connected directly to the computer via USB.

To select a printer

In the Print dialog (**Figure 28**) choose a printer from the Printer pop-up menu (**Figure 29**).

✔ Tips

■ The Printer pop-up menu (**Figure 29**) should list all of the printers that appear in the Printer Setup Utility's Printer List window (**Figure 2**), with a submenu that lists any shared printers.

■ Choosing Edit Printer List from the Printer pop-up menu (**Figure 29**) opens Printer Setup Utility, which is discussed earlier in this chapter.

To set Copies & Pages options

1. In the Print dialog, choose Copies & Pages from the third pop-up menu (**Figure 30a** or **30b**) to display Copies & Pages options (**Figure 28**).

2. In the Copies field, enter the number of copies of the document to print.

3. To collate multiple copies, turn on the Collated check box.

4. In the Pages area, select either the All radio button to print all pages or enter values in the From and To fields to print specific pages.

To set Layout options

1. In the Print dialog, choose Layout from the third pop-up menu (**Figure 30a** or **30b**) to display Layout options (**Figure 31**).

2. To set the number of pages that should appear on each sheet of paper, choose an option from the Pages per Sheet pop-up menu (**Figure 32**). The preview area of the dialog changes accordingly (**Figure 33**).

3. To indicate the order in which multiple pages should print on each sheet of paper, select a Layout Direction option. The preview area of the dialog changes accordingly (**Figure 33**).

4. To place a border around each page, choose an option from the Border pop-up menu (**Figure 34**).

To set Output options

1. In the Print dialog, choose Output Options from the third pop-up menu (**Figure 30a** or **30b**) to display the Output Options pane (**Figure 35**).

2. To save the document as a file (instead of printing it), turn on the Save as File check box, then choose an option from the Format pop-up menu:

    ▲ **PDF** creates a Portable Document Format (PDF) file that can be read with Preview on Mac OS X or Adobe Acrobat Reader on any computer.

    ▲ **PostScript** writes PostScript language code to a file that can then be downloaded to and interpreted by a PostScript printer or imagesetter.

✔ Tips

■ When you turn on the Save as File check box, the Print button in the Print dialog turns into a Save button.

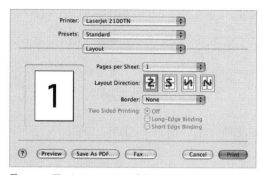

Figure 31 The Layout pane of the Print dialog.

Figure 32
The Pages per Sheet pop-up menu.

Figure 33
The Preview area indicates the number of pages to be printed per sheet, as well as the page order.

Figure 34
The Border pop-up menu.

Figure 35 The Output Options pane of the Print dialog.

■ Another way to create a PDF file is to click the Save As PDF button. I explain how later in this chapter.

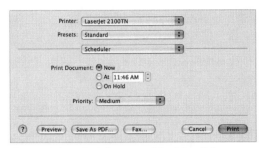

Figure 36 The Scheduler pane of the Print dialog.

Figure 37
Use the Priority pop-up menu to tell the printer how important your print job is.

To schedule a print job

1. In the Print dialog, choose Scheduler from the third pop-up menu (**Figure 30a** or **30b**) to display the Scheduler pane (**Figure 36**).

2. Select one of the Print Document options:

   ▲ **Now** prints the document immediately.

   ▲ **At** enables you to specify a time at which the job should be printed. Be sure to enter a time in the box beside this option.

   ▲ **On Hold** sends the document to the print queue on hold. You must manually release the document for printing for it to print.

3. Choose one of the options from the Priority pop-up menu (**Figure 37**).

✔ Tips

■ The ability to set scheduling options for a print job is brand new in Mac OS X 10.3.

■ The Priority option in step 3 determines when your print job will print when you send it to a printer that already has print jobs waiting in the queue.

■ If you're one of many people printing to a shared network printer, don't abuse the Priority feature by setting the highest priority for all of your documents. Believe it or not, other people print important stuff, too!

■ I tell you about print queues, including how to work with print jobs that are on hold, later in this chapter.

To set Paper Handling options

1. In the Print dialog, choose Paper Handling from the third pop-up menu (**Figure 30a** or **30b**) to display the Paper Handling pane (**Figure 38**).

2. To print pages in reverse order (last page first), turn on the Reverse page order check box.

3. Select one of the Print options:
   ▲ **All pages** prints all pages.
   ▲ **Odd numbered pages** prints only odd numbered pages.
   ▲ **Even numbered pages** prints only even numbered pages.

✔ Tips

- Paper Handling options are brand new in Mac OS X 10.3.

- The Reverse page order option is useful if your printer places documents face up in the printer tray when printed. In fact, if your printer does this, this option may already be turned on by default.

- Some paper handling options may also be offered in application-specific print settings. For example, Microsoft Word enables you to print just odd or just even pages.

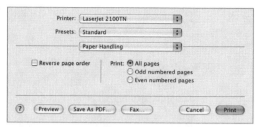

Figure 38 The Paper Handling pane of the Print dialog.

SETTING PAPER HANDLING OPTIONS

Figure 39 The ColorSync preferences pane in the Print dialog.

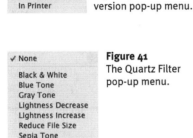

Figure 40 The Color Conversion pop-up menu.

Figure 41
The Quartz Filter pop-up menu.

To set ColorSync options

1. In the Print dialog, choose ColorSync from the third pop-up menu (**Figure 30a** or **30b**) to display the ColorSync pane (**Figure 39**).

2. Choose an option from the Color Conversion pop-up menu (**Figure 40**):

   ▲ **Standard** tells the application you're using to control the color.

   ▲ **In Printer** tells the printer to control the color.

3. If desired, choose an option from the Quartz Filter pop-up menu (**Figure 41**).

✔ Tips

■ ColorSync is a color matching technology that enables you to see accurate color on screen for documents that you print.

■ Quartz filters can modify printer output by adjusting color, adding visual effects, or changing resolution.

■ I discuss ColorSync and the ColorSync Utility briefly in **Chapter 19**.

■ To learn more about ColorSync, visit www.apple.com/colorsync/.

SETTING **C**OLOR**S**YNC **O**PTIONS

To set Cover Page options

1. In the Print dialog, choose Cover Page from the third pop-up menu (**Figure 30a**) to display Cover Page options (**Figure 42**).

2. Select one of the Print Cover Page options:

   ▲ **None** does not print a cover page. If you select this option, you can skip the remaining steps.

   ▲ **Before Document** prints a cover page at the beginning of the document.

   ▲ **After Document** prints a cover page at the end of the document.

3. Choose an option from the Cover Page Type pop-up menu (**Figure 43**).

4. If desired, enter information in the Billing Info box. Whatever you enter will print on the cover page.

✔ Tips

■ A cover page is a single sheet of information about the print job that can be printed at the beginning or end of the job.

■ Cover pages waste paper! If you don't need a cover page, don't print one!

■ The Cover Page options are not available for all printers.

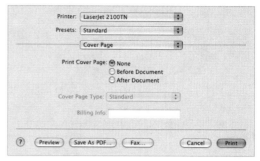

Figure 42 The Cover Page pane of the Print dialog.

✔ Standard	**Figure 43**
Classified	If you indicate that you
Confidential	want to print a cover
Secret	page, you can choose
Top Secret	from several formats.
Unclassified	

Figure 44 The Error Handling pane of the Print dialog.

Figure 45 The Paper Feed pane of the Print dialog.

Figure 46
Use this pop-up menu to choose the paper source.

To set Error Handling options

1. In the Print dialog, choose Error Handling from the third pop-up menu (**Figure 30a**) to display Error Handling options (**Figure 44**).

2. To specify how the printer should report PostScript errors, select one of the PostScript Errors options.

3. To specify how the printer should handle an out-of-paper situation for a multiple-tray printer, select one of the Tray Switching options.

✔ Tips

■ These options are only available for PostScript printers.

■ Tray switching options are only available for printers with multiple paper trays.

To set Paper Feed options

1. In the Print dialog, choose Paper Feed from the third pop-up menu (**Figure 30a**) to display Paper Feed options (**Figure 45**).

2. To specify how paper trays should be used for paper feed, select one of the radio buttons.

3. To specify which paper tray(s) should be used for paper feed, choose options from the pop-up menu(s) (**Figure 46**).

✔ Tip

■ The options offered in the Paper Feed pane of the Print dialog (**Figure 45**) vary depending on your printer. The options here are for an HP LaserJet 2100TN printer.

To set Image Quality options

1. In the Print dialog, choose Image Quality from the third pop-up menu (**Figure 30a**) to display Image Quality options (**Figure 47**).

2. Use the pop-up menus to set image quality options.

✔ Tips

- The options offered in the Image Quality pane of the Print dialog (**Figure 47**) vary depending on your printer. The options here are for an HP LaserJet 2100TN printer.

- To get more information about image quality options offered by your printer, consult the manual that came with your printer.

To set Print Settings options

1. In the Print dialog, choose Print Settings from the third pop-up menu (**Figure 30b**) to display the Print Settings pane (**Figure 48**).

2. Select the type of paper you will print on from the Media Type pop-up menu (**Figure 49**).

3. For a color printer, select an Ink option.

4. Set Mode options as desired. These options vary from printer to printer; check the documentation that came with your printer for details.

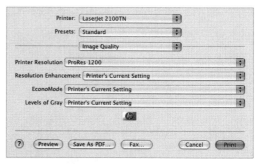

Figure 47 The Image Quality pane of the Print dialog for an HP LaserJet 2100TN printer.

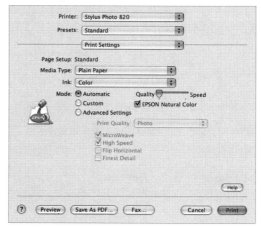

Figure 48 The Print Settings pane of the Print dialog for an Epson Stylus Photo printer.

✓ Plain Paper
Bright White Paper
360dpi Ink Jet Paper
Photo Quality Ink Jet Paper
Matte Paper – Heavyweight
Photo Paper
Glossy Photo Paper
Premium Glossy Photo Paper
Photo Quality Glossy Film
Ink Jet Transparencies
ColorLife Photo Paper
Premium Luster Photo Paper
Premium Semigloss Photo Paper

Figure 49
The Media Type pop-up menu for an Epson Stylus Photo printer.

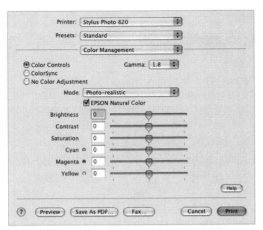

Figure 50 The Color Management pane of the Print dialog with Color Controls selected.

To set Color Management options

1. In the Print dialog, choose Color Management from the third pop-up menu (**Figure 30b**) to display Color Management options (**Figure 50**).

2. To indicate the color management method, select one of the radio buttons near the top of the pane.

3. If you selected Color Controls, set options in the dialog as desired.

✔ Tips

- Color management methods and options are far beyond the scope of this book.

- ColorSync is discussed in **Chapter 19**.

SETTING COLOR MANAGEMENT OPTIONS

To save settings as a preset

1. In the Print dialog (**Figure 28**), choose Save As from the Presets pop-up menu (**Figure 51**).

2. Enter a name for the settings in the Save Preset dialog that appears (**Figure 52**).

3. Click OK.

   The name you entered is added to the Presets pop-up menu and chosen (**Figure 53**).

✔ Tip

■ It's a good idea to save settings if you often have to change the Print dialog's settings. This can save time when you need to print.

To save changes to preset settings

In the Print dialog (**Figure 28**), choose Save from the Presets pop-up menu (**Figure 53**). Your changes to the preset settings are saved.

To use preset settings

In the Print dialog (**Figure 28**), choose the name of the preset settings you want to use from the Presets pop-up menu (**Figure 54**).

All Print dialog settings are set according to the saved settings.

To delete a preset setting

1. In the Print dialog (**Figures 28**), choose the name of the preset settings you want to delete from the Presets pop-up menu (**Figure 53**).

2. Choose Delete from the Presets pop-up menu (**Figure 53**).

   The preset setting is deleted.

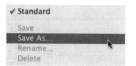

Figure 51 Choose Save As from the Presets pop-up menu.

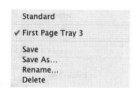

Figure 52 The Save Preset dialog.

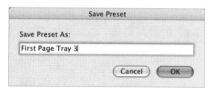

Figure 53 The preset is added to the menu and chosen as the current preset.

Figure 54 The Preset pop-up menu with several presets added.

WORKING WITH PRESETS

Figure 55 The Preview button displays the document in a Preview window. You can use controls in the window's toolbar or commands in the View menu to scroll through document contents.

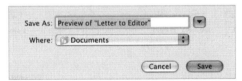

Figure 56 Use a standard Save Location dialog to save the document as a PDF file.

Previewing Documents

The Print dialog enables you to create and view previews of your documents. You might want to use this feature to check the appearance of a document before printing it.

To preview a document

1. Set options as desired in the Print dialog's panes.

2. In the Print dialog (**Figure 28**), click the Preview button. The Print dialog disappears and Mac OS opens Preview. A moment later, the document appears in a Preview window (**Figure 55**).

3. When you're finished previewing the document, you have three options:

   ▲ Choose File > Print, press ⌃⌘P, or click the Print button at the bottom of the Preview window (**Figure 55**) to display the Print dialog and print the document from Preview.

   ▲ Choose File > Save As or press ⇧⌃⌘S to display a Save dialog (**Figure 56**) and save the document as a PDF file from within Preview.

   ▲ Choose Preview > Quit Preview or press ⌃⌘Q to quit Preview and return to the original document.

✔ Tips

- Preview is covered in **Chapter 6**. The Save dialog is covered in **Chapter 5**.

- Some applications, such as Microsoft Word, include a Print Preview command on their File menu. This displays a preview of the document from within the application and does not use Preview.

Saving Documents as PDF Files

PDF, which stands for Portable Document Format, is a standard file format that can be opened and read by Preview, Adobe Acrobat Reader, and other PDF reader software. PDF is a good format for distributing a formatted document when you're not sure what software the document's recipient has. Most computer users have some kind of PDF reader software; if they don't, they can download Adobe Acrobat Reader for free.

The Print dialog offers two methods for saving a document as a PDF file: the quick way and the almost-as-quick way.

To save a document as a PDF file

1. Set options as desired in the Print dialog's panes.

2. In any pane of the Print dialog (**Figure 28**), click the Save As PDF button.

    or

    In the Output Options pane of the Print dialog, turn on the Save as File check box and choose PDF from the Format pop-up menu (**Figure 57**).

3. Use the Save to File dialog that appears (**Figure 58**) to enter a name and select a disk location for the PDF file.

4. Click Save.

✔ Tip

■ Using the Save dialog is covered in **Chapter 5**.

Figure 57 When you turn on the Save as File check box, the Print button turns into a Save button.

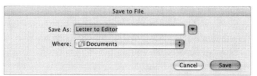

Figure 58 Use this dialog to enter a name, select a location, and Save a document as a file.

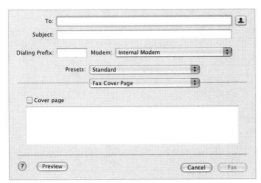

Figure 59 Use this dialog sheet to set options for faxing a document from within the Print dialog.

Figure 60 As you enter a recipient's name, your computer attempts to match it to Address Book entries.

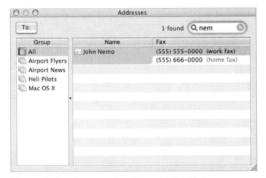

Figure 61 Another way to add a recipient is to use the searchable Addresses window. This is especially useful when a recipient has more than one fax number; double-click the one you want.

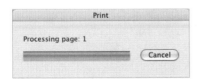

Figure 62 A progress window like this appears as a print job is spooled to a fax or print queue.

Faxing Documents

Mac OS X 10.3 added the ability to fax documents from within the Print dialog. All you need is a computer with a faxmodem connected to a telephone line.

To fax a document

1. Set options as desired in the Print dialog's panes.

2. In any pane of the Print dialog (**Figure 28**), click the Fax button. The Print dialog changes to offer options for faxing the document (**Figure 59**).

3. Enter the name of the person you are faxing the document to in the To box. As you type, your computer attempts to match what you're typing to entries in your Address Book file (**Figure 60**). If you prefer, you can click the Addresses button to display a searchable Addresses window (**Figure 61**); double-click a fax number to enter it in the window.

4. Enter a subject in the Subject box.

5. If you need to dial a number to get a dial tone (like in an office or hotel) or a 1 for long distance, enter these numbers in the Dialing Prefix box.

6. If you have multiple faxmodems, choose one from the Modem pop-up menu.

7. To include a cover page, turn on the Cover page check box and enter a message in the big box beneath it.

8. Click Fax. A Print status dialog (**Figure 62**) appears briefly as the document is spooled to the faxmodem's queue. A moment later, the computer dials and sends the fax.

Continued on next page...

Continued from previous page.

✔ Tips

■ In step 3, you don't have to enter a name. Instead, just enter a fax phone number. You might find this quicker when sending a one-time fax to someone whose fax number is not in your Address Book.

■ In step 3, you can enter multiple recipients in the To box. Separate each one with a comma (,).

■ Before step 8, you can click the Preview button to see what your fax will look like in Preview (**Figure 63**). Clicking the Fax button in the Preview window sends the fax.

■ The header on each page of the faxes you send includes the date, time, and page number.

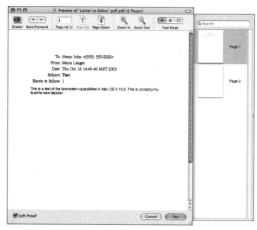

Figure 63 You can click the Preview button to display a preview of your fax, including the cover page.

Printing Documents

The Print dialog also enables you to send a document to a printer to be printed.

To print a document

1. Set options as desired in the Print dialog's panes.

2. In any pane of the Print dialog (**Figure 28**), click Print.

   The print job is sent to the print queue, where it waits for its turn to be printed. A progress window like the one in **Figure 62** appears as it is sent or *spooled*.

✔ Tips

- You can normally cancel a print job as it is being spooled to the print queue or printer by pressing ⌘.. Any pages spooled *before* you press ⌘., however, may be printed anyway.

- Canceling a print job that has already been spooled to a print queue is discussed later in this chapter.

Desktop Printers

Mac OS X 10.3 brings back a printing feature found in Mac OS 9.2 and earlier: desktop printers. With this feature, you create an icon for a printer you use frequently. Then, when you want to print a document, simply drag the document icon onto the printer icon.

To create a desktop icon for a printer

1. Open Printer Setup Utility and display the Printer list.

2. Select the printer you want to create a desktop printer icon for (**Figure 64**).

3. Choose Printers > Create Desktop Printer, or press ⟨Shift⟩⟨⌘⟩⟨D⟩.

4. Use the Save As dialog that appears (**Figure 65**) to enter a name and choose a location for the desktop printer icon.

5. Click Save. An alias for the printer appears in the location you specified (**Figure 66**).

✔ Tip

■ Although Desktop is the default location in the Save As dialog (**Figure 65**), you can save a desktop printer anywhere on disk.

To print with a desktop printer

1. Drag the icon for the document you want to print onto the printer icon (**Figure 67**).

2. When you release the mouse button, the document is sent to the print queue and prints.

✔ Tip

■ You can drag any number of document icons onto the printer icon. They will all be spooled to the printer.

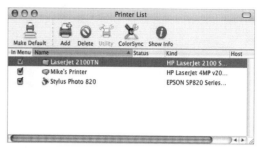

Figure 64 Select the printer you want to create an icon for in the Printer List window.

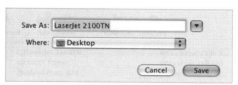

Figure 65 Use this dialog to name and save the printer icon.

Figure 66 Here's an example of a printer icon on the desktop.

Figure 67 To print, simply drag the document icon onto the printer icon.

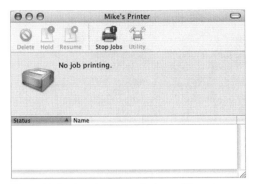

Figure 68 A printer's queue window, with no documents in the queue...

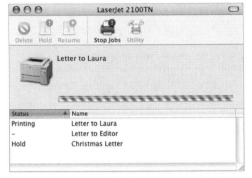

Figure 69 ...and the same printer's queue window with three documents in the queue: one printing, one waiting to be printed, and one on hold.

Figure 70 When print jobs are in a printer's queue, an icon for the printer appears in the Dock.

Print Queues

As mentioned earlier in this chapter, Printer Setup Utility can also be used to manage print queues. A *print queue* is a list of documents or *print jobs* waiting to be printed. When you click the Print button to send a document to a printer, you're really sending it to the printer's queue, where it waits its turn to be printed.

Printer Setup Utility's queue windows enable you to check the progress of print jobs that are printing; to stop printing; and to hold, resume, or cancel a specific print job.

✔ Tip

- Although this section discusses printer queues, your faxmodem also has a queue that works exactly the same way.

To open a printer's queue window

1. Open Printer Setup Utility and display the Printer List window (**Figure 2**).

2. Double-click the name of the printer for which you want to open the queue.

   or

   Select the name of the printer for which you want to open the queue, and choose Printers > Show Jobs (**Figure 3**) or press ⌘O.

   or

   Double-click the desktop icon for a printer (**Figure 66**).

   The printer's queue window appears (**Figure 68** or **69**).

✔ Tips

- When a document is in a print queue, the icon for the Printer that will print it appears in the Dock (**Figure 70**). Click the icon to view the printer's print queue.

OPENING A PRINTER'S QUEUE WINDOW

To stop all print jobs

Click the Stop Jobs button in the Print Queue window (**Figures 68** and **69**).

or

Choose Printer > Stop Jobs (**Figure 71a**).

Any printing stops and the words "Jobs Stopped" appear in the print queue window (**Figure 72**).

To restart print jobs

Click the Start Jobs button in the Print Queue window (**Figure 72**).

or

Choose Printers > Start Jobs (**Figure 71b**).

The next print job starts printing.

To hold a specific print job

1. In the printer's queue window (**Figure 69**), select the print job you want to hold.

2. Click the Hold button (**Figure 73**).

   or

   Choose Jobs > Hold Job (**Figure 74a**).

   The word *Hold* appears in the Status column beside the job name in the queue window (**Figure 69**). If the job was printing, printing stops and another job in the queue begins to print.

Figures 71a & 71b The Printers menu with a print queue window open. The last command will either stop (left) or start (right) the print jobs, depending on whether the queue is stopped.

Figure 72 The queue status appears in the queue window.

Figure 73 When you select a print job that is not on hold, the Delete and Hold buttons become active.

Figures 74a & 74b The Jobs menu with a print job that is waiting or printing selected (left) and the Jobs menu with a print job that is on hold selected.

Figure 75 When you select a print job that is on hold, the Resume button becomes active.

To resume a specific print job

1. In the printer's queue window (**Figure 69**), select the print job you want to resume.

2. Click the Resume button (**Figure 75**).

   or

   Choose Jobs > Resume Job (**Figure 74b**).

   The word *Hold* disappears from the Status column beside the job name in the queue window. If no other jobs are printing, the job begins to print.

✔ Tip

- You can also use this technique to start printing a job that you put on hold or scheduled for a later time using the Scheduler options in the Print dialog (**Figure 36**).

To cancel a specific print job

1. In the printer's queue window (**Figure 69**), select the print job you want to cancel.

2. Click the Delete button (**Figure 73** or **75**).

   or

   Choose Jobs > Delete Job (**Figure 74a** or **74b**).

   The job is removed from the print queue. If it was printing, printing stops.

MANAGING THE PRINT QUEUE & PRINT JOBS

Connecting to the Internet

Connecting to the Internet

The *Internet* is a vast, worldwide network of computers that offers information, communication, online shopping, and entertainment for the whole family.

There are two ways to connect to the Internet:

◆ In a *direct* or *network connection*, your computer has a live network connection to the Internet all the time. This is relatively common for workplace computers on companywide networks. For home use, *cable modems* and *DSL*, which work like direct connections, are gaining popularity.

◆ In a *modem* or *dial-up connection*, your computer uses its modem to dial in to a server at an *Internet Service Provider* (*ISP*), which gives it access to the Internet. Access speed is limited by the speed of your modem.

This chapter explains how to configure your system for an Internet connection, connect to the Internet, and use the Internet applications and utilities included with Mac OS X.

✔ Tips

■ An ISP is a business that provides access to the Internet for a fee.

■ The *World Wide Web* is part of the Internet. The Web and the *Web browser* software you use to access it are covered later in this chapter.

TCP/IP, PPP, & Internet Connect

Your computer accesses the Internet via a TCP/IP connection. *TCP/IP* is a standard Internet *protocol*, or set of rules, for exchanging information.

A TCP/IP connection works like a pipeline. Once established, Internet applications—such as your Web browser and e-mail program—reach through the TCP/IP pipeline to get the information they need. When the information has been sent or received, it stops flowing through the pipeline. But the pipeline is not disconnected.

If you have a direct or network connection to the Internet, the Internet is accessible all the time. But if you connect via modem, you need to use Internet Connect software. This software, which comes with Mac OS, uses PPP to connect to TCP/IP networks via modem. *PPP* is a standard protocol for connecting to networks.

When you connect via modem using Internet Connect, you set up a temporary TCP/IP pipeline. Internet applications are smart enough to automatically use Internet Connect to connect to the Internet when necessary. When you're finished accessing Internet services you should tell Internet Connect to disconnect.

✔ Tip

■ Internet Connect replaces the Remote Access software found in Mac OS 9.x and earlier.

Figure 1 Network Status information in the Network preferences pane.

Setting Internet Options in Network Preferences

If you set up your Internet connection as part of the setup process discussed in **Chapter 1**, your computer should be ready to connect to the Internet and you can skip ahead to the sections that discuss Internet connection software. But if you didn't set up your connection or your Internet connection information has changed since setup, you may have to do some manual configuration.

The Network pane of System Preferences displays information about your Internet connection (**Figure 1**)and enables you to configure your modem or network connection:

◆ For **modem or network connections**, you can set options to configure your TCP/IP address and proxy information.

◆ For **modem connections only**, you can set options for your PPP connection to the Internet and your modem.

◆ For **network connections only**, you can set options for your PPPoE connection to a cable or DSL server and AppleTalk and Ethernet connections to an internal network.

This part of the chapter explains how you can manually set Internet options in the Network preferences pane.

✔ Tips

■ If your Internet configuration is working fine, don't change it! Internet connections follow one of the golden rules of computing: *If it ain't broke, don't fix it.*

■ *PPPoE*, which stands for *Point to Point Protocol over Ethernet*, is a connection method used by some cable and DSL ISPs.

■ Before you set Network preferences, make sure you have all the information you need to properly configure the options. You can get all of the information you need from your ISP or network administrator.

■ I tell you more about networking in **Chapter 14**.

SETTING NETWORK PREFERENCES

To open Network preferences

1. Choose Apple > System Preferences or click the System Preferences icon on the Dock.

2. In the System Preferences window that appears (**Figure 2**), click the Network icon to display the Network pane (**Figure 1**).

3. Choose an option from the Show pop-up menu (**Figure 3**) to view and modify connection details:

   ▲ **Network Status** shows a summary of your network connections and their status (**Figure 1**).

   ▲ **Internal Modem** shows the settings for an internal modem (**Figure 4**).

   ▲ **Built-In Ethernet** shows the settings for the built-in Ethernet port (**Figure 12**).

   ▲ **Network Port Configurations** is an advanced option that enables you to add, enable, configure, and disable other network ports.

✔ Tips

■ Depending on your computer model and its features, other options may appear on the Show pop-up menu. For example, my 12-inch PowerBook also includes options for USB Bluetooth Modem Adaptor and AirPort. The options for these devices are very similar to the options for modem and Ethernet connections.

■ You can also view the details for a specific type of connection by double-clicking it in the Network Status pane of Network preferences (**Figure 1**).

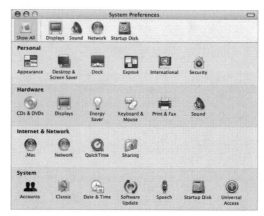

Figure 2 The System Preferences window.

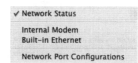

Figure 3 Use this pop-up menu to choose the type of connection you want to set up.

Figure 4 The PPP pane of Network preferences for a modem connection should include all of the information your computer needs to dial in and log on to the ISP's server. (The information here is not real.)

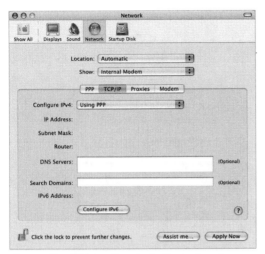

Figure 5 The TCP/IP options in the Network preferences pane for a modem connection to the Internet.

Figure 6 The Configure IPv4 pop-up menu in the TCP/IP tab of the Network preferences pane.

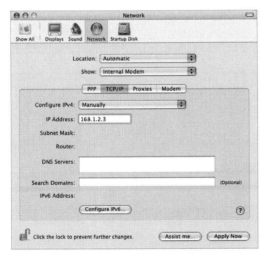

Figure 7 If your ISP has provided you with a static IP address, you must enter that address in the IP Address field.

To set up a modem connection

1. In the Network pane of System Preferences (**Figure 1**), choose Modem or Internal Modem from the Show pop-up (**Figure 3**).

2. If you are connecting through a regular ISP, click the PPP button to display PPP options (**Figure 4**).

   or

   If you are connecting through AOL, skip ahead to the third option of step 5.

3. Enter the dialup information provided by your ISP. **Figure 4** shows an example.

4. Click the TCP/IP button to display TCP/IP options (**Figure 5**).

5. If your ISP's instructions say that IP address and domain name information will be assigned automatically (for example, you have a *dynamic* IP address), choose Using PPP from the Configure IPv4 pop-up menu (**Figure 6**). Then enter the domain information in the fields. (This is the most commonly used option for dial-up connections to ISPs.)

   or

   If your ISP provided a *static* IP address and domain name server information for your connection, choose Manually from the Configure IPv4 pop-up menu (**Figure 6**) and enter the information provided in each of the fields that appear. **Figure 7** shows an example.

   or

   If you plan to use an AOL connection for accessing the Internet, choose AOL Dialup from the Configure pop-up menu (**Figure 6**). You can then skip the remaining steps.

Continued on next page...

SETTING UP A MODEM CONNECTION

Continued from previous page.

6. Click the Modem button to display Modem options (**Figure 8**).

7. Choose your modem type from the Modem pop-up menu.

8. To minimize errors and speed up data transfer, turn on the "Enable error correction and compression in modem" check box.

9. To instruct your computer to wait until it "hears" a dial tone before it dials, turn on the "Wait for dial tone before dialing" check box.

10. Select a dialing radio button:

   ▲ **Tone** enables you to dial with touch-tone dialing.

   ▲ **Pulse** enables you to dial with pulse dialing. Select this option only if touchtone dialing is not available on your telephone line.

11. Select a Sound radio button:

   ▲ **On** plays dialing and connection sounds through the modem or computer speaker.

   ▲ **Off** dials and connects silently.

12. If you have call waiting and want to be alerted for incoming calls, turn on the check box labeled "Notify me of incoming calls while connected to the Internet." You can then toggle settings two options:

   ▲ **Play alert sound when receiving a call** plays an audible alert when an incoming call is detected while you're connected to the Internet.

   ▲ **Remind me *n* seconds before disconnecting me** displays a reminder dialog the number of seconds you specify before disconnecting you from the Internet to answer the incoming call.

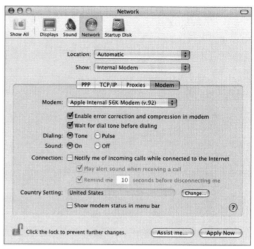

Figure 8 The Modem pane of the Network preferences pane enables you to set options for your modem.

Modem status icon

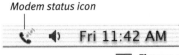

Figures 9 & 10
You can display a modem status icon in the menu bar (top). Clicking the icon displays a menu of commands for accessing the Internet.

13. To change the Country Setting for your location, click the Change button beside Country Setting. This displays the Date & Time preferences pane so you can set country options.

14. To include a modem status icon and menu in the menu bar (**Figures 9** and **10**), turn on the "Show modem status in menu bar" check box.

15. Click the Apply Now button in the bottom of the Network preferences pane (**Figure 8**) to save your changes to Network preferences.

✔ Tips

- Do not use the settings illustrated here. Use the settings provided by your ISP.

- In step 3, if you turn on the Save password check box, you won't have to enter your password when you connect to the Internet. Be aware, however, that anyone who accesses your computer will be able to connect to the Internet with your account.

- The Modem menu in step 7 includes dozens of modems, so yours should be listed. If it isn't, choose another model from the same manufacturer.

- The "Enable error correction and compression in modem" option in step 8 is not available for all modems.

- In step 11, you may want to keep modem sounds on until you're sure you can connect. This enables you to hear telephone company error recordings that can help you troubleshoot connection problems. You can always turn sound off later.

- If you do not have call waiting or don't want to be bothered by incoming calls if you do, keep the Notify me check box turned off in step 12.

To set up a network connection

1. In the Network pane of System Preferences (**Figure 1**), choose Built-in Ethernet from the Show pop-up (**Figure 3**).

2. If necessary, click the TCP/IP button to display TCP/IP options.

3. Choose one of the options from the Configure IPv4 pop-up menu (**Figure 11**). The option you select determines the appearance of the rest of the tab. **Figures 11** through **15** show examples.

4. Enter the appropriate IP addresses and domain names in the fields.

5. If you have a DSL connection via PPPoE, click the PPPoE button to display PPPoE options. Turn on the Connect using PPPoE check box and enter the connection information provided by your ISP. **Figure 16** shows an example.

6. Click the Apply Now button at the bottom of the Network preferences pane (**Figure 12**) to save your changes to Network preferences.

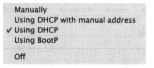

Figure 11 The Configure menu in the TCP/IP pane for a network connection offers several options.

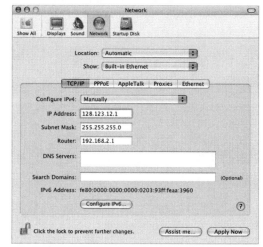

Figure 12 Examples of various configurations for a network TCP/IP connection: manual ...

Figure 13 ... DHCP ...

SETTING UP A NETWORK CONNECTION

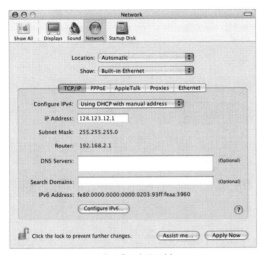

Figure 14 ... DHCP with a fixed IP address ...

✔ Tips

- Do not use the settings illustrated here. Use the settings provided by your ISP or network administrator.

- DHCP is a type of network addressing system.

- If you're not sure which option to choose in step 3, ask your network administrator.

- In step 5, if you turn on the Save password check box, you won't have to enter your password when you connect to the Internet. Be aware, however, that anyone who accesses your computer with your login will also be able to connect to the Internet with your account.

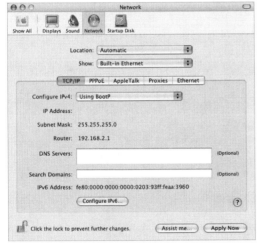

Figure 15 ... and using BootP.

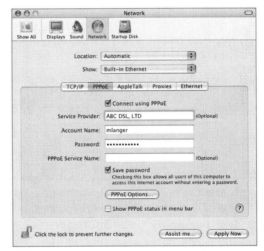

Figure 16 You can use the PPPoE tab to set up a PPPoE connection to a DSL server.

To set proxy options

1. In the Network pane of System Preferences, click the Proxies button to display Proxies options (**Figure 17**).

2. Turn on the check box beside each proxy option you need to set up. Then enter appropriate information for each one.

3. Click Apply Now to save your changes to Network preferences.

✖ Warning!

■ Do not change settings in the Proxies tab of Network preferences unless instructed by your ISP or network administrator. Setting invalid values may prevent you from connecting to the Internet.

✔ Tips

■ Proxies options are the same for modem connections as they are for network connections.

■ Proxies are most often required for network connections; they are seldom required for dialup connections.

■ Proxies tab options are the same for modems as for network connections.

■ Proxies enable your Internet connection to work with security setups such as firewalls that protect network computers from hackers. For more information about proxy settings on your network, consult your network administrator.

Figure 17 The Proxies pane of the Network preferences pane.

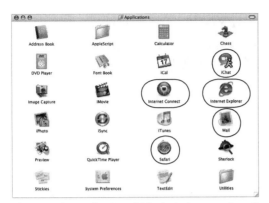

Figure 18 The Applications folder includes a number of applications for accessing the Internet.

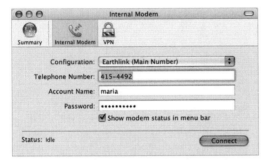

Figure 19 Internet Connect's Internal Modem pane.

Figure 20 The Status area displays connection status information while you are connecting...

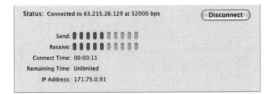

Figure 21 ...and after you have connected.

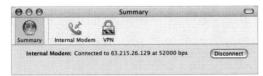

Figure 22 You can collapse Internet Connect's window to show only connection status.

Connecting to an ISP

You can establish a PPP connection to your ISP by using Internet Connect to dial in.

✔ Tip

■ If you have a network connection to the Internet—including a cable modem or DSL connection—you are always connected and can skip this section.

To connect to an ISP

1. Open the Internet Connect icon in the Applications folder (**Figure 18**).

2. If necessary, click the Internal Modem button to display its settings (**Figure 19**).

3. Check the settings and make changes as necessary. (These settings come from the PPP pane of the Network preferences pane for a modem connection (**Figure 4**).

4. Click the Connect button. Internet Connect dials your modem. It displays the connection status in its Status area (**Figure 20**).

   When Internet Connect has successfully connected, the Connect button turns into a Disconnect button and the Status area fills with connection information (**Figure 21**).

✔ Tips

■ Click the Summary button in Internet Connect's window to display only the status area (**Figure 22**).

■ Internet Connect does not have to be open while you are connected to the Internet.

To disconnect from an ISP

1. Open or switch to Internet Connect.

2. Click the Disconnect button (**Figures 21 and 22**). The connection is terminated.

Internet Applications

Mac OS X includes four applications for accessing the Internet:

◆ **Mail** is an Apple program that enables you to send and receive e-mail messages.

◆ **iChat** is an Apple program that enables you to exchange instant messages and conduct audio or video conferences with .Mac and AIM (AOL Instant Messenger) users.

◆ **Safari** is an Apple program that enables you to browse Web sites and download files from FTP sites.

◆ **Internet Explorer** is a Microsoft program that enables you to browse Web sites and download files from FTP sites.

This section provides brief instructions for using these four programs—just enough to get you started. You can explore the other features of these programs on your own.

✔ Tips

■ Mail and Safari are set as the default e-mail and Web browser programs.

■ Mac OS 9.x, which is bundled with Mac OS X to handle Classic applications, includes Outlook Express, an e-mail application, and Netscape Communicator, a Web browser.

To open an Internet application

Use one of the following techniques:

◆ Open the icon for the application in the Applications folder (**Figure 18**).

◆ Click the icon for the application in the Dock (**Figure 23**).

Figure 23 You can open Safari, Mail, and iChat by clicking their icons in the Dock.

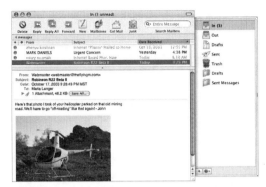

Figure 24 The Mail main window with the Mailbox drawer and an incoming message displayed.

Mail

Mail (**Figure 24**) is an e-mail application from Apple Computer, Inc. It enables you to send and receive e-mail messages using your Internet e-mail account.

Here's how it works. Imagine having a mailbox at the post office. As mail comes in, the postmaster sorts it into the boxes—including yours. To get your mail, you need to go to the post office to pick it up. While you're there, you're likely to drop off any letters you need to send.

E-mail works the same way. Your e-mail is delivered to your e-mail server—like the post office where your mailbox is. The server software (like the postmaster) sorts the mail into mailboxes. When your e-mail client software (Mail, in this case) connects to the server via the Internet, it picks up your incoming mail and sends any outgoing messages it has to send.

If you set up your Internet connection and provided e-mail information when you first configured Mac OS X, that information is automatically stored in Mail so it's ready to use. Just open mail and it automatically makes that virtual trip to the post office to get and send messages.

In this part of the chapter, I explain how to set up an e-mail account with Mail, just in case you need to add an account. I also explain how to compose, send, read, and retrieve e-mail messages.

✔ Tip

■ The first time you open Mail, a dialog appears, asking if you want to import e-mail addresses from another e-mail program. If you do, click Yes and follow the instructions that appear onscreen to perform the import.

To set up an e-mail account

1. Choose Mail > Preferences, or press ⌃ ⌘ , .

2. In the Mail Preferences window that appears, click the Accounts button to display its options (**Figure 25**).

3. Click the + button beneath the list of accounts.

4. A new, untitled account appears in the list (**Figure 26**). Enter account and server information for the account on the right side of the window.

5. Click the window's close button.

6. Click Save the Save Changes dialog that appears.

✔ Tips

- You only have to set up an e-mail account once. Mail will remember all of your settings.

- Your ISP or network administrator can provide all of the important information you need to set up an e-mail account, including the account name, password, and mail servers.

- If you have a .Mac account and want to set up another account, you must use the Outgoing Mail Server (SMTP) pop-up menu's Add Server command to add an outgoing mail server for that account. A .Mac account will only send e-mail messages for a .Mac account. SMTP server information should be provided by your ISP.

- You can set other options for an account by clicking the Special Mailboxes and Advanced buttons in the Accounts pane (**Figure 25**). Explore these options on your own.

Figure 25 The Accounts pane of Mail Preferences.

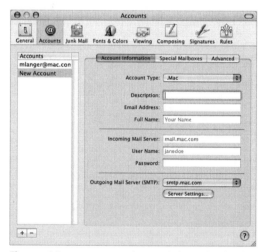

Figure 26 Enter account and server information for the new account.

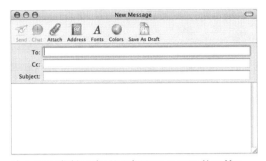

Figure 27 Clicking the New button opens a New Message window like this one.

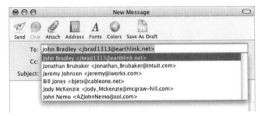

Figure 28 When you begin to type in a name, Mail tries to match it to entries in Address Book.

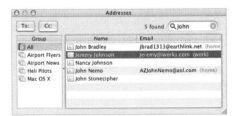

Figure 29 You can also use an Addresses window to enter a recipient's e-mail address.

Figure 30 Here's a short message ready to be sent.

To create & send a message

1. Click the New button at the top of the main Mail window (**Figure 23**). The New Message window appears (**Figure 27**).

2. Use one of the following techniques to enter the recipient's address in the To box:

    ▲ Type in the recipient's e-mail address.

    ▲ If the recipient is someone in your Address Book file or someone you have received an e-mail message from in the past, enter the person's name. As you type, Mail attempts to match the name (**Figure 28**). Click the correct entry.

    ▲ Click the Address button. Use the searchable Addresses window that appears (**Figure 29**) to locate the recipient's name and double-click it.

3. Repeat step 2 to add additional names. When you are finished, click Tab twice.

4. Enter a subject for the message in the Subject field, and press Tab.

5. Type your message into the large box at the bottom of the window. When you are finished, the window might look like the one in **Figure 30**.

6. Click the Send button near the top of the window. The message window closes and Mail sends the message.

✔ Tips

■ Address Book is covered in **Chapter 6**.

■ To add a file as an attachment to the message, drag the file's icon from a Finder window into the message body.

■ If you have a modem connection to the Internet, you must connect before you can send a message.

To retrieve e-mail messages

1. Click the Get Mail button at the top of the main window (**Figure 24**).

2. Mail connects to the Internet (if necessary), then connects to your e-mail server and downloads messages waiting for you. Incoming messages appear in a list when you select the In icon in the Mailbox drawer (**Figure 24**).

✔ Tips

- A blue bullet character appears beside each unread e-mail message (**Figure 24**).

- Messages that Mail thinks are junk mail are colored brown. You can set junk mail filtering options in the Junk Mail preferences window (**Figure 31**). Choose Mail > Preferences and click the Junk Mail button to get started. You'll find that Mail's junk mail filter can weed out at least 75% of the junk mail that you get.

- You can toggle the display of the Mailbox drawer by clicking the Mailboxes button in the main Mail window (**Figure 24**).

- You can configure Mail to have multiple mailboxes to organize your incoming e-mail more effectively. Use commands under the Mailbox menu to create and customize mailboxes.

- The Mac OS X 10.3 version of Mail gives you the ability to connect to a Microsoft Exchange server. Ask your network administrator for the information you need to set up and use this feature.

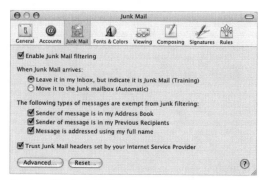

Figure 31 The Junk Mail preferences window enables you to set options that weed out junk mail messages.

RETRIEVING E-MAIL MESSAGES

Figure 32 Double-click a message to open it in its own window.

Figure 33 Clicking the Attachments triangle displays icons for attachments. In this example, there's only one attachment: a JPEG image file.

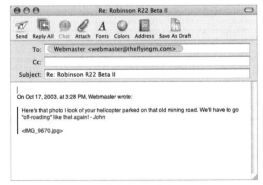

Figure 34 When you click the Reply button, a pre-addressed message window appears.

To read a message

1. Click the message that you want to read. It appears in the bottom half of the main Mail window (**Figure 24**).

2. Read the message.

✔ Tips

- You can also double-click a message to display it in its own message window (**Figure 32**).

- To view a list of message attachments (when present), click the triangle beside the paper clip icon in the message header. The header expands to show icons for each attachment (**Figure 33**). You can save a single attachment by dragging its icon from the message window to the desktop or a Finder window. You can save all attachments by clicking the Save All button and using the Save dialog that appears to choose a disk location.

- To reply to the message, click Reply. A preaddressed message window with the entire message quoted appears (**Figure 34**). Type your reply, and click Send.

- To forward the message to another e-mail address, click Forward. A message window containing a copy of the message appears. Enter the e-mail address for the recipient in the To field, and click Send.

- To add a message's sender to the Address book, select the message (**Figure 24**) and choose Message > Add Sender To Address Book or press ⌘Y. Mail automatically adds the person's name and e-mail address to Address Book's entries. You can open Address Book and add additional information for the record as desired. Address Book is covered **Chapter 6**.

iChat AV

iChat AV enables you to conduct live chats or audio or video conferences with .Mac and AIM (AOL Instant Messaging) users.

Here's how it works. The first time you open iChat, you configure it with your .Mac or AIM account information, as well as the information for your buddies who use iChat or AIM. Then, while you're connected to the Internet with iChat running, iChat does two things:

◆ It tells iChat and AIM users that you're available to receive instant messages and participate in chats.

◆ It tells you when your buddies are connected via iChat or AIM and available to receive instant messages and participate in chats.

When a buddy is available, sending him an instant message is as easy as clicking a button and typing what you want to say. If more than one buddy is available, you can open a chat window and invite them to participate together.

For Mac OS X 10.3, Apple enhanced iChat by adding AV (audio and video conferencing) features. If you have a microphone or a compatible video camera (including the iSight camera made by Apple), you can have live audio or video chats with your buddies.

In this part of the chapter, I explain how to configure iChat for your account, set up an iChat buddy list, invite a buddy to a chat, participate in text or video chats.

✔ Tips

■ To use iChat, you must have a .Mac or AIM account. To use the AV features, you must have a microphone (for audio only) or compatible video camera (for audio and video) and a fast Internet connection.

■ To learn more about iChat, visit www.apple.com/ichat/. To learn more about the iSight camera, check out www.apple.com/isight/.

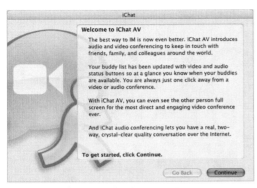

Figure 35 The Welcome to iChat AV window tells you a little about iChat AV.

Figure 36 Use this dialog to enter information about your iChat account.

✓ .Mac Account
   AIM Account

Figure 37
The Account Type pop-up menu.

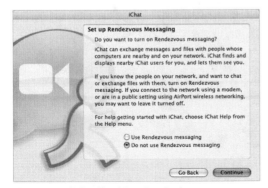

Figure 38 A dialog like this asks whether you want to enable Rendezvous messaging.

To set up iChat

1. Open iChat as discussed earlier in this chapter.

2. Read the information in the Welcome to iChat AV dialog that appears (**Figure 35**) and click Continue.

3. In the Set up a new iChat Account dialog (**Figure 36**), enter your name and .Mac or AIM account information. Be sure to select the correct option from the Account Type pop-up menu (**Figure 37**). Then click Continue.

4. In the Set up Rendezvous Messaging dialog (**Figure 38**), select one of the options and click Continue:

   ▲ **Use Rendezvous messaging** turns on Rendezvous messaging. This enables you to use iChat with local network users.

   ▲ **Do not use Rendezvous messaging** leaves Rendezvous messaging turned off. Choose this option if you are not connected to a local network or you do not plan to use iChat with other people on your network.

5. The Set up iChat AV dialog appears next. If you have a compatible video camera attached to your computer and turned on, you'll see an image (**Figure 39**). Otherwise, a message will say that there is no camera attached to the computer. If you have a microphone, you'll also see a sound level indicator that moves as you make noise. Click Continue.

6. Read the information in the Conclusion dialog (**Figure 40**). and click Done.

Continued on next page...

SETTING **U**P I**C**HAT

Continued from previous page.

7. A Buddy List window with a "Connecting" message appears next. Wait while iChat connects to AIM. The Buddy List expands to list your buddies and their online status (**Figure 41**).

✔ Tips

- In step 3, if you don't have a .Mac account or AIM account, click the Get an iChat Account button. This launches your Web browser and connects you to the Internet so you can sign up for a free .Mac iChat screen name.

- In step 5, if a message appears stating that your camera is in use by another application, disconnect the camera, wait a moment, and reconnect it. This usually solves this problem with my iChat AV and iSight setup; it should work for you, too.

- Rendezvous is a type of networking that's part of Mac OS X. You can learn more about networking in **Chapter 14**.

- If you have enabled Rendezvous messaging, two windows appear—a Buddy List window (**Figure 41**) and a Rendezvous window that looks just like it. The instructions in this chapter should help you get started using iChat with Rendezvous, too.

- If you set a picture for yourself in Address Book, that picture automatically appears for you in iChat (**Figure 41**). I explain how to use Address Book in **Chapter 6**.

- If you have used any version of iChat before—even if you used it on another computer—iChat retrieves your previous buddy list from the Internet and displays it in the Buddy List window (**Figure 41**).

Figure 39 If you have a compatible video camera attached, you'll see what it sees in this dialog. (I look pretty strung out today, don't I? Must be that deadline!)

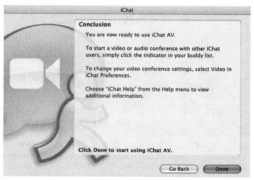

Figure 40 The Conclusion dialog at the end of the iChat setup process.

Figure 41
Your Buddy list window shows all of your buddies and their status.

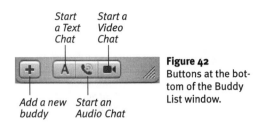

Start a Text Chat

Start a Video Chat

Figure 42
Buttons at the bottom of the Buddy List window.

Add a new buddy

Start an Audio Chat

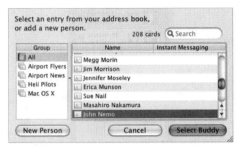

Figure 43 To add a person from your Address Book to your Buddy List, select his or her record and click Select Buddy.

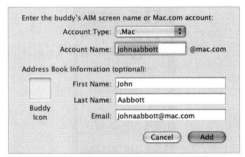

Figure 44 To add a new person (or my dog, in this example) to your Buddy List, fill in this form.

Figure 45
Buddies who are available appear in black type with a color-coded bullet beside their names. Buddies who are offline appear in gray type. A telephone or camera icon beside a buddy name indicates audio or video capabilities.

To add a buddy

1. Click the Add a new buddy button at the bottom of the Buddy List window (**Figure 42**).

   or

   Choose Buddies > Add a Buddy, or press Shift⌃⌘A.

2. A dialog sheet like the one in **Figure 43** appears. You have two choices:

   ▲ To add a person in your Address Book to your Buddy List, select a name in the dialog and click Select Buddy.

   ▲ To add a person not in your Address Book to your Buddy List, click the New Person button. Then fill out the form that appears by entering information about the person you want to add (**Figure 44**). Click Add.

✔ Tips

■ You can add as many .Mac and AIM accounts as you like to your buddy list.

■ A buddy's online status and audio or video capabilities is indicated in the buddy list with a color-coded bullet and phone or camera icons. **Figure 45** shows some examples.

■ If your Buddy List remains empty after adding buddies, you may have the list configured to show only available buddies. Choose View > Show Offline Buddies to display all buddies in the list, regardless of availability.

To remove a buddy

1. Select the name of the buddy you want to remove.

2. Press Delete.

3. Click OK in the confirmation dialog that appears.

ADDING & REMOVING BUDDIES

To conduct a text chat

1. In the Buddy List, select the name of a buddy who is available for chatting (**Figure 46**).

2. Click the Start a Text Chat button at the bottom of the Buddy List window (**Figure 42**). A window like the one in **Figure 47** appears.

3. Enter your message in the box at the bottom of the window. As you type, a "cloud" appears beside your icon to indicate that you're writing something (**Figure 48**).

4. Press [Return]. The comment appears in the top half of the window beside your icon (**Figure 49**).

5. Wait for your buddy to answer. His comments appear in the top half of the window beside his icon (**Figure 50**). If your buddy starts typing again, a "cloud" appears beside his icon (**Figure 51**).

6. Repeat steps 3 through 5 to continue your instant message conversation in the window. **Figure 52** shows an example of a conversation between a deadline-racing author and a sympathetic buddy.

Figure 46
Select a buddy who is available for chatting. If the buddy has a custom icon, it appears when he becomes available. From that point forward, it is saved in iChat.

Figure 47
As you prepare to type, a "cloud" appears beside your icon.

Figure 48
Type your message in the box.

Figure 49 When you press [Return], your message appears in the top half of the window.

Figure 50 When your buddy responds, his message appears beside his icon.

Figure 51
A "cloud" appears beside your buddy's icon as he types.

Figure 52
The start of a conversation.

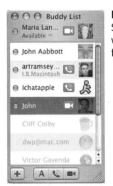

Figure 53
Select a buddy
who is available
for video chatting.

Figure 54 Try to be patient while you wait for the buddy to respond. (I should have worn makeup today.)

Figure 55 When the buddy appears, start talking! (This is John from California. I caught him just before he went out to wash the dog.)

To conduct a video chat

1. In the Buddy List, select the name of a buddy who is available for video chatting (**Figure 53**).

2. Click the Start a Video Chat button at the bottom of the Buddy List window (**Figure 42**). A window like the one in **Figure 54** appears.

3. Wait until your buddy responds. When he accepts the chat, the window changes to show his live image, with yours in a small box (**Figure 55**).

4. Talk!

✔ Tips

- To conduct a video chat, both you and your buddy must have video capabilities. Look for a camera icon beside a buddy's name (**Figure 53**).

- Video chats work best when both parties are accessing the Internet at speeds of 256Kbps or faster. You will notice an annoying time delay if you access at slow speed.

- I chatted with a bunch of people when I wrote this book and took screenshots of all of them. Unfortunately, I couldn't fit all the screenshots on this page. You can see some more of my video chat buddies on this book's companion Web site, www.marialanger.com/booksites/macosx/. Maybe your picture is there!

To end a chat

Click the close button in the chat window (**Figures 52** and **55**). (Be sure to say "Bye" first!)

To respond to a text chat invitation

1. When another iChat user invites you to a text chat, his message appears in a window on your desktop (**Figure 56**). Click the window to display an Instant Message window (**Figure 57**).

2. To accept the invitation, enter a message in the box at the bottom of the window (**Figure 58**) and click Accept or press Return. The message appears in the main window, which expands to display the chat (**Figure 59**).

   or

   To decline the invitation, click the Decline button or click the window's close button. The Instant Message window disappears.

   or

   To prevent the person from ever bothering you again with an invitation, click the Block button. Then click Block in the confirmation dialog that appears (**Figure 60**). The Instant Message window disappears.

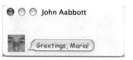

Figure 56 A chat invitation appears in a little window like this.

Figure 57 Click the window to expand it.

Figure 58 Enter your message in the bottom of the window.

Figure 59 When you accept a chat, the window expands so you can read and write messages.

Figure 60 Click Block in this dialog to prevent an annoying person from bothering you.

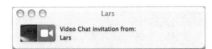

Figure 61 When you get a video chat invitation, you'll hear the sound of a ringing phone and a dialog like this appears.

Figure 62 Use one of the buttons at the bottom of the window to respond to the invitation.

Figure 63 When you accept an invitation, the caller's smiling face appears and you can start talking. (This is Lars from Arizona, who had to invite me twice so I could take these screen shots.)

To respond to a video chat invitation

1. When another iChat user invites you to a text chat, an invitation window like the one in **Figure 61** appears and iChat makes a phone ringing sound. Click the window to display a Video Chat window (**Figure 62**).

2. To accept the invitation, click Accept or press [Return]. iChat establishes a connection with the caller and the window changes to show his live image, with yours in a small box (**Figure 63**). Start talking!

   or

   To decline the invitation, click the Decline button or click the window's close button. The Video Chat window disappears.

RESPONDING TO A VIDEO CHAT INVITATION

Safari

Safari is a new Web browser application from Apple. It enables you to view, or *browse*, pages on the World Wide Web.

A Web *page* is a window full of formatted text and graphics (**Figures 64** and **65**). You move from page to page by clicking text or graphic links or by opening *URLs* (*uniform resource locators*) for specific Web pages. These two methods of navigating the World Wide Web can open a whole world of useful or interesting information.

✔ Tips

- You can easily identify a link by pointing to it; the mouse pointer turns into a pointing finger (**Figure 64**).

- You can change the default home page by specifying a different page's URL in Safari's General preferences (**Figure 66**). Choose Safari > Preferences and click the General button to get started.

To follow a link

1. Position the mouse pointer on a text or graphic link. The mouse pointer turns into a pointing finger (**Figure 64**).

2. Click. After a moment, the page or other location for the link you clicked will appear (**Figure 65**).

Mouse pointer when pointing to a clickable link

Figure 64 When you launch Safari, it displays the default home page.

Figure 65 Clicking the link in **Figure 64** displays this page.

Figure 66 You can change the default Home page and other settings in Safari's preferences window.

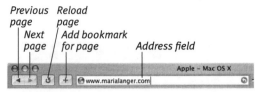

Previous page
Next page
Reload page
Add bookmark for page
Address field

Figure 67 Enter the URL in the Address field at the top of the Safari window, and press Return.

Figure 68
The Bookmarks menu.

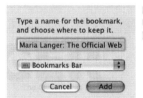

Figure 69
Use this dialog to set bookmark options.

Figure 70
This pop-up menu offers a variety of locations in which to save a bookmark.

To view a specific URL

Enter the URL in the address field near the top of the Safari window (**Figure 67**), and press Return or Enter.

To bookmark a page

1. Display the Web page that you want to create a bookmark for.

2. Click the Add bookmark for page button (**Figure 67**), choose Bookmarks > Add Bookmark (**Figure 68**), or press ⌘D.

3. A dialog sheet like the one in **Figure 69** appears. Enter a name for the bookmark in the box, then choose a location for it from the pop-up menu (**Figure 70**) and click Add.

   The name you specified is added in the location you specified (**Figures 71** and **72**).

✔ Tips

- Once a page has been added to the Bookmarks menu, you can display it by selecting its name from the menu.

- Microsoft Internet Explorer, which is discussed briefly on the next page, refers to bookmarks as *favorites*.

- iSync, which I discuss in **Chapter 8**, can automatically synchronize Safari bookmarks between computers.

Figure 71 In this example, I added a bookmark for my Home page to the bookmarks bar.

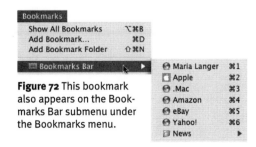

Figure 72 This bookmark also appears on the Bookmarks Bar submenu under the Bookmarks menu.

VIEWING URLS, CREATING BOOKMARKS

Internet Explorer

Internet Explorer (**Figure 73**) is a Web browser application by Microsoft. It does the same thing that Safari does with minor variations in how it does it. It's safe to say that if you know how to use Safari (or any other Web browser), you can use Internet Explorer.

Figure 73 The default Home page for Microsoft Internet Explorer. It shouldn't surprise you that it displays a Microsoft Web site.

✔ Tips

- The instructions for browsing Web pages and viewing URLs are the same for Internet Explorer as they are for Safari. Consult the previous two pages if you need more information.

- Previous versions of Mac OS X included Internet Explorer as the only Web browser. With the release of Safari in 2003, Apple added Safari and made it the default Web browser.

- To make Internet Explorer your default Web browser, open Safari, choose Safari > Preferences and click General to display Safari's General preferences (**Figure 66**), and choose Internet Explorer from the Default Web Browser pop-up menu. Close the General preferences window and quit Safari.

.Mac

Figure 1 The .Mac Home page explains what .Mac is all about and enables you to get more information about its features.

.Mac

Apple has embraced the Internet revolution and encourages Mac OS users to get connected to the Internet. One of the ways it does this is with .Mac (pronounced *dot Mac*).

.Mac, which can be found on the mac.com part of Apple's Web site (**Figure 1**), offers a wide range of features for Macintosh users, including:

◆ **Mail** gives you an e-mail address in the .mac domain that can be accessed via Apple's Mail software, any other e-mail client software, or a Web browser.

◆ **Address Book** puts all your Address Book entries on your .Mac account, where you can access them from any computer.

◆ **Bookmarks** puts all of your Safari bookmarks on your .Mac account, where you can access and use them from any computer.

◆ **iDisk** gives you 100 MB of hard disk space on Apple's server for saving or sharing files.

◆ **HomePage** lets you create and publish a custom Web site hosted on Apple's Web server, using easy-to-use, online Web authoring tools.

◆ **Backup** enables you to perform manual or automatic backups to iDisk, CD, or DVD.

Continued on next page...

Continued from previous page.

◆ **Virex** is McAfee Virex software, which protects your computer from viruses, "Trojan horses," worms, and other computer infections.

◆ **Support** enables you to access a variety of Web-based support services and features, including the AppleCare KnowledgeBase, and a member-only support forum.

◆ **iCards** lets you send custom greeting cards to anyone with an e-mail address.

There are two levels of .Mac membership:

◆ **Trial Membership** lets you work with .Mac features for 60 days. Not all features are available to Trial Members, but the price is right: it's free!

◆ **Full Membership** gives you full access to all .Mac features. When this book went to press, the annual fee was $99.95 per year.

Although this chapter explains how to sign up for and use the Full Membership features of a .Mac account, it provides enough information for you to explore a Trial Membership.

✔ Tips

■ To use .Mac, you must have an Internet connection. I explain how to set up an Internet connection and connect to the Internet in **Chapter 11**.

■ You can learn more about .Mac at www.mac.com (**Figure 1**).

■ .Mac features are relatively easy to use, with step-by-step instructions and lots of online help.

■ A .Mac account also enables you to use iChat for chatting with other .Mac members or AIM users. I explain how to use iChat in **Chapter 11**.

Figure 2 To join .Mac, start by filling out the Sign Up form.

Figure 3 Use the Billing Information form to enter credit card information to pay for your membership.

Figure 4 When your membership has been processed, all of your membership information appears on a page like this.

Joining & Accessing .Mac

In order to use .Mac features, you must become either a Trial or Full member. These instructions explain how to join .Mac with a full membership.

✔ Tips

- You must be 13 years of age or older to join .Mac.

- If you are already a member of .Mac, you can skip this section.

To join .Mac

1. Use your Web browser to view the .Mac Home page at www.mac.com (**Figure 1**).

2. Click the Join Now button.

3. Fill in the Sign Up form that appears in your Web browser window (**Figure 2**).

4. Click the Continue button at the bottom of the form.

5. Fill in the Billing Information form that appears (**Figure 3**).

6. Click the Continue button at the bottom of the form.

7. When your account has been set up, a Print your information page like the one in **Figure 4** appears. Use your browser's Print command to print the information for future reference.

8. Click Continue.

9. A Thank You page appears next. It summarizes the features of .Mac. Click the Start Using .Mac button at the bottom of the page to go to the .Mac Home page, where you're already logged in (**Figure 5**).

Continued on next page...

Continued from previous page.

✔ Tips

- After step 6, if the Member name you selected is already in use, you'll be prompted to enter a different member name. Follow the instructions that appear to continue.

- You'll need the e-mail address and server information that appears in the Print your information window to set up your .Mac e-mail account in an e-mail client application other than Mail.

To log in to .Mac

1. Use your Web browser to view the .Mac Home page at www.mac.com (**Figure 1**).

2. Click the Log in link.

3. Enter your member name and password in the appropriate boxes of the log in form (**Figure 6**) and click Enter. The .Mac Home page appears (**Figure 5**).

✔ Tip

- Your member name may automatically be entered in the Log In form (**Figure 6**).

To log out

Click the Log Out link on the .Mac Home page (**Figure 5**) or the Log Out button at the top of any .Mac page.

✔ Tip

- If you do not log out of .Mac, anyone using your computer will have access to your .Mac account. It's a good idea to log out after using .Mac when you're working on a shared computer.

Figure 5 The .Mac page when you're logged in to your account. The page changes daily (if not more often), so what you see probably won't look exactly like this.

Figure 6 Use this log-in form to log into your .Mac account.

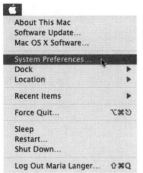

Figure 7
Choose System Preferences from the Apple menu.

Figure 8 Enter .Mac log in information in the .Mac preferences pane.

To configure .Mac preferences

1. Choose Apple > System Preferences (**Figure 7**), or click the System Preferences icon in the Dock.

2. In the System Preferences window that appears, click the .Mac icon to display the .Mac preferences pane.

3. If necessary, click the .Mac button to display its options (**Figure 8**).

4. Enter your .Mac member name and password in the appropriate boxes.

5. Choose System Preferences > Quit System Preferences or press ⌃⌘Q to save your changes.

✔ Tip

■ If you created a .Mac account when you registered Mac OS X, .Mac preferences (**Figure 8**) should already contain your .Mac login information.

Mail

Figure 9 A Mail Inbox with messages.

Mail is .Mac's e-mail feature. When you set up a .Mac account, you automatically get an e-mail account in the mac.com domain name. For example, if your member name is *johnjones*, your email account would be *johnjones@mac.com*.

Your .Mac e-mail account can be accessed with Mac OS X's Mail application or any other e-mail client software—such as Entourage or Eudora. Simply set it up as a IMAP account using the following information:

User Name: *your .Mac member name*
Password: *your password*
Incoming Mail Server: mail.mac.com
Outgoing Mail Server: smtp.mac.com

Your .Mac e-mail account can also be accessed via the Web on the .Mac Web site. This feature enables you to read and reply to your e-mail from any computer with a connection to the Internet.

This part of the chapter explains the basics of reading and sending e-mail messages using Mail on the .Mac Web site.

✔ Tip

- I explain how to use the Mail application in **Chapter 11**.

To access your Mail account

1. Log in to your .Mac account on the .Mac Web site.

2. Click the Mail button on the .Mac home page (**Figure 5**).

3. If a log in form appears (**Figure 6**), enter your password and click Enter.

4. Your Mail Inbox window appears (**Figure 9**).

Figure 10 When you click a message subject, the message appears in a Web browser window.

Figure 11
Use this pop-up menu to move a message to a different folder.

To read & work with messages

1. Click the subject of the message you want to read. The message appears in the Web browser window (**Figure 10**).

2. To read the next or previous message, click the up or down arrow beneath the toolbar.

   or

   To return to the folder you were viewing, click the blue link for the folder name beneath the toolbar.

   or

   Click one of the buttons in the toolbar to work with the message:

   ▲ **Delete** deletes the message.

   ▲ **Reply** opens a reply form (**Figure 15**) and addresses it to the message sender.

   ▲ **Reply All** opens a reply form (**Figure 15**) and addresses it to the sender, as well as anyone else the message was originally addressed to.

   ▲ **Forward** opens a message forwarding form with the body of the original message copied to the body of the form.

   ▲ **Add Sender** adds the sender's name and e-mail address to your .Mac Address Book.

   or

   To move the message to a specific folder, choose the folder name from the Move Message To pop-up menu (**Figure 11**)

✔ Tips

- A blue bullet beside the From column in the message list indicates that that message has not yet been read.

- I tell you about the .Mac Address Book feature later in this chapter.

To update the Inbox

Click the Get Mail button (**Figure 9**). The Inbox is updated to include any new messages that have been received since the Inbox's contents were last displayed.

To view a specific folder

Choose the folder name from the Go To pop-up menu (**Figure 12**) in any folder list window (**Figure 9**).

To delete messages in a folder

1. Turn on the check box beside the message(s) you want to delete.

2. Click the Delete button in the toolbar. The message(s) is deleted and the window reappears with the message(s) gone.

To send a message

1. Click the Compose button in the toolbar to display a new message form (**Figure 13**).

2. Fill in the To, Cc (if desired), and Subject fields in the form.

3. To save a copy of the form in the Sent Messages folder, turn on the Save a Copy check box.

4. Enter the body of the message in the large box at the bottom of the form.

5. Click Send. The message is sent.

✔ Tips

- To look up and insert e-mail addresses from Address Book, click the Address Book button, use the pop-up menus beside a person's name to specify a message form field (**Figure 14**), and click Apply.

- To include more than one e-mail address in the To or Cc field, separate each address with a comma.

Figure 12
Use this pop-up menu to display the contents of a specific folder.

Figure 13 A new message form, all ready to be filled in.

Figure 14 You can use the Address Book to address a message.

Figure 15 A message reply form already has the To and Subject fields filled in.

To reply to a message

1. With the message you want to reply to displayed (**Figure 10**), click the Reply or Reply All button.

2. A message reply form appears (**Figure 15**). Its To and Cc fields are already filled in with the appropriate e-mail addresses.

3. If desired, change the contents of the Subject field.

4. To save a copy of the form in the Sent Messages folder, turn on the Save a Copy check box.

5. Insert your reply in the large text field at the bottom of the form.

6. Click Send. The message is sent.

✔ Tips

- By default, the body of the original message is quoted in the reply. You can edit or delete this text if desired.

- If the original message was very long, it may be included with the reply as an attachment.

Address Book

Address Book, a relatively new feature of .Mac, enables you to synchronize your computer's Address Book with your .Mac account Address Book. This makes it possible to get information from your Address Book from any computer with an Internet connection.

✔ Tip

■ Like all information for your .Mac account, your Address Book is accessible only to you—you must log in to .Mac to view it.

To set up .Mac Address Book synchronization

1. On the .Mac Home page (**Figure 5**), click the Address Book link.

2. A .Mac Address Book Synchronization page appears (**Figure 16**). Click the Turn On Syncing button.

   A "Sync in progress" message appears (**Figure 17**) while your computer synchronizes its Address Book entries with the .Mac Address Book. When it's finished, the entries appear (**Figure 18**).

✔ Tips

■ If the page in **Figure 16** does not appear in step 2, and you don't see your Address Book information, click the Address Book button on the .Mac Home page. Enter your password, if prompted, and click Enter. Click the Preferences button in the Address Book window. Turn on the Turn on .Mac Address Book synchronization check box and then click Save. .Mac will sync your Address Book.

Figure 16 This page appears the first time you access the Address Book feature on .Mac.

Figure 17 A progress dialog appears while the Address Book data on .Mac and your computer are synchronized for the first time.

Figure 18 The first page of your .Mac Address Book appears.

■ Once Address Book syncing has been set up as instructed here, the Address Books will automatically be synced each time you use iSync. I explain how to use iSync in **Chapter 8**.

ADDRESS BOOK

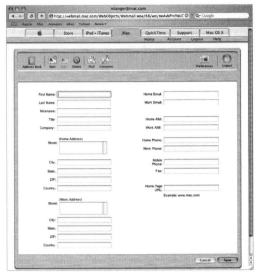

Figure 19 Fill in this form to create a new entry.

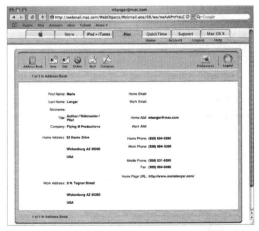

Figure 20 A confirmation page appears when you try to delete Address Book entries.

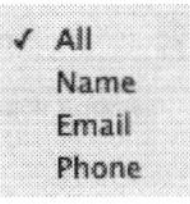

Figure 21 Use this pop-up menu to specify which fields should be searched.

Figure 22 Details for an entry appear in a page like this.

To work with the Address Book list

Use buttons, check boxes, and other elements in the Address Book list (**Figure 18**) to work with entries:

◆ To add an Address Book entry, click the New button. Then fill out the form that appears (**Figure 19**) and click Save.

◆ To edit an entry, turn on the check box to the left of the entry name and click Edit. A form similar to the one in **Figure 19** appears, with some fields already filled in. Make changes as necessary and click Save.

◆ To delete one or more entries, turn on the check box to the left of entry names and click the Delete button. A confirmation window like the one in **Figure 20** appears. Click Yes to delete the entries. If syncing is turned on, the entries will also be deleted from that Address Book data on your computer when you use iSync.

◆ To access Mail, click the Mail button (to display your Inbox; **Figure 9**) or the Compose button (to display a new message form; **Figure 13**).

◆ To search for an entry, enter search criteria in the text box and choose a field from the pop-up menu (**Figure 21**). Then click the magnifying glass button. A list of matches appears.

◆ To see all details for an entry, click the entry name. A page with all recorded information for the entry appears (**Figure 22**).

◆ To set Address Book preferences, click the Preferences button and set options on the page that appears.

Bookmarks

.Mac's Bookmarks feature enables you to synchronize your Safari bookmarks between your computer and .Mac. Once the bookmarks are stored on .Mac, you can access them from any computer with an Internet connection, making it easy to surf your favorite Web sites, even when you're away from your computer.

To set up Bookmarks synchronization

1. On the .Mac Home page (**Figure 5**), click the Bookmarks link.

2. A Sync Your .Mac Bookmarks page appears (**Figure 23**). Click the Sync Now button.

   A "Sync in progress" message appears (**Figure 24**) while your computer synchronizes its Safari bookmarks with .Mac's Bookmarks. When it's finished, the .Mac Home page reappears (**Figure 5**).

✔ Tips

- If the page in **Figure 23** does not appear in step 2, you have already synchronized your bookmarks. You can skip these instructions.

- Once bookmark syncing has been set up as instructed here, bookmarks will automatically be synced each time you use iSync. I explain how to use iSync in **Chapter 8**.

Figure 23 The first time you access .Mac Bookmarks, a page like this appears.

Figure 24 This message appears while the bookmarks are being synchronized.

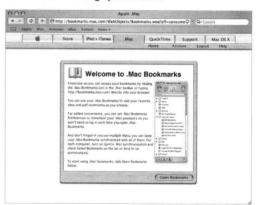

Figure 25 You may see a Welcome message like this when you access .Mac Bookmarks.

Figure 26 Your bookmarks appear in a customized Safari window.

Figure 27
You can use this pop-up menu to select one of your bookmark collections.

Figure 28
Bookmarks within a collection or folder appear in this window.

Add Bookmark   Add Folder   Delete

Figure 29 Enter information and click Add to create a new bookmark.

Figure 30 Click an X button to delete a bookmark or folder.

To open .Mac Bookmarks

1. After synchronizing bookmarks for the first time as discussed on the previous page, click the Bookmarks link on the .Mac Home page (**Figure 5**).

2. An introductory page like the one in **Figure 25** may appear. Read it and click Open Bookmarks.

   A Safari window like the one in **Figure 26** appears. It lists all bookmark collections.

To work with the Bookmarks list

Use buttons and menus within the Bookmarks list window (**Figure 26**) to work with your bookmarks:

◆ To open a collection, choose its name from the pop-up menu (**Figure 27**) or double-click its folder in the list. A list of bookmarks within that collection appears (**Figure 28**).

◆ To open a bookmarked page, click the bookmark's icon or name. The page opens in a new Safari window.

◆ To add a new bookmark, click the Add Bookmark button (**Figure 28**). Enter bookmark information in the fields that appear (**Figure 29**) and click Add.

◆ To add a new bookmark folder, click the Add Folder button (**Figure 28**). Enter folder information in the fields that appear and click Add.

◆ To delete a bookmark or folder, display it in the bookmarks list, click the Delete button (**Figure 28**), and then click the X beside the item you want to delete (**Figure 30**). Click the Delete button that appears to confirm the deletion.

◆ To set Bookmarks preferences, click the Preferences button, set options in the window that appears, and click Save.

iDisk

iDisk is 100 MB of private hard disk space on an Apple Internet server that you can use to store files and publish a Web site. But rather than deal with complex FTP software to access your iDisk space, Apple gives you access from within the Finder's Sidebar (**Figure 31**) and within Open and Save dialogs (**Figures 47** and **48**). Best of all, you manage files in your iDisk storage space just like you manage files on any other mounted volume.

Your iDisk storage space (**Figure 31**) is preorganized into folders, just like your Mac OS X home folder:

◆ **Documents** is for storing documents. This folder is completely private; only you have access to it.

◆ **Music**, **Pictures**, and **Movies** are for storing various types of media. By storing multimedia files in these folder, they're available to other .Mac programs, including iCard and HomePage.

◆ **Public** is for storing files you want to share with others. This folder can only be opened by a .Mac member who knows your member name.

◆ **Sites** is for storing Web pages that you want to publish on the World Wide Web. HomePage, a .Mac program I discuss later in this chapter, automatically stores Web pages here. You can also create Web pages with another authoring tool and publish them by placing them in this folder.

◆ **Backup** is for data files that have been backed up using the Backup feature of .Mac, which I discuss later in this chapter. It is a read-only folder, so you cannot manually add anything to it. This folder does not appear until you use the Backup feature.

Figure 31 The contents of your iDisk home folder.

◆ **Software** is a read-only folder maintained by Apple Computer. It contains Apple software updates and other download-able third-party applications that might interest you. The contents of this folder do not count toward the 100 MB of disk space iDisk allows you—which is a good thing, because many of these files are very large!

This part of the chapter tells you how you can access your iDisk storage space from your computer.

✔ Tips

■ iDisk is a great place to store secondary backups of important files. For example, if you're a Quicken 2003 user, you probably let Quicken automatically back up your financial data at the end of each Quicken session. But also consider putting a copy of the data on your iDisk space as an off-premises backup for added protection against data loss. As a .Mac member, you can automate this process with the Backup feature of .Mac, which I discuss later in this chapter.

■ You can purchase additional iDisk space from Apple if you need it. I explain how on the next page.

■ I cover file management operations such as copying and deleting files in **Chapters 2 through 4**.

■ Your iDisk home folder (**Figure 31**) also includes a text file called About your iDisk, which has more information about iDisk. You can open this file with TextEdit.

iDISK

To set iDisk preferences

1. Choose Apple > System Preferences (**Figure 7**), or click the System Preferences icon in the Dock.

2. In the System Preferences window that appears, click the .Mac icon to display the .Mac preferences pane.

3. Click the iDisk button. Your computer connects the Internet to retrieve iDisk information. When it's finished, your iDisk settings appear (**Figure 32**).

4. To buy more iDisk storage space, click the Buy More button. Your computer's default Web browser opens and displays a log in page for the .Mac Web site. Follow the instructions that appear onscreen to complete the transaction. The storage space is made available to you almost immediately.

5. To copy the contents of your iDisk storage space to your computer's hard disk, turn on the Create a local copy of your iDisk check box. You can then choose one of the Synchronize options:

   ▲ **Automatically** automatically syncs your iDisk and its local copy when you connect to the Internet.

   ▲ **Manually** requires you to initiate a synchronization.

6. Set options to control Public folder access:

   ▲ **Allow others to** enables you to specify whether other users can only read the contents of your public folder or both read and save files to your public folder.

   ▲ **Use a Password to Protect Your Public Folder** enables you to set a password that users must enter to access your Public folder. When you turn on this option, a password dialog sheet appears (**Figure 33**). Enter the same password twice and click OK.

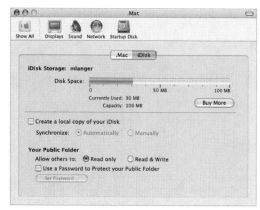

Figure 32 The iDisk pane of the .Mac preferences pane.

Figure 33 Use this dialog to set a password to protect your Public folder on iDisk.

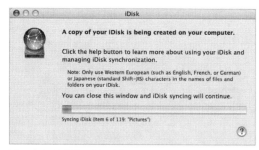

Figure 34 A dialog like this may appear when you enable iDisk synchronization.

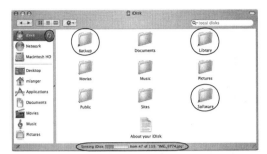

Figure 35 The iDisk window after synchronization is enabled.

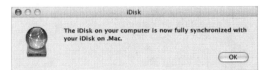

Figure 36 Your computer tells you when a manual sync is finished.

Figure 37 You can see sync status in iDisk's Finder window.

Figure 38 Use the Actions pop-up menu to manually initiate a sync.

7. Choose System Preferences > Quit System Preferences or press ⌃⌘Q to save your changes.

✔ Tips

- Creating a copy of your iDisk on your computer is a great way to quickly access most iDisk items, even when you're not connected to the Internet.

- If you enabled iDisk synchronization in step 5, a dialog like the one in **Figure 34** may appear when you quit System Preferences. You can close the window without interrupting the syncing process.

- When your iDisk is being synchronized, spinning arrows appear beside the iDisk icon in the Sidebar and a progress bar appears at the bottom of the window (**Figure 35**). When syncing is complete, a dialog tells you (**Figure 36**), the icon stops spinning and a bullet appears inside it, and the sync status appears in the status bar (**Figure 37**)

- When you create a copy of your iDisk, your entire iDisk is not copied to your computer. Instead, your computer makes aliases to the Backup, Library, and Software folders (**Figure 34**), which can be rather large and which cannot be modified by you anyway.

- To manually sync your iDisk, choose Sync Now from the Actions pop-up menu (**Figure 38**) when iDisk is selected in the Sidebar.

- You can change the password you set up in step 6 by clicking the Set Password button (**Figure 32**).

To open your iDisk storage space from the Finder

Click the iDisk icon in the Sidebar (**Figure 31** or **37**).

or

Choose Go > iDisk > My iDisk (**Figure 39**) or press Shift Ô ⌘ I .

A Finder window with your iDisk contents appears (**Figure 31** or **37**) and an iDisk icon appears on the desktop (**Figure 40**).

✔ Tip

■ The status bar of the Finder window (**Figure 31** or **37**) tells you how much space is left in your iDisk storage space. To display the status bar, make sure the window is active and then choose View > Show Status Bar.

To open another user's iDisk

1. Choose Go > iDisk > Other User's iDisk (**Figure 39**).

2. In the Connect to iDisk dialog that appears (**Figure 41**), enter the user's .Mac member name and password to open the iDisk. Then click Connect.

A window displaying the contents of the user's iDisk appears (**Figure 42**) and an icon for that iDisk appears on the desktop (**Figure 40**).

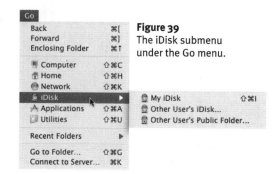

Figure 39
The iDisk submenu under the Go menu.

Figure 40
Volume icons representing iDisk storage space appear on your desktop when you access iDisk.

Figure 41 Use this dialog to enter the user's member name and password.

Figure 42 A window displaying the contents of the user's iDisk appears.

Figure 43 Use this dialog to enter the member's name.

Figure 44 If a Public folder is password-protected, a dialog like this appears.

Figure 45 A window containing the contents of the user's Public folder appears.

To open a user's Public folder

1. Choose Go > iDisk > Other User's Public Folder (**Figure 39**).

2. In the Connect to iDisk Public Folder dialog that appears (**Figure 43**), enter the .Mac member name and click Connect.

3. If the Public folder is password-protected, a WebDAV File System Authentication dialog like the one in **Figure 44** appears. Enter the password to access the folder and click OK.

A window displaying the contents of the user's Public folder appears (**Figure 45**) and an icon for that folder appears on the desktop (**Figure 40**).

To save a file to iDisk from within an application

1. Choose File > Save As (**Figure 46**) to display the Save dialog.

2. If necessary, click the triangle beside the Save As box to display the Sidebar and file locations (**Figure 47**).

3. In the Sidebar, click iDisk and choose a location on iDisk in which to save the file.

4. Enter a name for the file in the Save As box.

5. Click Save. The file is saved to the folder you selected in your iDisk storage space.

To open a file on iDisk from within an application

1. Choose File > Open (**Figure 46**) to display the Open dialog.

2. In the Sidebar, click iDisk (**Figure 48**) and choose the folder in which the file you want to open resides.

3. In the list of files, select the file you want to open.

4. Click Open. The file is opened in a document window.

Figure 46
Like most other applications, TextEdit's File menu includes commands for saving and opening files.

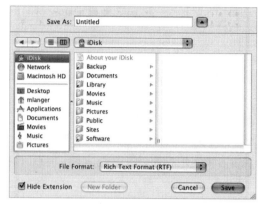

Figure 47 Click iDisk in the Save dialog's Sidebar to open the iDisk folder.

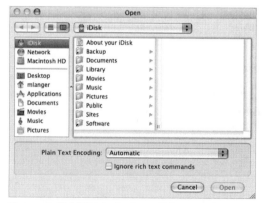

Figure 48 Click iDisk in the Open dialog's Sidebar to access folders and files stored on your iDisk.

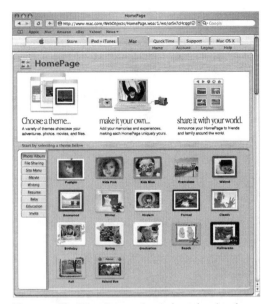

Figure 49 The HomePage main window, showing the Photo Album templates.

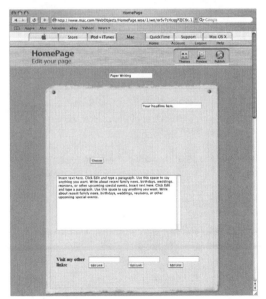

Figure 50 Clicking the Edit button near the top-right corner of the preview page enables you to edit the default text on the page.

HomePage

HomePage is a Web-based authoring tool that you can access from the .Mac Web site. With it, you can create Web pages for a variety of purposes, all without knowing a single tag of HTML.

This part of the chapter explains how you can use the templates included in HomePage to create a Web page or site and announce it to your friends and family members.

✔ Tip

■ HomePage uses images and other media already saved in your iDisk storage space. For that reason, it's a good idea to copy the images, movies, and other media you want to appear on your Web pages to appropriate locations on iDisk *before* creating a page.

To create a Web page or site

1. Use your Web browser to open the .Mac home page and, if necessary, log in.

2. Click the HomePage button.

3. In the HomePage main window (**Figure 49**), select one of the themes listed in tabs along the left side of the window. The template previews change to show templates in that theme.

4. Click the template preview you want to use.

5. HomePage begins by displaying a series of pages that prompt you for information, such as a folder in your iDisk storage space that contains images or text that you want to appear on the page. Follow the instructions that appear onscreen. You'll need to click an Edit button to edit any text that appears onscreen and a

Continued on next page...

Continued from previous page.

Preview button to see the results of your edits. **Figures 50** through **52** show some of the screens for creating an article using the paper-writing template.

6. When you're satisfied with your finished page or site, click the Publish button. HomePage saves its Web page files to your iDisk storage space and displays a Congratulations screen, which includes the URL for the site (**Figure 53**).

7. To announce your page or site to your friends or family members, click the iCard link. Then select an image, fill out the form, and click Send iCard in the page that appears (**Figure 54**).

✔ Tips

- It's impossible for me to cover every single instruction for creating every single type of Web page. The information presented here should be enough to get you started creating any type of Web page. Don't be afraid to experiment!

- I provide more information about using iCards next.

- Once a page has been created, it will be listed near the top of the HomePage main page. You use buttons beneath the list to add, delete, or edit pages.

Figure 51 You can add photos from your iDisk.

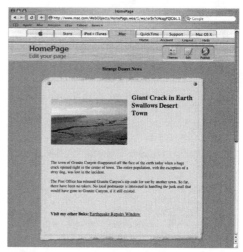

Figure 52 Here's a preview of the completed page before it has been published.

Figure 54 Fill out a form like this to send an iCard announcing the Web page to your family and friends.

Figure 53 HomePage confirms that your page has been published and provides its URL. It also offers a link you can click to announce the page with an iCard.

Figure 55 iCards' main page on the .Mac Web site.

Figure 56 If a theme has multiple categories, you can select the category you want.

Figure 57 Choose the image that you want to appear on your card.

iCards

iCards is a .Mac feature that enables you to send postcard-like e-mail messages to anyone with an e-mail address. The cards you send can use one of many photos available within iCards or a photo or other image from your iDisk storage space.

✔ Tips

- You do not need to be a member of .Mac to send or receive iCards. However, only .Mac members can send custom iCards that utilize their own images.

- The announcement feature of HomePage (**Figure 54**) utilizes iCards to tell people about the Web sites you publish with HomePage.

To send an iCard

1. Use your Web browser to open the .Mac home page and, if necessary, log in.

2. Click the iCards button.

3. In the iCards main window (**Figure 55**), click to select one of the theme buttons.

4. If a page with categories appears (**Figure 56**), click to select one of the categories.

5. On the next page that appears (**Figure 57**), click to select one of the stock images.

6. On the Personalize your very own iCard page (**Figure 58**), enter a message in the box near the top of the window. Then select a radio button for the font you want applied.

7. Click Continue to display the addressing window (**Figure 59**).

Continued on next page...

Continued from previous page.

8. Enter an e-mail address in the Recipient's Email Address box and click Add Recipient. Repeat this process for each person you want to send the card to.

9. When you are finished entering addresses, click Send Your Card.

10. A Thank You page appears, confirming that your card has been sent. Buttons on the page enable you to return to iCards categories or send the same card to someone else.

✔ Tip

■ If you choose one of the Create Your Own options, a page that enables you to browse through pictures in your iDisk storage space appears (**Figure 60**). Use the file list, Open, and Preview buttons to locate and preview your images. When the image you want appears in the Image Preview area, click the Select this Image button to use it on your iCard. Then follow steps 6 though 10 to complete and send your card.

Figure 58 Use this page to enter a message and select a font for your iCard.

Figure 59 Finally, use this page to enter the e-mail addresses of card recipients.

Figure 60 Use a page like this to locate and select an image from your iDisk storage space.

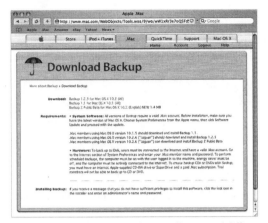

Figure 61 Backup's download page offer several different versions. As you can see, Backup 2 was still in beta when I wrote about it.

Figure 62
The disk image icon for the Backup installer disk, along with the mounted disk image.

Figure 63 The contents of the Backup installer disk.

Backup

Backup is an application that works with a .Mac account. It enables you to back up all or part of your hard disk to CD, DVD, or your iDisk storage space.

To use Backup, you must download and install the Backup software. You can get it from the Backup main page on the .Mac Web site. Once installed, you set options to determine what should be backed up and where it should be backed up to.

✔ Tip

- This part of the chapter covers Backup 2.0, which was still in beta when I wrote this book.

To download & install Backup

1. Use your Web browser to open the .Mac home page and, if necessary, log in.

2. Click the Backup button to display the Backup main page.

3. Click the Download Backup button.

4. On the Download Backup page that appears (**Figure 61**), click the link for the version of Backup that you want to download. Make sure you download a version that is compatible with your version of Mac OS X (10.3 Panther).

5. Wait while Backup downloads. If you display the Downloads window of Safari, you can see its progress.

6. If necessary, double-click the Backup disk image file icon to mount the installer disk (**Figure 62**). (It should appear on your desktop, unless you changed your browser's default download location.)

Continued on next page...

DOWNLOADING & INSTALLING BACKUP

Continued from previous page.

7. If necessary, double-click the Backup disk to open its window (**Figure 63**).

8. Double-click the Backup.pkg icon to launch the Installer.

9. If a dialog appears, asking if the Installer package can run a program, click Continue.

10. Follow the instructions that appear in installer windows (**Figure 64**) to install the software on your hard disk. Along the way, an Authenticate dialog like the one in **Figure 65** may appear. Enter an administrator's name and password and click OK.

11. Click the Close button in the final Installer window to quit the installer.

12. Drag the Backup installer disk to the Trash to unmount it.

✔ Tips

- Backup is installed in your Applications folder (**Figure 66**).

- After installing backup, you can delete the Backup installer disk image file. Personally, I like to archive software like this on CD in case I ever need to reinstall it from scratch.

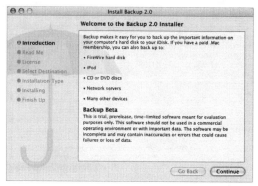

Figure 64 The first screen of Backup's installer window. The installer works just like any other Mac installer.

Figure 65 Before you can install Backup, you may need to prove that you have administrator privileges.

Figure 66 Backup and Virex are installed in your Applications folder.

Figure 67 The first time you run Backup, it may display a dialog thanking you for joining .Mac.

Figure 68 Backup's main window.

Figure 69 To add an item to the Backup list, simply drag its icon into the Backup window.

Figure 70
Choose a backup or restore location from this pop-up menu.

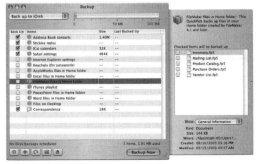

Figure 71 Double-clicking an item in Backup's window displays a drawer that itemizes contents.

To configure Backup

1. Double-click the Backup icon in the Applications folder (**Figure 66**).

2. Backup connects to the Internet and confirms that you have a valid .Mac account. When it's finished, it may display a dialog like the one in **Figure 67**. Click OK to dismiss it.

3. The main Backup window appears (**Figure 68**). It lists all the predefined items that Backup can recognize. Modify the item list as follows:

   ▲ To determine whether a listed item should be backed up, toggle the Back Up check box beside it.

   ▲ To add an item to be backed up, drag the icon for the item from a Finder window into the Backup window (**Figure 69**).

   ▲ To remove an item from the list, select it and press Delete.

4. Choose a backup location from the pop-up menu at the top of the window (**Figure 70**).

✔ Tips

■ You must have your .Mac account information properly entered in the .Mac preferences pane (**Figure 8**) for Backup to complete step 2.

■ List items with tiny package icons (**Figure 68**) are called *QuickPicks*. They make it possible to quickly locate and back up specific types of files, no matter where they are located in your Home folder.

■ If you double-click an item in the list, a drawer slides out and displays a list of files that will be backed up (**Figure 71**).

To schedule backups to iDisk

1. In the main Backup window (**Figure 68**), make sure Backup to iDisk is chosen from the pop-up menu (**Figure 70**).

2. Click the Schedule automatic backups to your iDisk button, which looks like a calendar, at the bottom of the window.

3. Then set options in the dialog sheet that appears (**Figure 72**) to set the frequency and time of the Backup.

4. Click OK.

✔ Tips

- Although you can set automatic backups to any location on the pop-up menu in **Figure 70**, that location must be available at the time of backup for the backup to occur.

- For a scheduled backup to occur:
  - ▲ Your computer must be turned on and not set to sleep.
  - ▲ You must be logged in to the computer. (You can use Fast User Switching, as discussed in **Chapter 15** so others can log in without logging you out.)
  - ▲ The Backup application cannot be running.

- Scheduled backups are completed in the background as you work and do not disrupt your normal work session.

- I've been using the automatic backup feature of Backup for over a year now and I love it! It takes care of backing up the little files I'd normally neglect, like my Address Book and iCal calendars, as well as folders full of important documents I wouldn't want to lose.

Figure 72 Use this dialog to schedule automatic backups to iDisk.

Figure 73 A window like this appears as Backup works.

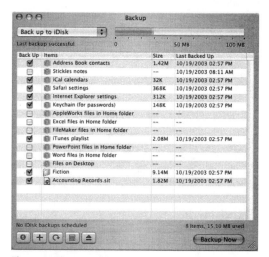

Figure 74 The main backup window indicates the status of the previous backup.

SCHEDULING BACKUPS TO iDISK

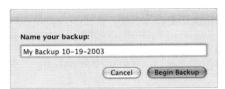

Figure 75 Use this dialog to specify a name for the backup disc.

Figure 76 The Burn Disc dialog after a disc has been inserted.

Figure 77 Backup shows the backup progress.

Figure 78 A dialog like this one confirms that the backup was successful.

To manually back up to iDisk

1. In the main Backup window (**Figure 68**), make sure Backup to iDisk is chosen from the pop-up menu (**Figure 70**).

2. Click the Backup Now button. A backup window like the one in **Figure 73** appears to indicate the progress of the backup. When it's finished, Backup's main window reappears, indicating the last backup date for all of the backed up files (**Figure 74**).

To manually back up to CD or DVD

1. In the main Backup window (**Figure 68**), choose Back up to CD/DVD from the pop-up menu (**Figure 70**).

2. If necessary, select the items you want to back up as discussed earlier in this section.

3. Click the Backup Now button.

4. A dialog like the one in **Figure 75** appears. Enter a name for the backup and click Begin Backup.

5. The Burn Disc dialog appears and the CD/DVD drive opens. Insert a blank CD or DVD and close the drive.

6. Click Burn in the Burn Disc dialog (**Figure 76**).

7. A backup window like the one in **Figure 77** appears to indicate the progress of the backup, CD or DVD burn, and verification. When Backup is finished, the CD/DVD drive opens and a dialog like the one in **Figure 78** appears. Remove the CD or DVD from the drive and Click OK to dismiss the dialog.

✔ Tips

■ Backing up to CD or DVD rather than iDisk makes it possible to restore damaged files from backups when an Internet connection is not available.

■ If a backup requires more than one CD or DVD, Backup will prompt you to insert them.

To manually back up to another drive

1. In the main Backup window (**Figure 68**), choose Back up to Drive from the pop-up menu (**Figure 79**).

2. Click the Set button and use the Save dialog that appears (**Figure 80**) to choose a disk location and enter a name for the backup file. Click Save.

3. If necessary, select the items you want to back up as discussed earlier in this section.

4. Click the Backup Now button.

5. A backup window like the one in **Figure 81** appears to indicate the progress of the backup. When Backup is finished, the main Backup window reappears.

✔ Tips

- In step 2, if a backup file already exists on disk, you can click the Select button and use the Open dialog that appears to locate, select, and open an existing backup file.

- Although you can back up to the same disk on which the files reside, that backup won't do you much good if the disk crashes. It's always a good idea to back up to a separate disk—and the farther away from your computer, the better!

Figure 79 When you choose Back up to Drive, a Set button appears at the top of the Backup window.

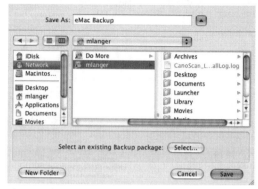

Figure 80 Use this Save dialog to specify a name and location for the backup file. In this example, I'm setting up to back up to my Home folder on another computer on my network.

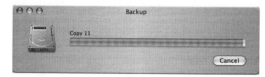

Figure 81 A disk icon appears in the Backup window when it backs up to a disk.

Figure 82 When you restore from a CD or DVD, Backup displays a dialog like this one with instructions on which disc to insert.

Figure 83 Turn on the check boxes beside each item you want to restore.

Figure 84 Backup asks whether you want to overwrite existing files with the backup copies.

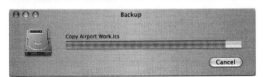

Figure 85 A progress dialog like this one appears as the files are restored.

To restore files

1. In the main Backup window (**Figure 68**), choose a Restore option from the pop-up menu (**Figure 70**).

2. If you chose Restore from CD/DVD, a dialog like the one in **Figure 82** appears. Click the eject button to open the CD or DVD drive. Insert the CD or DVD containing the backup you want to restore from and close the drive.

3. In the main Backup window, click to place a check box beside each item you want to restore (**Figure 83**).

4. Click the Restore Now button.

5. If the file you are restoring already exists, a dialog like the one in **Figure 84** appears. Click Replace or Skip to either replace the existing copy with the backup or keep the existing copy. Repeat this step each time the dialog appears.

   A restore progress dialog like the one in **Figure 85** appears. When it disappears, the restore is finished.

Virex

Virex (**Figure 86**) gives .Mac members access to McAfee Virex virus protection software, Virex updates, and other virus protection resources. This .Mac feature can prevent a lot of headaches if used correctly.

In this part of the chapter, I explain how to download, install, configure, use, and update Virex software.

✔ Tips

- This feature was known as Anti-Virus in some past versions of .Mac, but it always included Virex software.

- Virus protection software is only good if you keep it updated and use it regularly.

- You can help prevent viruses from harming your computer with a little common sense. Since most viruses are transmitted by opening files, don't open files that you receive via e-mail from strangers. This simple safeguard can protect your computer and help prevent the further spread of viruses.

- When it comes to viruses, Mac OS users are lucky. There are far fewer viruses that affect Macintoshes than Wintel systems.

Figure 86 The Virex main page on .Mac.

Figure 87
The Virex installer disk image and mounted disk on the Desktop.

Figure 88 The contents of the Virex installer disk.

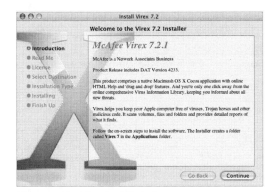

Figure 89 The Virex Installer's first screen.

Figure 90 You can find Virex and some documentation files in the Virex 7 folder installed in your Applications folder.

To download & install Virex

1. Use your Web browser to open the .Mac home page and, if necessary, log in.

2. Click the Virex button to display the Virex main page (**Figure 86**).

3. Click the Download Virex button.

4. On the Download Virex page that appears, click the link for the version of Virex that you want to download.

5. Wait while Virex downloads. If you display the Downloads window of Safari, you can see its progress.

6. If necessary, double-click the Virex disk image file icon to mount the installer disk (**Figure 87**). (It should appear on your desktop, unless you changed your browser's default download location.)

7. If necessary, double-click the Virex disk to open its window (**Figure 88**).

8. Double-click the Virex 7.2.pkg icon to launch the Installer.

9. Follow the instructions that appear in installer windows (**Figure 89**) to install the software on your hard disk. If an Authenticate dialog appears (**Figure 65**), enter an administrator name and password and click OK.

10. Click the Close button in the final Installer window to quit the installer.

11. Drag the Virex installer disk to the Trash to unmount it.

✔ Tips

- Virex is installed in the Virex 7 folder (**Figure 90**) in your Applications folder (**Figure 66**).

- After installing Virex, you can delete the Virex installer disk image file.

To scan for viruses

1. Open the Virex 7.2 icon in the Virex 7 folder (**Figure 90**) in your Applications folder (**Figure 66**).

2. If Virex displays a dialog like the one in **Figure 91**, it needs to check the Internet for virus definition updates. Enter an administrator's password and click OK. Virex connects to the Internet and checks for virus updates. If it finds any, it automatically installs them. You can monitor its status in the bottom right corner of Virex's main window (**Figure 92**).

3. In the main Virex window (**Figure 93**), choose a location to scan from the Scan pop-up menu (**Figure 94**).

4. To automatically clean any virus-infected files, turn on the check box marked Clean any files affected with a virus.

5. Click Scan.

6. Wait while Virex scans for viruses. It displays its progress in its main window as it works (**Figure 95**). When it's finished, it displays a Summary report (**Figure 96**).

✔ Tips

- You can manually initiate an eUpdate by clicking the eUpdate button in Virex's toolbar (**Figure 93**).

- The more you scan, the longer the scan will take. For example, scanning your hard disk will take far longer than scanning just your Home folder.

- You can continue using your computer while Virex scans.

- By default, Virex will scan your Home folder every time you start up or log in. I explain how to set preferences like this one next.

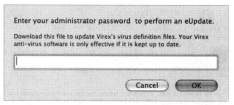

Figure 91 Virex displays a dialog sheet like this when it needs to check for virus definition updates using its eUpdate feature.

Figure 92
Monitor eUpdate progress in the corner of the window.

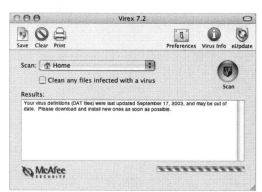

Figure 93 The Virex main window. When you first launch Virex, it provides the date of the last update.

Figure 94
Use this menu to tell Virex what you want to scan.

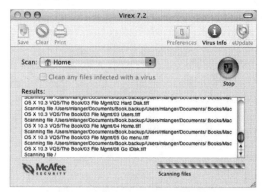

Figure 95 As Virex scans, it displays its progress.

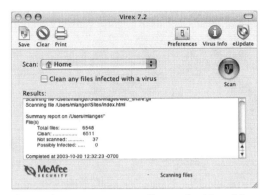

Figure 96 A summary report tells you what Virex did and found.

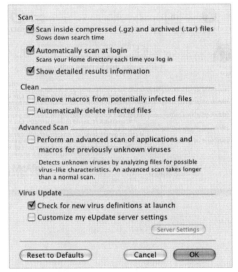

Figure 97 Virex's preferences appear in a dialog sheet like this one.

✔ Tip

■ Microsoft Word macros are a popular way of distributing viruses to both Mac OS and Windows users. You can help protect your computer against macro viruses by enabling macro virus protection in Word's preferences.

To set Virex preferences

1. If Virex isn't already running, launch it.

2. Choose Virex 7.2 > Preferences to display a dialog sheet of Virex preferences (**Figure 97**).

3. Set options as desired:

   ▲ **Scan inside compressed (.gz) and archived (.tar) files** tells Virex to look inside compressed and archived files to scan their contents.

   ▲ **Automatically scan at login** tells Virex to automatically scan your Home folder when you start up or log in.

   ▲ **Show detailed results information** provides details of what Virex found in its summary report (**Figure 96**).

   ▲ **Remove macros from potentially infected files** tells Virex to remove macros from Microsoft Office documents, such as Word files.

   ▲ **Automatically delete infected files** tells Virex to delete any file it believes contains a virus.

   ▲ **Perform an advanced scan of applications and macros for previously unknown viruses** tells Virex to analyze applications and macros using its knowledge of virus-like characteristics rather than just the virus definitions file.

   ▲ **Check for new virus definitions at launch** enables the automatic eUpdate feature.

   ▲ **Customize my eUpdate server settings** enables you to create custom server settings for the eUpdate feature. Do not use this advanced option unless you have received specific instructions from your network administrator to do so.

4. Click OK to save your settings.

Support

Support is a series of additional support options, some of which are available only to .Mac members. These include:

◆ **Tips and Tricks** are short articles with how-to instructions for tasks that'll increase your productivity.

◆ **Discussion Boards** are online discussions among .Mac members about .Mac and Macintosh computing issues. It's a great place to learn from and help users just like you.

◆ **FAQ's** are answers to frequently asked questions about .Mac.

◆ **AppleCare KnowledgeBase** is a searchable database of technical documents written by Apple support staff about Apple products. It includes information, software downloads, manuals, answers to frequently asked questions, and troubleshooting tips.

◆ **Feedback** is a way you can send your comments about .Mac to Apple.

◆ **Help Links** are links to online help for .Mac features, including iDisk, Email, HomePage, iCards, Backup, and Virex.

To access Support

1. Use your Web browser to open the .Mac Home page and, if necessary, log in.

2. Click the Support button to display the Support main page (**Figure 98**).

3. Follow links on the Support page to explore Support and get the information you need.

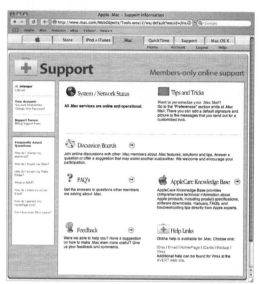

Figure 98 The main Support page offers access to a number of members-only support options.

Using Sherlock

Figure 1 Sherlock's Channels window.

Figure 2 You can launch Sherlock by opening its icon in the Applications folder.

Sherlock

Sherlock (**Figure 1**), which has been revised for Mac OS X 10.3, is Apple's Internet search utility. It enables you to search for information found on Web sites all over the world, including stock quotes and news, business listings, movie show times in your area, and flight information.

This chapter explain show to use Sherlock's search features to search the Internet.

✔ Tips

- The version of Sherlock that was part of Mac OS X 10.1 and earlier included disk searching capabilities. These features were moved from Sherlock to the Finder's Find command, which I discuss in **Chapter 4**.

- To use Sherlock, your computer must have access to the Internet. **Chapter 11** covers accessing the Internet.

To launch Sherlock

Open the Sherlock icon in the Applications folder (**Figure 2**).

Sherlock opens and displays a list of channels in its Toolbar collection (**Figure 1**).

Channels & Collections

Sherlock's interface (**Figure 1**) includes a feature called *channels,* which enables you to organize search sites based on the types of information they can find for you. Sherlock comes preconfigured with ten primary Apple-provided channels:

Figure 3
You can open a channel by choosing its name from the Channel menu.

- **Internet** lets you search the Internet for general information.

- **Pictures** enables you to search for pictures of people, places, and things.

- **Stocks** enables you to track prices and get news about stocks in your portfolio.

- **Movies** enables you to get information about movie locations and show times, as well as watch movie trailers.

- **Phone Book** enables you to search for businesses and get driving directions.

- **eBay** lets you participate in online auctions on eBay.

- **Flights** enables you to get information about flight arrivals.

- **Dictionary** lets you look up words and acronyms to get their meanings and synonyms.

- **Translation** enables you to translate words and phrases between several languages.

- **AppleCare** let's you search for Macintosh products and technical information.

Channels are organized by *collection.* A collection is a group of channels. Sherlock comes preconfigured with several collections:

- **Toolbar** includes channels that appear on Sherlock's toolbar. When you customize the toolbar, the list changes accordingly.

Figure 4 The Apple Channels collection lists channels provided by Apple.

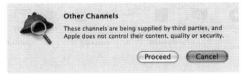

Figure 5 The first time you try to view the Other Channels collection, a dialog like this may appear.

Figure 6 Here's an example of what the Other Channels collection might look like.

◆ **Channels Menu** includes channels that appear on the Channels menu (**Figure 3**). When you add a shortcut to the Channels menu, the list changes accordingly.

◆ **Apple Channels** includes channels provided by Apple Computer, Inc.

◆ **Other Channels** includes channels from third-party providers.

◆ **My Channels** is a user-customizable list of channels where you can store your favorite channels.

✔ Tip

■ I explain how to customize Sherlock by adding channels, collections, and Channels menu shortcuts near the end of this chapter.

To view a collection

Click the name of the collection in the Collections list. A list of the channels in that collection appears in the main part of the window (**Figures 1** and **4**).

✔ Tip

■ When you select the Other Channels collection for the first time, a dialog like the one in **Figure 5** appears. Click Proceed to view the collection contents (**Figure 6**).

To open a channel

Use one of the following techniques:

◆ Double-click the name of the channel in the channels list (**Figures 1**, **4**, and **6**).

◆ Click the icon for the channel in the toolbar at the top of any Sherlock window (**Figures 1**, **4**, and **6**).

◆ Choose the name of the channel from the Channel menu (**Figure 3**).

The Internet Channel

You can use Sherlock to search the Internet for Web sites with information about topics that interest you. Unlike most other Internet search engines, Sherlock can search multiple directories (or *search sites*) at once. Best of all, you don't need to know special search syntax. Just enter a search word or phrase in plain English, select the search sites you want to use, and put Sherlock to work. It displays matches in order of relevance, so the most likely matches appear first.

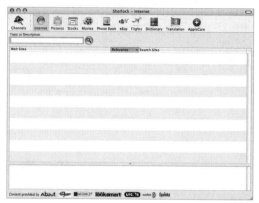

Figure 7 Use Sherlock's Internet channel to search the Internet for general information.

✔ Tip

■ Sherlock utilizes the search sites that are listed at the bottom of the Internet window (**Figure 7**). These sites may change.

Figure 8 Enter a search word or phrase in the box.

To search for Web content

1. Open the Internet channel (**Figure 7**).

2. Enter a search word or phrase in the Topic or Description box near the top of the window (**Figure 8**).

3. Click the magnifying glass button to begin the search.

4. After a moment, the matches begin to appear. You can begin working with matches immediately or wait until Sherlock has finished searching (**Figure 9**).

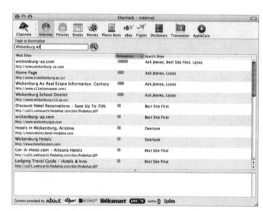

Figure 9 Sherlock displays matches, in order of relevance, in its window.

✔ Tips

■ When entering words in step 2, enter at least two or three words you expect to find in documents about the topic you are searching for. This helps narrow down the search, resulting in more useful matches.

■ To perform a new search, follow steps 2 and 3. A new results list replaces the original list.

Figure 10 Double-clicking the name of a Web page displays the page in your Web browser window. Here's my favorite Web site for my favorite western town.

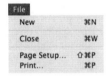

Figure 11
Sherlock's
File menu.

To work with found sites

1. Scroll through the list of items found (**Figure 9**) to locate an item that interests you.

2. To open an item's Web page, double-click it. Your Web browser launches and displays the page in its window (**Figure 10**).

✔ Tips

■ You can sort the items found list in the Sherlock window (**Figure 9**) by clicking one of its column headings. To reverse the sort order, just click the same column heading again.

■ To open a separate Sherlock window to perform a new search (without disturbing the items found list), choose File > New (**Figure 11**) or press ⌃ ⌘ N.

WORKING WITH FOUND SITES

The Pictures Channel

Sherlock's Pictures channel enables you to search for pictures of people, places, and things. You can use these pictures for a variety of things, from writing school reports to building Web pages to creating advertising campaigns.

✔ Tip

- Most of the photos that Sherlock finds are stock photography images that are protected by U.S. copyright law. These images must be licensed or purchased before they can be used.

To search for pictures

1. Open the Pictures channel (**Figure 12**).

2. Enter a search word or phrase in the Picture Topic or Description box near the top of the window.

3. Click the magnifying glass button to begin the search.

4. After a moment, the matches begin to appear as thumbnail images. You can begin working with matches immediately or wait until Sherlock has finished searching (**Figure 13**).

✔ Tip

- To perform a new search, follow steps 2 and 3. A new results list replaces the original list.

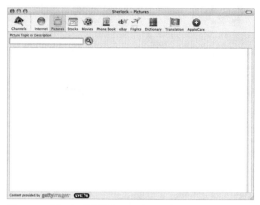

Figure 12 Sherlock's Pictures channel.

Figure 13 A search using the word *cowboy* results in pictures of cowboys (of all ages).

Figure 14 When you select a photo's thumbnail, the URL for its location on the Web appears in the bottom of the Sherlock window.

Figure 15 Double-clicking a thumbnail image displays a Web page with more information about the photo, including licensing information.

To work with found photos

1. Scroll through the thumbnail images found (**Figure 13**) to locate a photo that interests you.

2. Click the photo to select it. The URL for the photo's location on the Web appears in the bottom of the Sherlock window (**Figure 14**).

3. To open a photo Web page, double-click it. Your Web browser launches and displays the page in its window (**Figure 15**). The page will include licensing information if it applies.

✔ Tip

■ To open a separate Sherlock window to perform a new search (without disturbing the items found list), choose File > New (**Figure 11**) or press ⌘N.

The Stocks Channel

Sherlock's Stocks channel lets you get stock quotes, news headlines and stories, and charts for stocks. You enter the company name or ticker symbol and put Sherlock to work. It retrieves the information and displays it in the Stocks window.

✔ Tip

- Although the stock quotes are delayed 15 minutes, they are constantly updated as long as the Stocks window is open.

To look up stock information for a company

1. Open the Stocks channel. Sherlock connects to the Internet and retrieves information about the last companies you looked up, which it displays in its window (**Figure 16**).

2. Enter the name or ticker symbol for a company in the Company Name or Ticker Symbol box near the top of the window (**Figure 17**).

3. Click the magnifying glass button to begin the search.

   The company name and information is added to the list and appears in the window (**Figure 18**).

✔ Tips

- In step 1, the first time you open the Stocks channel, it displays information for Apple Computer, Inc.

- After step 3, if you entered a company name or ticker symbol that Sherlock does not recognize, it displays a "Company name or ticker symbol not found" message beside the magnifying glass icon. Repeat steps 2 and 3 to try again.

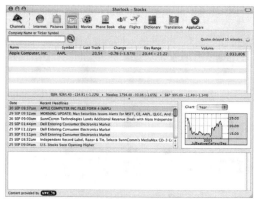

Figure 16 Sherlock's Stocks channel.

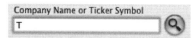

Figure 17 Enter a ticker symbol (like this) or a company name.

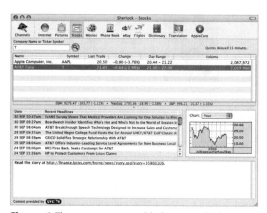

Figure 18 The company you added appears in the window.

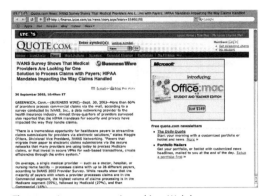

Figure 19 A news story viewed in a Web browser window.

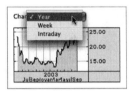

Figure 20 The Chart menu offers three charting options.

To view news stories

1. Click a headline in the Stocks window. The story appears in the bottom of the window (**Figure 18**).

2. Click the link. Sherlock launches your Web browser to display the article on the Web (**Figure 19**).

✔ Tip

■ In some instances, clicking a story's headline displays the story in the bottom half of Sherlock's window.

To view a different chart

Choose an option from the Chart pop-up menu (**Figure 20**). The chart changes accordingly.

To remove a company from the list

1. Select the company you want to remove from the list.

2. Press Delete. The company disappears.

✔ Tip

■ The fewer companies in the list, the quicker Sherlock can display and update information. This also speeds up the Stocks channel's loading time.

The Movies Channel

Sherlock's Movies channel (**Figures 21** and **24**) offers a great way to get local movie listings and show times, without picking up the phone.

To search for movie show times

1. Open the Movies channel.

2. Choose a recent entry from the Find Near drop-down list.

    or

    Enter an Address Book entry name or city and state in the Find Near box.

3. If necessary, click the Movies button on the far left side of the window. After a moment, a list of current movies appears in the leftmost list (**Figure 21**).

4. Select the name of a movie that you'd like to see. A list of theaters showing the movie appears in the middle list and information about the movie, including a movie poster and QuickTime movie trailer, appears in the bottom of the window (**Figure 22**).

5. Select the name of the theater where you'd like to see the movie. A list of showtimes appears in the rightmost list and the theater location appears in the bottom of the window (**Figure 23**).

6. Repeat steps 4 and 5 to find other show-times for movies.

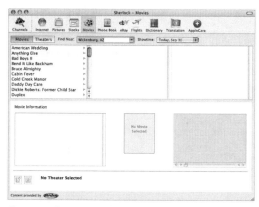

Figure 21 The Movies channel with the Movies option selected.

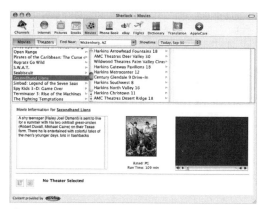

Figure 22 When you select a movie, a list of nearby theaters appears, along with movie info.

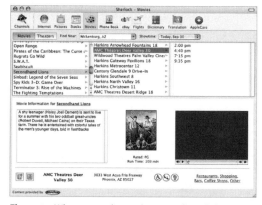

Figure 23 When you select a theater, a list of show-times and theater location information appears.

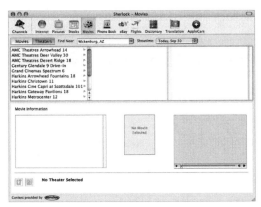

Figure 24 The Movies channel with the Theaters option selected.

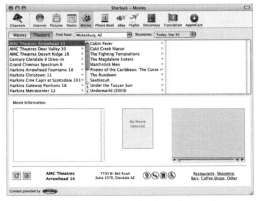

Figure 25 Select a theater to display a list of what's playing there.

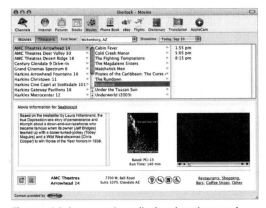

Figure 26 Select a movie to display showtimes and movie information.

To search theater schedules

1. Open the Movies channel.

2. Choose a recent entry from the Find Near drop-down list.

   or

   Enter an Address Book entry name or city and state in the Find Near box.

3. If necessary, click the Theaters button on the far left side of the window. After a moment, a list of nearby theaters appears in the leftmost list (**Figure 24**).

4. Select the name of a theater you'd like to see the schedule for. A list of movies playing at that theater appears in the middle list and additional information about the theater appears in the bottom left of the window (**Figure 25**).

5. Select the name of the movie you'd like to see. A list of showtimes appears in the rightmost list and information about the movie, including a QuickTime movie trailer, appears in the bottom right of the window (**Figure 26**).

6. Repeat steps 4 and 5 to find other theater schedules.

To work with the results window

1. Follow the instructions on one of the previous two pages to view movie listings and showtimes (**Figures 23** and **26**).

2. Perform any of the following tasks:

   ▲ To play the movie trailer, click the play button when the movie is finished downloading from the Internet. I explain how to play QuickTime movies in **Chapter 6**.

   ▲ To see theater show times for a different day, choose the date from the Showtime pop-up menu near the top of Sherlock's window.

   ▲ To add the theater to Address Book, click the Add this theater to your Address Book button on the lower left corner of the window.

   ▲ To get a map and driving directions to the theater, click the See a map with driving directions to this theater button in the lower left corner of the window. Sherlock switches to the Phone Book channel to get the information for you. (I tell you about the Phone Book Channel next.)

   ▲ To learn about restaurants, shopping, bars, coffee shops, and other businesses in the area, click one of the blue underlined links in the lower right corner of the window. Sherlock switches to the Phone Book channel to get the information for you (**Figure 27**).

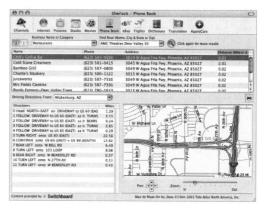

Figure 27 Clicking the restaurants link in **Figure 26** displays a list of restaurants near the theater. Selecting one of the restaurants displays directions and a map.

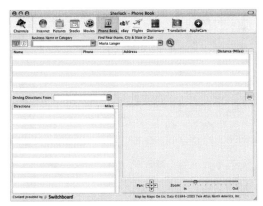

Figure 28 Sherlock's Phone Book channel.

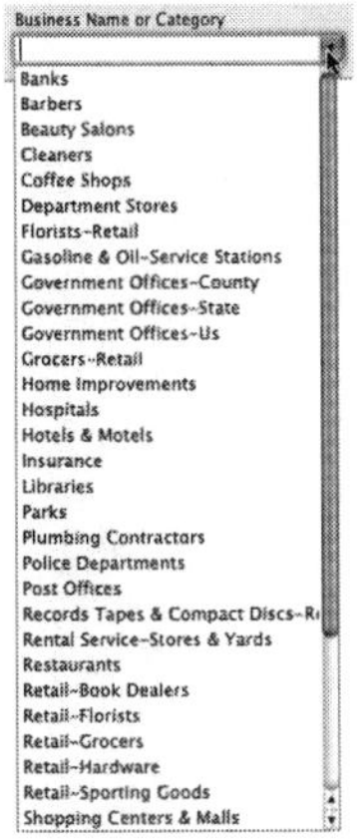

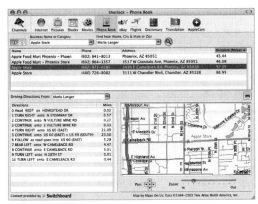

Figure 29
The Business Name or Category drop-down list includes standard categories, as well as recently accessed business names.

The Phone Book Channel

The Phone Book channel (**Figure 28**) is a great way to find local businesses and get the directions you need to find them.

✔ Tip

- The Phone Book channel was known as the Yellow Pages channel in previous versions of Sherlock.

To search for a business listing

1. Open the Phone Book channel (**Figure 28**).

2. Choose a recent entry from the Find Near drop-down list.

   or

   Enter an Address Book entry name or city and state in the Find Near box.

3. Enter a business name or category in the Business Name or Category box.

   or

   Choose a category or recent business name from the Business Name or Category drop-down list (**Figure 29**).

4. Click the magnifying glass button to begin the search.

5. After a moment, search results begin to appear. Select a listing to view driving directions and a map in the bottom half of the window (**Figure 30**)

✔ Tip

- In many instances, driving directions are for the shortest route, which may not be the quickest or most convenient. If I followed the driving directions in **Figure 30**, for example, I'd hit at least 50 traffic lights; I know a slightly longer but quicker route with only four traffic lights. Which do you think I'd take?

Figure 30 Select a business to display driving directions and a map.

The eBay Channel

The eBay channel (**Figure 31**) enables you to search for items available for sale on eBay, an online auction Web site. You enter search criteria, and Sherlock retrieves a list of found items from eBay. You can then track the auction within Sherlock or visit the auction's Web page, where you can bid on it.

To search for items on eBay

1. Open the eBay channel and make sure the Search button is selected (**Figure 31**).

2. Enter search criteria in the top part of the window, right beneath the toolbar.

3. Click the magnifying glass button to start the search.

4. After a moment, search results begin to appear. The first item is selected and information about it appears in the bottom half of the window (**Figure 32**).

5. To see information about another item in the list, click it to select it.

6. To get more information about an item, double-click it. Your Web browser launches and displays the item's page on eBay (**Figure 33**).

✔ Tip

■ Use search criteria to narrow down the search. The more entries you make in the search criteria area, the fewer matches will appear in the list of matches.

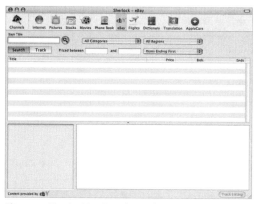

Figure 31 Sherlock's eBay channel.

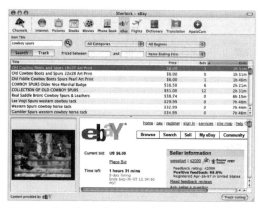

Figure 32 Search results for an eBay search include basic listing info, as well as auction details and a photo.

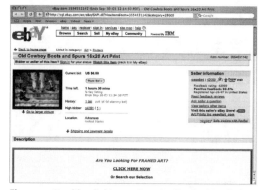

Figure 33 Double-clicking an item in Sherlock's window displays its Web page on eBay.

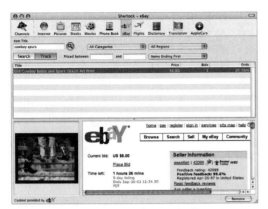

Figure 34 Clicking the Track button at the top of Sherlock's eBay channel displays a list of the auctions you are tracking.

To track an eBay auction item

1. Select the item you want to track in the list of found items (**Figure 32**).

2. Click the Track Listing button at the bottom of the Sherlock window.

3. The item is added to the Track list in the eBay channel; click the Track button near the top of the window to see it (**Figure 34**).

✔ Tip

■ Items you track on eBay remain in the Track list (**Figure 34**) until the auction is over.

To bid on an eBay item

1. Double-click the item you want to bid on in the list of found items (**Figure 32**) or the list of items you are tracking (**Figure 34**) to display its Web page (**Figure 33**).

2. Read the information on the page carefully.

3. Enter your bid in the form near the bottom of the page.

✔ Tip

■ You must have an account on eBay to bid on items. Setting up an account is free. Follow the instructions on the eBay Web site to learn more.

TRACKING & BIDDING ON EBAY ITEMS

The Flights Channel

The Flights channel (**Figure 35**) enables you to get departure and arrival information for airline flights. Enter search criteria in the top of the window and Sherlock displays results from a database of flights. This is handy for checking the status of a flight you think might be delayed—it could prevent you from waiting longer than you need to at the airport!

✔ Tip

■ The Flights channel provides information about current day flights only.

To search for flight information

1. Open the Flights channel (**Figure 35**).

2. Enter search criteria in the top part of the window, right beneath the toolbar.

3. Click the magnifying glass button to start the search.

4. After a moment, search results begin to appear. Click a flight to get information about it (**Figure 36**).

✔ Tip

■ In step 4, if a check mark appears in the Chart column for a flight, a graphic of the flight's position and weather appears in the bottom right of the window (**Figure 36**). Is this cool or what?

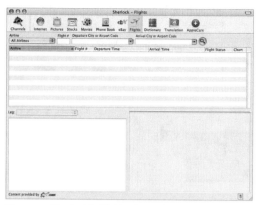

Figure 35 Sherlock's Flights channel.

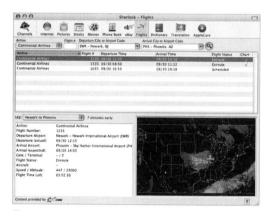

Figure 36 Sherlock displays information about a flight when you select it.

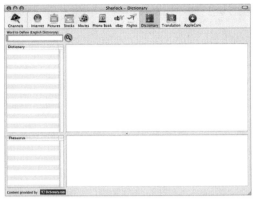

Figure 37 Sherlock's Dictionary channel.

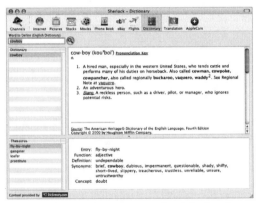

Figure 38 Sherlock looks up a word and displays its definition and synonyms. (I don't think too many of the cowboys around here would like being referred to by any of the listed synonyms.)

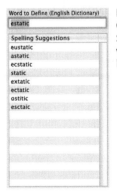

Figure 39
Can't spell? Not a problem. Sherlock displays a list of words it thinks you might have been trying to spell.

The Dictionary Channel

The Dictionary channel (**Figure 37**) enables you to get definitions and synonyms for words and acronyms. Enter the word you want to learn about and let Sherlock look it up on Dictionary.com.

To define a word

1. Open the Dictionary channel (**Figure 37**).

2. Enter the word or acronym you want to define in the Word to Define box.

3. Click the magnifying glass button to look up the word.

4. Wait while Sherlock looks up the word. After a moment, search results appear in the window (**Figure 38**):

   ▲ The Dictionary list displays words that either exactly match what you entered or are related to what you entered. Select the word to see a definition in the box beside it.

   ▲ The Thesaurus list displays synonyms for the word you selected in the list above it. Select a synonym to see more information and synonyms.

✔ Tips

■ To look up one of the words in the Dictionary or Thesaurus list, double-click it.

■ If Sherlock can't find the word because you misspelled it (heck, I did it twice while experimenting!), the Spelling Suggestions list appears in place of the Dictionary list (**Figure 39**). Double-click a word in the list to look it up.

The Translation Channel

Sherlock's Translation channel (**Figure 40**) uses online software tools to translate words and phrases between several languages, including: English, Chinese (Simplified and Traditional), Dutch, French, German, Greek, Italian, Japanese, Korean, Portuguese, Russian, and Spanish. Type in what you want to translate, click a button, and let Sherlock do the rest.

✔ Tip

■ Because translations are handled by software tools and not by human translators, they should not be relied upon for complete accuracy.

To translate a word or phrase

1. Open the Translation channel (**Figure 40**).

2. Enter the word or phrase you want to translate in the Original Text box.

3. Select a translation option from the pop-up menu (**Figure 41**).

4. Click the Translate button between the top and bottom halves of the Translation window. The translation and a fine-print disclaimer appear in the bottom half of the window (**Figure 42**).

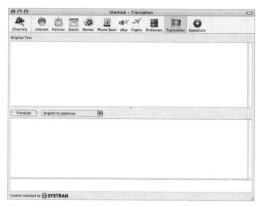

Figure 40 Sherlock's Translation channel.

Figure 41
The pop-up menu offers quite a few translation options.

Figure 42 A completed translation. I wonder how accurate this is?

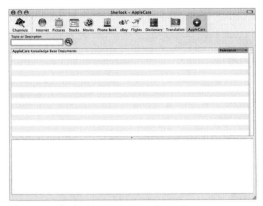

Figure 43 Sherlock's AppleCare channel.

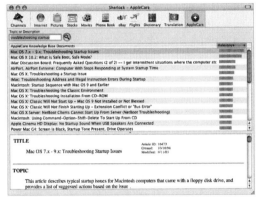

Figure 44 Sherlock displays a list of KnowledgeBase documents in the window. Click a document name to display it in the bottom half of the window.

The AppleCare Channel

Sherlock's AppleCare channel (**Figure 43**) is your direct connection to Apple's Knowledge-Base of information about Macintosh computers and software. It's a great place to learn more about your hardware and the Mac OS.

To search the AppleCare KnowledgeBase

1. Open the AppleCare channel (**Figure 43**).

2. Enter a search word or phrase in the Topic or Description box near the top of the window.

3. Click the magnifying glass button to start the search.

4. After a moment, search results begin to appear. Click an item in the list to display its document in the bottom half of the window (**Figure 44**).

SEARCHING THE APPLECARE KNOWLEDGEBASE

397

Customizing Sherlock

There are a number of ways you can customize Sherlock so it works the way you want it to. Make your own collections of channels, customize the toolbar, and add channels to the Channels menu. This part of the chapter explains how.

✔ Tip

■ You cannot modify the Apple Channels or Other Channels collections.

To move or copy a channel from one collection to another

1. Display the collection in which the channel you want to move or copy appears.

2. Drag the channel name from the channel list to the name of the collection you want to move or copy it to (**Figure 45**). The channel appears in that collection list.

✔ Tips

■ Dragging a channel from the Apple Channels or Other Channels collection copies the channel. Dragging a channel from any other collection list moves the channel.

■ You can force a channel to be copied (rather than moved) by holding down Option while dragging it to the destination collection.

■ Modifying the Toolbar or Channels Menu collection automatically modifies the toolbar or Channels menu.

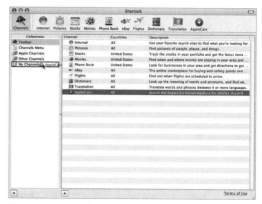

Figure 45 Drag a channel from one collection to another to move or copy it.

MOVING & COPYING CHANNELS

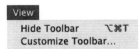

Figure 46 Sherlock's View menu.

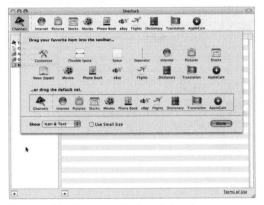

Figure 47 The Customize Toolbar dialog sheet.

✓ Icon & Text
Icon Only
Text Only

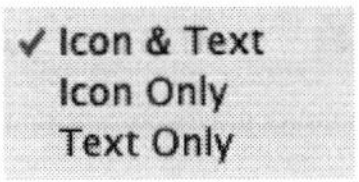

Figure 48
The Show pop-up menu lets you specify how the toolbar should appear.

To remove a channel from a collection

1. Display the collection you want to modify.

2. Select the channel you want to remove.

3. Press `Delete`. The channel is removed from the collection.

To customize the toolbar

Follow the instructions on the previous page and this page to add or remove channels in the Toolbar collection.

or

1. Choose View > Customize Toolbar (**Figure 46**). A dialog sheet like the one in **Figure 47** appears.

2. To change toolbar icons, use any combination of the following techniques:

   ▲ To add a button to the toolbar, drag its icon from the dialog to the toolbar.

   ▲ To remove a button, drag it off the toolbar.

   ▲ To restore the toolbar to the default buttons, drag the default set of buttons to the toolbar.

3. To change the way icons are displayed on the toolbar, choose an option from the Show pop-up menu (**Figure 48**).

4. To display smaller icons, turn on the Use Small Size check box.

5. When you're finished making changes, click Done.

✔ Tip

■ It is not necessary to display the Customize Toolbar dialog sheet (**Figure 47**) to add channel buttons to the toolbar. Simply drag a channel from any list to the toolbar to add an icon for it.

REMOVING CHANNELS, CUSTOMIZING TOOLBAR

To create a shortcut for a channel

1. Open the channel you want to create a shortcut for.

2. Choose Channel > Make a Shortcut (**Figure 3**), or press ⌃⌘L.

3. A dialog like the one in **Figure 49** appears. Enter a name and choose a disk location for the shortcut file.

4. Click Make. A shortcut file is saved in the location you specified with the name you entered (**Figure 50**).

✔ Tips

■ Sherlock shortcuts offer a quick way to open a specific Sherlock channel. Simply double-click the file's icon to launch Sherlock and display the channel.

■ I explain how to use a Save As dialog like the one in **Figure 49** in **Chapter 5**.

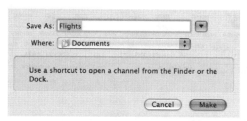

Figure 49 Use a dialog like this one to name and save a channel shortcut.

Figure 50
Here's what a shortcut for the Flights channel looks like.

Flights

Networking

Networking

Networking uses direct connections and network protocols to connect your computer to others on a network. Once connected, you can share files, access e-mail, and run special network applications on server computers.

This chapter looks at *peer-to-peer networking,* which uses the built-in features of Mac OS X to connect to other computers for file and application sharing. It also covers some of the advanced network configuration tools available as Mac OS X utilities.

✔ Tips

- If you use your computer at work, you may be connected to a companywide network; if so, you'll find the networking part of this chapter very helpful. But if you use your computer at home and have only one computer, you won't have much need for the networking information here.

- A discussion of Mac OS X Server, which is designed to meet the demands of large workgroups and corporate intranets, is beyond the scope of this book.

- This chapter touches only briefly on using networks to connect to the Internet. Connecting to the Internet is discussed in detail in **Chapter 11**.

Basic Networking Terms

Before I explain how to use your Mac on a network, let me take a moment or two to introduce and define some of the networking terminology used throughout this chapter. You'll find these words used again and again whenever you deal with networking features.

AppleTalk

AppleTalk is a networking protocol used by Macintosh computers to communicate over a network. It's the software that makes networking work. Fortunately, it's not something extra you have to buy—it's part of Mac OS X.

TCP/IP

TCP/IP is a networking protocol that is used for connecting to the Internet. Mac OS X computers can use both AppleTalk to communicate with local networks and TCP/IP to communicate with the Internet.

Rendezvous

Rendezvous is a networking technology introduced by Apple with Mac OS X 10.2. It simplifies network setup by enabling your computer to automatically recognize other Rendezvous-compatible network devices. Rendezvous works over both Ethernet and AirPort.

✔ Tips

■ Rendezvous can be used with iChat to initiate live chats with other Mac OS X users on your network. iChat is covered in **Chapter 11**.

AirPort

AirPort is the name for Apple's wireless networking technology. (It is also called *Wi-Fi*.) Through AirPort, your Mac can join wireless networks.

Ethernet

Ethernet is a network connection method that is built into all Mac OS X-compatible computers. It uses Ethernet cables that connect to the Ethernet ports or network interface cards of computers and network printers. Additional hardware such as *transceivers* and *hubs* may be needed, depending on the network setup and device.

Ethernet comes in three speeds: 10, 100 (also called *Fast Ethernet*), and 1000 (also called *Gigabit Ethernet*) megabits per second. The maximum speed of the computer's communication with the rest of the network is limited by the maximum speed of the cable, hub, and other network devices.

✔ Tips

■ Network hardware configuration details are far beyond the scope of this book. The information here is provided primarily to introduce some of the network terms you might encounter when working with your computer and other documentation.

■ *LocalTalk* is an older Mac OS-compatible network method. Slow and supported only by older Macintosh models with serial ports, it is rarely used in today's networks and is not covered in this book.

Figure 1 You configure sharing with two System Preferences panes: Network and Sharing.

Setting Up Network Sharing

To share files, applications, and printers with other network users, you must set options in two System Preferences panes (**Figure 1**):

◆ **Network** allows you to enable AppleTalk and choose your AppleTalk zone and configuration.

◆ **Sharing** allows you to name your computer, enable types of sharing and access, and control how other users can run applications on your computer.

This part of the chapter explains how to set up sharing via an Ethernet connection. It also explains how to share files and applications once the configuration is complete.

✔ Tips

■ Although file and application sharing is possible with other protocols and types of connections, it is impossible for me to cover all configuration options here. If you're using a different type of network and don't have instructions for using it with Mac OS X, read through the instructions here. Much of what you read may apply to your setup.

■ If your computer is on a large network, consult the system administrator before changing any network configuration options.

SHARING FILES & APPLICATIONS

To set AppleTalk Network preferences

1. Choose Apple > System Preferences (**Figure 2**), or click the System Preferences icon in the Dock.

2. In the System Preferences window that appears (**Figure 1**), click the Network icon in the toolbar or in the Internet & Network row.

3. In the Network preferences pane that appears, choose an Ethernet option (such as Built-in Ethernet) from the Show menu (**Figure 3**).

4. If necessary, click the AppleTalk button to display AppleTalk options (**Figure 4**).

5. Turn on the Make AppleTalk Active check box.

6. If necessary, choose a zone from the AppleTalk Zone pop-up menu.

7. Choose an option from the Configure pop-up menu:

   ▲ **Automatically** automatically configures your computer with the correct network identification information.

   ▲ **Manually** displays Node ID and Network ID boxes for you to enter network identification information (**Figure 5**).

8. Click Apply Now.

✔ Tips

- AppleTalk zones are normally only present in large networks.

- In step 7, if you choose Manually, you must enter the correct information for AppleTalk to work.

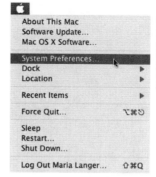

Figure 2
Open the System Preferences window by choosing System Preferences from the Apple menu.

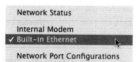

Figure 3
Choose an Ethernet option from the Show pop-up menu.

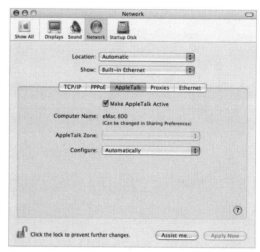

Figure 4 The AppleTalk options in the Network preferences pane.

Figure 5 If you choose Manually, you have to enter correct network identification information.

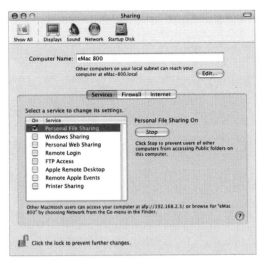

Figure 6 The Services options in the Sharing preferences pane.

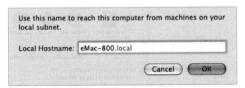

Figure 7 Use this dialog to change the identifier of your computer on the local subnet.

To set the computer's identity

1. Choose Apple > System Preferences (**Figure 2**), or click the System Preferences icon in the Dock.

2. In the System Preferences window that appears (**Figure 1**), click the Sharing icon in the Internet & Network row to display the Sharing preferences pane (**Figure 6**).

3. Enter a name in the Computer Name box.

4. To change the identifier for your computer on the local subnet, click the Edit button to display a dialog like the one in **Figure 7**. Enter a new name in the Local Hostname box; the name you enter must end in *.local*, which cannot be changed. Click OK.

✔ Tips

■ By default, the local subnet identifier is the computer name with dashes substituted for spaces, followed by *.local*.

■ Your computer name is not the same as your hard disk name.

■ If your computer is on a large network, give your computer a name that can easily distinguish it from others on the network. Ask your system administrator; there may be organization-wide computer naming conventions that you need to follow.

SETTING THE COMPUTER'S IDENTITY

To enable sharing services

1. Choose Apple > System Preferences (**Figure 2**), or click the System Preferences icon in the Dock.

2. In the System Preferences window that appears (**Figure 1**), click the Sharing icon in the Internet & Network row to display the Sharing preferences pane.

3. If necessary, click the Services tab to display its options (**Figure 6**).

4. Turn on the check box beside each sharing service you want to enable:

   ▲ **Personal File Sharing** lets Macintosh users access Public folders on your computer.

   ▲ **Windows Sharing** lets Windows users access shared folders using SMB, a Windows file sharing technology.

   ▲ **Personal Web Sharing** enables others to view Web pages in your Sites folder.

   ▲ **Remote Login** lets others access your computer using Secure Shell (SSH) client software, such as Terminal.

   ▲ **FTP Access** enables others to exchange files with your computer using FTP client software.

   ▲ **Apple Remote Desktop** enables others to access the computer using Apple Remote Desktop software, a program that makes it possible to run one computer from another.

   ▲ **Remote Apple Events** lets applications on other Mac OS computers send Apple Events to your computer.

   ▲ **Printer Sharing** enables others to use printers connected to your computer.

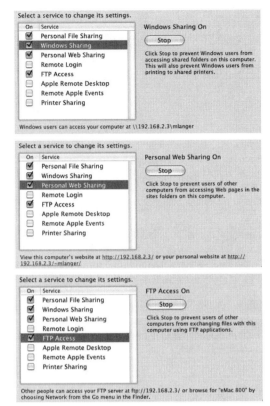

Figures 8, 9, & 10 A note beneath the services list explains how to access the selected service. These examples show Windows Sharing (top), Personal Web Sharing (middle), and FTP Access (bottom).

✔ Tips

- In step 4, turning on the check box beside an item is the same as selecting the item and clicking the Start button that appears beside it. Likewise, turning off an item's check box is the same as selecting it and clicking the Stop button.

- When you select a service that is turned on, a note beneath the list of services explains how your computer can be accessed by that service. **Figures 6, 8, 9**, and **10** show examples.

- With Personal Web Sharing enabled, the contents of the Sites folder within your home folder are published as Personal Web Sharing Web sites. To access a user's Web site, use the following URL: http://*IPaddress*/~*username*/ where *IPaddress* is the IP address or domain name of the computer and *username* is the name of the user on that computer.

- When a user accesses your computer via Remote Login, he accesses the Unix shell underlying Mac OS X. Keep in mind that turning on this option can open your computer to hackers who can use the Unix command-line interface to modify your system setup. Unix is covered in **Chapter 17**.

- Apple Remote Desktop is not part of Mac OS X and is not covered in this book. You can learn more about it at www.apple.com/remotedesktop/.

ENABLING SHARING SERVICES

To disable sharing services

1. Choose Apple > System Preferences (**Figure 2**), or click the System Preferences icon in the Dock.

2. In the System Preferences window that appears (**Figure 1**), click the Sharing icon in the Internet & Network row to display the Sharing preferences pane.

3. If necessary, click the Services tab to display its options (**Figure 6**).

4. Turn off the check box beside the sharing service you want to disable.

5. If a dialog sheet like the one in **Figure 11** appears, enter the number of minutes in which sharing will be disabled in the top box and click OK.

✔ Tips

- In step 5, the value you enter determines how long before sharing is disabled. If you're in a hurry, enter a smaller value than the default value, which is 10.

- When you disable file sharing, a dialog like the one in **Figure 12** appears on the screen of each connected user, warning them that the server (your computer) will be shutting down.

- In step 5, you can also enter a message in the bottom box to send to connected users. **Figures 11** and **12** show examples.

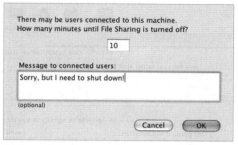

Figure 11 You can use a dialog like this to specify how long before sharing shuts down and include a personal message.

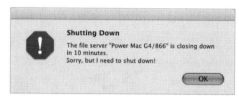

Figure 12 Here's what a connected user sees when you shut down file sharing, using the settings shown in **Figure 11**.

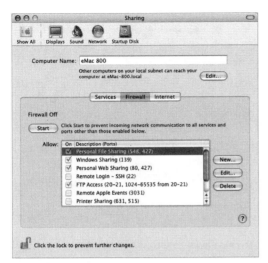

Figure 13 The Firewall tab of the Sharing preferences pane lets you configure and enable Mac OS X's built-in firewall.

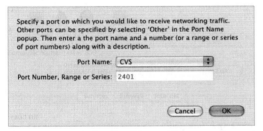

Figure 14 Use a dialog like this to add a port to the Firewall tab's list.

Figure 15 Mac OS X comes preconfigured with many commonly used ports.

To set firewall options

1. Choose Apple > System Preferences (**Figure 2**), or click the System Preferences icon in the Dock.

2. In the System Preferences window that appears (**Figure 1**), click the Sharing icon in the Internet & Network row to display the Sharing preferences pane.

3. If necessary, click the Firewall button to display Firewall options (**Figure 13**).

4. To start firewall protection, click Start.

5. Turn on the check box beside each type of sharing you want to *exclude* from firewall protection. The options are the same as those discussed in the section titled "To enable sharing services" earlier in this chapter, plus:

   ▲ **iChat Rendezvous** enables network users to conduct chats with you via Rendezvous networking.

   ▲ **iTunes Music Sharing** enables network users to listen to your iTunes playlists.

✔ Tips

- A *firewall* is security software that prevents incoming network access to your computer.

- In step 5, each type of sharing corresponds to one or more network ports.

- To add a port to the Description (Ports) list, click the New button. In the dialog that appears (**Figure 14**), choose an option from the Port Name pop-up menu (**Figure 15**), enter a port number in the box beneath it, and click OK. The port is added to the list.

- To stop firewall protection, click Stop in step 4 and skip step 5. (The Stop button appears in place of the Start button when the firewall is enabled.)

To share an Internet connection with other network users

1. Choose Apple > System Preferences (**Figure 2**), or click the System Preferences icon in the Dock.

2. In the System Preferences window that appears (**Figure 1**), click the Sharing icon in the Internet & Network row to display the Sharing preferences pane.

3. If necessary, click the Internet button to display Internet sharing options (**Figure 16**).

4. Choose an option from the pop-up menu to specify which Internet connection you want to share.

5. Turn on the check box to specify how the computers you are sharing the Internet connection with are connected to your computer.

6. A Caution dialog like the one in **Figure 17** may appear. If you're sure you want to share the connection, click OK.

7. Then click Start.

✔ Tips

- When you share an Internet connection, the total connection speed is divided among each active connection. So, for example, if two computers are actively sharing a 128 Kbps ISDN connection with you, the speed of each connection will only be about 42 Kbps.

- To stop sharing an Internet connection with other network users, follow steps 1 through 3 above, then click the Stop button.

Figure 16 Internet sharing options make it possible to share an Internet connection with other computers on a network.

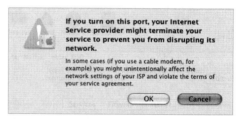

Figure 17 A dialog like this may appear if you try to share a built-in Ethernet connection.

Figure 18
The Go menu.

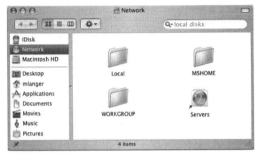

Figure 19 Clicking the Network icon in the Sidebar displays the network browser.

Connecting to Another Computer for File Sharing

Once network and sharing options have been set up for sharing, you can connect to another computer and access its files. Mac OS X 10.3 offers two ways to do this:

◆ The Go menu's Connect to Server command (**Figure 18**) prompts you to enter the address of the server you want to connect to. You enter a user name and password to connect, choose the volume you want to access, and display its contents in Finder windows.

◆ The new network browser feature enables you to use the Network icon in the Sidebar (**Figure 19**) to browse the computers on the network—from the Finder and from within Open and Save dialogs. You open an alias for another computer and you're prompted for a user name and password. Enter login information, choose the volume you want to access, and work with the files just as if they were on your computer.

The main difference between these two methods is that the Connect to Server command mounts the other computer's shared volume and the network browser does not. In addition, the Connect to Server command makes it possible to connect to servers that are not listed in the network browser.

The next few pages provide instructions for connecting to other computers using both methods, along with some tips for speeding up the process in the future.

✔ Tips

■ I tell you about mounting volumes in **Chapter 3**.

■ Mac OS X's networking features refer to network-accessible computers as *servers*.

■ The access privileges you have for network volumes varies depending on the privileges set for that volume or folder. I tell you about privileges later in this chapter.

To use the network browser

1. Choose Go > Network (**Figure 18**), press
   Shift ⌘ K, or click the Network icon in
   the Sidebar. The Network window opens
   (**Figure 19**).

2. To see servers in your local network or
   subnet, open the Local folder (**Figure 20**).

   or

   To see servers in a specific network area
   or workgroup, click the folder for that
   area or workgroup (**Figure 21**).

3. To open a server, double-click its alias
   icon.

4. A dialog like the one in **Figure 22** appears.
   Enter a user name and password that is
   recognized by the server and click Connect.

5. A window for the server opens. It lists the
   volumes available for access (**Figure 23**).
   Double-click the volume you want to
   access.

   The contents of the volume you opened
   appear in the window (**Figure 24**). You
   can work with the volume as you would
   any other disk.

✔ Tips

- Mac OS X remembers that you accessed
  a server throughout your work session.
  If you access the same server again
  before shutting down or logging out, it
  does not prompt you for a user name
  and password.

- Servers you have accessed during a work
  session have blue icons. Computers you
  have not yet accessed during a work
  session have gray icons.

Figure 20 The servers on my local subnet.

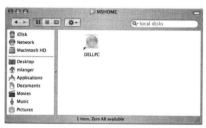

Figure 21 The MSHOME workgroup on my
network includes the lone Dell PC I use
when they make me write Windows books.

Figure 22
Use a dialog
like this to
log in to the
server.

Figure 23 The server's available volumes appear.

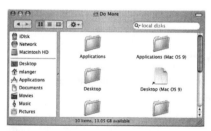

Figure 24 Opening a volume displays its contents.

Figure 25 The Connect To Server dialog.

Figure 26 Use this dialog to enter login information.

Figure 27 Use this dialog to select the volume you want to work with.

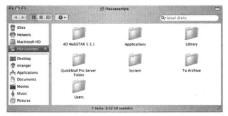

Figure 28 The contents of the volume you selected appear in a window.

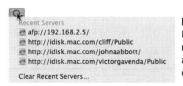

Figure 29
Use this pop-up menu to choose a recently opened server.

To use the Connect to Server command

1. In the Finder, choose Go > Connect to Server (**Figure 18**), or press ⌃⌘K.

2. In the Connect To Server dialog that appears (**Figure 25**), enter the network address of the server you want to connect to.

3. Click Connect.

4. A login dialog like the one in **Figure 26** appears.

   ▲ If you are registered as a user on the other computer, select the Registered User radio button (**Figure 26**) and enter your user name and password.

   ▲ If you are not registered as a user on the other computer and it allows Guest access, select the Guest radio button.

5. Click Connect.

6. A dialog like the one in **Figure 27** appears next. Select the volumes you want to mount.

7. Click OK.

   An icon for the mounted volume appears on your desktop and in the top half of the Sidebar and a window for the volume opens (**Figure 28**). You can work with the volume as you would any other disk.

✔ Tips

■ After step 2, you can click the Add to Favorites button to add the server address to the Favorite Servers list in the Connect to Server dialog (**Figure 25**). You can the access the server by double-clicking its address in the list.

■ In step 2, to open a recently opened server, choose its address from the Recent Servers pop-up menu (**Figure 29**).

To set login options as a registered user

1. Follow steps 1 through 4 on the previous page. Make sure you select the Registered User radio button and enter your login information in step 4.

2. Click the Options button (**Figure 26**) to display login options (**Figure 30**).

3. Toggle check boxes in the Preferences area as desired and click the Save Preferences button:

   ▲ **Add Password to Keychain** adds your login information to your keychain.

   ▲ **Allow Clear Text Password** allows your password to be sent over the network without encryption.

   ▲ **Warn when sending password in Clear Text** warns you before sending your password without encryption.

   ▲ **Allow Secure Connections using SSH** enables you to establish a secure connection when using a Secure Shell client such as Terminal.

4. To change your password on the server, click the Change Password button. A dialog like the one in **Figure 31** appears. Enter your current password in the Old Password box, then enter the new password in each of the other boxes. Click OK to return to the login window (**Figure 26**).

   or

   Click OK to dismiss the login options dialog (**Figure 30**) and return to the login window (**Figure 26**).

5. Follow the remaining steps on the previous page to complete the login process.

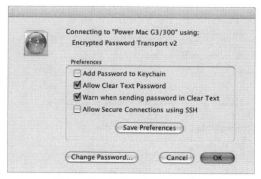

Figure 30 Clicking the Options button in the login window (**Figure 26**) displays login options.

Figure 31 Use this dialog to change your password on the server.

✔ Tip

■ Once you've added your server password to your keychain, you will no longer be prompted to enter a password when you connect to that server. I tell you about keychain access in **Chapter 15**.

Users, Groups, & Privileges

Network file and application sharing access is determined by the users and groups set up for the computer, as well as the privileges settings for each file or its enclosing folder.

Users & Groups

Each person who connects to a computer (other than with Guest access) is considered a *user*. Each user has his own user name or ID and a password. User names are set up by the computer's system administrator, using the Accounts preferences pane. The password is also assigned by the system administrator, but in most cases, it can be changed by the user in the My Account preferences pane. This enhances security.

Each user can belong to one or more groups. A *group* is one or more users who have the same privileges. Some groups are set up automatically by Mac OS X when you install it and add users with the Users preferences pane. Other groups can be set up by the system administrator using a program such as NetInfo Manager.

✔ Tips

- Setting up users is discussed in detail in **Chapter 15**. Setting up groups is an advanced network administration task that is beyond the scope of this book.

- I discuss NetInfo Manager briefly near the end of this chapter.

Privileges

Each file or folder can be assigned a set of privileges. Privileges determine who has access to a file and how it can be accessed.

There are four possible privileges settings:

◆ **Read & Write** privileges allow the user to open and save files.

◆ **Read only** privileges allow the user to open files but not save files.

◆ **Write only (Drop Box)** privileges allow the user to save files but not open them.

◆ **No Access** means the user can neither open nor save files.

Privileges can be set for three categories of users:

◆ **Owner** is the user or group who can access and set access privileges for the item. In Mac OS X, the owner can be you (if it's your computer and you set it up), system, or admin.

◆ **Group** is the group that has access to the item.

◆ **Others** is everyone else on the network, including users logged in as Guest.

✔ Tips

■ In previous versions of Mac OS, which were not designed as multiuser systems, you were the owner of most (if not all) items on your computer.

■ You can check or set an item's privileges in the Ownership & Permissions area of the Info window for the item (**Figures 33, 34,** and **35**).

Figure 32
Choose Get Info from the File menu.

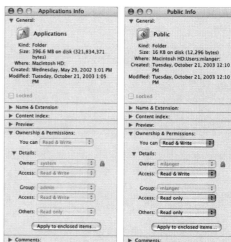

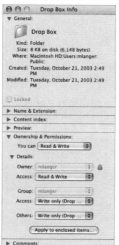

Figures 33, 34, & 35
Privileges settings for the Applications folder (top left), Public folder (above), and Drop Box folder inside my public folder (left).

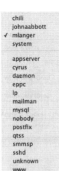

Figure 36
The Owner pop-up menu includes users I created (at the top of the list) and those created by Mac OS X.

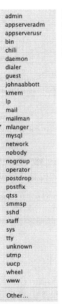

Figure 37
When I installed Mac OS X 10.3, it created all of these groups.

✓ Read & Write
Read only
Write only (Drop Box)
No Access

Figure 38 Use this pop-up menu to set privileges for each category of user.

To set an item's owner, group, & privileges

1. Select the icon for the item for which you want to change privileges.

2. Choose File > Get Info (**Figure 32**), or press ⌘ I.

3. In the Info window that appears, click the triangle beside Ownership & Permissions to expand the window and display permissions information (**Figures 33, 34, and 35**).

4. To change the owner and group for an item, choose an option from the Owner (**Figure 36**) or Group (**Figure 37**) pop-up menu. You may need to click the lock icon beside an item to unlock it or enter an administrative password before the change can be made.

5. To change the privileges for an item, choose options from the Access and Others pop-up menus (**Figure 38**).

6. If the item is a folder, to apply the settings to all folders within it, click the Apply to enclosed items button.

7. Close the Info window to save your changes.

✔ Tips

- You cannot change privileges for an item if you are not the owner (**Figure 33**) unless you have an administrator password.

- The Write only (Drop Box) privilege is only available for folders and disks.

- The privileges you assign to one category of users will affect which privileges can be assigned to another category of user. For example, if you make a folder Read only for Everyone, you can only make the same folder Read & Write or Read only for the Group and Owner.

SETTING PRIVILEGES

AirPort

AirPort is Apple's wireless local area network technology. It enables your computer to connect to a network or the Internet via radio waves instead of wires.

Most AirPort configurations consist of two components:

◆ **AirPort Base Station** is an external device that can connect to a network via Ethernet cable or can act as a modem for connecting to the Internet via phone lines.

◆ **AirPort card** is a networking card inside your computer that enables your computer to communicate with a base station or another AirPort-equipped computer.

There are two ways to use AirPort for wireless networking:

◆ Use an AirPort-equipped computer to connect to other AirPort-equipped computers.

◆ Use a base station to link an AirPort-equipped computer to the Internet or to other computers on a network. This makes it possible for a computer with an AirPort card to communicate with computers without AirPort cards.

Mac OS X includes two programs for setting up an AirPort network (**Figure 36**):

◆ **AirPort Setup Assistant** offers an easy, step-by-step approach for configuring a base station. In most cases, this is the only tool you'll need to set up a base station.

◆ **AirPort Admin Utility** enables you to set advanced options that cannot be set with the AirPort Setup Assistant.

This part of the chapter explains how to configure an AirPort base station and connect to an AirPort network with an AirPort-equipped computer.

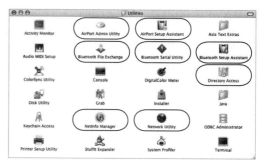

Figure 39 The Utilities folder includes a number of utility applications for working with networks.

✔ Tips

■ AirPort is especially useful for PowerBook and iBook users who may work at various locations within range of a base station.

■ An AirPort network can include multiple base stations and AirPort-equipped computers.

■ You can learn more about AirPort networking at Apple's AirPort home page, www.apple.com/airport/.

■ The current version of AirPort hardware is referred to as *AirPort Extreme*. AirPort Extreme hardware is fully compatible with the original AirPort hardware.

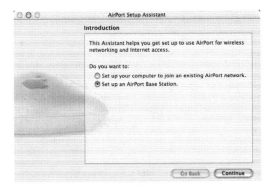

Figure 40 In the Introduction window, tell the Assistant what you want to do.

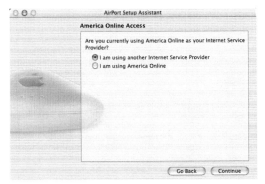

Figure 41 The Assistant asks whether AOL is your ISP.

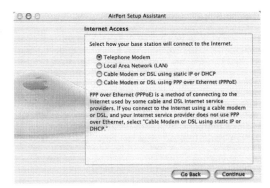

Figure 42 Indicate how you connect to the Internet.

To set up an AirPort base station

1. Open the AirPort Setup Assistant icon in the Utilities folder (**Figure 39**) inside the Applications folder.

2. The AirPort Setup Assistant uses the computer's AirPort card to scan for base stations. It then displays the Introduction window (**Figure 40**). Select the Set up an AirPort Base Station radio button and click Continue.

3. The America Online Access window appears next (**Figure 41**).

    ▲ If America Online is not your Internet service provider, select the first radio button and continue following instructions with step 4.

    ▲ If America Online is your Internet service provider, select the second radio button and skip ahead to step 7.

4. The Internet Access window appears next (**Figure 42**). Select the radio button for the type of Internet access you have and click Continue.

5. The window that appears next depends on what you selected in Step 4:

    ▲ If you selected Telephone Modem, the Modem Access window appears (**Figure 43**). Enter information needed to access the Internet via modem.

    ▲ If you selected Local Area Network (LAN) or Cable Modem or DSL using static IP or DHCP, the Ethernet Access window appears (**Figure 44**). Enter information needed to access the Internet via LAN or cable modem.

Continued on next page...

SETTING UP AIRPORT BASE STATIONS

Continued from previous page.

▲ If you selected Cable Modem or DSL using PPP over Ethernet (PPPoE), the PPPoE Access window appears (**Figure 45**). Enter the information needed to access the Internet via PPPoE.

6. Click Continue and skip ahead to step 8.

7. The America Online Access window changes to display options for setting up an AOL account (**Figure 46**). Enter dialup information and click Continue.

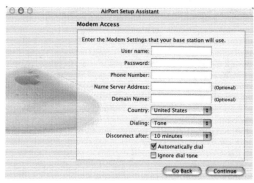

Figure 43 If the AirPort base station's modem will provide Internet access, enter the information it will need to dial in and connect to the Internet.

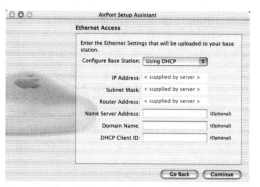

Figure 44 If you'll be connecting to the Internet via LAN and Ethernet, enter network information.

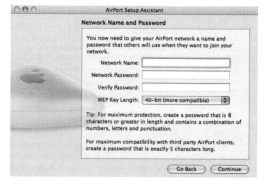

Figure 45 If you'll be connecting to the Internet via PPPoE, enter login information.

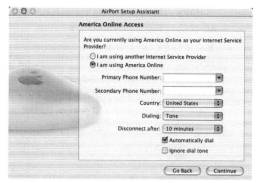

Figure 46 If you'll be connecting to the Internet via AOL, enter dialup information.

Figure 47 Enter a name and password for the AirPort network.

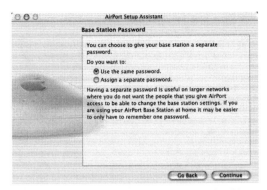

Figure 48 Indicate whether the base station should have a different password than the AirPort network.

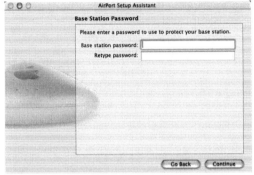

Figure 49 If you want the base station to have a different password, enter it twice here.

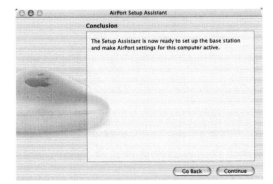

Figure 50 The first Conclusion window tells you the assistant is ready to configure the base station.

8. The Network Name and Password window appears next (**Figure 47**). Enter a name for the network in the Network Name box and then enter the same password in each of the Password boxes.

9. The Base Station Password window appears next (**Figure 48**). Select one of the options and click Continue:

   ▲ **Use the same password** uses the same password for the base station as you entered for the AirPort network.

   ▲ **Assign a separate password** enables you to enter a different password for the Base Station than the AirPort network. When you click Continue, a different Base Station Password window appears (**Figure 49**). Enter the same password in each box and click Continue.

10. The Conclusion window appears next (**Figure 50**). Click Continue.

    Wait while the settings are copied to the base station and the station is reset.

11. The second Conclusion window summarizes what was done (**Figure 51**). Click Done.

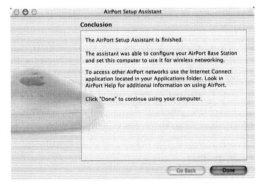

Figure 51 The second Conclusion window tells you what has been done.

SETTING UP AIRPORT BASE STATIONS

✔ Tips

- You can only use the AirPort Setup Assistant on a computer with an AirPort card installed. If a card is not installed, the Assistant will tell you (**Figure 52**).

- If your base station has already been configured, after step 2, you may be prompted to enter the Network and Base Station passwords. Enter the correct passwords as required in the windows that appear (**Figure 53**) and click Continue. Then continue with step 3.

- If your Airport Base Station was used with a previous version of Mac OS, a dialog sheet may appear after step 2, telling you that its software must be updated. Click Update to update the software.

- In step 5, you can get the access information you need from your ISP or network administrator.

- In step 7, you can get the access information you need from your AOL software's dialup configuration settings.

- In step 8, its best to assign a five-character password. This prevents wireless users who don't have Apple equipment from having to enter a different, encoded password.

- If you are the only user of your AirPort network, it's okay to have the same password for the network as the base station. But if multiple users will be using the network, you should assign a different password to the base station to prevent other users from changing base station settings.

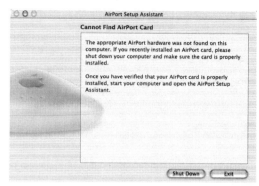

Figure 52 You must use the AirPort Setup Assistant on a computer that has an AirPort card installed.

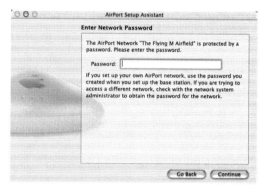

Figure 53 If the base station has already been set up, you'll have to enter network and base station passwords to access it.

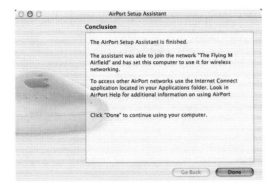

Figure 54 At the end of the setup process, the Assistant tells you what it has done.

To set up an AirPort-equipped computer to access an AirPort network

1. Open the AirPort Setup Assistant icon in the Utilities folder (**Figure 39**) inside the Applications folder.

2. The AirPort Setup Assistant uses the computer's AirPort card to scan for base stations. It then displays the Introduction window (**Figure 40**). Select the Set up your computer to join an existing AirPort network radio button, and click Continue.

3. The Enter Network Password window appears next (**Figure 53**). Enter the password for the AirPort network and click Continue.

4. In the Conclusion window that appears, click Continue.

5. The Assistant sets your computer to access the network and reports its results in the Conclusion window (**Figure 54**). Click Done.

To view & modify AirPort base station settings

1. Open the AirPort Admin Utility icon in the Utilities folder (**Figure 39**) inside the Applications folder.

2. The AirPort Admin Utility uses the computer's AirPort card to scan for base stations. It then displays the Select Base Station window (**Figure 55**). Select the base station you want to work with and click Configure.

3. In the password dialog that appears (**Figure 56**), enter the base station's password and click OK.

4. The Summary window for the base station appears (**Figure 57**). Click buttons on the left side of the window to view and modify setup information:

   ▲ **Show Summary** (**Figure 57**) summarizes the base station's configuration information.

   ▲ **Name and Password** (**Figure 58**) displays the name of the base station and network and enables you to change the password for either one.

   ▲ **Internet Connection** (**Figure 59**) displays information about the Internet connection.

   ▲ **Show All Settings** (**Figure 60**) gives you access to all base station settings. Click a button along the top of the window to access and change different categories of information.

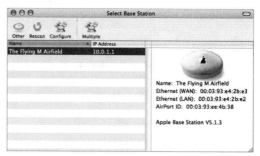

Figure 55 Use this dialog to select the base station you want to work with.

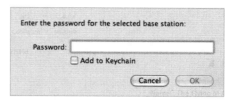

Figure 56 Enter the base station password in this dialog.

Figure 57 Show Summary displays a summary of the base station's configuration information.

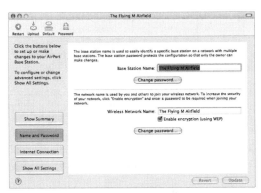

Figure 58 Change the name and password for the base station or the AirPort network in this window.

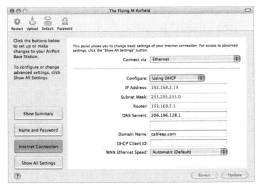

Figure 59 Use the Internet Connection window to change options for the base station's Internet connection.

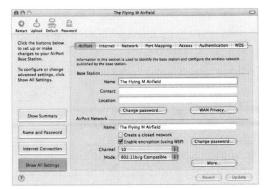

Figure 60 Show All Settings includes buttons for accessing various categories of configuration options, some of which are quite advanced.

5. If you make changes in step 4, click the Update button to send changes to the base station. A status window like the one in **Figure 61** appears while it works.

6. When you're finished viewing and modifying settings, choose AirPort Admin Utility > Quit Airport Admin Utility or press ⌃ ⌘ Q.

✔ Tips

■ The AirPort Admin Utility can also be used to configure a base station from scratch. But I think you'll find it much easier to use the AirPort Setup Utility as instructed earlier in this section. I know I do!

■ I tell you more about connecting to the Internet in **Chapter 11**.

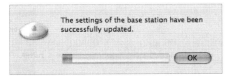

Figure 61 When you click Update, the configuration information is uploaded to the base station.

VIEWING BASE STATION SETTINGS

To use the AirPort status menu

Choose commands on the AirPort status menu (**Figure 62**) to perform the following tasks:

◆ **Turn AirPort Off** disables AirPort on your computer.

◆ *Network Name* connects you to that network. If multiple networks are within range, all of them will appear on the menu.

◆ **Other** displays the Closed Network dialog (**Figure 63**), which you can use to join a network that doesn't appear on the AirPort Status menu. Enter the name of the network and its password (if necessary) and click OK.

◆ **Create Network** displays the Computer to Computer dialog (**Figure 64**), which you can use to create a network between your computer and another AirPort-equipped computer. When you click OK in this dialog, the new network appears on the menu (**Figure 65**) on your computer, as well as the other computer. Choose the new network on both computers to connect.

◆ **Use Interference Robustness** helps improve signal reliability when the base station is operating near a microwave oven or other source of interference.

◆ **Open Internet Connect** opens the Internet Connect application, which I discuss in **Chapter 11**.

✔ Tips

■ The number of curves in the AirPort status menu's icon indicates the signal strength. The more curves, the stronger the signal.

Figure 62
The AirPort status menu shows signal strength (in the menu bar icon) and offers options for working with AirPort networks.

Figure 63 Use the Closed Network dialog to connect to an AirPort network that does not appear on the AirPort Status menu.

Figure 64 Use this dialog to create a computer-to-computer network.

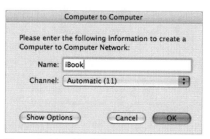

Figure 65
The name of the network appears on the AirPort status menu.

■ If the base station has a dial-up connection to the Internet, a Connect command will also appear on this menu. Use this command to connect to the Internet.

USING THE AIRPORT STATUS MENU

Bluetooth

Bluetooth is a very short-range—30 feet or less—wireless networking technology. It enables you to connect Bluetooth-enabled computers, personal digital assistants (PDAs), and mobile phones to each other and to the Internet. It also let you connect Bluetooth-enabled input devices, such as a mouse or keyboard, to your Mac.

Mac OS X comes with three utilities for working with Bluetooth devices:

◆ **Bluetooth Setup Assistant** makes it easy to pair your computer with another Bluetooth device.

◆ **Bluetooth File Exchange** enables you to send files from one Bluetooth device to another.

◆ **Bluetooth Serial Utility** enables you to set up serial ports on Bluetooth devices for communicating with your computer. (This is an advanced feature that is not covered in this book.)

In addition, you can use the Bluetooth preferences pane to set options that customize the way Bluetooth works.

To use Bluetooth with Mac OS X, your computer must have built-in Bluetooth or a Bluetooth adapter. Bluetooth adapters are available from the Apple Store (www.apple.com/store/) and other sources. You must also have a Bluetooth-enabled device to connect to.

This part of the chapter explains how to configure and use Bluetooth to exchange files between two computers. It also tells you about some of the options in the Bluetooth preferences pane. Although this chapter does not go into specifics about using other devices, it should be enough to get you started using your Bluetooth device with Mac OS X.

✔ Tips

■ Don't confuse Bluetooth with AirPort. These are two similar yet different technologies. AirPort enables an AirPort-enabled computer to connect to and exchange information with computers and devices on an entire network. Bluetooth, however, enables your computer to connect to and exchange information with a single Bluetooth-enabled device.

■ You can find a complete list of currently available devices on the official Bluetooth Web site, www.bluetooth.com.

■ For detailed information about using your Bluetooth-enabled device with Mac OS X, consult the documentation that came with the device or its manufacturer's Web site.

BLUETOOTH

To use the Bluetooth Setup Assistant

1. Open the Bluetooth Setup Assistant icon in the Utilities folder (**Figure 39**) inside the Applications folder.

2. The Bluetooth Setup Assistant Introduction screen appears (**Figure 66**). Click Continue.

3. In the Select Device Type screen (**Figure 67**), select the type of device you will be using and click Continue.

4. The Bluetooth Device Set Up screen appears next. The Assistant locates all Bluetooth devices within range and displays them in a list (**Figure 68**). Select the device you want to work with and click Continue.

5. The next screen prompts you to enter a passkey (**Figure 69**). Enter any number—you don't have to keep it secure or even remember it—and click Continue.

Figure 66 The Introduction screen for the Bluetooth Setup Assistant.

Figure 67 The Bluetooth Setup Assistant prompts you to select a type of device.

Figure 68 Select the device you want to set up.

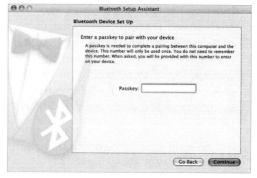

Figure 69 Enter a passkey in this screen.

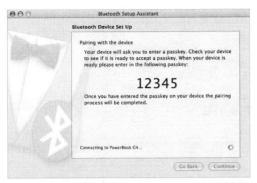

Figure 70 Your computer displays the passkey in big numbers (so you can see it from 30 feet away, I guess).

Figure 71 On the device, you'll see a prompt like this one. In this example, I'm setting up my eMac to exchange files via Bluetooth with my Power-Book. This is what I see on the PowerBook.

Figure 72 When you've successfully entered the passkey, the devices are paired.

6. The next screen displays your passkey and provides instructions (**Figure 70**). Look at the device you want to configure. It should display a message prompting you to enter the passkey (**Figure 71**). Enter the passkey and click Pair.

7. A Conclusion screen appears next (**Figure 72**). To set up another device, click the Set Up Another Device button and follow steps 3 though 6 above. Otherwise, click Quit.

✔ Tips

- ■ This process may be different for other Bluetooth devices. But the Assistant makes the process easy to complete, so you should be able to figure it out.

- ■ You can modify or delete device pairings in the Devices pane of the Bluetooth preferences pane (**Figure 82**).

To send a file from one Bluetooth device to another

1. Open the Bluetooth File Exchange icon in the Utilities folder (**Figure 39**) inside the Applications folder.

2. If necessary, choose File > Send File to display the Select File to Send dialog (**Figure 73**).

3. Locate and select the file you want to send. Then click Send.

4. A Send File dialog appears (**Figure 74**). In the Device list, select the device you want to send the file to and click Send.

5. A dialog like the one in **Figure 75** appears while your computer waits for the device to accept the file. On the device, you'll see an Incoming File Transfer message (**Figure 76**). Click Accept.

   When the file has been transferred, the device displays a dialog with information about it (**Figure 77**).

✔ Tips

- In step 3, you can select multiple files by holding down ⌘ while clicking each one.

- In step 4, you can narrow down the list of devices in the Device list (**Figure 74**) by choosing options from the Device Type and Device Category pop-up menus.

- In step 5, you can turn on the Accept all without warning check box to receive all files without giving you an opportunity to accept or decline.

- You can click the magnifying glass button in the Incoming File Transfer window (**Figure 77**) to open the folder where the file has been saved.

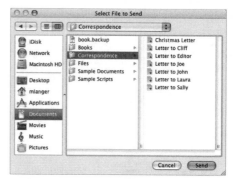

Figure 73 Use this dialog to select the file you want to send.

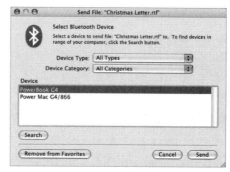

Figure 74 Select the device you want to send the file to.

Figure 75 Your computer waits for a response.

Figure 76 Tell the device to accept the file.

Figure 77 The device displays information about the received file.

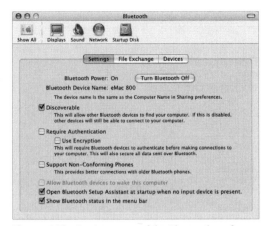

Figure 78 The Settings pane of the Bluetooth preferences pane.

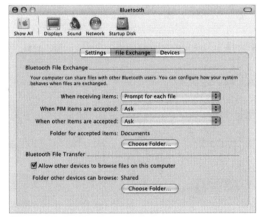

Figure 79 The File Exchange pane of the Bluetooth preferences pane.

To set Bluetooth preferences

1. Choose Apple > System Preferences (**Figure 2**), or click the System Preferences icon in the Dock.

2. In the System Preferences window that appears (**Figure 1**), click the Bluetooth icon in the Hardware row.

3. Click the Settings button in the Bluetooth preferences pane that appears (**Figure 78**) and set options as desired:

   ▲ **Discoverable** enables other Bluetooth devices to easily find your computer.

   ▲ **Require Authentication** requires you to enter a password on the Bluetooth device before connecting to your computer. If you turn on the **Use Encryption** check box, all data that is sent is encrypted to prevent unauthorized interception.

   ▲ **Support Non-Conforming Phones** makes Bluetooth on your computer more compatible with older Bluetooth phone models.

   ▲ **Allow Bluetooth devices to wake this computer** makes it possible for a Bluetooth device to wake the computer. This option is not supported by all computer models.

   ▲ **Open Bluetooth Setup Assistant at startup when no input device is present** tells your computer to launch the Bluetooth Setup Assistant if no keyboard or mouse is connected; this assumes that you're going to set up a Bluetooth input device.

   ▲ **Show Bluetooth status in the menu bar** displays the Bluetooth status menu (**Figure 83**).

Continued on next page...

4. Click the File Exchange button (**Figure 79**) and set options to customize the way Bluetooth File Exchange and File Transfer works:

   ▲ Choose an option from each of the pop-up menus (**Figure 80**) to determine what your computer does when it receives and accepts items.

   ▲ To change the folder into which accepted items are saved, click the Choose Folder button under Folder for accepted items. Then use the Open dialog that appears (**Figure 81**) to locate and open the folder you want to save files into.

   ▲ To specify a folder that other Bluetooth devices can browse, click the bottom Choose Folder button and use the Open dialog that appears (**Figure 81**) to locate and open a folder.

5. Click the Devices button to view a list of Bluetooth devices you have set up. Select one of the devices in the list to learn about it (**Figure 82**). Use buttons on the right side of the window to work with the list.

✔ Tip

■ The Bluetooth icon only appears in System Preferences if a Bluetooth adapter is connected to your computer.

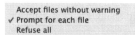

Figure 80 Use this pop-up menu to tell Bluetooth how to handle incoming items.

Figure 81 Use a standard Open dialog to select a new folder for accepted items or browsing by Bluetooth devices.

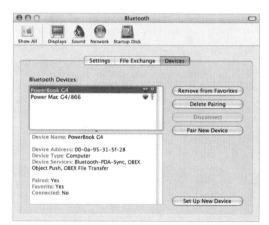

Figure 82 The Devices pane of the Bluetooth preferences pane with two devices set up.

Figure 83
The Bluetooth status menu offers commands for working with Bluetooth devices.

To use the Bluetooth status menu

Choose commands on the Bluetooth status menu (**Figure 83**) to perform the following tasks:

◆ **Turn Bluetooth Off** disables Bluetooth on your computer.

◆ **Discoverable** enables other Bluetooth devices to easily find your computer

◆ **Set up Bluetooth Device** launches the Bluetooth Setup Assistant, which I discuss earlier in this section, so you can set up a Bluetooth Device.

◆ **Send File** launches Bluetooth File Exchange, which I discuss earlier in this section, so you can send a file to a Bluetooth device.

◆ **Browse Device** launches Bluetooth File Exchange so you can browse the contents of a Bluetooth device.

◆ **Open Bluetooth Preferences** opens the Bluetooth preferences pane (**Figure 78**).

✔ Tip

■ The Bluetooth status menu only appears if the Show Bluetooth status in the menu bar option is turned on in the Settings pane of Bluetooth preferences (**Figure 78**).

Advanced Network Administration Tools

The Utilities folder inside the Applications folder includes three powerful utilities you can use to modify and monitor a network (**Figure 39**): Directory Access, NetInfo Manager, and Network Utility. Although a complete discussion of these utilities is beyond the scope of this book, here's an overview so you know what they do.

Directory Access

Directory Access enables you to select the directory services your computer can access and configure how it connects to them.

Directory Access has three panes of options:

◆ **Services** (**Figure 84**) are the types of directory services your computer can access. Toggle a check box to turn access on or off.

◆ **Authentication** (**Figure 85**) enables you to specify where your computer should look for administrator user name and password information.

◆ **Contacts** (**Figure 86**) enables you to specify where your computer should look for contact information, including names and addresses.

✔ Tips

■ Don't understand what all this is about? Then don't change the settings in Directory Access! This is an administrative tool that, if misused, can mess up your computer.

■ When you open Directory Access, it is locked. You must click the lock button at the bottom of the window and enter an administrator's name and password to make any changes.

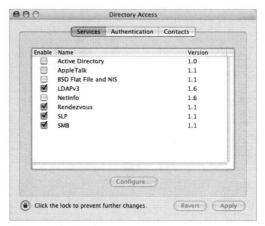

Figure 84 The Services options of Directory Access.

Figure 85 The Authentication options of Directory Access.

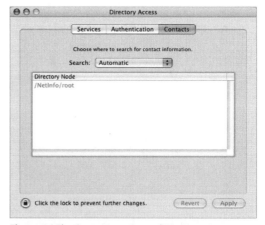

Figure 86 The Contacts options of Directory Access.

Figure 87 NetInfo Manager's main window.

NetInfo Manager

NetInfo Manager (**Figure 87**) enables you to explore and, if you have administrative access, modify the network setup of your computer. With it, you can create and modify network users, groups, and domains and manage other network resources.

NetInfo Manager works by opening the NetInfo data hidden away within Mac OS X's configuration files. Although these files can also be explored and modified with command-line interface tools, NetInfo Manager's interface is a bit easier to use.

NetInfo Manager is a network administrator tool that requires advanced knowledge of the inner workings of Mac OS X networks.

✖ Caution!

- Making changes with NetInfo Manager when you don't know what you're doing is a good way to damage NetInfo data files. If you do enough damage, you could make it impossible to use your computer.

✔ Tip

- If you want to learn more about NetInfo data and NetInfo Manager, look for the document titled "Using NetInfo," which is available on Apple's Mac OS X Server resources page, www.apple.com/server/ resources.html.

NETINFO MANAGER

Network Utility

Network Utility is an information-gathering tool to help you learn more about and troubleshoot a network. Its features are made available in eight tabs:

◆ **Info** (**Figure 88**) provides general information about the network interfaces.

◆ **Netstat** (**Figure 89**) enables you to review network performance statistics.

◆ **AppleTalk** (**Figure 90**) provides information about your AppleTalk network.

◆ **Ping** (**Figure 91**) enables you to test your computer's access to specific domains or IP addresses.

◆ **Lookup** (**Figure 92**) uses a domain name server to convert between IP addresses and domain names.

◆ **Traceroute** (**Figure 93**) traces the route from your computer to another IP address or domain.

◆ **Whois** (**Figure 94**) uses a whois server to get information about the owner and IP address of a specific domain name.

◆ **Finger** (**Figure 95**) gets information about a person based on his e-mail address.

◆ **Port Scan** (**Figure 96**) scans a specific IP address for active ports.

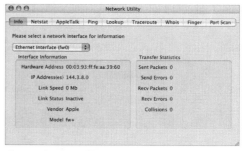

Figure 88 Use the Info button to get information about a network interface.

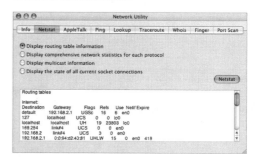

Figure 89 Use the Netstat button to get network performance statistics.

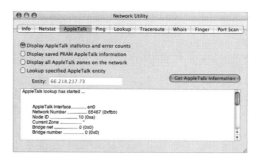

Figure 90 Use AppleTalk button to get information about AppleTalk on your network.

Figure 91 Use the Ping button to "ping" another computer on the network or Internet.

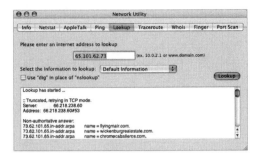

Figure 92 Use the Lookup button to get the IP address for a specific domain name.

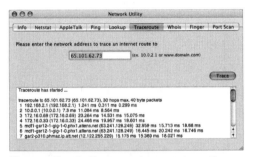

Figure 93 Use the Traceroute button to trace the routing between your computer another IP address.

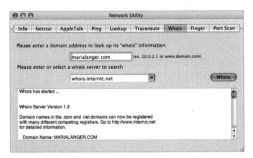

Figure 94 Use the Whois button to look up information about a domain name.

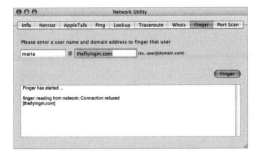

Figure 95 Use the Finger button to look up information about a person based on his e-mail address.

✔ Tips

■ The tools within Network Utility are used primarily for troubleshooting network problems and getting information about specific users or systems.

■ Many of these utilities are designed to work with the Internet and require Internet access.

■ In this day and age of increased privacy and security, you'll find that the Finger utility (**Figure 95**) is seldom successful in getting information about a person. (Heck, I couldn't even get information out of my own server!)

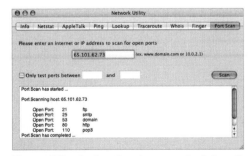

Figure 96 Use the Port Scan button to check for active ports on another IP address or domain name.

Multiple Users & Security

Multiple Users & Security

Mac OS X is designed to be a multiple-user system. This means that different individuals can log in and use a Mac OS X computer. Each user can install his own applications, configure his own desktop, and save his own documents. User files and setup is kept private. When each user logs in to the computer with his account, he can access only the files that belong to him or are shared.

In addition to login passwords to protect each user's private files, each user can take advantage of the keychain access feature, which enables him or her to store passwords for accessing data online or on a network. And for those users who are serious about security, Mac OS X's new FileVault feature enables them to encrypt their Home folders, thus making it virtually impossible for anyone to hack in and read their files.

In this chapter, I discuss both the multiple-user and keychain access features of Mac OS X.

✔ Tips

- Using a multiple-user operating system doesn't mean that you can't keep your computer all to yourself. You can set up just one user—you.

- **Chapters 3** and **17** provide some additional information about how Mac OS X's directory structure is set up to account for multiple users.

Configuring Mac OS X for Multiple Users

In order to take advantage of the multiple users feature of Mac OS X, you need to set up user accounts.

The Mac OS X Setup Assistant does part of the setup for you. Immediately after you install Mac OS X, the Setup Assistant prompts you for information to set up the Admin user. If you are your computer's only user, you're finished setting up users. But if additional people—coworkers, friends, or family—will be using your computer, it's in your best interest to set up a separate user account for each one, then specify what each user is allowed to do on the computer. You do all this with the Accounts preferences pane (**Figure 2**).

In this section, I explain how to add, modify, set capabilities for, and delete user accounts.

✔ Tips

- I tell you more about accessing another user's folders and files later in this chapter.

- You also use the Accounts preferences pane to modify settings for your own account and to set up log in options and startup items. In previous versions of Mac OS X, you did this with the My Account and Login Items preferences panes, which no longer exist.

To open the Accounts preferences pane

1. Choose Apple > System Preferences (**Figure 1**) or click the System Preferences icon on the Dock.

2. In the System Preferences window that appears, click the Accounts icon (in the System area) to display the Accounts preferences pane (**Figure 2**).

Figure 1
The Apple menu.

Figure 2 The Accounts preferences pane with the Admin user selected. (I'm not telling you my password hint!)

Figure 3 Creating a new user account is as simple as filling in a form.

Figure 4 Use the Picture pane to select or drag in a user picture.

To add a new user

1. In the Accounts preferences pane (Figure 2), click the + button at the bottom of the accounts list to add an unnamed user (Standard) to the list and display a blank Password form **Figure 3**.

2. Enter the name of the user in the Name box.

3. Enter an abbreviated name for the user in the Short Name box. This name should be in lowercase characters and should not include spaces.

4. Enter a password for the user in the Password and Verify boxes. The password must be at least four characters long.

5. If desired, enter a hint for the password in the Password Hint box.

6. To change the user's picture, click the Picture button. Then do one of the following in the Picture pane (**Figure 4**):

   ▲ Click to select one of the pictures in the scrolling list.

   ▲ Drag an image file from a Finder window onto the Picture well.

7. Choose System Preferences > Quit System Preferences or press ⌘Q to save your settings and dismiss the Accounts preferences pane.

   A folder for the user appears in the Users folder (**Figure 13**).

✔ Tip

■ To modify an existing user's settings, display the Accounts preferences pane, select the user account in the accounts list, and make changes as desired.

ADDING NEW USERS

To give a user Administrator privileges

1. In the Accounts preferences pane, click to select the name of the user you want to set give Administrator privileges to (**Figure 5**).

2. Click the Limitations button to display Limitations options. Make sure the No Limits button is selected (**Figure 6**).

3. Click the Security button to display Security options.

4. Turn on the check box labeled Allow user to administer this computer. The word *Admin* appears under the user name in the account list (**Figure 7**).

✖ Warning!

■ Only give Administrator privileges to individuals you trust and who have a good understanding of how Mac OS X works. An Administrator has access to the entire computer and can make changes that lock you out or prevent the computer from working properly.

To limit a user's access

1. In the Accounts preferences pane, click to select the name of the user you want to set limitations for (**Figure 5**).

2. Click the Limitations button to display Limitations options.

3. Click the Some Limits button to display its options (**Figure 8**).

4. Turn on the check boxes for each task the user is allowed to perform:

   ▲ **Open all System Preferences** enables the user to open and make changes in all System Preferences.

Figure 5 Select the user account you want to change.

Figure 6 No limits, the default setting, has no options.

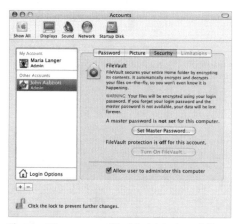

Figure 7 When you enable Administrator privileges for a user, the word *Admin* appears under his name.

Figure 8 The Some Limits pane enables you to specify what a user can do and which programs he can access.

Figure 9 Clicking the triangle beside a folder name displays a list of all the applications within that folder. You can then enable or disable specific applications.

▲ **Modify the Dock** enables the user to add or remove Dock items. (This only affects the Dock as it appears for the user's account.)

▲ **Change password** lets the user change his password. To enable this option, you must turn on the Open all System Preferences check box.

▲ **Burn CDs and DVDs** enables the user to burn CDs and DVDs, if the computer is capable of doing so.

5. To specify which applications a user is allowed to work with, turn on the check box beside This user can only use these applications. Then:

▲ To allow the user to access all applications within a specific folder, turn on the check box beside the folder name. (*Others* refers to applications that are not in any of the other folders.)

▲ To allow the user to access some of the applications within a specific folder, click the triangle beside the folder name to display a list of all applications within the folder (**Figure 9**). Then turn on the check box beside each application the user can access.

✔ Tip

■ The Limitations button does not appear for the account on which you are logged into the computer. Instead, you'll see the Startup Items button, which I discuss later in this chapter.

To enable Simple Finder for a user

1. In the Accounts preferences pane, click to select the name of the user you want to enable Simple Finder for (**Figure 5**).

2. Click the Limitations button to display Limitations options.

3. Click the Simple Finder button to display Simple Finder options (**Figure 10**).

4. Specify which applications a user is allowed to work with:

   ▲ To allow the user to access all applications within a specific folder, turn on the check box beside the folder name. (*Others* refers to applications that are not in any of the other folders.)

   ▲ To allow the user to access some of the applications within a specific folder, click the triangle beside the folder name to display a list of all applications within the folder (**Figure 8**). Then turn on the check box beside each application the user can access.

✔ Tip

■ Simple Finder (**Figure 11**), as the name suggests, is a highly simplified version of the Finder. Designed for users with little or no knowledge of computers, it offers a safe, highly controlled environment for kids and novices. If you want to try Simple Finder, create a new user with Simple Finder enabled, then log in as that user. If you've been using a Mac for more than a few years, I guarantee you'll go nuts in about five minutes. (I didn't even last two.)

Figure 10 Simple Finder options for a user account.

Figure 11 Simple Finder is an extremely simple version of the Finder.

Figure 12 Mac OS X confirms that you really do want to delete the user and offers two options for doing it.

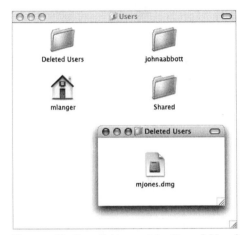

Figure 13 The Users folder contains Home folders for each current user and a Shared folder that all users can access. If any users have been deleted, you may also find a Deleted Users folder which contains disk images of deleted users' Home folders.

To delete a user account

1. In the Accounts preferences pane, click to select the name of the user you want to delete.

2. Click the – button at the bottom of the accounts list.

3. A dialog sheet like the one in **Figure 12** appears. You have two options to delete the user:

   ▲ **Delete Immediately** removes all traces of the user from the computer. (This option is new in Mac OS X 10.3.)

   ▲ **OK** removes the user from the Account list and saves the contents of the user's Home folder as a file in the Deleted Users folder inside the Users folder (**Figure 13**).

DELETING USER ACCOUNTS

To set log in options

1. In the Accounts preferences pane, click the Login Options button at the bottom of the accounts list (**Figure 14**).

2. Select a Display Login Window option:

   ▲ **List of users** displays the name of each user. Click a name to display a password box for the user (**Figure 15**) and log in.

   ▲ **Name and password** displays boxes for the user name and password. Enter the user name and password to log in.

3. To prevent the Login window from appearing at startup, turn on the Automatically log in as check box and choose a user from the pop-up menu. If you choose a user other than the name already selected, a dialog sheet like the one in **Figure 16** appears. Enter the user's password and click OK.

4. To prevent the display of the Sleep, Restart, and Shut Down buttons in the Login window, turn on the Hide the Sleep, Restart, and Shut Down buttons check box.

5. To make it possible for a user to log in without logging out another user, turn on the Enable fast user switching check box. A Warning dialog like the one in **Figure 17** appears. If you trust other computer users, click OK.

Figure 14 The Login options in the Accounts preferences pane.

Figure 15 Clicking the name of a user in a login window's list of users displays the user name and a password box like this.

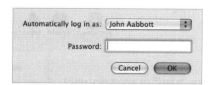

Figure 16 Enter the user's password in this dialog sheet.

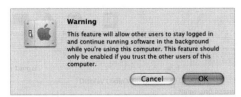

Figure 17 This Warning dialog tells you a little about the fast user switching feature.

✔ Tips

- Although I consider myself somewhat of a screenshot expert (there are over 2,000 shots in this book alone), I could not figure out a way to take a screenshot of every possible Login window in Mac OS X 10.3. Sorry!

- I explain how to log in and out of a Mac OS X computer in **Chapter 2**.

- The Name and Password option in step 2 is more secure, since it requires users to know user names to log in.

- Automatic log in is especially useful if you're the only person who uses your computer and it's in a secure location.

- With the automatic log in feature enabled, the log in window only appears when you log out or purposely display it via the fast user switching option.

- I tell you more about the fast user switching feature later in this chapter.

SETTING LOGIN OPTIONS

To specify startup items

1. In the Accounts preferences pane, click to select the name of the account you logged in with (**Figure 2**). Normally, this will be your account, but if you want to set startup items for another user, you must log in with that user's account.

2. Click the Startup Items button to display its options (**Figure 18**).

3. To add a startup item, drag its icon into the list (**Figure 19**) or click the + button at the bottom of the list and use the dialog sheet that appears (**Figure 20**) to locate, select, and open the item. The item you dragged or selected appears in the list.

   or

   To remove an item from the list, click to select it and then click the – button at the bottom of the list. The item disappears from the list.

4. To automatically hide an item when it launches, turn on the Hide check box beside it.

✔ Tips

- *Startup items*, which were referred to as *login items* in previous versions of Mac OS X, are applications, documents, folders, or other items that are automatically opened when you log in or start up the computer.

- You can set the order in which items open by dragging them up or down in the list.

Figure 18 Startup Items in the Account preferences pane.

Figure 19 One way to add an item to the Startup Items list is to drag it in.

Figure 20 You can use a dialog sheet like this one to locate, select, and open the item you want to add as a startup item.

SPECIFYING STARTUP ITEMS

Figure 21
Fast user switching puts a menu like this one on the far right end of the menu bar.

Fast User Switching

Mac OS X 10.3 introduces *fast user switching*, a feature that enables one user to log in and use the computer without another user logging out.

The benefit to this is that it's fast (hence the name). You don't need to close all open documents and quit all applications for another user to access his account. That means you don't have to reopen all those documents and applications when he's done and you can continue using the machine.

✔ Tip

■ Before you can use fast user switching, you must enable it. You can learn how in the section titled "To set login options" earlier in this chapter.

To use fast user switching

1. With the computer turned on and a user already logged in, choose a user account from the menu at the far right end of the menu bar (**Figure 21**).

2. In the Login window that appears (**Figure 15**), enter the account password and click Log In.

   The screen changes (using a cool graphic effect) to the account you logged in to.

✔ Tips

■ The user menu (**Figure 21**) indicates each user's status:

   ▲ A user name that cannot be selected (Maria Langer in **Figure 21**) is the active user.

   ▲ An orange check mark appears beside the name of any user that is logged in.

■ You must always enter a password to switch to another account, even if that account is already logged in.

The Home Folder

Mac OS X creates a Home folder for each user account in the Users folder (**Figure 13**), with the user's short name as the folder name. The icon for the folder appears as a house for the user who is currently logged in and as a regular folder for all other users. Each user's Home folder contains folders for storing his files (**Figure 22**):

Figure 22 Each user's Home folder is preconfigured with folders for storing documents and settings files.

◆ **Desktop** contains all items (other than mounted disks) on the user's desktop.

◆ **Documents** is the default file location for document files.

◆ **Movies**, **Music**, and **Pictures** are for storing video, audio, and image files.

◆ **Sites** is for the user's Web site, which can be put online with the Personal Web Sharing feature.

◆ **Library** is for storing various preferences files, as well as fonts.

◆ **Public** is for storing shared files.

◆ **Applications**, when present, is for storing applications installed by the user for his private use.

Figure 23 The Home folder in **Figure 21** when viewed by another user.

✔ Tips

■ You can quickly open your Home folder by clicking the name of your Home folder in the Sidebar (**Figure 22**).

■ Personal Web Sharing is discussed in **Chapter 14** and fonts are covered in **Chapter 9**.

■ Although a user can open another user's Home folder, he can only open the Public and Sites folders within that user's Home folder; all other folders are locked (**Figure 23**). A dialog like the one in **Figure 24** appears if you attempt to open a locked folder.

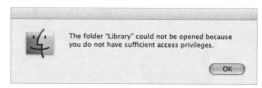

Figure 24 A dialog like this one appears if you try to open another user's private folder.

Figure 25 Each user's Public folder contains a Drop Box folder for accepting incoming files.

Sharing Files with Other Users

Mac OS X offers several ways for multiple users of the same computer to share files with each other:

◆ The **Shared** folder in the Users folder (**Figure 13**) offers read/write access to all users.

◆ The **Public** folder in each user's Home folder (**Figure 22**) offers read access to all users.

◆ The **Drop Box** folder in each user's Public folder (**Figure 25**) offers write access to all users.

✔ Tips

■ *Read* access for a folder enables users to open files in that folder. *Write* access for a folder enables users to save files into that folder.

■ File sharing over a network is covered in **Chapter 14**.

To make a file accessible to all other users

Place the file in the Shared folder in the Users folder (**Figure 13**).

or

Place the file in the Public folder in your Home folder (**Figure 22**).

✔ Tip

■ If your computer is managed by a system administrator, check to see where the administrator prefers public files to be stored.

To make a file accessible to a specific user

1. Drag the file's icon onto the Drop Box folder icon inside the Public folder in the user's Home folder (**Figure 25**).

2. A dialog like the one in **Figure 26** appears. Click OK. The file moves into the Public folder.

✔ Tips

- When you drag a file into a Drop Box folder, the file is moved—not copied— there. You cannot open a Drop Box folder to remove its contents. If you need to keep a copy of the file, hold down Option while dragging the file into the Drop Box folder to place a copy of the file there. You can then continue working with the original.

- To use the Drop Box, be sure to drag the file icon onto the Drop Box folder icon. If you drag an icon into the Public folder, a dialog like the one in **Figure 27** appears, telling you that you can't modify the Public folder. In Mac OS X 10.3, you can click the Authenticate button and enter an administrator password in the Authenticate dialog (**Figure 28**) to override this warning and put the file there anyway.

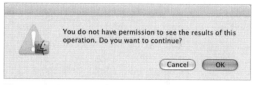

Figure 26 When you drag a file into a Drop Box folder, a dialog like this appears.

Figure 27 You can't place files into another user's Public folder or any other locked folder ...

Figure 28 ... unless you can prove you're an administrator.

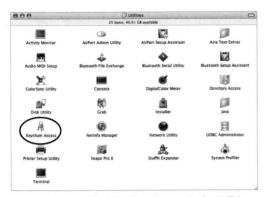

Figure 29 You can find Keychain Access in the Utilities folder inside the Applications folder.

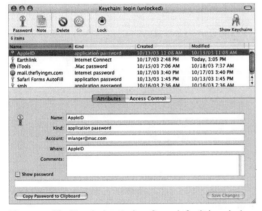

Figure 30 The Keychain window for a default keychain.

Keychain Access

The Keychain Access feature offers users a way to store passwords for accessing password-protected applications, servers, and Internet locations. Each user's keychain is automatically unlocked when he logs in to the computer, so the passwords it contains are automatically available when they are needed to access secured files and sites.

✔ Tips

- Mac OS X automatically creates a keychain for each user, using the user's short name as the keychain name. This is the default keychain.

- Keychain Access only works with applications that are keychain-aware.

- You can also use your keychain to store other private information, such as credit card numbers and bank personal identification numbers (PINs).

To open Keychain Access

Open the Keychain Access icon in the Utilities folder inside the Applications folder (**Figure 29**).

The keychain window for your default keychain appears (**Figure 30**). It lists all of the items in your keychain.

KEYCHAIN ACCESS

To add a keychain item when accessing a secure application, server, or Internet location

1. Follow your normal procedure for accessing the secure item.

2. Enter your password when prompted (**Figure 31**).

3. Turn on the Add Password to Keychain check box (**Figure 31**). (In some applications, you may have to click an Options button to see it.)

4. Finish accessing the secure item. When you open Keychain Access, you'll see that the password has been added to your keychain (**Figure 32**).

✔ Tip

- The exact steps for adding a keychain when accessing a secure item vary based on the item you are accessing and the software you are using to access it.

Figure 31 This example shows the authentication dialog for accessing someone else's iDisk.

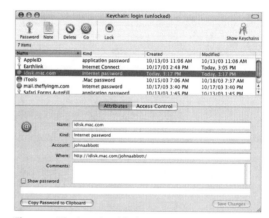

Figure 32 The item is added to your keychain.

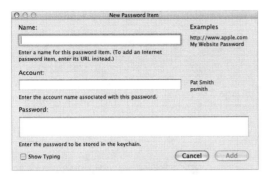

Figure 33 Use this dialog to manually enter password item information.

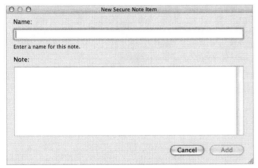

Figure 34 Use this dialog to enter other private information that you want to keep handy but secure.

Name		Kind	Created	Modified
AppleID		application password	10/13/03 11:08 AM	10/13/03 11:08 AM
Earthlink		Internet Connect	10/17/03 2:48 PM	Today, 3:05 PM
idisk.mac.com		Internet password	Today, 3:19 PM	Today, 3:19 PM
iTools		.Mac password	10/15/03 7:06 AM	10/18/03 7:37 AM
Mike's SS#		secure note	Today, 3:25 PM	Today, 3:25 PM
Safari Forms AutoFill		application password	10/13/03 1:45 PM	10/13/03 1:45 PM

Figure 35 Here's the Keychain Access item list for a keychain with several different types of items added.

To add a password item manually

1. Open Keychain Access (**Figures 30** and **32**).

2. Click the Password button in the upper-left corner to display the New Password Item dialog (**Figure 33**).

3. Enter an identifying name or Internet URL for the item in the Name box.

4. Enter the user ID or account name or number for the item in the Account box.

5. Enter the password for the item in the Password box.

6. Click Add. The new item is added to your keychain (**Figure 35**).

✔ Tip

- If you turn on the Show Typing check box in the New Password Item dialog (**Figure 33**), the password you enter will appear as text rather than as bullets. You may want to use this option to be sure that you're typing the password correctly, since you only enter it once.

To add a secure note

1. Open Keychain Access (**Figures 30** and **32**).

2. Click the Note button to display the New Secure Note Item dialog (**Figure 34**).

3. Enter an identifying name for the note in the Name box.

4. Enter the note in the Note box.

5. Click Add. The new item is added to your keychain (**Figure 35**).

To delete a keychain item

1. Open Keychain Access (**Figures** 30 and 32).

2. Select the keychain item you want to remove.

3. Click Delete.

4. A dialog like the one in **Figure 36** appears. Click Delete.

✔ Tip

- Removing a keychain item does not prevent you from accessing an item. It just prevents you from accessing it without entering a password.

To open a keychain item

1. Open Keychain Access (**Figures** 30 and 32).

2. Select the keychain item you want to open.

3. Click Go. The Web page, server volume, document file, or other item for which the keychain item applies opens.

✔ Tips

- The Open button is not available for all keychain items.

- In step 3, if you turn on the Show password check box, a dialog like the one in **Figure 37** may appear. To see the password, you must enter the keychain password (your user password, for the default keychain) and click the Allow Once or Always Allow button. I tell you more about this dialog later in this chapter.

Figure 36 A dialog like this appears when you delete a keychain item.

Figure 37 When an application that does not have permission to use a keychain item wants to use it, it displays a dialog like this. You click a button to determine whether to allow access.

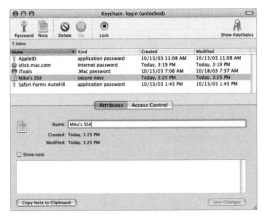

Figure 38 The Attributes tab of the Keychain Access window for a keychain with a note selected.

Figure 39 This dialog appears when you try to view the password or note in a keychain item.

To get general information about a keychain item

1. Open Keychain Access.

2. Select the keychain item you want to learn about.

3. If necessary, click the Attributes button . General information about the item appears in the bottom half of the window. **Figures 30**, **32**, and **38** show examples.

4. To see the item password, turn on the View password check box (**Figures 30** and **32**).

   or

   To see a note, turn on the Show note check box (**Figure 38**).

✔ Tip

- In step 4, if you turn on the Show password (**Figures 30** and **32**) or Show note (**Figure 38**) check box, a dialog like the one in **Figure 39** may appear. To see the password, you must enter the keychain password (your user password, for the default keychain) and click the Allow Once or Always Allow button. I tell you more about this dialog later in this chapter.

To set Access Control options

1. Open Keychain Access (**Figures 30, 32, or 38**).

2. Select the keychain item you want to set Access Control options for.

3. Click the Access Control button (**Figure 40**).

4. Select an access option:

   ▲ **Allow all applications to access this item** enables any application to access the item, without displaying a confirmation dialog. If you choose this option, skip ahead to step 6.

   ▲ **Confirm before allowing access** displays a confirmation dialog for each application that attempts to access the item (**Figure 37**). You can specify whether the dialog includes a password prompt (**Figure 39**) by toggling the Ask for Keychain password check box. Continue following the remaining steps.

5. If desired, use the Add and Remove buttons to modify the list of applications that can access the item without displaying the confirmation dialog:

   ▲ **Add** displays a dialog sheet like the one in **Figure 30**, which you can use to locate and choose an application to add to the list.

   ▲ **Remove** removes a selected application from the list.

6. Click Save Changes.

7. A dialog like the one in **Figure 41** appears. Enter the keychain password in the box and click Allow Once to save the change.

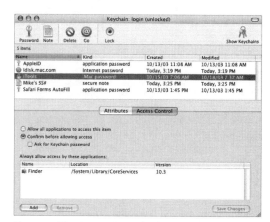

Figure 40 The Access Control information for a keychain item.

Figure 41 You must enter a password in this dialog to change Access Control settings.

SETTING ACCESS CONTROL OPTIONS

To use a keychain item

1. Follow your normal procedure for accessing the secure item.

2. If Access Control settings are set up to allow access to the item without confirmation, the item opens without displaying any dialog.

   or

   If Access Control settings are set up to require a confirmation, a dialog like the one in **Figure 37** or **39** appears. Enter a password (if necessary; **Figure 39**) and click a button:

   ▲ **Deny** prevents use of the keychain item. You will have to manually enter a password to access the secure item.

   ▲ **Allow Once** enables the keychain to open the item this time.

   ▲ **Always Allow** enables the keychain to open the item and adds the item to the Access Control application list so the dialog does not appear again.

✔ Tips

■ The only reason I can think of for denying access with a keychain is if you have another user name and password you want to use.

■ If a keychain item does not exist for the secure item, you'll have to go through the usual procedure for accessing the item.

To create a new keychain

1. Open Keychain Access (**Figures 30, 32, or 38**).

2. Choose File > New Keychain (**Figure 42**) or press Option ⌃ ⌘ N.

3. Enter a name for the keychain in the New Keychain dialog that appears (**Figure 43**) and click Create.

4. The New Keychain Password dialog appears (**Figure 44**). Enter the same password in each box and click OK.

✔ Tips

■ If you're an organization nut, you may want to use multiple keychains to organize passwords for different purposes. Otherwise, one keychain should be enough for you. (It is for me.)

■ Don't confuse the Add Keychain command with the New Keychain command (**Figure 42**). (I did, at first.) The Add Keychain command enables you to add keychain items from another keychain to the currently open keychain.

■ In step 3, although you can specify a different location to save the new keychain, it's a good idea to save it in the default location, the Keychains folder.

To view a different keychain

1. Open Keychain Access (**Figures 30, 32, or 38**).

2. If necessary, click the Show Keychains button in the window's toolbar to display the Keychains drawer (**Figure 45**).

3. Select the keychain you want to view (**Figure 45**).

Figure 42 Options under Keychain Access's File menu.

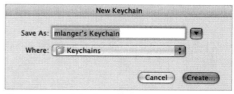

Figure 43 Use this dialog to name and save a new keychain.

Figure 44 Set the keychain's password by entering the same password or phrase in both edit boxes.

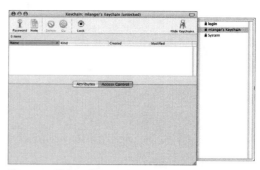

Figure 45 Clicking the Keychains button opens the Keychains drawer so you can see all keychains.

Figure 46 The Unlock Keychain dialog appears when you use Keychain Access to unlock a keychain.

Figure 47 The Unlock Keychain dialog also appears when you attempt to open an item for which a keychain item exists but the keychain is locked.

To unlock a keychain

1. Open Keychain Access and click the Show Keychains button to display the Keychain drawer (**Figure 45**).

2. Select the keychain you want to unlock.

3. Click the Unlock button.

4. The Unlock Keychain dialog appears (**Figure 46**). Enter the password for the keychain and click OK. The icon beside the keychain name changes so it looks unlocked.

✔ Tips

■ The password for the keychain Mac OS X automatically creates for you (the one named with your user short name) is the same as your login password.

■ By unlocking a keychain, you make its passwords available for use by applications as set in the keychain's access controls.

To lock a keychain

1. Open Keychain Access and click the Show Keychains button to display the Keychain drawer (**Figure 45**).

2. Select the keychain you want to lock.

3. Click the Lock button. The icon beside the keychain name changes so it looks locked.

✔ Tips

■ When a keychain is locked, when you try to open a secure item for which you have a keychain item, the Unlock Keychain dialog appears (**Figure 47**). You must enter your keychain password and click OK to unlock the keychain before the keychain item can be used.

■ To quickly lock all keychains, choose File > Lock All Keychains.

FileVault

FileVault, a new security feature of Mac OS X 10.3, enables you to encrypt your Home folder using Advanced Encryption Standard 128-bit (AES-128) encryption. This makes it virtually impossible for any hacker to access the files in your Home folder. Best of all, it's all done quickly and transparently—files are decrypted automatically when you log in and encrypted again when you log out.

✔ Tips

- I say "virtually impossible" above but that's just because I don't believe that anything is really *impossible*. But this comes pretty close—certainly close enough for most people!

- If you're worried about someone recovering one of your deleted files, use the Secure Empty Trash command when you empty the trash. I tell you more about deleting files in **Chapter 3**.

To enable FileVault for the computer

1. Make sure all other users are logged off.

2. Log in with an administrator account.

3. Choose Apple > System Preferences (**Figure 1**) or click the System Preferences icon in the Dock.

4. Click the Security button to display the Security preferences pane (**Figure 48**).

5. Click Set Master Password.

6. In the dialog sheet that appears (**Figure 49**), enter the same password in the top two boxes. Then enter a password hint in the bottom box and click OK. The Security preferences pane indicates that a master password has been set (**Figure 50**)

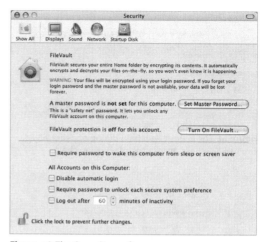

Figure 48 The Security preferences pane.

Figure 49 Use this dialog to set up a master password for the entire computer.

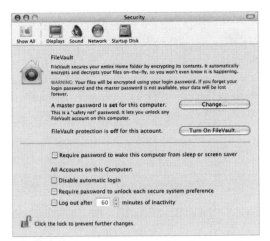

Figure 50 When a Master Password has been set, the Security preferences pane tells you.

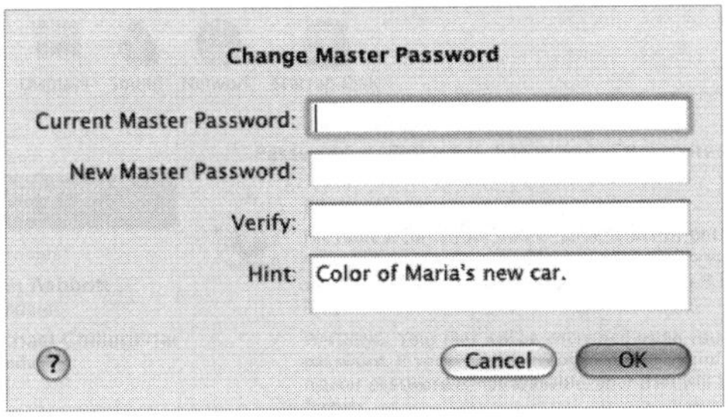

Change Master Password

Current Master Password:

New Master Password:

Verify:

Hint: Color of Maria's new car.

Cancel   OK

Figure 51 Use this dialog to change the master password.

✔ Tips

- By setting a master password, you make it possible for users to use the FileVault feature. You do not, however, enable it for any particular account.

- The master password is used as a "safety net" to help users who have forgotten their account password. After trying unsuccessfully to log in three times, you can click the Forgot Password button and enter the master password when prompted to reaccess your account.

- In step 7, don't forget to enter a password hint that'll help you remember the master password. If you forget the master password, you or other users could be locked out of your Home folder forever.

- To change the Master Password, follow steps 1 through 4, then click Change in the Security preferences pane (**Figure 50**) to display the Change Master Password dialog (**Figure 51**). Enter the current password in the top box and the new password and hint in the next three boxes. Click OK.

- Once you enter a master password, you cannot remove it.

- You can also perform this task in the Security options of the Accounts preferences pane (**Figure 7**) when an administrator account is selected.

SETTING THE MASTER PASSWORD

To protect your Home folder with FileVault

1. Log in to your account.

2. Choose Apple > System Preferences (**Figure 1**) or click the System Preferences icon in the Dock.

3. Click the Security button to display the Security preferences pane (**Figure 48**).

4. Click Turn On FileVault.

5. A dialog like the one in **Figure 52** appears. Enter your account password and click OK.

6. A dialog like the one in **Figure 53** appears next. Read it carefully! Then click the Turn On FileVault button.

   You are logged out and a FileVault window appears. It shows encryption progress and may display an estimate of how long it will take to finish.

7. When the encryption process is done, a Login window appears. Log in to your account.

   From that point forward, every time you open a file in your Home folder, your computer decrypts it before displaying it. When you close a file, your computer encrypts it.

✔ Tips

- If you are an administrator, you can turn on FileVault for another user in the Security pane of Account preferences (**Figure 7**).

- The initial encryption process can be time consuming, depending on how many files are in your Home folder.

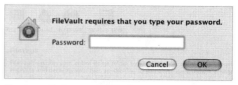

Figure 52 To turn on FileVault, enter your password in this dialog.

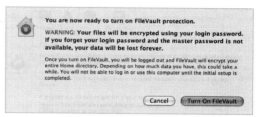

Figure 53 A dialog like this explains what happens when you turn on FileVault.

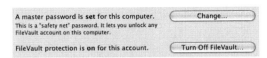

Figure 54 You can tell that FileVault is enabled by looking in the Security preferences pane.

Figure 55 This dialog appears when you turn off FileVault.

To turn off FileVault

1. Log in to your account.

2. Choose Apple > System Preferences (**Figure 1**) or click the System Preferences icon in the Dock.

3. Click the Security button to display the Security preferences pane, which indicates that FileVault is turned on (**Figure 54**).

4. Click Turn Off FileVault.

5. A dialog like the one in **Figure 52** appears. Enter your account password and click OK.

6. A dialog like the one in **Figure 55** appears next. Click the Turn Off FileVault button.

   You are logged out and a FileVault window appears. It shows decryption progress and may display an estimate of how long it will take to finish.

7. When the decryption process is done, a Login window appears. Log in to your account.

TURNING OFF FILEVAULT

465

Enhancing System Security

The Security preferences pane (**Figures 48** and **50**), which is new in Mac OS X 10.3, offers additional options for enhancing security on your computer. Here's how you can use them to make your computer more secure.

✔ Tip

- You must be logged in as an administrator to change Security preferences pane settings.

To set system security options

1. Log in to your account.

2. Choose Apple > System Preferences (**Figure 1**) or click the System Preferences icon in the Dock.

3. Click the Security button to display the Security preferences pane (**Figure 48** or **50**).

4. Set options in the bottom half of the window as desired:

   ▲ **Require password to wake this computer from sleep or screen saver** displays an Authenticate dialog when you wake your computer or deactivate the screen saver.

   ▲ **Disable automatic login** turns off the automatic login feature.

   ▲ **Require password to unlock each secure system preference** displays an Authenticate dialog when a user opens a System preferences pane that requires administrative privileges.

   ▲ **Log out after _n_ minutes of inactivity** automatically logs out a user when he has been inactive for the number of minutes you specify.

✔ Tip

- I tell you about the automatic login feature earlier in this chapter and about System preferences in **Chapter 18**.

The Classic Environment

The Classic Environment

One of the goals of the Mac OS X development team was to build an operating system that would allow for compatibility with most existing Mac application software. After all, who would buy Mac OS X if they couldn't use their favorite applications with it?

The developer's strategy was to make it possible for Mac OS 9.1 or later to run as a process within Mac OS X. Users could then run applications that had not yet been updated for Mac OS X within the Mac OS 9.x process, which is called the *Classic environment*.

The Classic environment utilizes a complete Mac OS 9.x System Folder that contains just about all the components you'd find on a computer that doesn't have Mac OS X installed. This System Folder is so complete, you can even start your computer from it—that means you can choose whether to boot from Mac OS 9.x or Mac OS X.

This chapter provides an overview of the Mac OS 9.x installation and configuration process, then explains how you can use the Classic environment and Mac OS 9.x to work with applications that aren't ready for Mac OS X.

✔ Tip

- In 2003, Apple began selling Macs that won't start from Mac OS 9.x. The Classic environment, however, is still available to run pre-Mac OS X applications.

Installing Mac OS 9.x

In order to use Mac OS 9.x and the Classic environment, you must install it. How you do this depends on how Mac OS X was installed on your computer:

◆ If you updated your computer from Mac OS 9.1 or later to Mac OS X and did not initialize your hard disk as part of the installation process, Mac OS 9.x is still installed on your computer, so you probably won't need to do a thing.

◆ If you updated your computer from Mac OS 9.0 or earlier to Mac OS X, you'll need to update the existing version of Mac OS to 9.1 or later.

◆ If you erased or initialized your hard disk when you installed or upgraded to Mac OS X, then only Mac OS X is installed. You'll need to install Mac OS 9.1 or later.

◆ If you purchased a new computer with both Mac OS X and Mac OS 9.1 or later preinstalled, you're all set and probably don't need to do a thing.

This section explains how to install or update to Mac OS 9.2.

✔ Tip

■ Although you can use Mac OS 9.1 with Mac OS X 10.3, the first time you start the Classic environment, Mac OS X displays a dialog like the one in **Figure 1**. If you have a Mac OS 9.2 updater disc, follow the instructions in the dialog to update to Mac OS 9.2. If you don't plan to update to Mac OS 9.2, you can turn on the Don't show again check box so the dialog doesn't bother you every time you launch the Classic environment.

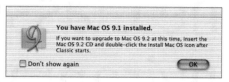

Figure 1 This dialog may appear the first time you run the Mac OS 9.1 Classic environment under Mac OS X 10.3.

Figure 2
The Mac OS Install icon.

Figure 3 The Welcome window appears when you launch the Mac OS 9.2 installer.

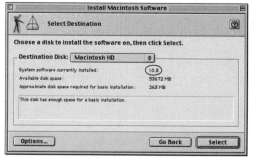

Figure 4 Use this window to select a destination location. The currently installed version of the System software is identified here.

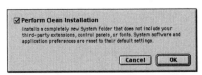

Figure 5 Be sure to perform a clean installation if you're installing Mac OS 9.2 on a system that only has Mac OS X installed.

Figure 6 Read this information before you continue the installation.

Figure 7 The Software License Agreement window.

Figure 8 You must click Agree in this dialog to complete the installation.

To install Mac OS 9.2 from an Install CD

1. Start your computer from the Mac OS 9.2 installation disc. The easiest way to do this is to insert the installation disc, then hold down C while restarting your computer.

2. If necessary, open the icon for the Install disc to display disc contents.

3. Double-click the Mac OS Install icon (**Figure 2**) to launch the installer.

4. In the Welcome window (**Figure 3**), click Continue.

5. In the Select Destination window (**Figure 4**), use the Destination Disk pop-up menu to select the disk on which you want to install Mac OS 9.2. Then:

   ▲ If Mac OS 9.0 or earlier is already installed on the disk, click Select. This tells the installer to update that version of Mac OS.

   ▲ If Mac OS X is the only system software installed on the disk, click the Options button, turn on the check box beside Perform Clean Installation (**Figure 5**), and click OK. Then click Select. This tells the installer to add a new System Folder for Mac OS 9.2.

6. Read the contents of the Important Information window (**Figure 6**), and click Continue.

7. Read the contents of the Software License Agreement window (**Figure 7**), and click Continue.

8. Click Agree in the dialog that appears (**Figure 8**).

9. Click Start in the Install Software window (**Figure 9**) to start the installation.

Continued on next page...

INSTALLING MAC OS 9.2

Continued from previous page.

10. When the installation is complete, click Quit in the dialog that appears.

11. Choose Special > Restart to restart your computer with Mac OS 9.2.

12. The Mac OS Setup Assistant Introduction window appears (**Figure 12**). Follow the instructions later in this chapter to configure Mac OS 9.2.

✔ Tips

■ If the computer was started with Mac OS X and holding down C won't start from the installer disc, follow these steps:

1. Choose Apple > System Preferences.

2. In the System Preferences window that appears, click the Startup Disk icon in the Toolbar.

3. In the Startup Disk preferences pane, select the folder icon for the Mac OS 9.2 installer disc (**Figure 10**).

4. Click Restart.

5. If a dialog sheet like the one in **Figure 11** appears, click Restart.

■ After step 3, if a message appears telling you that the application cannot run on your computer, you'll have to use the Restore CDs that came with your computer to install Mac OS 9.x. I explain how on the next page.

■ These instructions assume that you don't want to customize the installation.

■ I provide detailed instructions on how to install Mac OS 9.1 in *Mac OS 9.1: Visual QuickStart Guide*. That book's instructions also apply to installing Mac OS 9.2. The information provided here, however, should be enough to install Mac OS 9.2 for use with Mac OS X.

Figure 9 Click Start to begin the installation.

Figure 10 Use the Startup Disk preferences pane to select the Mac OS 9.2 installer disc's System Folder.

Figure 11 If this dialog appears, click Restart.

Figure 12
The contents of the first Restore CD for my "test mule," an eMac with SuperDrive.

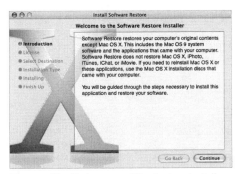

Figure 13 The first screen of the Restore Installer.

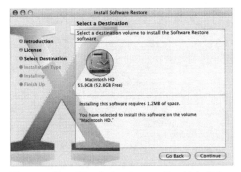

Figure 14 Use this window to specify which disk the installer should be installed on.

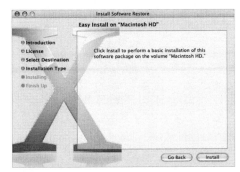

Figure 15 The last window before the Restore Installer is installed.

To install Mac OS 9.2 from Software Restore CDs

1. Insert the first Software Restore CD.

2. If necessary, open the icon for the Restore disc to display disc contents (**Figure 12**).

3. Double-click the SoftwareRestore.pkg icon to launch the installer.

4. If a dialog appears, telling you that the installer needs to run a program, click Continue.

5. In the Introduction window (**Figure 13**), click Continue.

6. Read the contents of the License window, and click Continue.

7. Click Agree in the dialog sheet that appears.

8. In the Select Destination window (**Figure 14**), click to select the icon for the disk on which you want to install Mac OS 9.2. Then click Continue.

9. In the Installation Type window (**Figure 15**), click Install.

10. An Authenticate dialog like the one in **Figure 16** appears. Enter an administrator's name and password and click OK.

11. Wait while the Restore Installer is installed. When a dialog appears, telling you it is finished, click Quit.

12. The Restore Installer's main window appears (**Figure 17**). Click Continue.

13. An Authenticate dialog like the one in **Figure 16** appears again. Enter an administrator's name and password and click OK.

14. The installer may prompt you to insert a specific restore disc. Follow the instructions that appear onscreen.

Continued on next page...

INSTALLING MAC OS 9.2 FROM RESTORE CDS

15. In the Restore Software window that appears, turn off all of the check boxes except the one marked Mac OS 9 (**Figure 18**). (You'll have to turn off the Restore All check box first.) Then click Continue.

16. Wait while Mac OS 9.2 is installed. As the installer works, it may eject discs and request different discs to be inserted. Follow all instructions that appear onscreen.

17. When the Restore Complete window appears (**Figure 19**), click Quit.

✔ Tips

■ If you read these instructions carefully, you'll note that it's a two-step process. The first step is to install the Restore Installer. The second step is to use the Restore Installer to install Mac OS 9.2.

■ This is the only way you can install Mac OS 9.2 on computers that won't start from Mac OS 9.x.

■ You cannot start your computer from a Software Restore disc. You must start in Mac OS 10.2 or later.

■ It is not necessary to erase your hard disk to install Mac OS 9 with the Restore discs. If the only option is to erase your hard disk, you're probably using the wrong restore disc.

■ When the installation process is finished, you should see two additional folders on your hard disk: System Folder and Applications (Mac OS 9).

Figure 16
Mac OS X requires that you prove you have administrative privileges before installing any software.

Figure 17 The first screen of the Restore Installer.

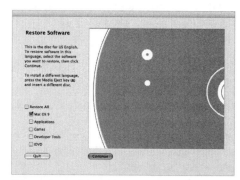

Figure 18 Use this window to specify what you want to install.

Figure 19 When the installation is complete, the Installer tells you.

Figure 20
The Apple menu.

Figure 21 You can also open System Preferences by clicking its icon on the Dock.

Using the Classic Preferences Pane

In Mac OS X, you set options for the Classic environment with the Classic preferences pane. This pane offers options in three areas:

◆ **Start/Stop** (**Figure 22**) enables you to launch the Classic environment within Mac OS X, or to restart or force quit the Classic environment once it is running.

◆ **Advanced** (**Figure 31**) enables you to set Startup and sleep options for the Classic environment and to rebuild the desktop files used by the Classic environment.

◆ **Memory/Versions** (**Figure 36**) displays information about Mac OS 9 processes currently running in the Classic environment.

This section explains how to use the Classic preferences pane.

To open the Classic preferences pane

1. Choose Apple > System Preferences (**Figure 20**), or click the System Preferences icon in the Dock (**Figure 21**).

2. In the System Preferences window that appears, click the Classic icon in the System row. The Classic preferences pane appears (**Figure 22**).

To select a startup volume for Classic

1. Open the Classic preferences pane.

2. Click the Start/Stop button to display its options (**Figure 22**).

3. Select the name of the disk or volume containing the Mac OS 9.x System Folder you want to use for the Classic environment.

✔ Tip

- In most cases, only one option will appear in the list of startup volumes. In that case, the volume that appears will automatically be selected and you can skip this procedure.

To manually start the Classic environment

1. Open the Classic preferences pane.

2. Click the Start/Stop button to display its options (**Figure 22**).

3. Click the Start button.

4. A dialog with a progress bar appears (**Figure 23**). The Classic icon bounces in the Dock (**Figure 24**).

   When Classic is finished starting, the progress bar and Dock icon disappear. In the Start/Stop tab of the Classic preferences pane (**Figure 25**), the words "Classic is running" appear and the Stop, Restart, and Force Quit buttons become active.

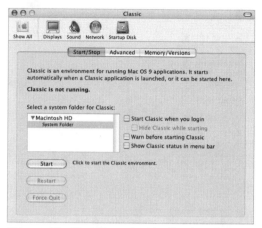

Figure 22 The Start/Stop tab of the Classic preferences pane.

Figure 23 This progress bar...

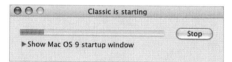

Figure 24 ...and a bouncing Classic icon appear when the Classic environment starts up.

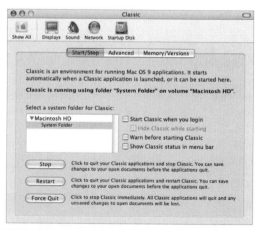

Figure 25 The Start/Stop tab indicates that Classic is running and offers options to stop it.

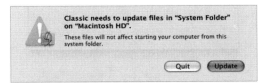

Figure 26 If this dialog appears, click Update.

Figure 27 You can expand the progress window to show the Mac OS 9.x startup screen. (For some people, it's like taking a trip down Macintosh Memory Lane.)

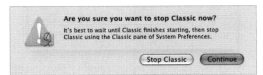

Figure 28 Although you can stop Classic while it's starting, it's best to wait until it's finished.

✔ Tips

- If a dialog appears, telling you that you need to upgrade QuickTime to version 6.0.3 or later, click Continue. I explain how to update software for Mac OS 9 later in this chapter.

- If a dialog appears, telling you that you need to update files (**Figure 26**), click Update. This dialog should only appear the first time you launch the Classic environment after installing or updating your system software.

- If you click the triangle beside Show Mac OS 9 desktop window in the Classic Environment is starting window (**Figure 23**), the window expands to show the Mac OS 9.x startup screen (**Figure 27**).

- If you change your mind while Classic is starting, you can click the Stop button beside the progress bar (**Figure 23**) to stop it. As the dialog that appears warns (**Figure 28**), it's better to let Classic finish starting up before you stop it.

- Remember, the Classic environment starts automatically when you launch a Classic application, so it isn't necessary to manually start it when you want to run a classic application.

STARTING CLASSIC

To automatically start the Classic environment when you log into Mac OS X

1. Open the Classic preferences pane.

2. Click the Start/Stop button to display its options (**Figure 22**).

3. Turn on the Start Classic when you log in check box.

4. If you don't want to see the Classic progress bar (**Figure 23**) or startup window (**Figure 27**), turn on the Hide Classic while starting check box.

✔ Tip

■ You may want to use this feature if you use Classic applications often. This makes Classic ready anytime you want to use it, so you don't have to wait for Classic to start up when you open a Classic application.

To be warned each time the Classic environment automatically starts

1. Open the Classic preferences pane.

2. Click the Start/Stop button (**Figure 16**).

3. Turn on the Warn before starting Classic check box.

✔ Tip

■ With this feature enabled, each time you attempt to open a Classic application when the Classic environment is not already running, a dialog like the one in **Figure 29** appears.

Figure 29 A dialog like this appears when you set the Warn before starting Classic option and start a Mac OS 9 application when the Classic environment isn't already running.

STARTING CLASSIC

🄆	◀))	Wed 1:09 PM

🄆	◀))	Wed 1:09 PM

Figures 30a & 30b A tiny Mac OS 9 icon indicates when the Classic environment is not running (top) and when it is (bottom).

To monitor Classic status in the menu bar

1. Open the Classic preferences pane.

2. Click the Start/Stop button (**Figure 22**).

3. Turn on the Show Classic status in menu bar check box.

✔ Tip

■ With this option enabled, a tiny Mac OS 9 icon appears in the menu bar. The icon is gray if the Classic environment is not running (**Figure 30a**) and black with a half filled-in background if it is running (**Figure 30b**).

To stop the Classic environment

1. Open the Classic preferences pane.

2. Click the Start/Stop button (**Figure 25**).

3. Click the Stop button.

4. If Classic applications with unsaved documents are open, your computer switches to the open applications, one at a time, and offers you an opportunity to save the unsaved documents. Save changes as desired.

   Your computer quits all open Classic applications and stops the Classic environment.

✔ Tip

■ If you're having trouble with the Classic environment and the Stop command won't work, you can click the Force Quit button in the Start/Stop tab to stop Classic. Doing so, however, quits all Classic applications without giving you an opportunity to save changes to documents. For this reason, you should only click Force Quit if you cannot stop Classic any other way.

MONITORING STATUS, STOPPING CLASSIC

To restart the Classic environment

1. Open the Classic preferences pane.

2. Click the Start/Stop button to display its options (**Figure 25**).

3. Click the Restart button.

4. If Classic applications with unsaved documents are open, your computer switches to the open applications, one at a time, and offers you an opportunity to save the unsaved documents. Save changes as desired.

   Your computer quits all open Classic applications and restarts the Classic environment.

✔ Tip

- Use the Restart button if a Classic application unexpectedly quits. This flushes out memory allocated to the Classic environment and can prevent other Classic applications from having related problems.

RESTARTING CLASSIC

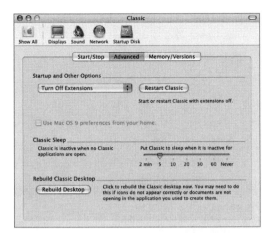

Figure 31 The Advanced tab of the Classic preferences pane.

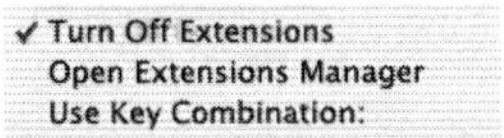

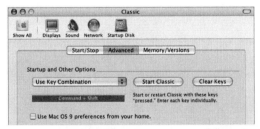

Figure 32 Use this pop-up menu to set startup options.

Figure 33 When you choose Use Key Combination, the dialog changes to display a box for entering your keystrokes.

To set Classic Startup options

1. Open the Classic preferences pane.

2. Click the Advanced button to display its options (**Figure 31**).

3. Choose an option from the pop-up menu in the Startup Options area (**Figure 32**):

   ▲ **Turn Off Extensions** turns off all Mac OS 9.x extensions when Classic starts or restarts. (This is the same as holding down Shift when starting from Mac OS 9.x.)

   ▲ **Open Extensions Manager** automatically opens Extensions Manager when Classic starts or restarts. (This is the same as holding down Spacebar when starting from Mac OS 9.x.)

   ▲ **Use Key Combination** enables you to enter up to five keys to start or restart Classic. If you choose this option, the window changes to display a box for your keystrokes and instructions (**Figure 33**). Press the keys, one at a time, to enter them in the box.

4. To use preference settings from your Home folder rather than the System Folder selected in the Start/Stop tab (**Figure 22**), turn on the Use preferences from home folder check box.

5. Click Start Classic (**Figure 31**) or Restart Classic (if Classic is already running) to start or restart Classic with your startup option set.

✔ Tip

■ The option you select in Step 3 only applies when Classic is started or restarted from the Advanced tab of the Classic preferences pane (**Figure 31**).

To set Classic sleep options

1. Open the Classic preferences pane.

2. Click the Advanced button to display its options (**Figure 31**).

3. Use the slider to specify how long Classic should be inactive before it sleeps.

✔ Tips

■ The Classic environment is said to be *inactive* when no Classic applications are running.

■ When the Classic environment is sleeping, it uses fewer system resources. This can increase performance on an older computer, especially one with a slow CPU or the minimum required amount of RAM.

■ If you launch a Classic application while the Classic environment is sleeping, it may take a moment or two for Classic to wake and the application to appear. This is still quicker than starting Classic.

To rebuild the Classic desktop

1. Open the Classic preferences pane.

2. Click the Advanced button to display its options (**Figure 31**).

3. Click Rebuild Desktop.

4. A dialog sheet like the one in **Figure 34** appears. Select the names of the disks you want to rebuild the desktop file for and click Rebuild.

   A status bar appears in the bottom half of the Advanced area (**Figure 35**). When it disappears, the process is complete.

Figure 34 Use this dialog sheet to choose the disks you want to rebuild the desktop for.

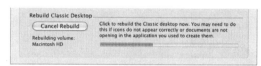

Figure 35 A progress bar appears in the Advanced tab of the Classic preferences pane when you rebuild the Mac OS 9.x desktop.

✔ Tips

■ You may want to rebuild the Mac OS 9.x desktop if icons are not properly displayed in the Classic environment or when starting your computer from Mac OS 9.x.

■ You can use the Rebuild Desktop feature to rebuild the Mac OS 9.x desktop even if the Classic environment is not running.

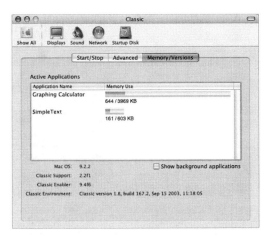

Figure 36 The Memory/Versions area of the Classic preferences pane, with two applications running.

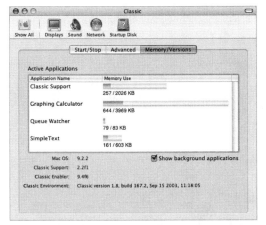

Figure 37 You can include background applications in the list of active applications.

To check Classic application memory usage & versions

1. Open the Classic preferences pane.

2. Click the Memory/Versions button. The window displays a list of all active Classic applications, as well as Mac OS and Classic version information (**Figure 36**).

3. To include background applications in the list (**Figure 37**), turn on the Show background applications check box.

✔ Tip

■ If you have Mac OS 9.x experience, this window's list should look familiar—it's very much like the list that appears in the About this Mac window of a Macintosh running Mac OS 9.

Using Classic Applications

When you open an icon for a Classic application or a document created with a Classic application, Mac OS X automatically starts the Classic environment and opens the application within it (**Figure 38**). The Mac OS X Aqua appearance disappears, replaced with the more sedate appearance of Mac OS 9.x.

While the Classic environment is in use, certain operations work differently than they do in Mac OS X:

◆ The Classic Apple (**Figure 39**) and File (**Figure 40**) menus contain different commands than they do in Mac OS X. In addition, Classic applications do not include a menu named after the application; the commands normally under that menu can be found on the File and Window (if available) menus.

◆ To print from the Classic environment, you must select and set up a printer with the Chooser (**Figure 41**). To open the Chooser, choose Apple > Chooser (**Figure 39**). The Print dialog (**Figure 42**) offers different options than those in Mac OS X.

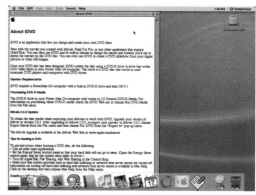

Figure 38 This example shows a SimpleText document open in the Classic environment on a Mac OS X system.

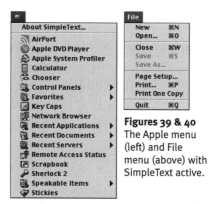

Figures 39 & 40
The Apple menu (left) and File menu (above) with SimpleText active.

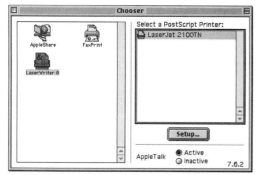

Figure 41 Use the Chooser to set up and select a printer for printing documents from Classic applications.

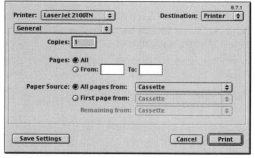

Figure 42 The Classic Print dialog offers different options than the one for Mac OS X.

USING CLASSIC APPLICATIONS

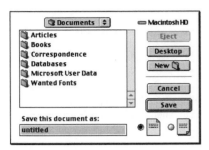

Figure 43 The Classic Save As ...

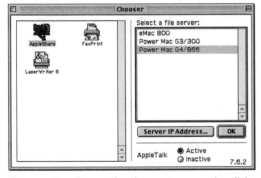

Figure 44 ...and Open dialogs look and work a little differently than in Mac OS X.

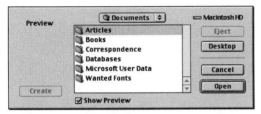

Figure 45 You also use the Chooser to open other disks available via network.

◆ Although you use a Save As dialog (**Figure 43**) to save a document and an Open dialog (**Figure 44**) to open a file, the dialogs look and work differently than in Mac OS X.

◆ To connect to a networked computer from the Classic environment, you must open one of its disks with the Chooser (**Figure 45**). To open the Chooser, choose Apple > Chooser (**Figure 39**).

◆ System preferences can be set with control panels (**Figure 46**).

These are just a few differences between Mac OS X and the Classic environment. As you work with Classic applications, you're likely to find more.

Continued on next page...

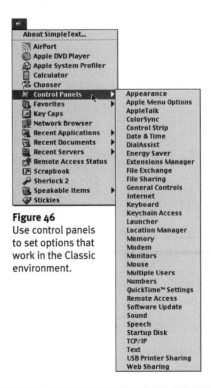

Figure 46
Use control panels to set options that work in the Classic environment.

USING CLASSIC APPLICATIONS

✔ Tips

- Not all applications are supported by the Classic environment. If you try to open an application that was not written for Mac OS X and a dialog like the one in **Figure 47** appears, you'll have to restart your computer with Mac OS 9.x to use it.

- You cannot access the Classic Finder from within Mac OS X. To use the Classic Finder, you must restart your computer from Mac OS 9.x, as instructed later in this chapter.

- Unfortunately, it is impossible to explore all differences between Mac OS 9 and Mac OS X without going into a complete discussion of Mac OS 9.x. If you feel that you need more Mac OS 9.x information, consider picking up a copy of *Mac OS 9.1: Visual QuickStart Guide*, which covers Mac OS 9.1 in detail. Mac OS 9.2 is very similar.

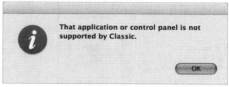

Figure 47 If an application cannot be opened in the Classic environment, Mac OS X tells you.

Starting Your Computer with Mac OS 9.x

If you plan to do a lot of work with Classic applications, you may want to start your computer with Mac OS 9.x and work without using Mac OS X at all. You can do this by selecting your Mac OS 9.x System Folder as the startup disk and restarting your computer.

✔ Tips

■ Not all Macintosh models can start from Mac OS 9.x. If you bought your computer in 2003 or later, it probably can't. You can, however, run Mac OS 9 applications in the Classic environment.

■ You may find that some large and complex Classic applications work a bit better on an older Macintosh model when you start with Mac OS 9.x.

■ If you start your computer from Mac OS 9.x, you cannot use Mac OS X features and applications. You must restart with Mac OS X to use Mac OS X.

■ All the differences discussed on the previous three pages apply when you start your computer from Mac OS 9.x *except* compatibility issues—all Mac OS 9.x applications will work when you start with Mac OS 9.x, even those that are not compatible with the Classic environment.

To restart with Mac OS 9.x

1. Choose Apple > System Preferences (**Figure 20**), or click the System Preferences icon in the Dock (**Figure 21**).

2. In the System Preferences window that appears, click the Startup Disk icon in the Toolbar or in the System row.

3. In the Startup Disk preferences pane, select the folder icon for the Mac OS 9.x System Folder (**Figure 48**).

4. Click Restart.

5. If a dialog sheet like the one in **Figure 49** appears, click Save and Restart.

   Your computer restarts from the Mac OS 9.x System Folder (**Figure 50**).

✔ Tip

■ If a Mac OS 9.x System Folder does not appear in step 3, your computer cannot start from Mac OS 9.

To restart with Mac OS X

1. Choose Apple > Control Panels > Startup disk (**Figure 46**).

2. In the Startup Disk control panel, select the folder icon for the Mac OS X System folder (**Figure 51**).

3. Click Restart.

   Your computer restarts from the Mac OS X System folder.

✔ Tip

■ In step 2, you may have to click the triangle beside the name of your hard disk to display the System folders inside it (**Figure 51**).

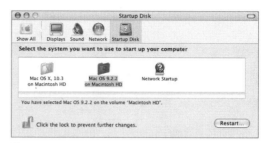

Figure 48 Mac OS X's Startup Disk preferences pane.

Figure 49 If this dialog appears, click Save and Restart.

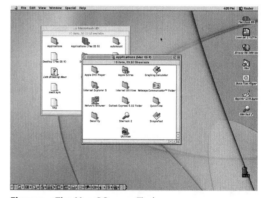

Figure 50 The Mac OS 9.2.2 Finder.

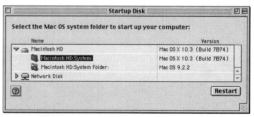

Figure 51 Mac OS 9.2.2's Startup Disk control panel.

Figure 52 The Introduction window for the Mac OS Setup Assistant.

Figure 53 If, for some reason, the Mac OS Setup Assistant doesn't launch automatically, you can open its icon to launch it.

Configuring Mac OS 9.2

When you start your computer for the first time with Mac OS 9.2, the Mac OS Setup Assistant may automatically launch (**Figure 52**). This program steps you through the process of configuring Mac OS 9.2.

✔ Tip

■ Use the Mac OS Setup Assistant to configure Mac OS 9.2, even if you are an experienced Mac OS user. The Setup Assistant can properly set all configuration options in Mac OS 9.2 control panels; setting control panels manually may interfere with the operation of Mac OS X.

To use the Mac OS Setup Assistant

1. If the Mac OS Setup Assistant does not automatically appear when you first restart your computer with Mac OS 9.x, open its icon. You can find it in *Hard Disk Name*: Applications (Mac OS 9):Utilities: Assistants (**Figure 53**).

2. Read the instructions that appear in each screen of the Mac OS Setup Assistant and enter information when prompted. Click the right-pointing triangle button to move from one screen to the next.

✔ Tip

■ If you need step-by-step instructions for configuring Mac OS 9.x with the Mac OS Setup Assistant, you can find it in *Mac OS 9.1: Visual QuickStart Guide* or online, on the companion Web site for *Mac OS X 10.3: Visual QuickStart Guide*, www.marialanger.com/booksites/macosx/.

Unix Basics for Mac OS X

17

BY RON HIPSCHMAN

Ron Hipschman has been playing with computers at the Exploratorium in San Francisco for more years than he wants to admit. At the Exploratorium he has also built exhibits, taught classes, written books, and created the Exploratorium's Web site (www.exploratorium.edu) way back in 1993 when it was among the first 600 sites on the Internet. This is where he learned his Unix (on a Sun Microsystems machine).

Ron's first "real" computer was an IMSAI 8080 that he soldered together from a kit and loaded software (initially) with the toggle switches on the front panel. That computer ran an operating system called CP/M. He became a Mac fanatic in 1985 (he waited for the Mac Plus). He's on his fifth Mac (a Power Mac G4). He sponsors a local Mac user group that meets at the Exploratorium (www.bmugwest.com). He is now very happy that he has his two favorite operating systems (Mac OS and Unix) all in one machine.

Unix & Mac OS X

You probably bought your Macintosh because it was powerful, easy to learn, and easy to use. Sure, more powerful machines were out there, but they all ran this crazy, cryptic Unix or Linux operating system. You thought that Unix was more a lifestyle choice than an operating system, and you swore that you'd never saddle yourself with the task of learning all those arcane commands.

Oops. Now you have Mac OS X.

Guess what? Even though you still have the ease of use for which we all love Apple, you now have the power of Unix under the hood, too. Although it's beyond the scope of this book to teach you everything there is to know about Unix (it really is a lifestyle!), the brief introduction in this chapter will get you going with some basics and point you to other resources you can explore on your own.

Unix Directories & Files

Before I start my discussion of Unix commands, let's take a look at the structure of the Unix file system.

The directory system

Like the Macintosh file system, the Unix file system starts at the top level with a *root* directory, which can contain files and *subdirectories*. The root directory in Mac OS 9 and earlier is named after your hard disk. The root directory in Unix is named / (a slash without any other characters following it). Subdirectories below the root directory are indicated by listing them after the root slash. Each subdirectory is separated from the subdirectory it resides within by a slash.

For example, my home directory is /Users/ronh. That means that in the root directory, /, is a subdirectory called *Users*, inside of which is a subdirectory called *ronh*.

✔ Tips

- On Mac OS, subdirectories are also known as *folders*.

- Unix uses a forward slash (/) to separate subdirectories, not a backslash (\) like in Windows or MS-DOS.

- I discuss the home directory later in this chapter. It is also covered in more detail in **Chapter 3**.

File names

There are two things about Unix file names that you should be aware of.

First, although Unix file names are normally case-sensitive, in the Mac OS Extended file system (HFS+), file names are not case-sensitive. What does this mean to you? Just that you need to be aware of the case of file names, especially if you move files to another Unix machine—for example, to a Unix Web server. Remember, on every other Unix machine in the known universe, upper- and lowercase are different. It's a good idea to pretend that this is the case on your Mac OS X machine, too.

Second, Unix file names do not normally include space characters. Although the Mac OS X Finder has no problem with spaces in file names, the underlying Unix uses spaces to separate commands, options, and operands. Spaces in Unix file names will cause you no end of grief because Unix will misinterpret them as operand separators in the commands you enter and your commands will perform unpredictably. If you need to enter a command that includes a file name with space characters, enclose the file name in single quotation marks so the system recognizes it as a single entity in the command.

Invisible files

File names that begin with a dot (.) are *hidden*. Programs such as the shell, mail, and editors use these files to store preferences and other data.

Note that Unix has two unusually named subdirectories, one with a single dot (.) and another with double dots (..). These are shorthand ways for Unix to refer to "the current directory" and "the directory above this one" (also called the *parent directory*). The Unix operating system gives these plain files special treatment, as you'll learn later in this chapter in the discussion of the cd command.

✔ Tip

- I explain how to include invisible files in a file list later in this chapter.

Terminal, the Shell, & Console

In the Utilities folder (**Figure 1**) inside the Applications folder is a utility called *Terminal* (**Figure 2**). This application is your window into the Unix world lurking deep inside Mac OS X. If you're old enough, you may remember using big, clunky video terminals to communicate with large mainframes. Terminal mimics the operation of those CRT terminals, but it uses your computer's screen, keyboard, and CPU instead of dumb-terminal hardware.

When you run Terminal, it connects to a communication process inside your Mac called a *shell*. The shell is a program that interprets human actions such as the typing of commands and the starting and stopping of jobs. It passes these requests to the computer and is responsible for sending the results of your actions to the Terminal window.

Each shell has its own set of features. The default shell that Mac OS X assigns to new accounts is called *bash*, which stands for Bourne-Again SHell (don't ask; there are far too many Unix in-jokes to deal with in this book). This is a change from Mac OS X 10.2 (Jaguar), which assigned *tcsh* (pronounced "t-shell") as the default shell.

Religious wars have been fought over which shell is best and the debate is certainly beyond the scope of this book. bash is a derivative of the *bourne* shell and tcsh is a derivative of the *csh* (c-shell). The bash shell is a powerful shell that includes many enhancements, some of which were borrowed from csh, such as a command line editor, file-name completion, and a command history. bash also contains a script command processor that allows you to build interactive programs and preprogrammed command series, similar to what you can do with AppleScript.

The Terminal application and the shell work together, allowing you to communicate with and control your computer. But they are separate entities. Terminal is responsible for accepting commands and displaying results, and the shell is responsible for interpreting and executing commands. You can use Terminal to talk to a variety of shells. You can open as many Terminal windows as you need—they each work independently.

Mac OS X also includes a utility called *Console* (**Figure 3**), which is an application that displays system messages. Keeping the console.log window open and watching it can tell you a lot about what's happening on your system.

✔ Tips

■ bash is an extended version of the standard *sh*, or "bourne-shell," that's part of Unix. You can get more information about bash by typing man bash at the shell prompt. (More on the man command later.)

■ If you are debugging programs, use Console to view error messages.

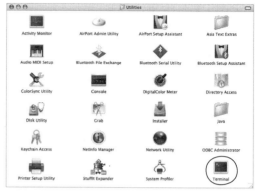

Figure 1 The contents of the Utilities folder includes applications for working with Unix.

Figure 2 A Terminal window with a shell prompt.

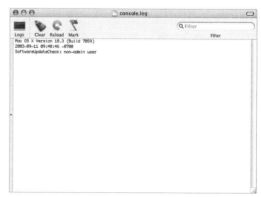

Figure 3 The console.log window displays system messages.

Unix Command Basics

You work with Unix by typing commands into a Terminal window at the shell prompt. Press Return after each command to enter it. The results of the command entry appear in the Terminal window, followed by a new shell prompt.

Most Unix commands can be used with options that make them do slightly different things. For instance, the ls command has 34 options in Mac OS X. To include an option with a command, enter the command followed by a space, a hyphen, and the option. For example, to use the l option with the ls command, you'd enter ls -l.

You can use more than one option at a time by stringing them together. Some commands, such as ls, let you put all the options together after a single hyphen. Other commands require that you use a separate hyphen for each option.

✔ Tips

■ Typing commands into a command-line interface (CLI) offers advantages beyond what is possible with a graphical user interface (GUI) like the Finder.

■ If, while working with Unix commands in the Terminal window, you are either flooded with output that you'd like to stop or faced with a command that seems stuck, try pressing Control C to break the current command. If that doesn't work, close the Terminal window and open a new one.

■ Throughout this chapter, an ellipsis (...) in command syntax means that you can repeat the previous operand as many times as you wish. For instance, rather than saying cp *source-file1 source-file2 source-fileN target-directory*, I'll say cp *source-file ... target-directory*, meaning that you can include as many source files as you like in the command.

Listing Directory Contents with the ls Command

ls is one of the most basic Unix commands. It enables you to list the contents of a directory.

✔ Tip

- The commands in this section assume that the shell prompt is displaying your home directory (~).

To list the contents of your home directory

Type ls and press Return.

A list of the contents of your home directory appears (**Figure 4**).

To list the contents of a subdirectory

Type ls followed by the subdirectory name (for example, ls Library) and press Return.

A list of the contents of the subdirectory you typed appears (**Figure 5**).

To view a long directory listing

Type ls -l and press Return.

A list of the contents of your home directory, including permissions, owner, size, and modification date information, appears (**Figure 6**).

✔ Tip

- I tell you more about permissions later in this chapter.

To include invisible items in a directory listing

Type ls -a and press Return.

A list of the contents of your home directory, including invisible items, appears (**Figure 7**).

Figure 4 A simple directory listing using the **ls** command.

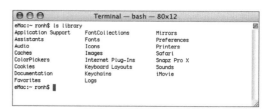

Figure 5 A listing for the library subdirectory.

Figure 6 The long version of a directory listing includes permission, owner, file size, and modification date information.

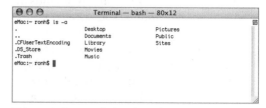

Figure 7 A directory listing that includes invisible subdirectories.

Table 1

man pages Sections	
Section	**Type of Command or File**
1	User commands
2	System calls
3	Library routines
4	I/O and special files
5	Administrative files
6	Games
7	Miscellaneous
8	Administrative and maintenance commands

Viewing man pages

One important Unix command tells you everything you ever wanted to know about Unix commands and files: the man command. It displays information about commands and files documented in the on-line manual pages. These *man pages* are included with every version of Unix.

The man pages present information about a command one page at a time. You can use keystrokes to advance to the next line or page of the man pages. You must quit the man pages feature to enter other Unix commands.

Like a book, man pages are broken into chapters called *sections* (**Table 1**). Each section is designed for a specific type of user. For example, a programmer will be interested in different man pages than a user or a system administrator. There are some man pages that document identical sounding items, yet are intended for different users.

✔ Tip

■ The man pages for commands and files can be lengthy and complex. Don't worry if you don't understand everything on a man page. Just take what you need. As you understand more about Unix, more will make sense.

To view man pages for a command

Type man followed by the name of the command (for example, man ls), and press [Return].

The first page of the reference manual for the command appears (**Figure 8**).

To view the next line of a man page

Press [Return].

The manual advances one line.

To view the next page

Press [Spacebar].

The manual advances one page (**Figure 9**).

To quit man pages

Press [Q].

Terminal returns you to the shell prompt.

To get man pages for man

Type man man and press [Return].

The first page of the reference manual for the online manual appears (**Figure 10**).

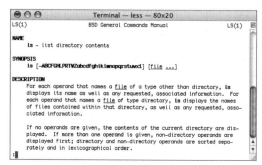

Figure 8 The first man page for the ls command.

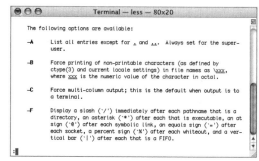

Figure 9 The second page for the ls command.

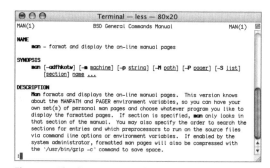

Figure 10 The first man page for man.

Moving Around with the cd Command

Up to now, you haven't moved around in the directory tree. You've been fixed in place in your home directory. Changing directories is easy—just use the cd (change directory) command, followed by the destination you want to move to.

You have two ways to indicate a destination: with an *absolute path* or a *relative path*.

◆ An absolute path specifies the location of a file or subdirectory, starting at the root directory and working downward.

◆ A relative path specifies the location of a file or subdirectory starting at your present location.

Let's look at an example. Suppose I'm currently in my home directory (/Users/ronh) and I want to move to the /usr/bin directory. I could specify the destination with its absolute path: /usr/bin. Or I could use the relative path to go up two directories to the root and then down two directories to the one I want. This is where the special "double-dot" (..) directory name that I discussed earlier comes into play; it indicates the directory above the current one. So the relative path from my home directory to /usr/bin would be ../../usr/bin.

✔ Tips

■ The cd command does not have any options and has no man page of its own because it's built in to the shell. You can find out more about the shell by using the man pages; enter man bash and press (Return).

■ Absolute paths, which always start with a forward slash (/), work no matter where you are located in the Unix file system because they start from the root directory.

■ Relative paths are especially useful if you are deep inside the directory structure and want to access a file or subdirectory just one level up. For example, it's a lot easier to type ../images/flower.jpg than /Users/ronh/Documents/ClipArt/Plants/Color/images/flower.jpg—and it's a lot easier to remember, too!

To change directories using an absolute path

Type cd followed by the absolute path to the directory you want (for example, cd /usr/bin) and press [Return].

The current directory changes and the path to the directory appears in the shell prompt (**Figure 11**).

To change directories using a relative path

Type cd followed by the relative path to the directory you want (for example, from your home directory, type cd ../../usr/bin) and press [Return].

The current directory changes and the path to the directory appears in the shell prompt (**Figure 12**).

To move to a subdirectory using an absolute path

Type cd followed by the absolute path to the subdirectory (for example, cd /Users/ronh/Sites) and press [Return].

The current directory changes and the path to the directory appears in the shell prompt (**Figure 13**).

To move to a subdirectory using a relative path

Type cd followed by the relative path to the subdirectory (for example, from your home directory, type cd Sites) and press [Return].

The current directory changes and the path to the directory appears in the shell prompt (**Figure 14**).

Figure 11 Here's how you can change the current directory to /usr/bin using an absolute path...

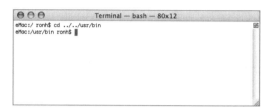

Figure 12 ...or a relative path from your home directory.

Figure 13 Here's how you can move to a subdirectory using an absolute path...

Figure 14 ...or with a relative reference.

✔ Tip

- Do not include a forward slash (/) before a subdirectory name. Doing so tells Unix to start at the root directory (as if you were entering an absolute path) and could result in an error message (**Figure 15**).

Figure 15 If you enter an incorrect path, an error message appears.

Figure 16 Once you're in a directory, using the **ls** command by itself displays the contents of that directory.

Figure 17 The **pwd** command displays the complete path to the current directory.

To list the contents of the current directory

Type ls and press (Return).

The contents of the directory appear in the Terminal window (**Figure 16**).

To return to your home directory

Type cd (without any arguments) and press (Return).

The current directory changes to your home directory and the tilde (~) character appears in the shell prompt.

✔ Tip

- The tilde character is Unix shorthand for "home directory." So, for example, if you wanted to change to the home directory for user name rosef, you could type cd ~rosef.

Getting the Directory Location with the pwd Command

You might be wondering how to find out exactly where you are after doing many cd commands. Unix has a spiffy little command just for this: pwd (present working directory).

To learn the current directory

Type pwd and press (Return).

The complete path to the current directory appears, followed by the shell prompt (**Figure 17**).

The cd & pwd COMMANDS

499

Wildcards in File Names & Directories

One frustrating activity in Mac OS 9.x and earlier was working with a group of files. Other than Shift-clicking or dragging to select the group, you had no good way to select group items by name—for example, to select all files that started with the characters *file* and ended with the characters *.doc*.

Unix, however, makes this easy by enabling you to use three special characters as wildcards:

- **Asterisk** (*), which is referred to as star, is a wildcard for zero or more characters— any character!

- **Question mark** (?) is a wildcard for any single character.

- **Brackets** ([and]) around one or more characters act as a wildcard for any of the enclosed characters.

You can place the wildcard wherever you want in the name you are searching for. As you can imagine, wildcards are powerful tools for selecting or listing files or subdirectories.

✔ Tip

- The brackets wildcard can include individual characters, such as [ABCD] or character ranges, such as [A-G] or [1-6].

Using wildcards

The best way to explain how you can use wildcards is to show you some examples.

Suppose your Documents subdirectory contained the following subdirectories and files:

dir1	file03.doc	file12.txt
dir2	file04.doc	file20.txt
dir30	file05.doc	file21.txt
file01.doc	file10.txt	file38.txt
file02.doc	file11.txt	file39.txt

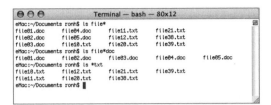

Figure 18 These examples show how you can use the asterisk wildcard to list specific files in a directory.

Figure 19 These examples show the question mark wildcard in action. (Both dir1 and dir2 are empty directories; that's why no files are listed for them.)

```
● ● ●        Terminal — bash — 80x12
eMac:~/Documents ronh$ ls file1[12].txt
file11.txt    file12.txt
eMac:~/Documents ronh$ ls file[01][02].*
file02.doc    file10.txt    file12.txt
eMac:~/Documents ronh$
```

Figure 20 Here are two examples for the bracket wildcard.

Here are some examples to illustrate the asterisk wildcard (**Figure 18**):

◆ To work with all the files that start with the characters *file*, you enter file*.

◆ To work with all the files that begin with the characters *file* and end with the characters *doc*, you enter file*doc.

◆ To work with all the files that end with the characters *txt*, you enter *txt.

These examples illustrate the question mark wildcard (**Figure 19**):

◆ To work with files named *file10.txt*, *file11.txt*, and *file12.txt*, you enter file1?.txt.

◆ To work with files named *file10.txt* and *file20.txt*, you enter file?0.txt.

◆ To work with subdirectories named *dir1* and *dir2*, you enter dir?.

◆ To work with files named *file01.doc*, *file11.txt*, and *file21.txt*, you enter file?1.*. (Okay, so that one uses two wildcards.)

And these examples illustrate the brackets wildcard in action (**Figure 20**):

◆ To work with files named *file11.txt* and *file12.txt* (but not *file10.txt*), you enter file1[12].txt.

◆ To work with files named *file01.doc*, *file10.txt*, and *file11.txt*, you enter file[01][01].*. (Yes, that's another one with multiple wildcard characters.)

To view a directory list using a wildcard

Type ls followed by the search string for the files or directories you want to display (see previous examples) and press (Return).

A list containing only the files and directories that match the search string appear (**Figures 18, 19,** and **20**).

WILDCARDS IN FILE NAMES & DIRECTORIES

Copying & Moving Files

Unix also includes commands for copying and moving files: cp and mv. These commands enable you to copy or move one or more source files to a target file or directory.

Figure 21 Here's the cp command in action.

✔ Tips

- Why copy a file? Usually, to make a backup. For instance, before you edit a configuration file, you should create a backup copy of the original. This way you can revert back to the original if your edits "break" something in the file.

- The mv command can also be used to rename a file.

- The cp and mv commands support several options. You can learn more about them in the man pages for these commands. Type man cp or man mv and press Return to view each command's man pages.

- Unix does not confirm that a file has been copied or moved when you correctly enter a command (**Figures 21** and **22**). To check to see if a file has been copied or moved to the correct destination, you can use the ls command to get a listing for the target directory. The ls command is covered earlier in this chapter.

To copy a file to the same directory

Type cp *source-file target-file* and press Return (**Figure 21**).

For example, cp file.conf file.conf-orig would duplicate the file named *file.conf* and assign the name *file.conf-orig* to the duplicate copy.

✔ Tips

- The *source-file* and *target-file* names must be different.

- The *source-file* operand can be a file or a directory.

Figure 22 Here's the **mv** command in use.

To copy files to another directory

Type cp *source-file ... target-directory* and press Return (**Figure 21**).

For example, cp file.conf /Users/ronh/Documents would copy the file named *file.conf* in the current directory to the directory named *Documents* in my home folder.

To copy files using a wildcard

Type cp followed by the wildcard search string for the source file and the name of the target directory and press Return (**Figure 21**).

For example, cp *.conf Originals would copy all files ending with *.conf* in the current directory to the subdirectory named *Originals*.

To rename a file

Type mv *source target* and press Return (**Figure 22**).

For example, mv file.conf file.conf-backup would rename *file.conf* as *file.conf-backup*.

To move files to another directory

Type mv *source ... directory* and press Return (**Figure 22**).

For example, mv file.conf Documents would move the file named *file.conf* in the current directory to the subdirectory named *Documents*.

To move a file to another directory & rename it

Type mv *source directory/filename* and press Return (**Figure 22**).

For example, mv file.conf-orig Documents/file.conf-backup2 would move the file named *file.conf-orig* in the current directory to the subdirectory named *Documents* and name it *file.conf-backup2* in its new location.

COPYING & MOVING FILES

Making Symbolic Links with ln

Mac OS enables you to make aliases to files. It should come as no surprise that Unix does, too. But in Unix, aliases are called *symbolic links*. And rather than use a menu command or shortcut key to create them, you use the ln (make links) command with its -s option.

Figure 23 These examples show the commands for creating symbolic links to a file and a directory.

✔ Tips

- Mac OS aliases and Unix symbolic links make it convenient to access deeply buried files or to organize files differently than the way the operating system organizes them.

- If you omit the -s option, the ln command creates a hard link. Hard links can't cross file systems (or partitions) and can't normally refer to directories.

- Unix does not tell you if the source file to which you want to create a symbolic link does not exist. As a result, it's possible to create an alias that doesn't point to anything.

- You can learn more about other options for the ln command in its man pages. Type man ln and press (Return) to display them.

To make a link to a file

Type ln -s *source-file target-file* and press (Return) (**Figure 23**).

For example, ln -s file1 alias1 creates an alias called *alias1* that points to the file called *file1*. In this example, both files (the source and the target) are in the current directory.

To make a link to a directory

Type ln -s *source-directory target-file* and press (Return) (**Figure 23**).

For example, ln -s ~ronh/Library/Favorites ./Favs creates a alias called *Favs* in the current directory (./) that points to the directory called *Favorites*, which is in the directory called *Library*, inside the home directory (~) of the user ronh.

Figure 24 The **rm** command in action, with and without the **-i** option.

Removing Files & Directories with rm & rmdir

Unix includes two commands that you can use to delete files and directories: rm (remove) and rmdir (remove directory).

✖ Caution

- rm may be the most dangerous command in Unix. Because Unix doesn't have a Trash that lets you recover mistakenly deleted files, when you delete a file, it's gone forever.

✔ Tips

- There are two options that you may want to use with the rm command:
  - ▲ -i tells the rm command to ask permission before deleting each file (**Figure 24**). You must press Ⓨ and then Return at each prompt to delete the file. This is especially useful when using the rm command with wildcard characters, since it can help prevent files from being accidentally deleted.
  - ▲ -R, which stands for *recursively*, tells the rm command to delete everything within a directory, including its subdirectories and their contents. The -R option can be very dangerous; you may want to use it in conjunction with the -i option to confirm each deletion.

- The rm command's *file* operand can be a file or a directory name. If you are deleting a non-empty directory, you must use the -R (recursive) option.

- You can learn more about the rm and rmdir commands and their options on their man pages. Type man rm or man rmdir and press Return to view each command's man pages.

To remove a file

Type rm *file* ... and press (Return). For example, rm file1 removes the file named *file1* from the current directory (**Figure 24**).

To remove files using a wildcard character

Type rm followed by the wildcard search string and press (Return). For example, rm *.bak removes all files ending with *.bak* from the current directory.

To remove all files in a directory

Type rm * and press (Return) (**Figure 25**).

✔ Tips

- You may want to include the -i option (for example, rm -i *) to confirm each deletion so you do not delete files by mistake.

- Since the rm command cannot remove directories without the -R option, an error message may appear when you use the rm * command string in a directory that contains subdirectories (**Figure 25**).

To remove all files & subdirectories in a directory

Type rm -R * and press (Return) (**Figure 25**).

✖ Caution

- This is the most dangerous command in all of Unix. If you enter this command in the root directory (/), you will erase the entire disk (if you have permission). Use this command with care!

✔ Tip

- You may want to include the -i option (for example, rm -Ri *; **Figure 25**) to confirm each deletion so you do not delete files or subdirectories by mistake.

Figure 25 Two more examples of the **rm** command. In the first, the **rm *** command string deletes all files in the directory, but not the subdirectory named dir30. In the second, the **-Ri** options delete all contents with confirmation; the only item still in the directory is the subdirectory named dir30.

USING rm & rmdir

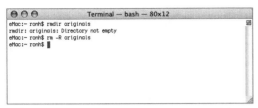

Figure 26 This example shows two attempts to delete a subdirectory. The first, using the **rmdir** command, is not successful because the directory is not empty. The second, using the **rm -R** command string, does the job.

Figure 27 In this example, the **mkdir** command is used to create three new subdirectories.

To remove an empty directory

Type rmdir *directory* ... and press Return. For example, rmdir Originals removes the subdirectory named *Originals* in the current directory (**Figure 26**).

✔ Tip

■ The rmdir command will result in an error message if the directory you are trying to remove is not empty (**Figure 26**).

To remove a directory & its contents

Type rm -R *directory* and press Return. For example, rm -R Originals removes the directory named *Originals* even if it is not empty (**Figure 26**).

Creating a New Directory with mkdir

You can also create new directories. You'll do this with the mkdir command.

✔ Tip

■ You can learn more about the mkdir command and its options on its man pages. Type man mkdir and press Return to view the command's man pages.

To create a new directory

Type mkdir *directory-name* ... and press Return. For example, mkdir Project1 Project2 Project3 makes three new subdirectories in the current directory: *Project1*, *Project2*, and *Project3* (**Figure 27**).

USING rmdir, rm, & mkdir

Viewing File Contents

Unix offers a few tools for examining the contents of files:

◆ cat (concatenate) lists one or more files to the Terminal window.

◆ less outputs files in page-size chunks, enabling you to view the contents of large files one screen at a time.

◆ head displays the first lines of a file.

◆ tail displays the last lines of a file.

◆ wc displays a count of the number of lines, words, and characters in a file.

✔ Tip

■ To learn more about these commands, check out their man pages. Type man cat, man less, man head, man tail, or man wc and press [Return] to display the command's man page.

To list a file's contents

Type cat *file* ... (for example, cat example.rtf) and press [Return]. cat lists the entire file in the Terminal window without stopping (**Figure 28**).

✔ Tips

■ Do not use cat to list binary executable files (that is, any non-text file, such as an application). Because they contain many nonprintable characters, they could cause Terminal to act strangely. If this happens, close the Terminal window and open a new one.

■ If you specify more than one file, cat lists them one after another without any indication that it has finished one file and started another one.

Figure 28 In this example, the **cat** command is used to view the contents of an RTF file. The first few lines of the file—which you wouldn't see when viewing the file with an RTF-compatible word processor (such as TextEdit)—are formatting codes.

■ I explain how to use the cat command and output redirection to combine multiple files and output them to a new file later in this chapter.

■ If you use cat to list a long file, Terminal may not be able to store all of the lines. You may prefer to use the more command to output the file in page-sized chunks.

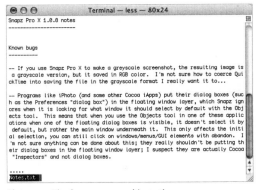

Figure 29 The **less** command in action.

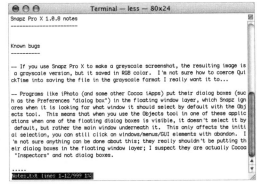

Figure 30 In this example, the **-m** option was used with the **less** command. See how the prompt at the bottom of the page changes?

To page through the contents of a file

1. Type less *file* (for example, less Notes.txt) and press ⟨Return⟩. The first page of the file appears in the Terminal window (**Figure 29**). The last line tells you the name of the file and what percentage of the file has been displayed.

2. Use one of the following keystrokes:
   ▲ Press ⟨Spacebar⟩ to advance one screen.
   ▲ Press ⟨Return⟩ to advance one line.
   ▲ Press ⟨D⟩ to advance one half screen.

3. Repeat step 2 to view the entire file.

   or

   Press ⟨Q⟩ to return to the shell prompt.

✔ Tips

■ When you reach the end of the file, you must press ⟨Q⟩ to return to the shell prompt.

■ You can use the -m option to display a more instructive prompt at the bottom of the screen (**Figure 30**).

■ You can also use wildcard characters to specify multiple files. When you reach the end of each file, tell less to proceed to the next file by typing :n. Less will display the file names at the start of each file.

■ Like the man command discussed earlier in this chapter, the less command is a *pager*. A pager displays information one screen at a time, enabling you to page through it.

■ Most Unix operating systems include an older paging program called more. In Mac OS X 10.2, Apple provided both more and less. In Mac OS X 10.3, Apple decided to take away your choice of pagers and made more a duplicate of the less program.

USING less

To show the first lines of a file

Type head [-n *count*] *file* ... and press (Return), where *count* is the number of lines at the beginning of the file that you want to display. For example, head -n 15 sample.txt displays the first 15 lines of the file named *sample.txt* (**Figure 31**).

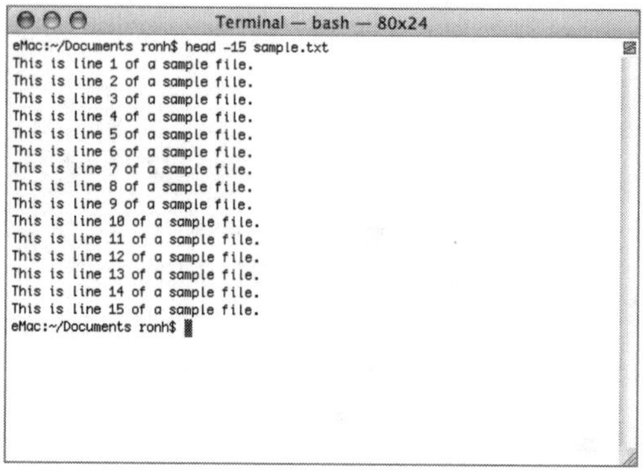

✔ Tips

- If you omit the -n *count* operand, head displays the first ten lines of the file.

- You can specify multiple files. If you do, head displays the file names at the start of each file.

To show the last lines of a file

Type tail [-n *count*] *file* ... and press (Return), where *count* is the number of lines at the end of the file that you want to display. For example, tail -n 15 sample.txt displays the last 15 lines of the file named *sample.txt* (**Figure 32**).

✔ Tips

- If you omit the -n *count* operand, tail displays the last ten lines of the file.

- You can specify multiple files. If you do, tail displays the file names at the start of each file.

- The -f option (for example tail -f log.txt) displays the last lines of the file but prevents the tail command from terminating. Instead, tail waits for the file to grow. As new lines are added to the file, tail immediately displays them. You may find this useful if you want to watch a log file grow and see the latest entries as they are added. You may also use it to watch an error log file when you are debugging a program. You cannot use the -f option if you specify multiple files; to monitor multiple files with the tail command, open multiple Terminal windows.

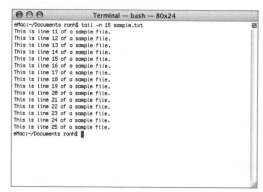

Figure 31 The **head** command displays the first bunch of lines in a file...

Figure 32 ...and the **tail** command displays the last bunch.

USING head & tail

Figure 33 The **wc** command shows the number of lines, words, and characters in a file.

To count the lines, words, & characters in a file

Type wc *file* ... (for example, wc Notes.txt), and press (Return). The number of lines, words, and characters (or bytes) in the file you specified is displayed in the Terminal window (**Figure 33**).

✔ Tip

■ You can use any combination of options for the wc command:

-c displays the number of characters

-w displays the number of words

-l displays the number of lines

With no options, wc displays all three pieces of information in this order: lines, words, characters, file name (**Figure 33**).

Creating & Editing Files with pico

Although it's easy to use a GUI text editor in Mac OS X, it's a good idea to know a little about Unix text editors and how they work. This way, if you ever find yourself sitting in front of a Unix system, you'll have a chance at making it usable.

Unix offers a number of text editors: the easy-to-use pico, the ever-present vi, and the geek-favorite emacs. Which one you use is a personal decision: Each has strengths and weaknesses. It is far beyond the scope of this chapter (or book) to help you master any one of these, let alone all three. Because pico is the easiest Unix text editor to use, I'll introduce it here.

✔ Tips

- The emacs and vi text editors are so powerful and complex that entire books have been written about them. You can learn a little more about them in their somewhat inadequate man pages; type man emacs or man vi and press Return to view them.

- pico is normally a piece of the pine email package, but Apple did not make pine part of the standard Mac OS X Unix installation. You can download the entire pine-pico package for Mac OS X from www.osxgnu.org/software/Email/pine/.

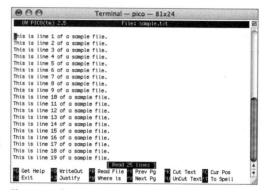

Figure 34 pico can open an existing file...

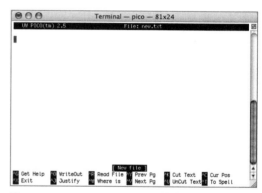

Figure 35 ...or create a new one with the name you specify.

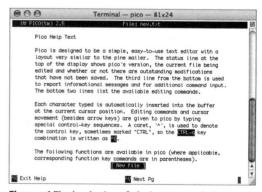

Figure 36 The beginning of **pico's** onscreen help.

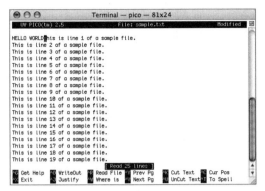

Figure 37 Text is inserted at the cursor.

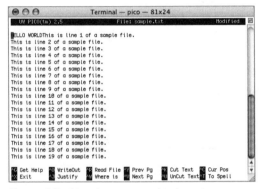

Figure 38 Position the cursor on the character you want to delete.

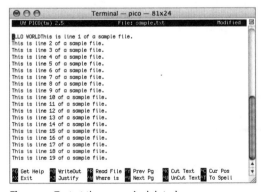

Figure 39 Text at the cursor is deleted.

To open a file with pico

Type pico *file* (for example, pico sample.txt) and press `Return`.

pico starts up in the Terminal window. If you entered the name of an existing file, the first 25 lines of the file appear (**Figure 34**). If you entered the name of a file that does not already exist, pico creates a new file for you (**Figure 35**). Either way, the pico menu appears at the bottom of the window. The cursor appears as a gray box at the beginning of the file.

To use pico menu commands

Press the keystroke for the command you want. Each command includes `Control` (indicated by ^). For example, you can view onscreen help by pressing `Control G` (**Figure 36**).

To navigate through text

To move one character in any direction, press the corresponding arrow key.

or

To move to the previous or next page, press `Control Y` or `Control V`.

To insert text

1. Position the cursor where you want to insert character(s) (**Figure 34**).

2. Type the character(s) you want to insert. The new text is inserted (**Figure 37**).

To delete text

1. Position the cursor on the character you want to delete (**Figure 38**).

2. Press `Control D`. The character disappears (**Figure 39**).

To cut & paste text

1. Use the arrow keys to position the cursor at the beginning of the text you want to cut (**Figure 34**).

2. Press (Control)(Shift)(^). *[Mark Set]* appears near the bottom of the window (**Figure 40**).

3. Use the arrow keys to position the cursor at the end of the block you want to cut. Text between the starting point and cursor turns black (**Figure 41**).

4. Press (Control)(K) (Cut Text). The selected text disappears (**Figure 42**).

5. Position the cursor where you want to paste the text (**Figure 43**).

6. Press (Control)(U) (Uncut Text). The cut text appears at the cursor (**Figure 44**).

✔ Tip

■ *[Mark Set]* (**Figure 40**) indicates that you have marked the beginning of a text selection.

Figure 40 *[Mark Set]* appears in the window.

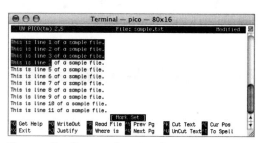

Figure 41 Use the arrow keys to select text.

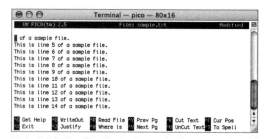

Figure 42 Using the Cut Text command removes the selected text.

Figure 43 Position the cursor where you want to paste the text.

Figure 44 Using the Uncut Text command pastes the text back into the document.

USING pico

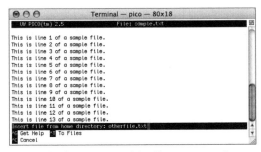

Figure 45 Enter the name of the file you want to insert at the Insert file prompt.

Figure 46 The file is inserted at the cursor.

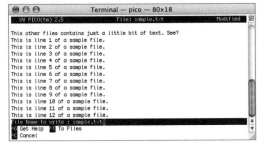

Figure 47 Use the File Name to write prompt to enter a name for the file.

Figure 48 The Save modified buffer prompt enables you to save changes to the file before you exit pico.

To insert an existing file

1. Position the cursor where you want to insert the file (**Figure 34**).

2. Press (Control)(R) (Read File).

3. The Insert file prompt appears at the bottom of the window. Enter the path name for the file you want to insert (**Figure 45**) and press (Return). The contents of the file appear at the cursor (**Figure 46**).

To save changes to a file

1. Press (Control)(O) (WriteOut). The File Name to write prompt appears at the bottom of the window, along with the name of the file you originally opened (**Figure 47**).

2. To save the file with the same name, press (Return).

   or

   To save the file with a different name, use (Delete) to remove the existing file name, enter a new file name, and press (Return). The file is saved.

To exit pico

1. Press (Control)(X) (Exit).

2. If you have made changes to the file since opening it, the Save modified buffer prompt appears at the bottom of the window (**Figure 48**).

   ▲ Press (Y) and then (Return) to save changes to the file and exit pico.

   ▲ Press (N) and then (Return) to exit pico without saving changes to the file.

USING pico

Output Redirection

In all of the Unix commands up to this point that produced output—such as man and ls—the command output appears in the Terminal window. This is called the *standard output device* of Unix.

But the shell can also redirect the output of a command to a file instead of to the screen. This *output redirection* enables you to create files by writing command output to a file.

Output redirection uses the greater-than character (>) to tell the shell to place the output of a command into a file rather than listing it to the screen. If the output file already exists, it is overwritten with the new information.

Similarly, a pair of greater-than signs (>>) tells the shell to append the output of a command to the end of a file rather than erasing the file and starting from the beginning. If the output file does not already exist, the shell creates a new file with the name you specified.

This section offers some examples of output redirection, using commands I covered earlier in this chapter.

To sort a file & output it to another file

Type sort *file* > *output-file* and press Return.

For example, sort sample.txt > alpha.txt would sort the lines in the file named *sample.txt* and write them to a file named *alpha.txt*.

To save a directory listing as a file

Type ls > *output-file* and press Return.

For example, ls -la > list.txt creates a file named *list.txt* that contains a complete directory listing in the long format (**Figure 49**).

Figure 49 This example shows how the **ls** command can be used to save a directory listing as a text file. The **cat** command was used in the illustration to display the contents of the new file.

Figure 50 This example uses >> to append another directory to the one in **Figure 49** and display the combined files with the **cat** command.

Figure 51 Using the **cat** command with an output file name starts **cat** and waits for text entry.

Figure 52 Enter the text you want to include in the file.

Figure 53 Press Control D to save the file.

To append output to an existing file

Type *command >> output-file* and press Return.

For example, ls -la Documents >> list.txt would append a directory listing for the Documents subdirectory to the list.txt file (**Figure 50**).

To create a text file with cat

1. Type cat > *output-file* (for example, cat > test.txt) and press Return. The cat command starts and waits for you to type text (**Figure 51**).

2. Enter the text you want to include in the file. You can press Return to start a new line if desired (**Figure 52**).

3. When you're finished entering text, press Control D (**Figure 53**). (Control D is the ASCII "End Of Transmission" character.)

   The new file is saved with the name you specified.

✔ Tip

■ Normally, the cat command uses a source-file argument; that is, you normally tell cat to list a specific file to the screen. If you do not specify a source-file for cat, it takes source data from the *standard input device*, which is usually the keyboard, and redirects it to the output-file.

To combine files with cat

Type cat *file1 ... > output-file* and press Return.

For example, cat firstfile.txt secondfile.txt thirdfile.txt > combinedfile.txt combines the files named *firstfile.txt*, *secondfile.txt*, and *thirdfile.txt*, in that order, and saves them as a file named *combinedfile.txt*.

USING OUTPUT REDIRECTION

Unix Passwords & Security

You may think, "I don't care if someone reads my mail" or "I don't store important files in my directory, so who needs a good password?"

This is exactly what *crackers* count on. Many times, these crackers don't want to read your mail or erase your files; they want to install their own programs that take up your computer time and Internet bandwidth. They steal resources from you and slow down your computer and Internet response time. They also install *Trojan horse* programs that allow them to break into your computer at a future date. These Trojan horses are designed to look and act exactly like other normal programs you expect to see on the machine.

When a cracker breaks into your computer system, your only course of action is to take the machine off the network and rebuild the operating system from scratch. It's virtually impossible to detect Trojan horses, which is why you must rebuild your system. The rebuild process can take days, and you lose communication during that time. Scared? Good. Your first line of defense is to use good passwords.

The object when choosing a password is to pick a password that is easy for you to remember but difficult for someone else to guess. This leaves the cracker no alternative but a brute-force search, trying every possible combination of letters, numbers, and punctuation. A search of this sort, even conducted on a machine that could try one million passwords per second (most machines can try less than one hundred per second), would require, on average, over one hundred years to complete. With this as your goal, here are some guidelines you should follow for password selection.

Dos

◆ Do use a password with nonalphabetic characters: digits or punctuation mixed into the middle of the password. For example, *ronh3;cat.*

◆ Do use a password that contains mixed-case letters, such as *ROnHCAt.*

◆ Do pick a password that is easy to remember, so you don't have to write it down. (And *never* write it on a sticky note and stick it on your monitor.)

◆ Do use a password that you can quickly type, without having to look at the keyboard. This makes it harder for someone watching over your shoulder to steal your password. If someone is watching, ask them to turn their head.

Don'ts

◆ Don't use your login name in any form— for example, as it is, reversed, capitalized, or doubled.

◆ Don't use your first name, last name, or initials in any form.

◆ Don't use your spouse's, child's, or pet's name.

◆ Don't use other information that is easily obtained about you. This includes license plate numbers, addresses, telephone numbers, social security numbers, the brand of your automobile, and the name of the street you live on.

◆ Don't use a password that consists of all digits or all the same letter. This significantly decreases the search time for a cracker.

◆ Don't use a word contained in dictionaries (either English or foreign language), spelling lists, or other lists of words (for example, the Star Trek series, movie titles, Shakespeare plays, cartoon characters, Monty Python episodes, the *Hitchhiker's Guide* series, myths or legends, place names, sports words, and colleges). These are all part of the standard dictionaries that come with cracking software, and the crackers can always add their own dictionaries.

◆ Don't use a word simply prefixed or suffixed with a number or a punctuation mark.

◆ Don't substitute a zero for the letter O or substitute a numeral one for the letter L or I.

◆ Don't use a password shorter than six characters.

Password ideas

Although these password rules may seem extreme, you have several methods for choosing secure, easy-to-remember passwords that also obey the rules. For example:

◆ Choose a line or two from a song or poem and then use the first letter of each word. For example, if you pick, "In Xanadu did Kubla Kahn a stately pleasure dome decree," you would have *IXdKKaspdd*. "Ding dong the Witch is dead" becomes *DdtWid*.

◆ Create a password by alternating between one consonant and one or two vowels, as long as eight characters. This provides nonsense words that are usually pronounceable and thus easily remembered. For example, *moatdup* and *jountee*.

◆ Choose two short words and concatenate them with a punctuation character. For example: *dog:rain* or *ray/gun* or *kid?goat*.

To change your password

1. In the Terminal window, type passwd and press (Return).

2. The shell prompts you to enter your old password (**Figure 54**). Enter it and press (Return).

3. The shell prompts you to enter your new password (**Figure 55**). Enter it, and press (Return).

4. The shell prompts you to enter your new password again (**Figure 56**). Enter it and press (Return).

✔ Tips

■ When you enter your old and new password, the cursor in the Terminal window does not move. This is an added security feature; someone looking over your shoulder as you type can't even see how many characters you typed.

■ The new password you select must be at least five characters in length.

■ You can also change your password in the My Account preferences pane. I explain how in **Chapter 14**.

Figure 54 First, the shell prompts you for your current password.

Figure 55 Next, it prompts you to enter your new password.

Figure 56 Finally, it prompts you to re-enter your new password.

```
  ● ● ●            Terminal — bash — 80x24
eMac:~ ronh$ ls -la
total 48
drwxr-xr-x  19 ronh   ronh    646 11 Sep 13:13 .
drwxrwxr-x   6 root   admin   204 11 Sep 09:36 ..
-rw-r--r--   1 ronh   ronh      3 11 Sep 09:36 .CFUserTextEncoding
-rwxr-xr-x   1 ronh   ronh   6148 11 Sep 13:06 .DS_Store
drwx------   6 ronh   ronh    204 11 Sep 12:03 .Trash
drwx------   3 ronh   ronh    102 11 Sep 09:36 Desktop
drwx------  26 ronh   ronh    884 11 Sep 12:59 Documents
lrwxr-xr-x   1 ronh   ronh     29 11 Sep 12:02 Favs -> /Users/ronh/Library/Favori
tes
drwx------  26 ronh   ronh    884 11 Sep 09:49 Library
drwx------   3 ronh   ronh    102 11 Sep 09:36 Movies
drwx------   3 ronh   ronh    102 11 Sep 09:36 Music
drwx------  12 ronh   ronh    408 11 Sep 13:19 Pictures
drwxr-xr-x   2 ronh   ronh     68 11 Sep 12:07 Project1
drwxr-xr-x   2 ronh   ronh     68 11 Sep 12:07 Project2
drwxr-xr-x   2 ronh   ronh     68 11 Sep 12:07 Project3
drwxr-xr-x   4 ronh   ronh    136 11 Sep 09:36 Public
drwxr-xr-x   5 ronh   ronh    170 11 Sep 09:36 Sites
-rw-r--r--   1 ronh   ronh   2486 11 Sep 13:11 list.txt
-rw-r--r--   1 ronh   ronh    131 11 Sep 13:15 test.txt
eMac:~ ronh$ █
```

Figure 57 A directory listing including permissions and other information for files.

File & Directory Permissions & Ownership

If you've ever used file sharing on your Mac, you probably noticed that you can set permissions for folders and files, giving certain users, groups of users, or everyone read-only, read-write, or no access. (This is covered in **Chapter 4**.) Unix has almost the same system with users, groups, and public permissions.

Through the ls command, which I cover earlier in this chapter, you can learn quite a bit more about the ownership and permissions of files on your system. For example, take a look at the ls -la listing for a home directory, in **Figure 57**. There's lots of useful information on each line.

The first line (starting with the word *total*) is the number of 512-byte blocks used by the files in the directories that follow. Below that, each line contains seven columns of information about each subdirectory and file.

Permissions

The group of characters at the beginning of the line (for example, drwxr-xr-x in the first entry) indicates the entry's type and permissions.

The first character indicates the type of entry:

◆ d indicates a directory.

◆ – indicates a file.

◆ l indicates a link to another file.

The next nine characters of the permissions can be broken into three sets of three characters each. The first set of three is permissions for the owner of the file, the second set is permissions for the group owner, and the third set is permissions for everyone else who has access to the entry.

Continued on next page...

Continued from previous page.

◆ r indicates read permissions. This permission enables the user to open and read the file or directory contents.

◆ w indicates write permissions. This permission enables the user to make changes to the file or directory contents, including delete it.

◆ x indicates execute permissions. For an executable program file, this permission enables the user to run the program. For a directory, this permission enables the user to open the directory.

◆ – indicates no permission.

For example, the file named *example.rtf* in **Figure 57** can be written to and read by the owner (ronh) and can only be read by the group (staff) and everyone else.

Links

The next column shows the number of links. This is a count of the files and directories contained within a directory entry. It's set to 1 for normal files.

Owner

The third column is the owner of the file or directory. Normally this will be the name of your account. Sometimes, the system creates files for you, and you may see another owner. For example, the .. directory in **Figure 57** was created by the system, which gave ownership to root, the superuser.

Group

The group is listed next. Just as in file sharing in Mac OS 9.x and earlier, you can create groups of users that have separate permissions. You are, by default, assigned to the staff group, so many of your files are also owned by that group.

When your account is created, a group is also created with the same name as your short name, with you as the sole member of the group. If you want special groups for people (for example, marketing, staff, sysadmins), you can set these up using NetInfo Manager if you are an administrator of the system.

File size

The number in the fifth column gives the size of the entry in bytes.

Modification date

The sixth column shows the date and time that the file or directory was last modified. A directory is modified whenever any of its contents are modified.

Filename

Last, you see the name of the file or directory.

More about File & Directory Ownership

Normally when you create a new file, you are given ownership of that file and it is assigned to your default group. Your default group is assigned to you when you are given your user account by the system administrator (sysadmin). You can belong to multiple groups at the same time. Unless the system administrator specifically assigns you to a different group, in Mac OS X, the default group is a unique group with the same name as your short name and with you as the sole member.

✔ Tip

■ The admin user can use the chown and chgrp commands to change the ownership of a file or directory. You can learn more about these commands by viewing their man pages. In the Terminal window, type man chown or man chgrp and press (Return) to view the command's man pages.

Changing Permissions for a File or Directory

Unix includes a command for setting file or directory permissions: chmod. Although this command can be a bit complicated, it is important. The security of your files and subdirectories depends on its proper usage.

The chmod command uses the following syntax:

    chmod *mode file* ...

The complex part of the chmod command is understanding what can go in the mode operand. This is where you specify the owner (also called user), group, and other (everyone else) permissions. You have two ways to do this: numerically and symbolically.

✔ Tip

■ You can learn more about the chmod command by viewing its man pages. In the Terminal window, type man chmod and press [Return].

Numeric permission modes

Numeric permission modes uses numbers to represent permissions options. The best way to explain this is to provide an example. Remember, the nine characters of the permissions coding in a directory listing can be broken down into three sets of three:

    rwx   rwx   rwx
    user   group   other

Each character can be represented with an octal digit (a number between 0 and 7) by assigning values to the r, w, and x characters, like this:

    421   421   421
    rwx   rwx   rwx
    user   group   other

So, if you want to give read and write permission for a file called *file1* to the owner, that would be a 4 (read) plus a 2 (write), which adds up to a 6. You could then give read only permission to the group and others by assigning the value 4 (read). The command to do all this is chmod 644 file1. (The 644 permission is one you'll see often on text files that are readable by everyone. A permission of 600 would make a file private.)

Symbolic permission modes

Symbolic permission modes enables you to add or remove privileges using symbols. For example, to remove write permission from the group and others, type chmod go-w file1. This translates to "take away write permissions from the group and others."

The ownership symbols you use for this are:

u user (owner) of the file or directory

g group owner of the file or directory

o others (everyone)

a all three (user, group, and others)

The symbols for the permissions you can add or take away are:

r read

w write

x execute

Finally, the operations you can perform are:

+ add the permission

– remove the permission

= set (add) the following permissions

You can combine more than one symbol in a mode and more than one "equation" if you separate them with commas. For example, chmod a+rwx,o-w file1 gives universal read, write, and execute access to all and then takes away write permission from others to file1. (The equivalent numerical permission would be 775.)

To change the permissions for a file or directory

In the Terminal window, type chmod *mode file* ... (for example, chmod 644 file1) and press Return.

✖ Warning!

- Do not change the ownership and permissions of files on your computer without reason or if you're not sure what you're doing. The operating system assumes that certain files belong to certain users and have specific privileges. If you change the ownership or permissions on some system files, you may render your computer unusable! It's usually safe to modify your own files—those that you create—but unless you know what you are doing, stay away from other files.

✔ Tip

- If you include the -R option in the command (for example, chmod -R 644 folder1), the change is made recursively down through the directory tree. In other words, the change is made to the folder and every file and folder within it.

Learning What's Happening on Your System

A few Unix commands can provide you with answers to questions about your system: "Who is logged in?" "What are they doing?" "What jobs are taking up all my CPU cycles?" "How long has my system been up?"

◆ uptime tells you how long it has been since you last restarted and what your workload is.

◆ who tells you who is logged in to your system, where they're logged in from, and when they logged in.

◆ w tells you who is online and what they are doing.

◆ last tells you who has logged into your computer.

◆ ps and top tell you what jobs are running on your computer.

This section explains how to use each of these commands and shows simulated output so you know what you might expect to learn.

✔ Tip

■ You can learn more about these commands by viewing their man pages. In the Terminal window, type man uptime, man who, man w, man last, man ps, or man top and press Return to view the command's man pages.

To learn your workload & how long since you last restarted

In the Terminal window, type uptime and press [Return].

The results might look something like what you see in **Code 1**. You see the current time, the time since the last restart, or boot (7 days, 17 hours, and 48 minutes), and load averages of how many active jobs were in the queue during the last 1, 5, and 15 minutes. The load shown here is high because my system is running the SETI@home screensaver. Normally these numbers will be less than 1.

To learn who is on your system

In the Terminal window, type who and press [Return].

The results might look something like what you see in **Code 2**. In this example, I'm logged in remotely twice from the machine with the IP address 192.168.2.1, once as root and once as myself. I'm also logged in from a remote location (isaac.exploratorium.edu) and at the system console.

To learn who is online & what they are doing

In the Terminal window, type w and press [Return].

The command's output looks something like **Code 3**. The w command first does an uptime command. Then it gives you information about each user, when they logged in, and how long it's been since they've done anything.

Code 1 The results of the **uptime** command.

```
⊝ ⊝ ⊝          Terminal — bash — 80x24
7:21PM  up 7 days, 17:48, 5 users, load
averages: 1.87, 1.80, 1.67
```

Code 2 The results of the **who** command.

```
⊝ ⊝ ⊝          Terminal — bash — 80x24
ronh    console  Sep 2 01:35
ronh    typ1     Sep 9 19:13   (192.168.1.2)
root    ttyp3    Sep 9 19:13   (192.168.1.2)
ronh    ttyp4    Sep 9 19:16   (isaac.explorator)
```

Code 3 The results of the **w** command.

```
⊝ ⊝ ⊝          Terminal — bash — 80x24
7:28PM  up 7 days, 17:55, 5 users, load averages: 1.90,
1.80, 1.67
USER  TTY FROM              LOGIN@   IDLE  WHAT
ronh  co  -                 02Sep01  7days  -
ronh  p1  192.168.1.2       7:13PM   0      -
ronh  p2  -                 Thu01AM  13     -
root  p3  192.168.1.2       7:13PM   0      -
ronh  p4  isaac.explorator  7:16PM   0      -
```

To learn who has logged in to your machine recently

◆ In the Terminal window, type last and press ⟨Return⟩.

The output should look similar to **Code 4**. The last command spews out a list of everyone who has logged in to your machine, when and from where they logged in, how long they stayed, and when you last shut down or restarted your machine.

or

◆ In the Terminal window, type last *user* (where *user* is the user name of a specific user) and press ⟨Return⟩.

If you specify a user, last will show only the logins for that user.

Code 4 The results of the **last** command.

● ● ●		Terminal — bash — 80x24			
ronh	ttyp4	isaac.explorator	Sun Sep 9	19:16	still logged in
root	ttyp3	192.168.1.2	Sun Sep 9	19:13	still logged in
ronh	ttyp1	192.168.1.2	Sun Sep 9	19:13	still logged in
ronh	ttyp1	192.168.1.2	Sat Sep 8	23:20 - 00:07	(00:46)
ronh	ttyp1	sodium.explorato	Sat Sep 8	16:05 - 16:13	(00:08)
ronh	ttyp1	192.168.1.2	Sat Sep 8	00:03 - 00:40	(00:36)
ronh	ttyp3	192.168.1.2	Thu Sep 6	22:19 - 00:01	(01:41)
ronh	ttyp1	192.168.1.2	Thu Sep 6	22:01 - 00:01	(02:00)
ronh	ttyp1	192.168.1.2	Thu Sep 6	10:13 - 10:37	(00:23)
ronh	ttyp2		Thu Sep 6	01:17	still logged in
ronh	ttyp1	192.168.1.2	Thu Sep 6	00:56 - 02:06	(01:09)
ronh	ttyp1	192.168.1.2	Mon Sep 3	23:47 - 01:51	(02:04)
ronh	ttyp1	192.168.1.2	Mon Sep 3	14:12 - 23:19	(09:06)
ronh	console	localhost	Sun Sep 2	01:35	still logged in
reboot	~		Sun Sep 2	01:35	
shutdown	~		Sun Sep 2	01:33	
ronh	ttyp2	192.168.1.2	Sun Sep 2	00:53 - 01:23	(00:30)

To learn what jobs are running

♦ In the Terminal window, type ps and press [Return].

The ps command tells you what you are running at the instant you run the command.

or

♦ In the Terminal window, type top and press [Return].

The top command gives you a running commentary of the top ten jobs. If you expand the size of the Terminal window, top shows more than the top ten jobs. Press [Q] to quit top.

✔ Tip

■ You may find Activity Viewer (in the Utilities folder) a more useful utility to see the processes that are running. Activity Viewer is covered in **Chapter 19**.

USING ps & top

Archive & Compression Utilities

Long before utilities such as StuffIt existed—long before the Mac existed, in fact!—Unix users could group files together into *archives* and compress the archives to take up less disk space, which was vastly more expensive then. Unix offers several archiving and compression tools:

- tar (short for *t*ape *ar*chive) was originally used to combine a collection of files into a single file, which was written to tape. But you don't have to write the file to tape; you can write it to any device your Unix system knows about: disks, tapes, CD-Rs, even Terminal.

- compress and uncompress do what you probably expect them to: compress and expand files. Text files are very compressible, sometimes 10 to 1. Files that have already been compressed such as JPEG and MPEG files and QuickTime movies, however, can actually become larger.

- gzip is a newer set of utilities that are like compress and uncompress on steroids. gzip includes more options and offers better compression ratios.

✔ Tips

- You can learn more about these commands by viewing their man pages. In the Terminal window, type man tar, man compress, man uncompress, or man gzip and press ⌐Return⌐ to view the command's man pages.

- Experienced Unix users often use tar and gzip together to produce a compressed archive with a name like *file.tar.gz* or *file.tgz*. A useful way to uncompress and untar a file uses pipes to string multiple commands together. For example, gzcat file.tar.gz | tar xf - uncompresses the gzipped file and pipes the output to the tar command for extraction. The – in the tar command is necessary to tell tar to expect its input from the pipe (its standard input device).

- It's useful to know something about these tools because you will encounter them if you download software from Internet archives. If you don't need the GUI interface of StuffIt, the tar/gzip utilities will do the same job for free!

To create an archive from an entire directory tree

Type tar [-cxtvpf] [-C *directory*] *archive file* ... and press [Return]. (Consult **Table 2** for tar options.)

Here are some examples using the tar command:

◆ tar -cf archive.tar file1 directory1 file2 creates and then writes to the archive named *archive.tar: file1, directory1* and all its contents, and *file2* in that order.

◆ tar -tvf old-archive.tar displays everything in the archive called *old-archive.tar* but does not extract anything. The t option just prints the contents of a tar archive.

◆ tar -xpvf old-archive.tar extracts the files and directories in the archive file called *old-archive.tar* and puts the resulting files in the current directory. The v option reports progress and the p option preserves the ownerships and modification dates of the original files. (The tar file is unaffected and remains on the disk.)

◆ tar -xpvf old-archive.tar -C /usr/local/src extracts the files and directories in the archive file called *old-archive.tar* and puts the resulting files in the directory */usr/local/src*.

✔ Tip

■ It's a standard procedure to end archive names with a .tar suffix, and you should honor this standard to keep evil spirits out of your computer.

Table 2

tar Options

Option	Description
-c	Creates a new archive
-x	Extracts files from the named archive
-t	Displays a list of files and directories in the named archive
-v	Verbose mode: Tells you everything tar is doing
-p	Preserves permissions, owners, and modification dates if possible
-f	Archives files to the following filename or extracts files from the following archive name
-C	Puts extracted files in the specified location

To compress & decompress with compress & uncompress

Type compress *file* ... (for example, compress file.txt), and press (Return).

or

Type uncompress *file* ... (for example, uncompress file.z), and press (Return).

✔ Tips

■ Your original file is removed if either of the commands successfully complete the compression or decompression.

■ By convention, compressed files should have a .Z extension. The compress command will automatically append this extension to the filename.

To compress or decompress with gzip & gunzip

Type gzip *file* ... and press (Return). This compresses the files, adds the .gz suffix to their names, and removes the original files.

or

Type gunzip *file* ... and press (Return). This uncompresses the files and removes the original archive.

✔ Tips

■ The gzip command has several options. The r option, for recursive, goes into specified subdirectories and compresses or uncompresses the files. The v option, for verbose, tells the command to report its progress.

■ zcat file lists the contents of a compressed file to Terminal (or pipes the content to another command) without altering the original archive.

System  Preferences

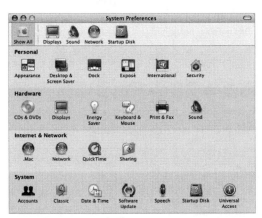

Figure 1 The System Preferences window, with icons for all panes displayed.

✔ **Tip**

■ Other Preferences panes are covered elsewhere in this book:

▲ Exposé, in **Chapter 4**.

▲ Network, in **Chapters 11** and **14**.

▲ .Mac, in **Chapter 12**.

▲ Sharing, in **Chapter 14**.

▲ Accounts and Security in **Chapter 15**.

▲ Classic, in **Chapter 16**.

▲ ColorSync, in **Chapter 19**.

System Preferences

One of the great things about Mac OS is the way it can be customized to look and work the way you want it to. Many customization options can be set within the System Preferences application (**Figure 1**). That's where you'll find a variety of preferences panes, each containing settings for a part of Mac OS.

System Preferences panes are organized into four categories:

◆ **Personal** preferences panes enable you to set options to customize various Mac OS X appearance and operation options for personal tastes. This chapter covers Appearance, Desktop & Screen Saver, Dock, and International.

◆ **Hardware** preferences panes control settings for various hardware devices. This chapter covers CDs & DVDs, Displays, Energy Saver, Keyboard & Mouse, Print & Fax, and Sound.

◆ **Internet & Network** preferences panes enable you to set options related to Internet and network connections. This chapter covers QuickTime.

◆ **System** preferences panes control various aspects of your computer's operation. This chapter covers Date & Time, Software Update, Speech, Startup Disk, and Universal Access.

To open System Preferences

Choose Apple > System Preferences (**Figure 2**).

or

Click the System Preferences icon in the Dock (**Figure 3**).

The System Preferences window appears (**Figure 1**).

To open a preferences pane

Click the icon for the pane you want to display.

or

Choose the name of the pane you want to display from the View menu (**Figure 4**).

✔ Tip

- You can customize the System Preferences window's toolbar. Simply drag an icon for a preferences pane into the toolbar. You can then access that pane no matter which pane is displayed in the window.

Figure 2
To open System Preferences, choose System Preferences from the Apple menu...

Figure 3 ...or click the System Preferences icon in the Dock.

Figure 4
The View menu lists all of the System Preferences panes.

Figure 5 System Preferences panes can also be displayed alphabetically.

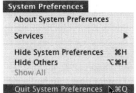

Figure 6
The System
Preferences
menu.

To show all preferences pane icons

Choose a command from the System Preferences' View menu (**Figure 4**):

▲ **Organize by Categories** (⌃⌘L) displays all icons organized by category (**Figure 1**).

▲ **Organize Alphabetically** displays all icons organized alphabetically by name (**Figure 5**).

or

Click the Show All button in the toolbar of the System Preferences window (**Figures 1 and 5**). This displays all icons in the last view used (by category or alphabetically).

To quit System Preferences

When you are finished setting Preference options, choose System Preferences > Quit System Preferences (**Figure 6**), press ⌃⌘Q, or simply click the System Preferences window's close button.

✔ Tip

■ The ability to quit System Preferences by clicking the close button on any System preferences pane window is new in Mac OS X 10.3.

Appearance

The Appearance preferences pane (**Figure 7**) enables you to set options for color, scroll bar functionality, recent items, and text smoothing.

✔ Tip

- In previous versions of Mac OS X, this was called the *General* preferences pane.

To set Appearance preferences

In the Appearance preferences pane (**Figure 7**), set options as desired:

- **Appearance** sets the color for buttons, menus, and windows throughout Mac OS X and Mac OS X applications.

- **Highlight Color** sets the highlight color for text in documents, fields, and lists.

- **Place scroll arrows** determines where scroll arrows should appear in windows and scrolling lists:
    - ▲ **At top and bottom** places a scroll arrow at each end of the scroll bar (**Figure 8**).
    - ▲ **Together** places both scroll arrows together at the bottom or right end of the scroll bar (**Figure 9**).

- **Click in the scroll bar to** determines what happens when you click in the scroll track of a scroll bar.
    - ▲ **Jump to the next page** scrolls to the next window or page of the document.
    - ▲ **Scroll to here** scrolls to the relative location in the document. For example, if you click in the scroll track two-thirds of the way between the top and bottom, you'll scroll two-thirds of the way through the document. (This is the same as dragging the scroller to that position.)

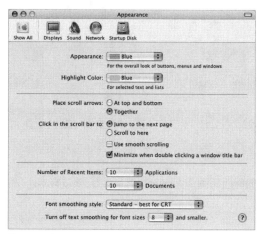

Figure 7 The Appearance preferences pane.

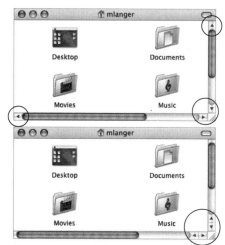

Figures 8 & 9 A window with scroll bars at top and bottom (top) and the same window with scroll bars together (bottom).

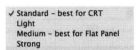

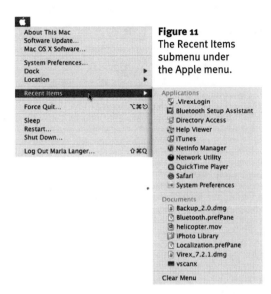

Figure 10 The Font smoothing style pop-up menu.

Figure 11
The Recent Items submenu under the Apple menu.

12-point text with text smoothing turned on.

12-point text with text smoothing turned off.

Figure 12 As these example show, text smoothing can change the appearance of text on screen.

▲ **Use smooth scrolling** scrolls the contents of a window smoothly, without jumping.

▲ **Minimize when double clicking a window title bar** minimizes a window when you double-click its title bar.

◆ **Applications** and **Documents** enables you to choose the number of items you want Mac OS X to consider "recent" when displaying recent Applications and Documents. Options range from None to 50.

◆ **Font smoothing style** (**Figure 10**) determines how Mac OS X smooths text onscreen.

◆ Choose a text smoothing font size option from the pop-up menu. The smaller the size, the more font smoothing is on screen. Your options are 8, 9, 10, and 12.

✔ Tips

■ Recent items appear on the Recent Items submenu under the Apple menu (**Figure 11**).

■ You can clear the Recent Items submenu by choosing Apple > Recent Items > Clear Menu (**Figure 11**).

■ Text smoothing uses a process called *antialiasing* to make text more legible onscreen. Antialiasing creates gray pixels between black ones and white ones to eliminate sharp edges. **Figure 12** shows what text looks like with text smoothing turned on and off.

SETTING APPEARANCE PREFERENCES

CDs & DVDs

The CDs & DVDs preferences pane lets you specify what should happen when you insert a CD or DVD. The options that appear vary depending on your computer's CD and DVD capabilities. **Figure 13** shows how this preferences pane appears for an eMac with a SuperDrive, which is capable of reading and writing both CDs and DVDs.

To specify what should happen when you insert a CD or DVD

Choose an option from the pop-up menu beside the event that you want to set. The menus are basically the same; **Figures 14** and 15 shows an example for inserting a blank CD and a music CD. Your options are:

◆ **Ask what to do** displays a dialog like the one in **Figure 16**, which enables you to tell your computer what to do each time you insert that type of disc. If you turn on the Make this action the default check box in the dialog, you will change the setting for that type of disc in the CDs & DVDs preferences pane.

◆ **Open** *application name* opens the specified application. Use this option if you always want to open a specific application when you insert that type of disc.

◆ **Open other application** displays a dialog like the one in **Figure 17**. Use it to select and open the application that should open when you insert that type of disc.

◆ **Run script** displays a dialog like the one in **Figure 17**. Use it to select and open an AppleScript applet that should open when you insert that type of disc. (I discuss AppleScript in **Chapter 6**.)

◆ **Ignore** tells your computer not to do anything when you insert that type of disc.

Figure 13 The CDs & DVDs preferences pane on an iMac with a SuperDrive.

Figure 14
The pop-up menu for inserting a blank CD...

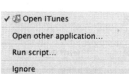

Figure 15
...and for inserting a music CD.

Figure 16 The Ask what to do option displays this dialog when you insert a disc.

Figure 17 Use this dialog to select an application or AppleScript applet to run when you insert a disc.

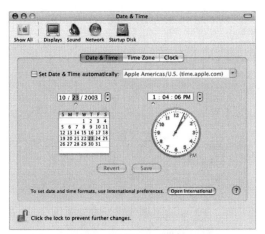

Figure 18 The Date & Time pane of the Date & Time preferences pane.

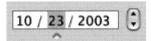

Figure 19 Click the part of the date that you want to change, then use the arrow buttons to change the value.

Date & Time

The Date & Time preferences pane (**Figures 18, 21,** and **22**) includes three panes for setting the system time and clock options:

◆ **Date & Time** (**Figure 18**) enables you to manually set the date and time.

◆ **Time Zone** (**Figure 21**) enables you to set your time zone.

◆ **Clock** (**Figure 22**) enables you to set options for the appearance of the clock.

To manually set the date & time

1. In the Date & Time preferences pane, click the Date & Time button (**Figure 18**).

2. To change the date, click the part of the date you want to change (**Figure 19**), then type in a new value or use the arrow buttons beside the date to change the value.

3. To change the time, click the part of the time that you want to change and type a new value or use the arrow buttons beside the time to change the value.

4. Click Save.

✔ Tips

■ You can't manually change the date or time if you have enabled the network time server feature; I tell you more about that on the next page.

■ Another way to change the time in step 3 is to drag the hands of the analog clock so they display the correct time.

SETTING THE DATE & TIME

To automatically set the date & time

1. In the Date & Time preferences pane, click the Date & Time button (**Figure 18**).

2. Turn on the Set Date & Time automatically check box.

3. Choose the closest time server from the drop-down list (**Figure 20**).

✔ Tip

■ With the network time server feature enabled, your computer will use its network or Internet connection to periodically get the date and time from a time server and update the system clock automatically. This ensures that your computer's clock is always correct.

To set the time zone

1. In the Date & Time preferences pane, click the Time Zone button (**Figure 21**).

2. Click your approximate location on the map. A white bar indicates the time zone area (**Figure 21**).

3. If necessary, choose the name of your time zone from the Closest City drop-down list beneath the map.

✔ Tips

■ In step 3, only those time zones within the white bar on the map are listed in the drop-down list. If your time zone does not appear, make sure you clicked the correct area in the map in step 2.

■ It's a good idea to choose the correct time zone, since Mac OS uses this information with the network time server (if utilized) and to properly change the clock for daylight saving time.

Figure 20 The drop-down list includes time servers all over the world.

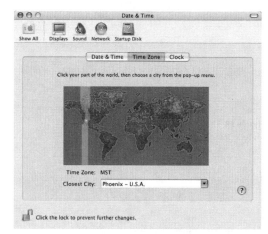

Figure 21 The Time Zone pane of the Date & Time preferences pane, with a time zone selected.

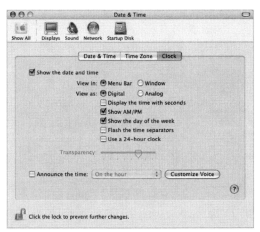

Figure 22 The Clock pane of the Date & Time preferences pane.

Figure 23
You can display the clock in a floating window. This example shows a digital clock.

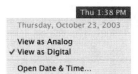

Figure 24
The menu bar clock is also a menu.

✔ Tips

- The menu bar clock is also a menu that displays the full date and time and offers options for changing the clock display (**Figure 24**).

- In Mac OS X 10.3, Apple incorporated the functionality of the old Clock application into the Clock pane of the Date & Time preferences pane. The Clock application is no longer part of Mac OS X.

To set clock options

1. In the Date & Time preferences pane, click the Clock button (**Figure 22**).

2. To enable the clock, turn on the Show the date and time check box.

3. Select a View in radio button:
   - ▲ **Menu Bar** puts the clock in the menu bar, which is the default location.
   - ▲ **Window** puts the clock in a floating window (**Figure 23**).

4. Select a View as radio button:
   - ▲ **Digital** displays the date and time with letters and numbers.
   - ▲ **Analog** displays the time on an analog clock. If you select this option, you cannot set options in step 5.

5. Toggle check boxes to customize the clock's appearance:
   - ▲ **Display the time with seconds** displays the seconds as part of the time.
   - ▲ **Show AM/PM** displays AM or PM after the time.
   - ▲ **Show the day of the week** displays the three-letter abbreviation for the day of the week before the time.
   - ▲ **Flash the time separators** blinks the colon(s) in the time every second.
   - ▲ **Use a 24-hour clock** displays the time as a 24-hour (rather than 12-hour) clock.

6. If you selected Window in step 3, you can use the Transparency slider to set the transparency of the clock window.

7. To instruct your computer to announce the time periodically, turn on the Announce the time check box and choose a frequency option from the pop-up menu.

Desktop & Screen Saver

The Desktop & Screen Saver preferences pane (**Figures 25** and **29**) enables you to set the background picture for the Mac OS X desktop and configure a screen saver that appears when your computer is idle.

✔ Tips

- In previous versions of Mac OS X, two separate System Preferences panes handled these tasks: Desktop and Screen Effects.

- Mac OS X's built-in screen saver doesn't really "save" anything. All it does is cover the normal screen display with graphics, providing an interesting visual when your computer is inactive.

- The Energy Saver preferences pane offers more protection for flat panel, PowerBook, and iBook displays than Screen Saver. Energy Saver is covered later in this chapter.

To set the desktop picture

1. In the Desktop & Screen Saver preferences pane, click the Desktop button to display Desktop options (**Figure 25**).

2. In the list on the left side of the window, select an image collection or folder. The images in the collection appear on the right side of the window.

3. Click to select the image you want. It appears in the image well above the collection list and the desktop's background picture changes (**Figure 26**).

4. To change the picture periodically, turn on the Change picture check box and select a frequency option from the pop-up menu (**Figure 27**). Turning on the Random order check box beside this displays the images in random order.

Figure 25 The Desktop pane of the Desktop & Screen Saver preferences pane.

Figure 26 In this example, I've selected a photo of the Grand Canyon from my iPhoto library.

Figure 27 Use this pop-up menu to set the picture changing frequency.

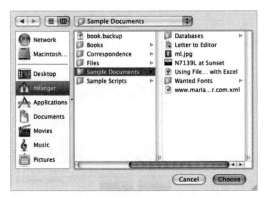

Figure 28 Use this dialog to locate, select, and choose a folder containing pictures.

✔ Tips

- For best results, use pictures that are the same size or larger than your screen resolution. For example, if your screen resolution is set to 1024 x 768, the image should be at least this size. You can check or change your screen resolution in the Displays preferences pane, which I discuss later in this chapter.

- The image collection list on the left side of the Desktop pane (**Figures 25** and **26**) include predefined collections installed with Mac OS X, as well as access to your Pictures folder, your iPhoto library, and any iPhoto albums you may have set up.

- In step 2, if you select Choose Folder, you can use a dialog like the one in **Figure 28** to locate, select, and open another folder that contains images.

- In step 4, you can only turn on the Change picture check box if you selected a collection above the divider line in the collection list in step 2—in other words, any image except an iPhoto library image.

- Although you can have your desktop display a virtual slide show by setting the picture changing frequency in step 4 to a low value like 5 seconds, you may find it distracting—and nonproductive—to have the background change that often. I know I would!

SETTING THE DESKTOP PICTURE

To configure the screen saver

1. In the Desktop & Screen Saver preferences pane, click the Screen Saver button to display Screen Saver options (**Figure 29**).

2. In the Screen Savers list, select a screen saver module. The preview area changes accordingly.

3. To set options for the screen saver, click Options. Not all screen savers can be configured and the options that are available vary depending on the screen saver you selected in Step 2. **Figures 30** and **31** show two examples.

4. To see what the screen effect looks like on your screen, click Test. The screen goes black and the screen effect kicks in. To go back to work, move your mouse.

5. To have the screen saver start automatically after a certain amount of idle time, drag the Start screen saver slider to the desired value.

6. To set "hot corners" that activate or deactivate the screen saver, click the Hot Corners button to display the Active Screen Corners dialog (**Figure 32**). Choose an option from each pop-up menu (**Figure 33**) to specify what should happen when you position the mouse pointer in the corresponding corner. When you're finished, click OK to save your settings.

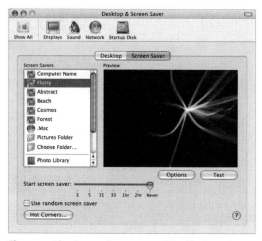

Figure 29 The Screen Saver pane of the Desktop & Screen Saver preferences pane.

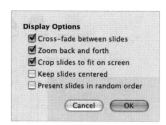

Figure 30 Display options for several of the screen savers.

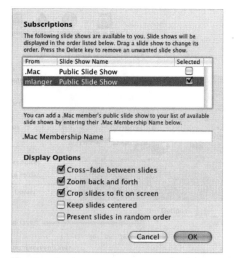

Figure 31 To view a .Mac user's public slide show as a screen effect, enter the member name in the .Mac Membership Name box and click OK.

Figure 32 Use this dialog to set hot corners for activating or deactivating the screen saver. In this example, it's set so that if I put my mouse pointer in the upper-left corner of the screen, the screen saver never goes on, and if I put my mouse pointer in the lower-right corner of the screen, the screen saver goes on immediately.

Figure 33
This pop-up menu includes both Screen Saver and Exposé options.

✔ Tips

■ If you're not picky about what screen saver appears, you can turn on the Use random screen saver check box after step 1 and skip steps 2 through 4.

■ In step 2, if you select Choose Folder, you can use a dialog like the one in **Figure 28** to locate, select, and open another folder that contains images.

■ The .Mac screen effects module enables you to display slides published on a .Mac member's iDisk with iPhoto. This requires a connection to the Internet. To publish your slides on iDisk, you must have a .Mac member account. I cover .Mac in **Chapter 11** and iPhoto in **Chapter 8**.

■ As shown in **Figure 33**, you can use the Active Screen Corners dialog to set up hot corners for Exposé, too. I tell you about Exposé in **Chapter 4**.

■ In step 6, you can configure the hot corners any way you like. For example, you can set it up so every corner starts the screen saver.

■ The Screen Saver and Screen Effects preference pane found in previous versions of Mac OS X included a feature that required you to enter your password to wake the computer. This feature can now be found in the Security preferences pane, which I discuss in **Chapter 15**.

CONFIGURING THE SCREEN SAVER

Displays

The Displays preferences pane enables you to set the resolution, geometry, colors, and other settings for your monitor. Settings are organized into panes; this section covers the Display (**Figure 34**) and Color (**Figure 38**) panes.

✔ Tip

■ The options that are available in the Displays preferences pane vary depending on your computer and monitor. The options shown in this chapter are for an eMac.

To set basic display options

1. In the Displays preferences pane, click the Display button (**Figure 34**).

2. Set options as desired:

   ▲ **Resolutions** control the number of pixels that appear on screen. The higher the resolution, the more pixels appear on screen. This makes the screen contents smaller, but shows more onscreen, as shown in **Figures 35** and **36**.

   ▲ **Colors** controls the number of colors that appear on screen. The more colors, the better the screen image appears.

   ▲ **Refresh Rate** controls the screen refresh rate, in hertz. The higher the number, the steadier the image.

   ▲ **Show displays in menu bar** displays a menu of recently used display settings in the menu bar (**Figure 37**). You can use the pop-up menu beneath this option to specify how many recent settings should appear in the menu.

   ▲ **Contrast** and **Brightness** enable you to adjust the display's contrast and brightness by dragging the sliders.

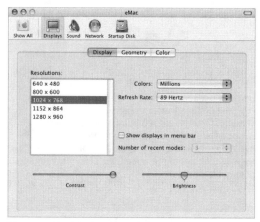

Figure 34 The Display pane of the Displays preferences pane for an eMac.

Figure 35 An eMac display set to 800 x 600 resolution ...

Figure 36 ... and the same display set to 1024 x 768 resolution.

SETTING DISPLAY OPTIONS

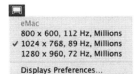

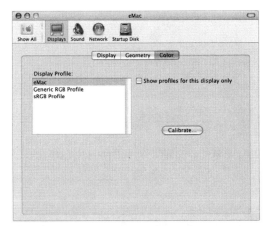

Figure 37
The Displays menu in the menu bar.

Figure 38 The Color pane of the Displays preferences pane for an eMac.

To set display color profile

1. In the Displays preferences pane, click the Color button (**Figure 38**).

2. Select one of the Display Profiles.

✔ Tips

■ Color profiles is an advanced feature of Mac OS that enables you to display colors onscreen as they will appear when printed.

■ Clicking the Calibrate button in the Color tab of the Displays preferences pane opens the Display Calibrator Assistant, which I discuss in **Chapter 19**.

Dock

The Dock preferences pane (**Figure 39**) offers several options for customizing the Dock's appearance and functionality.

To customize the Dock

In the Dock preferences pane (**Figure 39**), set options as desired:

◆ To set the size of the Dock and its icons, drag the Dock Size slider to the left or right.

◆ To enable Dock icon magnification (**Figure 40**), turn on the Magnification check box. Then drag the slider to the left or right to specify how large the magnified icons should become when you point to them.

◆ To change the Dock's position on the screen, select one of the Position on screen options: Left (**Figure 41**), Bottom (the default), or Right.

◆ To set the special effect Mac OS X uses to minimize a window to an icon in the Dock and maximize an icon from the Dock to a window, choose an option from the Minimize using pop-up menu:

▲ **Genie Effect**, the default option, shrinks the window into the Dock like a genie slipping into a magic lamp. (Well, how else could you describe it?)

▲ **Scale Effect** simply shrinks the icon into the Dock.

◆ To display the "bouncing icon" animation while a program is launching, turn on the Animate opening applications check box.

◆ To hide the Dock until you need it, turn on the Automatically hide and show the Dock check box. With this feature enabled, the Dock disappears until you move the mouse pointer to the edge of the screen where the Dock is positioned.

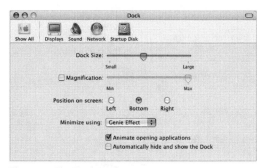

Figure 39 The Dock preferences pane.

Figure 40 With magnification enabled, when you point to an icon in the Dock, it grows so you can see it better.

Figure 41 When you set the Dock's position to Left, it appears as a vertical bar of icons on the left side of the screen, below the Apple menu.

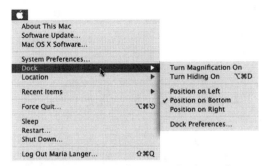

Figure 42 Use the Dock submenu under the Apple menu to set some Dock options.

✔ Tips

- You can use the Dock submenu under the Apple menu (**Figure 42**) to set some Dock options without opening the Dock preferences pane. (You can also use this submenu to open the Dock preferences pane.)

- If you think the Dock takes up too much valuable real estate on your screen, try one of these options:

  - ▲ Set the Dock size smaller, then enable magnification so the icons enlarge when you point to them.

  - ▲ Position the Dock on the right. In most cases, document and Finder windows won't need to cover that area of the screen.

  - ▲ Turn on the Automatically hide and show the Dock check box. (This is what I do and it works like a charm.)

- Although the Genie Effect is pretty cool, the Scale Effect requires fewer system resources and may improve performance when minimizing and maximizing windows and icons.

- You can add, remove, or rearrange icons on the Dock by dragging them, as discussed in **Chapter 4**.

Energy Saver

The Energy Saver preference pane (**Figures 43**, **44**, and **46**) enables you to specify settings for automatic system, display, and hard disk sleep. These settings can reduce the amount of power your computer uses when idle.

✔ Tips

- Energy Saver settings are especially important for PowerBook and iBook users running on battery power.

- To wake a sleeping display, press any key. A sleeping hard disk wakes automatically when it needs to.

- Display sleep is a better way to protect flat panel displays and displays on Power-Books and iBooks than a screen saver. Mac OS X's built-in screen saver is covered earlier in this chapter.

- Energy Saver has been improved for Mac OS X 10.3 with the reintroduction of the scheduling feature, which is available in Mac OS 9.2 and earlier.

To set Energy Saver sleep options

1. In the Energy Saver preferences pane, click the Sleep button to display its options (**Figure 43**).

2. Set options as desired:
   - ▲ To set the system sleep timing, drag the top slider to the left or right.
   - ▲ To set different display sleep timing, turn on the second check box and drag its slider to the left or right. (You cannot set display sleep for longer than system sleep.)
   - ▲ To tell your computer to put the hard disk to sleep when it isn't needed, turn on the bottom check box.

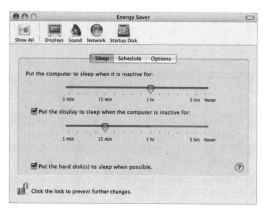

Figure 43 The Sleep pane of the Energy Saver preferences pane.

SETTING ENERGY SAVER SLEEP OPTIONS

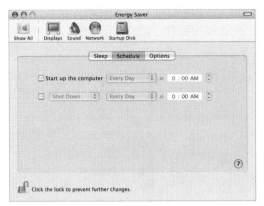

Figure 44 The new Schedule pane of the Energy Saver preferences pane.

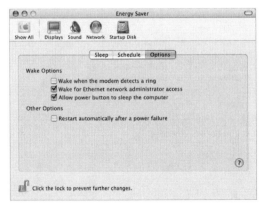

Figure 45
Use this pop-up menu to specify the days you want to start up or shut down the computer automatically.

Figure 46 The Options pane of the Energy Saver preferences pane.

✔ Tip

- If your computer is being used as a server, it's important to turn on the Restart automatically check box. This ensures that the computer is running whenever possible.

To schedule start up & shut down

1. In the Energy Saver preferences pane, click the Schedule button to display its options (**Figure 44**).

2. To start the computer automatically, turn on the top check box. Then choose an option from the pop-up menu (**Figure 45**) and enter a time beside it.

3. To shut down the computer automatically, turn on the second check box, choose an option from the second pop-up menu in that line (**Figure 45**), and enter a time beside it.

✔ Tip

- To set the computer to sleep rather than shut down, after step 3, choose Sleep from the first pop-up menu in the second line.

To set Energy Saver waking & restarting options

1. In the Energy Saver preferences pane, click the Options tab (**Figure 46**).

2. Set wake and other options as desired:

   ▲ **Wake when the modem detects a ring** wakes the computer from System sleep when the modem detects an incoming call.

   ▲ **Wake for Ethernet network administrator access** wakes the computer from System sleep when it detects a Wake-on-LAN packet.

   ▲ **Allow power button to sleep the computer** puts the computer to sleep when you press the power button. This option does not appear for all computers.

   ▲ **Restart automatically after a power failure** automatically restarts the computer when power is restored after a power failure.

SETTING OTHER ENERGY SAVER OPTIONS

International

The International preferences pane enables you to set options that control how Mac OS X works in an environment where U.S. English is not the primary language or multiple languages are used.

International preferences are broken down into three different categories: Language (**Figure 47**), Formats (**Figure 52**), and Input Menu (**Figure 56**).

To set the preferred language

1. In the International preferences pane, click the Language tab (**Figure 47**).

2. To set the preferred order for languages to appear in application menus and dialogs, drag languages up or down in the Languages list (**Figure 48**).

3. To set sort order, case conversion, and word definition behaviors for text, click the Customize Sorting button. Then use the dialog that appears (**Figure 49**) to select a script and choose a behaviors option. Click OK to save your settings.

✔ Tips

- You can edit the Languages list. Click the Edit button in the Language pane (**Figure 47**) to display a dialog sheet like the one in **Figure 50**. Turn on the check boxes beside each language you want to include in the list and click OK.

- The changes you make to the Languages list in step 2 take effect in the Finder the next time you restart or log in. Changes take effect in applications (**Figure 51**) the next time you open them.

- A *script* is a writing system or alphabet.

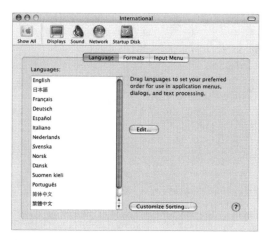

Figure 47 The Language pane of the International preferences pane.

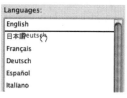

Figure 48 You can change the preferred language order by dragging a language up or down in the list.

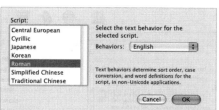

Figure 49 Use this dialog to set options for sorting text and converting case.

Figure 50 Turn on check boxes for the language you want to include in the Languages list.

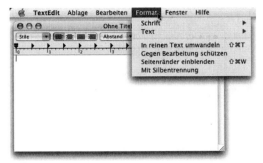

Figure 51 Changing the language of an application's menus and dialogs is as easy as dragging the language to the top of the Languages list (**Figure 48**). Here's TextEdit in German (Deutsch).

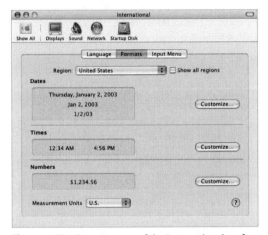

Figure 52 The Formats pane of the International preferences pane.

To set the date, time, & number formats

1. In the International Preferences pane, click the Formats button (**Figure 52**).

2. Choose an option from the Region pop-up menu.

3. To customize the date, time, or number format, click the Customize button in the appropriate area of the dialog. Then set options in the dialog sheets that appear (**Figures 53, 54,** and **55**) and click OK.

4. To change the measurement unit, choose an option from the Measurement Units pop-up menu.

✔ Tips

- Changes in this pane affect how dates, times, and numbers are displayed throughout Mac OS X and its applications.

- The sample dates, times, and numbers in the customize dialogs (**Figures 53, 54,** and **55**) show the effect of your changes.

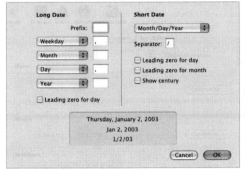

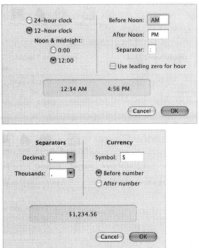

Figures 53, 54, & 55 Use these dialogs to customize the date (above), time (top-right), and number formats (bottom-right).

To create & customize an input menu

1. In the International Preferences pane, click the Input Menu button (**Figure 56**).

2. Turn on the check boxes beside each keyboard layout you may want to use with Mac OS X. If more than one keyboard is selected, an Input menu appears on the menu bar (**Figure 57**).

3. To customize the way the keyboard menu feature works, click the Options button. A dialog sheet like the one in **Figure 58** appears. Toggle check marks beside options as desired and click OK:

   ▲ **Input Menu Shortcuts** enables you to switch from one keyboard layout or input method to the next by pressing ⌃ ⌘ Option Spacebar. (The ⌃ ⌘ Spacebar shortcut to switch toggle between the last two keyboard layouts cannot be disabled.)

   ▲ **Try to match keyboard with text** automatically switches to the keyboard layout a font is synchronized to. The switch occurs when you click in or select text formatted with that font.

✔ Tips

■ To switch from one language's keyboard to another's, select the language from the Input menu (**Figure 57**).

■ The Input menu also appears on the menu bar when you use the Special Characters command in an application.

■ I explain how to use the Character palette in **Chapter 9**.

■ Font and keyboard synchronization is handled internally by international bundle resources included in font files. You cannot change synchronization options; you can only disable this feature.

Figure 56 The Input Menu pane of the International preferences pane.

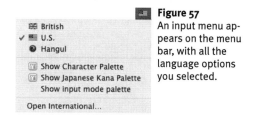

Figure 57 An input menu appears on the menu bar, with all the language options you selected.

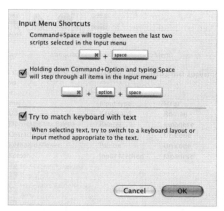

Figure 58 Use this dialog sheet to customize the way the Input menu feature works.

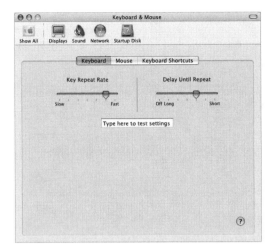

Figure 59 The Keyboard pane of the Keyboard & Mouse preferences pane.

Keyboard & Mouse

The Keyboard & Mouse preferences pane enables you to customize the way the keyboard and mouse (or trackpad) work. Options can be set in three panes: Keyboard (**Figure 59**), Mouse (**Figure 60**), and Keyboard Shortcuts (**Figure 61**).

✔ Tip

■ The Keyboard & Mouse preferences pane combines the options of two separate preferences panes in previous versions of Mac OS X: Keyboard and Mouse.

To set keyboard options

1. In the Keyboard & Mouse preferences pane, click the Keyboard button (**Figure 59**).

2. Set options as desired:
   ▲ **Key Repeat Rate** sets how fast a key repeats when held down.
   ▲ **Delay Until Repeat** sets how long a key must be pressed before it starts to repeat.

3. Test your settings by typing in the test field at the bottom of the pane. If necessary, repeat step 2 to fine-tune your settings for the way you type.

✔ Tip

■ Key Repeat settings are especially useful for heavy-handed typists.

SETTING KEY REPEAT OPTIONS

To set mouse speeds

1. In the Keyboard & Mouse preferences pane, click the Mouse button (**Figure 60**).

2. Set options as desired:

   ▲ **Tracking Speed** enables you to set the speed of the mouse movement on your screen.

   ▲ **Double-Click Speed** enables you to set the amount of time between each click of a double-click. You can test the double-click speed by double-clicking in the test area; make changes as necessary to fine-tune the speed.

✔ Tip

■ If you're just learning to use a mouse, try setting the tracking and double-click speeds to slower than the default settings.

To customize keyboard shortcuts

1. In the Keyboard & Mouse preferences pane, click the Keyboard Shortcuts button (**Figure 61**).

2. To enable or disable a specific keyboard shortcut, toggle the On check box beside it.

3. To change a keyboard shortcut, double-click the shortcut to select it, then hold down the new keys to change it.

4. To access onscreen items with the keyboard (as well as the mouse), turn on the check box marked Turn on full keyboard access.

✔ Tips

■ You can add custom shortcut keys for applications. Click the + button at the bottom of the list to get started.

■ With full keyboard access enabled, you can use the shortcut keys in **Table 1** to activate onscreen items. Then use ⤒, ←, →, ↓, Tab, and Return to select and accept items.

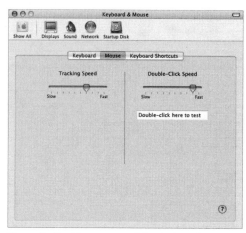

Figure 60 The Mouse pane of the Keyboard & Mouse preferences pane.

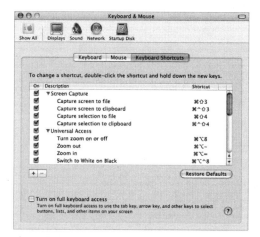

Figure 61 The Keyboard Shortcuts pane of the Keyboard & Mouse preferences pane.

Table 1

Full Keyboard Access Keys	
To do this	**Press these keys**
Turn full keyboard access on or off	Control F1
Highlight the menu bar	Control F2
Highlight the Dock	Control F3
Highlight the active window or the window behind it	Control F4
Highlight the toolbar	Control F5
Highlight a tool palette, then each palette in order	Control F6
Access all controls in the current dialog	Control F7

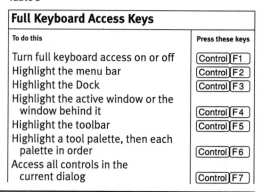

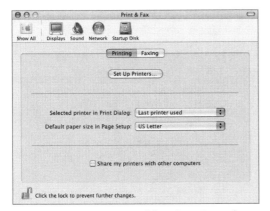

Figure 62 The Printing pane of the Print & Fax preferences pane.

Print & Fax

The Print & Fax preferences pane (**Figures 62** and **63**), which is brand new in Mac OS X 10.3, enables you to set options for printing and faxing from within applications.

✔ Tip

■ I cover printing and faxing in **Chapter 10**.

To set printing options

1. In the Print & Fax preferences pane, click the Printing button to display its options (**Figure 62**).

2. Set options as desired:

   ▲ **Selected printer in the Print Dialog** is the default printer. Choose a printer from the pop-up menu.

   ▲ **Default paper size in Page Setup** is the default paper size in the Page Setup dialog. Choose an option from the pop-up menu. The options that appear vary depending on the default printer.

   ▲ **Share my printers with other computers** turns on printer sharing.

✔ Tip

■ Clicking the Set Up Printers button launches the Printer Setup Utility. I explain how to use that application in **Chapter 10**.

SETTING PRINTING OPTIONS

To set up your computer to receive faxes

1. In the Print & Fax preferences pane, click the Faxing button to display its options (**Figure 63**).

2. Turn on the check box marked Receive faxes on this computer.

3. Set other options as desired:

   ▲ **My Fax Number** is the fax phone number that will appear in fax headers.

   ▲ **Answer after** is the number of rings before the computer answers the phone.

   ▲ **Save to** enables you to choose a folder in which faxes should be saved. The options are Faxes and Shared Faxes, but you can choose Other Folder and use the dialog that appears (**Figure 28**) to choose a different folder.

   ▲ **Email to** tells your computer to e-mail a copy of the fax to the address you enter in the box.

   ▲ **Print on printer** tells your computer to print the fax on the printer you choose from the pop-up menu.

✔ Tips

■ To receive faxes, your computer must have a modem that is connected to a telephone line.

■ If your computer shuts down or goes to sleep, it cannot receive faxes.

■ I explain how to send faxes from your computer in **Chapter 10**.

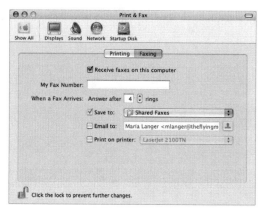

Figure 63 The Faxing pane of the Print & Fax preferences pane.

QuickTime

The QuickTime preferences pane enables you to set options that control the way QuickTime works. The pane's options are broken down into five tabs:

◆ **Plug-In** (**Figure 64**) controls the way the QuickTime Plug-in works with your Web browser.

◆ **Connection** (**Figure 66**) lets you specify a connection speed for downloading and playing QuickTime content.

◆ **Music** (**Figure 70**) enables you to specify a music synthesizer to play QuickTime music and MIDI files.

◆ **Media Keys** (**Figure 71**) allows you to add, modify, or remove keys for accessing secured QuickTime media files.

◆ **Update** (**Figure 73**) enables you to update or install Apple or third-party QuickTime software.

✔ Tips

■ For the most part, these options affect how QuickTime works within your Web browser. You can customize the way the QuickTime Player application works by setting options in its Player Preferences dialog; choose QuickTime Player > Preferences > Player Preferences while the QuickTime Player application is active.

■ Using the QuickTime Player is covered in **Chapter 6**.

QUICKTIME PREFERENCE OPTIONS

To set QuickTime Plug-in options

1. In the QuickTime preferences pane, click the Plug-In tab (**Figure 64**).

2. Set options as desired:

   ▲ **Play movies automatically** plays QuickTime movies automatically as they are downloaded to your Web browser. With this option turned on, the movie will begin to play as it downloads to your computer. With this option turned off, you'll have to click the Play button on the Quick-Time controller to play the movie after it has begun to download.

   ▲ **Save movies in disk cache** saves a copy of downloaded movies in your Web browser's disk cache whenever possible. This makes it possible to replay the movie at another time without reloading it. This feature is limited by the size of your Web browser's disk cache; as soon as the cache is full, old movies are deleted to make room for new downloaded pages, images, and other media.

   ▲ **Enable kiosk mode** hides the options to save movies and to change Quick-Time settings from within your Web browser. With this option turned off, you can hold down [Control] and click a QuickTime movie to display a con-textual menu with commands for working with the movie or QuickTime settings.

3. To associate document types with Quick-Time, click the MIME settings button. Then use the dialog that appears (**Figure 65**) to turn on check boxes beside docu-ment types that the QuickTime Plug-in should handle. (You can click a triangle to display options beneath it.) When you're finished, click OK.

Figure 64 The Plug-In tab of the QuickTime preferences pane.

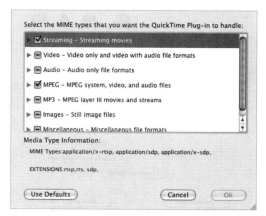

Figure 65 Use the MIME settings dialog to specify the types of documents that should be handled by the QuickTime Plug-In.

SETTING QUICKTIME PLUG-IN OPTIONS

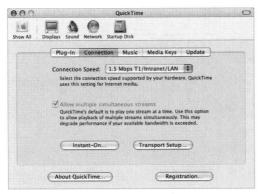

Figure 66 The Connection tab of the QuickTime preferences pane.

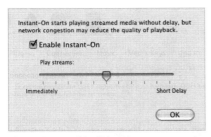

Figure 67
The Connection
Speed pop-up menu.

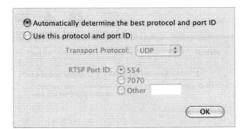

Figure 68 Use this dialog sheet to set options for media streaming.

To set QuickTime connection options

1. In the QuickTime preferences pane, click the Connection tab (**Figure 66**).

2. Choose the speed at which you connect to the Internet from the Connection Speed pop-up menu (**Figure 67**).

3. To play multiple data streams at the same time, turn on the Allow multiple simultaneous streams check box.

4. To enable QuickTime to play streamed media without delay, click the Instant-On button. Then turn on the Enable Instant-On check box in the dialog sheet that appears (**Figure 68**). Use the slider to indicate the length of delay before streaming media begins playing and click OK to save your settings.

5. To select a streaming video transport protocol and port number, click the Transport Setup button. Then set options in the dialog sheet that appears (**Figure 69**) and click the close button.

✔ Tip

■ Because of performance issues, the simultaneous streams feature should only be enabled if your connection speed exceeds 112 Kbps. (In fact, it is turned on by default at 112 Kbps or higher.) When used with slower connection speeds, QuickTime media may not play back smoothly.

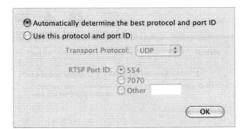

Figure 69 Use this dialog sheet to set streaming transport protocol and port options.

To set the QuickTime music synthesizer

1. In the QuickTime preferences pane, click the Music tab (**Figure 70**).

2. Select one of the options in the list.

3. Click Make Default.

✔ Tips

- The options that appear in the list vary depending on the synthesizers installed in your computer.

- The Audio MIDI Setup application, which you can find in the Utilities folder inside the Applications folder, enables you to fine-tune a MIDI setup for use with Mac OS X.

To add, remove, or modify QuickTime media keys

1. In the QuickTime preferences pane, click the Media Keys tab (**Figure 71**).

2. Modify the list of media keys as desired:

   ▲ To add a media key, click Add. Then use the dialog sheet that appears (**Figure 72**) to enter the category and key and click OK.

   ▲ To modify a media key, select the key in the list and click Edit. Then use the dialog sheet that appears (**Figure 72**) to modify the key's information.

   ▲ To remove a media key, select the key in the list and click Delete. Then click Delete in the confirmation dialog that appears.

✔ Tip

- You must have a media key set up to access secured QuickTime media.

Figure 70 The Music tab of the QuickTime preferences pane.

Figure 71 The Media Keys tab of the QuickTime preferences pane.

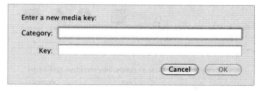

Figure 72 Use this dialog sheet to enter media key information.

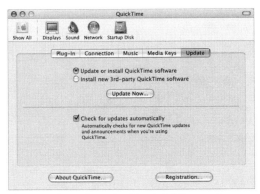

Figure 73 The Update tab of the QuickTime preferences pane.

Figure 74 The QuickTime Component Install dialog tells you whether an update is necessary.

To update QuickTime software

1. In the QuickTime preferences pane, click the Update tab (**Figure 73**).

2. Select one of the update/install options:

   ▲ **Update or install QuickTime software** searches the QuickTime Web site for QuickTime software released by Apple.

   ▲ **Install new 3rd-party QuickTime software** searches the QuickTime Web site for third-party software that works with QuickTime.

3. Click Update Now to launch the Software Update or QuickTime Updater application.

4. A dialog warning you that the updater has to connect to the Internet may appear. Click Continue.

5. A progress dialog may appear while the updater searches for update information. When it's finished, the QuickTime Component Install dialog (**Figure 74**) appears to tell you whether you need to update.

   ▲ If an update is available, click Update Now and follow the instructions that appear onscreen.

   ▲ If no update is necessary, click Quit.

✔ Tips

■ You must have an Internet connection to update QuickTime with this feature.

■ If an update is available in step 5, you can click the Custom button to pick and choose among the updates to install.

■ If you turn on the Check for updates automatically check box in the Update tab of the QuickTime preferences pane (**Figure 73**), your computer automatically checks for updates and displays the QuickTime Component Install dialog (**Figure 74**) when an update is available.

To upgrade to QuickTime Pro

1. Display any tab of the QuickTime preferences pane (**Figure 64, 66, 70, 71,** or **73**).

2. Click the Registration button.

3. In the dialog sheet that appears (**Figure 75**), click Register Online.

   or

   If you already have a QuickTime Pro key, skip ahead to step 5.

4. Your Web browser launches, connects to Apple's Web site, and displays the Get QuickTime Pro page. Follow the instructions that appear onscreen to purchase a QuickTime Pro key. Then switch back to System Preferences.

5. In the registration information dialog sheet (**Figure 75**), enter your registration information in the appropriate boxes and click OK.

✔ Tips

- A QuickTime Pro upgrade adds features to the QuickTime Player software, including the ability to edit and save QuickTime files.

- You can confirm that your registration information has been properly entered by clicking the Registration button in any tab of the QuickTime preferences pane (**Figure 64, 66, 70, 71,** or **73**). The QuickTime version information should appear right above the buttons in the registration information dialog that appears (**Figure 76**).

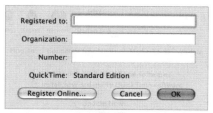

Figure 75 Use this dialog to enter, edit, and check registration information.

Figure 76 Once QuickTime has been upgraded, the version number appears in the registration information window.

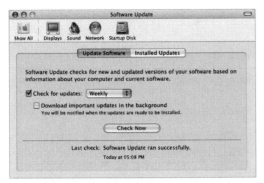

Figure 77 The Update Software pane of the Software Update preferences pane.

Software Update

The Software Update preferences pane (**Figure 77**) enables you to configure the Mac OS software update feature. This program checks Apple's Internet servers for updates to your Mac OS X software and enables you to download and install them.

✔ Tip

- You must have an Internet connection to update Mac OS X software with this feature.

To set automatic update options

1. In the Software Update preferences pane, click the Update Software button (**Figure 77**).

2. Turn on the Check for updates check box.

3. Use the pop-up menu to specify how often your computer should check for updates: Daily, Weekly, or Monthly.

4. To automatically download important updates without asking you, turn on the check box labeled Download important updates in the background.

✔ Tip

- When your computer checks for updates and finds one or more, it displays a window like the one in **Figure 79**. Follow the instructions in step 2 on the next page to install software and/or dismiss the window.

To manually update software

1. In the Update Software tab of the Software Update preferences pane (**Figure 77**), click Check Now.

   Your computer connects to the Internet and checks Apple's servers for updates (**Figure 78**).

2. When the check is complete, the Software Update window appears (**Figure 79**). It contains information about whether any updates are available.

   ▲ To install updates, turn on the check marks beside them. Then click Install. Follow any additional instructions that appear onscreen.

   ▲ To quit Software Update without installing updates, choose Software Update > Quit Software Update or press ⌘Q. Then click Quit in the confirmation dialog that appears.

✔ Tips

■ You can learn about an update before you install it by selecting it in the top half of the window to display a description in the bottom half of the window (**Figure 79**).

■ If you don't install a listed update, it will appear in the Software Update window (**Figure 79**) again the next time you check for updates. To remove it from the list without installing it, select it and choose Update > Ignore Update or press ⌘Delete.

■ Updates may require that you provide an administrator password before installation. If so, an Authenticate dialog will appear. Enter administrator login information as prompted and click OK.

■ To view a log of installed updates, click the Installed Updates tab in the Software Update preferences pane (**Figure 80**).

Figure 78 A progress bar appears in the bottom of the Software Update preferences pane while your computer checks for updates.

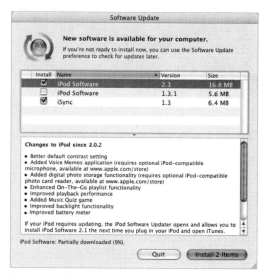

Figure 79 A list of software updates appears in the Software Update window.

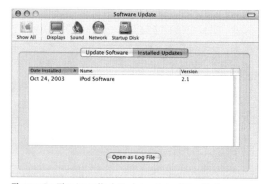

Figure 80 The Installed Updates tab of the Software Update preferences pane shows a log of recent software update installations.

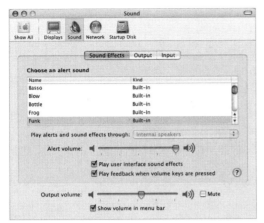

Figure 81 The Sound Effects pane of the Sound preferences pane.

Figure 82
The Sound volume menu appears in the menu bar beside the menu bar clock.

Sound

The Sound preferences pane enables you to set options to control the system and alert sounds, output device, and input device.

Sound settings can be change in three panes:

◆ **Sound Effects** (**Figure 81**) lets you set options for alert sounds and sound effects.

◆ **Output** (**Figure 83**) allows you to set the output device and balance.

◆ **Input** (**Figure 84**) enables you to set the input device and volume.

✔ Tip

■ The options that appear in the Sound preferences pane vary depending on your computer and the devices connected to it. The figures on these pages show options on an eMac.

To set system volume

1. Display any tab of the Sound preferences pane (**Figure 81, 83, or 84**).

2. Set options in the bottom of the window:

   ▲ **Output volume** is the system volume. Drag the slider to the left or right.

   ▲ **Mute** keeps your computer quiet.

   ▲ **Show volume in menu bar** displays a sound volume menu in the menu bar (**Figure 82**).

✔ Tips

■ The output volume is the maximum volume for all sounds, including alerts, games, QuickTime movies, and iTunes music.

■ Each time you move and release the Main volume slider in step 2, an alert sounds so you can hear a sample of your change.

■ The Sound volume menu appears on the right end of the menu bar, just to the left of the menu bar clock (**Figure 82**). To use the menu, click to display the slider and drag it up or down. You can rearrange the menus on the right end of the menu bar by holding down ⌘ while dragging them.

SETTING SYSTEM SOUND VOLUME

To set sound effects options

1. In the Sound preferences pane, click the Sound Effects tab (**Figure 81**).

2. To set the alert sound, select one of the options in the scrolling list.

3. Set other options as desired:

   ▲ **Play alerts and sound effects through** enables you to set the output device for alert and sound effect sounds. (This option may not be accessible if the Sound preferences pane includes an Output tab.)

   ▲ **Alert volume** is the volume of alert sounds. Drag the slider to the left or right.

   ▲ **Play user interface sound effects** plays sound effects for different system events, such as dragging an icon to the Trash.

   ▲ **Play feedback when volume keys are pressed** enables you to hear the new volume each time you press one of the volume keys on the keyboard.

✔ Tips

■ Each time you move and release the slider or select a different alert sound, an alert sounds so you can hear a sample of your change.

■ Alert volume depends partly on the main volume setting, which is discussed on the previous page. An alert sound cannot be louder than the main sound.

■ Volume keys, when present, are located above the numeric keypad on USB keyboards. Not all Macintosh keyboards include volume keys.

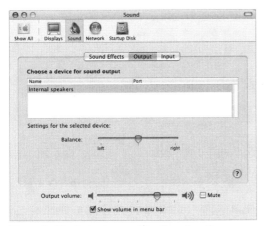

Figure 83 The Output pane of the Sound preferences pane.

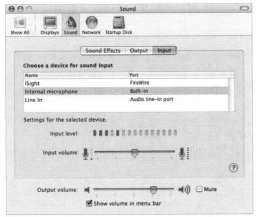

Figure 84 The Input pane of the Sound preferences pane.

To set output device options

1. In the Sound preferences pane, click the Output button (**Figure 83**).

2. To set the output device, select one of the options in the scrolling list.

3. To set the speaker balance for the selected device, drag the Balance slider to the left or right.

✔ Tip

- Each time you move and release the slider, an alert sounds so you can hear a sample of your change.

To set input device options

1. In the Sound preferences pane, click the Input tab (**Figure 84**).

2. To set the input device, select one of the options in the scrolling list.

3. To set the input volume for the selected device, drag the Input volume slider to the left or right. The further to the right you drag the slider, the more sensitive the microphone will be.

✔ Tips

- Input device and volume are especially important if you plan to use Mac OS X's speech recognition features. I discuss speech recognition later in this chapter.

- The Input Level area of the Input tab (**Figure 84**) graphically represents the current volume levels, including the peak level. You might find this helpful when setting the Input volume.

SETTING INPUT & OUTPUT DEVICE OPTIONS

Speech

Mac OS X's Speech preferences pane includes three panes of options:

◆ **Speech Recognition** lets you enable and configure speech recognition features.

◆ **Default Voice** allows you to set the default system voice for the text-to-speech feature.

◆ **Spoken User Interface** lets you enable and configure talking alerts and other spoken items.

In this section, I explain how to set up and use these features.

✔ Tips

■ Speech recognition requires a microphone (either built-in or plug-in).

■ The speech recognition feature works best in a relatively quiet work environment.

To enable & configure speech recognition

1. In the Speech preferences pane, click the Speech Recognition button (**Figure 85**).

2. Choose Apple Speakable Items from the Recognition System pop-up menu. (It may be the only option.)

3. If necessary, click the On/Off button to display its options (**Figure 85**).

4. Select the On radio button.

5. A dialog sheet may appear with instructions for using Apple Speakable Items (**Figure 86**). If this is your first time using this feature, read the contents of the dialog and click Continue to dismiss it.

   The round Feedback window appears (**Figure 87**).

Figure 85 The On/Off pane for Speech Recognition settings in the Speech preferences pane.

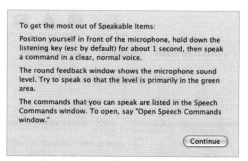

Figure 86 This dialog sheet provides brief instructions for using Apple Speakable Items.

Figure 87
The Feedback window.

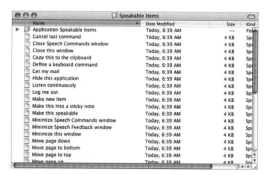

Figure 88 The contents of the Speakable Items folder.

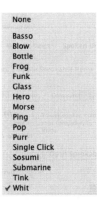

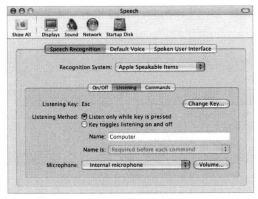

Figure 89
Use this pop-up menu to select a sound to indicate that your computer recognizes a spoken command.

Figure 90 The Listening pane of the Speech Recognition settings in the Speech preferences pane.

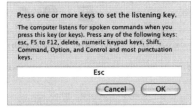

Figure 91 Use this dialog to enter a new listening key.

Optional before commands
✓ Required before each command
  Required 15 seconds after last command
  Required 30 seconds after last command

Figure 92 This pop-up menu enables you to specify how the computer name should be used for listening.

6. Set options and click buttons as desired:

   ▲ **Turn on Speakable Items at login** enables the speech recognition feature when you start or log in to your computer.

   ▲ **Helpful Tips** displays the dialog sheet with information about speakable items (**Figure 86**).

   ▲ **Open Speakable Items Folder** opens the Speakable Items folder (**Figure 88**).

   ▲ **Play sound** enables you to select a system sound to play when your computer recognizes the spoken command. Choose a sound from the pop-up menu (**Figure 89**).

   ▲ **Speak confirmation** instructs your computer to repeat the command that it heard.

7. Click the Listening button to display its options (**Figure 90**).

8. Set options and click buttons as desired:

   ▲ **Listening key** is the keyboard key you must press to either listen to spoken commands or toggle listening on or off. By default, the key is Esc. To change the key, click the Change Key button, enter a new key in the dialog that appears (**Figure 91**), and click OK.

   ▲ **Listening method** enables you to select how you want your Mac to listen for commands. **Listen only while key is pressed** requires you to press the listening key to listen. **Key toggles listening on and off** uses the listening key to turn listening on or off. If you select this second option, you can enter a name for your computer (the default name is Computer) and use the Name is pop-up menu (**Figure 92**) to specify whether the

Continued on next page...

ENABLING & CONFIGURING SPEECH RECOGNITION

Continued from previous page.

name must be spoken before each command.

▲ **Microphone (Figure 93)** enables you to select which microphone you will use to issue commands. The options vary depending on your computer model and the microphones attached to it.

▲ **Volume** enables you to check and adjust the microphone volume. Click the button to display the Microphone Volume dialog (**Figure 94**). Then speak phrases listed on the left side of the window. As a phrase is recognized, it blinks. Use the slider to change the volume as necessary. When you're finished, click Done.

9. Click the Commands button to display its options (**Figure 95**).

10. Turn on the check box beside each set of commands that should be available when Speakable Items is on.

✔ Tips

■ Each user has his or her own Speakable Items folder, which can be found at /Users/*username*/Library/Speech/Speakable Items.

■ For best results, either set the Listening method to Listen only while key is pressed or require the computer name before each spoken command. Otherwise, your computer could interpret background noise and conversations as commands.

■ An external microphone—especially one on a headset—will work more reliably than a built-in microphone, such as the one on the front of the computer.

Figure 93 The Microphone pop-up menu lists all the sound input devices connected to your computer.

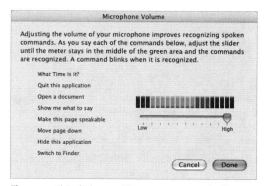

Figure 94 This dialog enables you to test and adjust the microphone volume.

Figure 95 The Commands pane of the Speech preferences pane for Speech Recognition.

Figure 96
When your computer recognizes a spoken command, the command appears above the Feedback window.

Figure 97
When a command has feedback, the response appears beneath the Feedback window.

✔ Tips

- The technique you use in step 1 will vary depending on how you set up speech recognition.

- The Speakable Items folder (**Figure 88**) contains preprogrammed Speakable Items. Each file corresponds to a command. Say the file name to issue the command.

- The Application Speakable Items folder inside the Speakable Items folder (**Figure 88**) contains Speakable Items commands that work in specific applications.

- If it is not possible to execute a command, nothing will happen after the command appears above the Feedback window. For example, if you use the "Close this window" command and no window is active, nothing will happen.

To use Speakable Items

1. Hold down the listening key and speak the command you want your computer to perform.

   or

   Use the listening key to turn listening on, then speak the command you want your computer to perform. If the computer name is required before or after the command, be sure to include it.

2. If your computer understands the command, the sound you specified during setup will play and the command will appear above the Feedback window (**Figure 96**). The command is executed (if possible).

   or

   If your computer did not understand the command, nothing happens. Wait a moment and try again.

- If the command you issued results in feedback (for example, the "What Day Is It?" command) and you set up speech recognition to speak feedback, your computer displays (**Figure 97**) and speaks the results of the command.

- To add a Speakable Item, use AppleScript to create a script for the command. Save the script as a compiled script in the appropriate location in the Speakable Items folder. Be sure to name the script with the words you want to use to issue the command. AppleScript is discussed in **Chapter 6**.

USING SPEAKABLE ITEMS

To set the default speaking voice

1. In the Speech preferences pane, click the Default Voice button (**Figure 98**).

2. Select one of the voices in the Voice list. The description on the right side of the window changes for that voice and your computer speaks so you can hear it.

3. To change the speed at which the voice speaks, use the Rate slider. You can then click the Play button to hear the effect of your change.

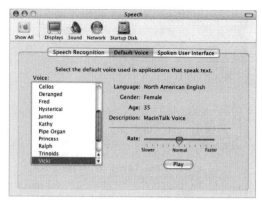

Figure 98 The Default Voice tab of the Speech preferences pane.

✔ Tips

■ As you try some of the voices, you'll see that some of them are more fun than practical.

■ The settings you make in the Default Voice tab affect any application that can speak text.

To set spoken user interface options

1. In the Speech preferences pane, click the Spoken User Interface tab (**Figure 99**).

2. Set Talking Alerts options as desired:

   ▲ **Speak the phrase** tells your computer to speak a certain phrase when an alert appears. If you turn on this check box, choose an option from the pop-up menu beside it (**Figure 100**).

   ▲ **Speak the alert text** tells your computer to read the contents of alert dialogs that appear. If you choose this option, use the pop-up menu beside it to select an alert voice. The options are the same as those in the Default Voice tab of the Speech preferences pane, which I discuss on the previous page.

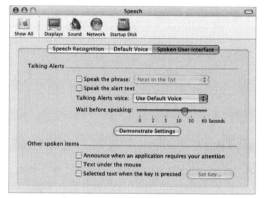

Figure 99 The Spoken User Interface pane of the Speech preferences pane.

Figure 100
As this pop-up menu indicates, your computer can be very polite when it tells you about alerts.

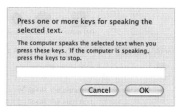

Figure 101 Use this dialog sheet to specify a keystroke that will speak or stop speaking selected text.

Figure 102 You can customize the way your computer alerts you by editing the Alert Phrases it uses.

▲ **Wait before speaking** enables you to set a delay between the time an alert appears and your computer starts talking. Use the slider to set the delay.

▲ **Demonstrate Settings** displays an alert using the settings so you can see how you like them.

3. Set other spoken items options as desired:

▲ **Announce when an application requires your attention** tells your computer to verbally announce when an application needs your attention. (Normally, the icon for an application needing attention bounces in the dock.)

▲ **Text under the mouse** reads the text that appears under your mouse pointer when you point to a menu, button, or other interface element.

▲ **Selected text when the key is pressed** reads any text you select when you press a key combination. When you turn on this check box, a dialog sheet like the one in **Figure 101** appears. Press the keystroke you want to use to speak or stop speaking selected text and click OK. You can change the keystroke by clicking the Change Key button to display this dialog sheet again.

✔ Tip

■ In step 2, you can choose Edit Phrase List from the Speak the phrase pop-up menu (**Figure 100**) to display the Alert Phrases dialog (**Figure 102**). Click the Add or Remove buttons to add a new phrase or remove a selected one. When you're finished, click OK to save your changes.

Startup Disk

The Startup Disk preferences pane (**Figure 103**) enables you to select a startup disk and, if desired, restart your computer. You might find this helpful if you want to start your computer under Mac OS 9.2 or from a bootable CD-ROM disc, such as a Mac OS installer disc.

Figure 103 The Startup Disk preferences pane.

✔ Tips

- Starting your computer under Mac OS 9.x is discussed in **Chapter 16**.

- Mac OS X enables you to have multiple System folders on a single disk or partition. Startup Disk is the tool you use to select which System folder should be used at startup.

To select a startup disk

1. Display the Startup Disk preferences pane (**Figure 103**).

2. Click the icon for the startup folder or disk you want to use.

3. To immediately restart your computer, click the Restart button.

    or

    Quit System Preferences. Click the Change button in the confirmation dialog sheet that appears to save your change.

✔ Tips

- If you choose Network Startup in step 2, your computer will look for a NetBoot startup volume when you restart. This makes it possible to boot your computer from a Mac OS X server on the network. Do not select this option unless a Net-Boot volume is accessible; doing so could cause errors on restart.

- If you do not immediately restart your computer with the new startup disk selected, that disk will be used the next time you restart or start up your computer.

SELECTING A STARTUP DISK

Figure 104 The Seeing pane of the Universal Access preferences pane

Universal Access

The Universal Access preferences pane enables you to set options for making your computer easier to use by people with disabilities.

Universal Access's features can be set in four different tabs:

◆ **Seeing** (**Figure 104**) enables you to set options for people with visual disabilities.

◆ **Hearing** (**Figure 105**) allows you to set options for people with aural disabilities.

◆ **Keyboard** (**Figure 106**) lets you set options for people who have difficulty using the keyboard.

◆ **Mouse** (**Figure 108**) enables you to set options for people who have difficulty using the mouse.

To set global Universal Access options

1. Display any pane of the Universal Access Preferences pane (**Figure 104, 105, 106,** or **108**).

2. Toggle check boxes at the bottom of the window as desired:

   ▲ **Enable access for assistive devices** allows you to use an assistive device, such as a screen reader, with Mac OS X.

   ▲ **Enable text-to-speech for Universal Access preferences** automatically reads items you point to on screen while working with the Universal Access preferences pane.

To set visual options

1. In the Universal Access preferences pane, click the Seeing button (**Figure 104**).

2. To enable or disable the Zoom feature, click the large Turn On Zoom or Turn Off Zoom button.

3. To enable or disable the White on Black display, click the large Switch to White on Black or Switch to Black on White button.

4. Drag the Enhance contrast slider to the left or right to decrease or increase contrast.

✔ Tips

- You can click the Zoom Options button to set additional options for using the Zoom feature.

- Clicking the Set Display to Grayscale button turns colors into shades of gray on the screen. Click the button again to return to a color display.

- Other options in the Display preferences pane may help you set your computer monitor so you can see it better. I tell you about the Display preferences pane earlier in this chapter.

To set hearing options

1. In the Universal Access preferences pane, click the Hearing button (**Figure 105**).

2. To visually display an alert sound, turn on the Flash the screen whenever an alert sound occurs check box.

3. To change the volume, click the Adjust Volume button, Then use the Sound preferences pane, which I discuss earlier in this chapter, to adjust the volume.

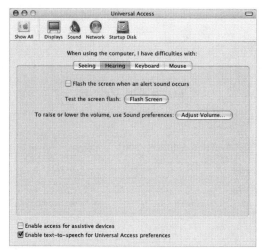

Figure 105 The Hearing pane of the Universal Access preferences pane.

✔ Tip

- Clicking the Flash Screen button shows you what the screen will look like when visually displaying an alert sound. Try it and see for yourself.

SETTING VISUAL & HEARING OPTIONS

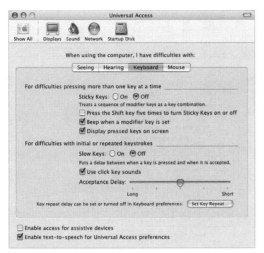

Figure 106 The Keyboard pane of the Universal Access preferences pane.

Figure 107
Universal Access can show you which keys you pressed—in this example, ⌃ ⌘ and Shift.

To enable & configure Sticky Keys & Slow Keys

1. In the Universal Access preferences pane, click the Keyboard tab (**Figure 106**).

2. To enable Sticky Keys, select the On radio button beside Sticky Keys. Then set options as desired:

   ▲ **Press the Shift key five times to turn Sticky Keys on or off** enables you to toggle Sticky Keys by pressing Shift five times.

   ▲ **Beep when a modifier key is set** plays a sound when a modifier key you press is recognized by the system.

   ▲ **Display pressed keys on screen** shows the image of the modifier key on screen when it is recognized by the system (**Figure 107**).

3. To enable Slow Keys, select the On radio button beside Slow Keys. Then set options as desired:

   ▲ **Use click key sounds** plays a sound when a key press is accepted.

   ▲ **Acceptance delay** enables you to adjust the amount of time between the point when a key is first pressed and when the keypress is accepted.

✔ Tips

- Sticky Keys makes it easier for people who have trouble pressing more than one key at a time to use modifier keys, such as Shift, ⌃ ⌘, and Option.

- Slow Keys puts a delay between when a key is pressed and when it is accepted by your computer. This makes it easier for people who have trouble pressing keyboard keys to type.

- Clicking the Set Key Repeat button displays the Keyboard preferences pane, which is discussed earlier in this chapter, so you can set other options for making the keyboard easier to use.

SETTING STICKY KEYS & SLOW KEYS

To enable & configure Mouse Keys

1. In the Universal Access preferences pane, click the Mouse button (**Figure 108**).

2. To enable Mouse Keys, select the On radio button. Then set options as desired:

   ▲ **Press the option key five times to turn Mouse Keys on or off** enables you to toggle Mouse Keys by pressing (Option) five times.

   ▲ **Initial Delay** determines how long you must hold down the key before the mouse pointer moves.

   ▲ **Maximum Speed** determines how fast the mouse pointer moves.

✔ Tips

■ To move the mouse with Mouse Keys enabled, hold down a key on the numeric keypad. Directions correspond with the number positions (for example, ⑧ moves the mouse up and ③ moves the mouse diagonally down and to the right).

■ Mouse Keys does not enable you to "click" the mouse button with a keyboard key. Full Keyboard Access, however, does. You can set up this feature with the Keyboard preferences pane; click the Open Keyboard Preferences button to open it.

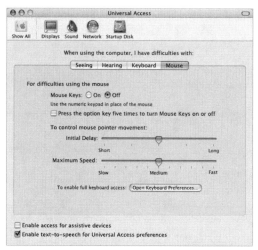

Figure 108 The Mouse pane of the Universal Access preferences pane.

SETTING UP MOUSE KEYS

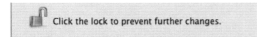

Click the lock to prevent further changes.

Figure 109 when a preferences pane is unlocked, the padlock icon at the bottom of its window looks unlocked.

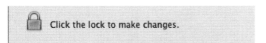

Click the lock to make changes.

Figure 110 When a preferences pane is locked, the padlock icon at the bottom of its window looks locked.

Figure 111 Enter an administrator's user name and password in the Authenticate dialog to unlock the preferences pane.

Locking Preference Settings

Most preferences panes include a lock button that enables you to lock the settings. Locking a preferences pane's settings prevent them from being changed accidentally or by users who do not have administrative privileges.

To lock a preferences pane

Click the lock button at the bottom of a preferences pane window (**Figure 109**).

The button changes blue and the icon within it looks like a locked padlock (**Figure 110**).

To unlock a preferences pane

1. Click the lock button at the bottom of a locked preferences pane window (**Figure 110**).

2. Enter an administrator's name and password in the Authenticate dialog that appears (**Figure 111**) and click OK.

   The button changes to gray and the icon within it looks like an unlocked padlock.

LOCKING & UNLOCKING PREFERENCES PANES

Mac OS Utilities

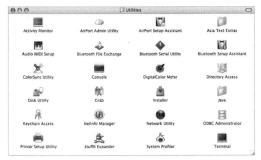

Figure 1 The Utilities folder contains a bunch of utility applications for working with your computer and files.

✔ Tips

- This chapter does not cover the following utilities, which are discussed elsewhere in this book:
  - ▲ Printer Setup Utility, in **Chapter 10**.
  - ▲ AirPort Admin Utility, AirPort Setup Assistant, Bluetooth File Exchange, Bluetooth Serial Utility, Bluetooth Setup Assistant, Directory Access, NetInfo Manager, and Network Utility, in **Chapter 14**.
  - ▲ Keychain Access, in **Chapter 15**.
  - ▲ Terminal, in **Chapter 17**.
- Coverage of Asia Text Extras, Java, and ODBC Administrator is beyond the scope of this book.

Mac OS Utilities

The Utilities folder inside the Applications folder (**Figure 1**) includes a number of utility applications you can use to work with your computer and its files.

This chapter covers the following utilities:

- ◆ **Activity Monitor** displays information about your computer CPU's workload.

- ◆ **Audio MIDI Setup** enables you to set options for audio and MIDI devices connected to your Macintosh.

- ◆ **ColorSync Utility** enables you to check and repair ColorSync profiles and to assign profiles to hardware devices.

- ◆ **Console** displays technical messages from the system software and applications.

- ◆ **Digital Color Meter** enables you to measure and translate colors on your display.

- ◆ **Disk Utility** allows you to check, format, partition, and get information about disks, as well as create and open disk image files.

- ◆ **Grab** enables you to capture screen images and save them as image files.

- ◆ **Installer** enables you to install software.

- ◆ **StuffIt Expander** opens compressed or archived files in a variety of formats.

- ◆ **System Profiler** provides information about your Mac's installed software and hardware.

Activity Monitor

Activity Monitor enables you to get information about the various processes running on your computer. It also displays, in graphical format, CPU activity, memory usage, and disk and network statistics. You may find this information helpful if you are a programmer or network administrator or you are trying to troubleshoot a computer problem.

✔ Tips

- A *process* is a set of programming codes that performs a task.

- Activity Monitor combines the features of the CPU Monitor and Process Viewer utilities that were available in previous versions of Mac OS X.

To monitor computer activity

1. Open the Activity Monitor icon in the Utilities folder (**Figure 1**). The Activity Monitor window appears (**Figure 2**).

2. To view only specific types of processes, choose an option from the pop-up menu at the top of the window (**Figure 3**). The list of processes in the top half of the window changes accordingly.

3. Click a button at the bottom of the window to view other information:

   ▲ **CPU** (**Figure 2**) displays current CPU activity.

   ▲ **System Memory** (**Figure 4**) displays RAM usage.

   ▲ **Disk Activity** (**Figure 5**) displays disk access activity.

   ▲ **Disk Usage** (**Figure 6**) displays free and utilized space on disk. You can use the pop-up menu to choose other disks, if available.

   ▲ **Network** (**Figure 7**) displays network activity.

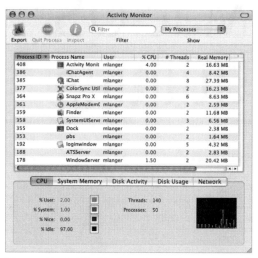

Figure 2 The Activity Monitor window shows a list of all processes running on your computer.

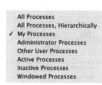

Figure 3
Use this pop-up menu to choose the type of processes to display.

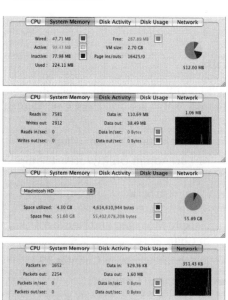

Figures 4, 5, 6, & 7 The bottom half of the Activity Monitor window can show System Memory, Disk Activity, Disk Usage, and Network information.

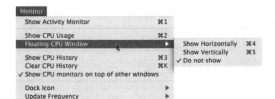

Figure 8 The Monitor menu and its Floating CPU Monitor submenu.

Figure 9
This tiny window displays a live, graphical representation of current CPU usage.

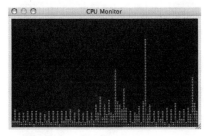

Figure 10 This window displays CPU usage over time.

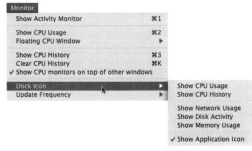

Figure 11 The Dock Icon submenu offers options for displaying computer activity information in the Dock.

✔ Tip

■ To sort processes in the Activity Monitor window (**Figure 2**), click the column you want to sort by. You can reverse the sort order by clicking the same column again.

To display other monitor windows

Choose an option from the Monitor menu (**Figure 8**) or one of its submenus (**Figures 8** and **11**):

◆ **Show Activity Monitor** displays the Activity Monitor window (**Figure 2**).

◆ **Show CPU Usage** displays a graphical representation of current CPU usage (**Figure 9**).

◆ **Floating CPU Window** submenu commands (**Figure 8**) display a horizontal or vertical bar with a graphical representation of current CPU usage.

◆ **Show CPU History** displays a window with a chart of CPU usage over time (**Figure 10**).

◆ **Dock Icon** submenu commands (**Figure 11**) display graphical representations of usage and activity in the Dock. **Figure 12** shows an example of the Dock with a Network display icon.

✔ Tip

■ You can use the Update Frequency submenu under the Monitor menu to change how often monitor windows are updated.

Figure 12 Activity Monitor can display activity graphs, such as Network Activity, as an icon in the Dock.

MONITORING COMPUTER ACTIVITY

Audio MIDI Setup

Audio MIDI Setup enables you to configure audio and MIDI devices for use with a MIDI music system. It offers two panes of settings:

◆ **Audio Devices (Figure 13)** enables you to configure input and output devices, including internal and external microphones and speakers.

◆ **MIDI Devices (Figure 14)** enables you to configure MIDI devices, such as MIDI keyboards and other instruments, that are connected to your Macintosh.

This section provides a quick overview of Audio MIDI Setup.

✔ Tips

■ If you don't use MIDI devices with your Macintosh, you probably won't ever need to use Audio MIDI Setup.

■ Some audio or MIDI devices require additional software to be used with your computer. Make sure any required drivers or other software is installed before setting audio or MIDI options.

To configure audio devices

1. Open the Audio MIDI Setup icon in the Utilities folder (**Figure 1**).

2. Click the Audio Devices button in the Audio MIDI Setup window that appears (**Figure 13**).

3. Choose the devices you want to use and configure from the pop-up menus. Only those devices connected to your computer will appear in the menus.

4. Set other options as desired.

5. When you are finished, choose Audio MIDI Setup > Quit Audio MIDI Setup. Your settings are automatically saved.

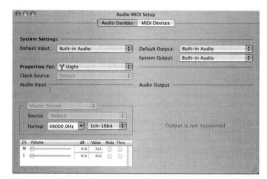

Figure 13 The Audio Devices pane of Audio MIDI Setup.

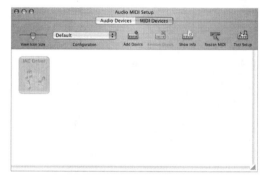

Figure 14 The MIDI Devices pane of Audio MIDI Setup, before any devices have been added.

Figure 15
An icon like this appears when you click the Add Device button.

Figure 16 Use this dialog to enter basic information about your MIDI device.

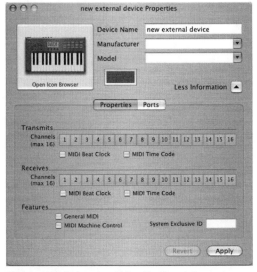

Figure 17 Click the triangle beside More Information to expand the dialog sheet and set Properties ...

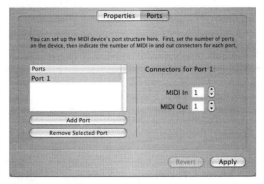

Figure 18 ... and Ports options.

To configure a MIDI setup

1. Connect your MIDI interface device to your computer as instructed in its documentation and turn it on.

2. Open the Audio MIDI Setup icon in the Utilities folder (**Figure 1**).

3. Click the MIDI Devices button in the Audio MIDI Setup window that appears (**Figure 14**).

4. Click the Add Device button. A new external device icon appears in the window (**Figure 15**).

5. Double-click the new external device icon to display a dialog like the one in **Figure 16**.

6. Enter information about the device in the appropriate boxes. You may be able to use the pop-up menus to select a Manufacturer and Model.

7. To enter additional information about the device, click the triangle beside More Information to expand the dialog. Then use the Properties (**Figure 17**) and Ports (**Figure 18**) panes to enter information.

8. Click OK to save the device settings.

9. Repeat steps 4 through 8 for each device you want to add.

10. When you are finished, choose Audio MIDI Setup > Quit Audio MIDI Setup. Your settings are automatically saved.

✔ Tips

- Your MIDI devices may appear automatically in step 3, depending on how they are connected.

- Don't change default for a device unless you know what you're doing! Consult the documentation that came with the device if you need help.

The ColorSync Utility

ColorSync is an industry-standard technology that helps designers match the colors they see onscreen to those in devices such as scanners, printers, and imagesetters. For the average user, color matching may not be very important, but for a designer who works with color, correct reproduction makes it possible to complete complex projects on time and within budget.

To use ColorSync, you must set it up and then instruct your software to use it. In this section, I explain how to use the ColorSync utility to set ColorSync preferences and work with ColorSync profiles and devices.

✔ Tips

- Previous versions of Mac OS X included a ColorSync preferences pane. The functionality of that preferences pane has been rolled into ColorSync Utility in Mac OS X 10.3.

- A complete discussion of ColorSync is far beyond the scope of this book. To learn more about ColorSync features and settings, visit www.apple.com/colorsync.

COLORSYNC

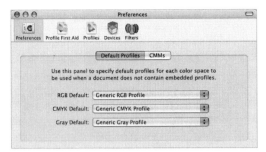

Figure 19 The Default Profiles pane for ColorSync preferences.

Figure 20 The CMMs pane for ColorSync preferences.

To set ColorSync preferences

1. Open the ColorSync Utility icon in the Utilities folder (**Figure 1**).

2. In the window that appears, click the Preferences icon.

3. Click the Default Profiles button to display its options (**Figure 19**).

4. Choose the desired option from the pop-up menu for each type of color space.

5. Click the CMMs button to display its options (**Figure 20**).

6. Select a color matching method from the Preferred CMM pop-up menu.

✔ Tips

- A ColorSync or ICC *profile* is a standard file format that provides output color information for a device based on a specific input.

- *ICC* stands for *International Color Consortium*, a group that sets standards for color profiles.

- A *color space* is a range of color coordinates that defines the hues and shades a device can print or display.

- *CMM* stands for *Color Matching Method*. ColorSync includes a default CMM provided by Apple that produces excellent results and is very fast.

- If an application that utilizes ColorSync enables you to set profile information within the application, those selections will override the ones set in the ColorSync preferences pane.

SETTING COLORSYNC PREFERENCES

To verify and/or repair ColorSync profiles

1. Open the ColorSync Utility icon in the Utilities folder (**Figure 1**).

2. In the window that appears, click the Profile First Aid icon (**Figure 21**).

3. Click Verify to check all installed profiles for errors.

   or

   Click Repair to repair any errors in installed profiles.

4. Wait while ColorSync Utility checks or repairs installed profiles. When it's finished, it displays results in its window (**Figure 22**).

✔ Tip

■ You might want to use this feature to check or fix ColorSync Profiles if you notice a difference between what you see on your monitor and what you see on printed documents.

To view a list of installed profiles

1. Open the ColorSync Utility icon in the Utilities folder (**Figure 1**).

2. In the window that appears, click the Profiles icon (**Figure 23**).

3. If necessary, click triangles beside a folder pathname to view a list of the items in the folder.

✔ Tip

■ Clicking an item displays information about it in the right side of the window, as shown in **Figure 23**, including the file's disk location (path) and *lab plot*—a graphic representation of the profile's settings.

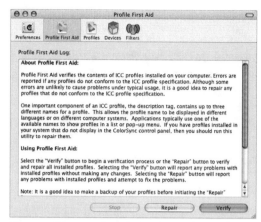

Figure 21 When you first display the Profile First Aid pane of the ColorSync Utility, a window full of instructions appears.

Figure 22 Here's what the results of a profile verification might look like.

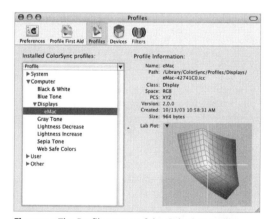

Figure 23 The Profiles pane of the ColorSync utility displays a list of all installed profiles. Click a profile to learn more about it.

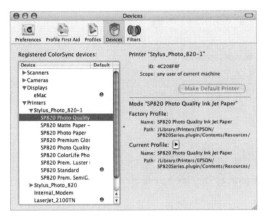

Figure 24 The Devices pane of the ColorSync utility displays a list of all registered devices. Click a device to learn more about it.

To view a list of registered devices

1. Open the ColorSync Utility icon in the Utilities folder (**Figure 1**).

2. In the ColorSync Utility window that appears, click the Devices icon (**Figure 24**).

3. If necessary, click the triangle beside a device type to view a list of the devices of that type.

✔ Tips

- A registered device is one that is recognized by the system software and has a ColorSync profile assigned to it.

- Clicking an item displays information about it in the right side of the window, as shown in **Figure 24**, including the profile.

- You can change an item's profile by choosing an option from the Current Profile pop-up menu when the item is displayed.

- If there is more that one device for a type of device, you can make one of the devices the default. Simply select it in the list (**Figure 24**) and click the Make Default *Type* button. (The exact label on the button varies depending on what type of item is selected.)

VIEWING REGISTERED DEVICES

To view filter information

1. Open the ColorSync Utility icon in the Utilities folder (**Figure 1**).

2. In the ColorSync Utility window that appears, click the Filters icon (**Figure 25**).

3. Select a filter from the Filters list.

4. Click a button in the Filter Details area to get information about the filter.

✔ Tips

- The filters that are installed with Mac OS X 10.3 are locked and cannot be changed.

- You can create a new filter by clicking the Add button at the bottom of the Filters list or by selecting a filter and then clicking the Duplicate button at the bottom of the Filters list. You can then set filter options in the various Filter details panes.

- To see what an image looks like with a filter applied, select a filter in the Filters list and click the View file with Filter button. Use the Open dialog that appears to locate, select, and open an image file. Then work with settings in the window that appears (**Figure 26**). Be sure to turn on the Preview check box to see how the settings affect the image.

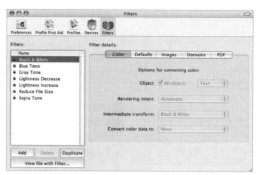

Figure 25 The Filters pane of the ColorSync Utility.

Figure 26 A great new feature of the ColorSync Utility is the ability to preview a picture with a filter applied.

Figure 27 The console.log window records messages sent by Mac OS and its applications. (What may look like a bunch of gibberish to you and me can help a programmer or troubleshooter debug a Mac.)

Figure 28 The Font palette enables you to change the appearance of text in the console.log window.

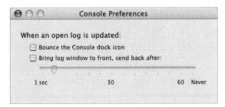

Figure 29 The Console Preferences window.

Console

The Console application enables you to read messages from the Mac OS X system software and applications. You might find this useful if you are a programmer or are troubleshooting a problem. (If not, you'll probably think it looks like a bunch of gibberish.)

To view system messages

1. Open the Console icon in the Utilities folder (**Figure 1**).

2. The console.log window appears (**Figure 27**). Scroll through its contents to read messages.

✔ Tips

- The most recent console.log entries appear at the end of the document.

- You can choose Format > Font > Show Fonts to display the Font palette (**Figure 28**) and change the appearance of text in the window. I explain how to use the Font palette in **Chapter 9**.

To set Console preferences

1. Choose Console > Preferences.

2. In the Console Preferences window (**Figure 29**), set options as desired:

   ▲ **Bounce the Console dock icon** bounces the log's icon in the Dock when a new message is recorded in the log.

   ▲ **Bring log window to front, send back after** brings the console.log window to the foreground when a new message is added. (Console must be running for this to work.) The window returns to the background after the number of seconds you specify with the slider has passed.

3. Click the close button to save your preference settings.

DigitalColor Meter

The DigitalColor Meter (**Figure 30**) enables you to measure colors that appear on your display as RGB, CIE, or Tristimulus values. This enables you to precisely record or duplicate colors that appear onscreen.

✔ Tip

- A discussion of color technology is far beyond the scope of this book. To learn more about how your Mac can work with colors, visit the ColorSync page on Apple's Web site, www.apple.com/colorsync/.

To measure color values

1. Open the DigitalColor Meter icon in the Utilities folder (**Figure 1**) to display the DigitalColor Meter window (**Figure 30**).

2. Point to the color onscreen that you want to measure. Its values appear in the right side of the DigitalColor Meter window (**Figure 30**).

3. If desired, choose a different option from the pop-up menu above the measurements (**Figure 31**). The value display changes to convert values to that measuring system (**Figure 32**).

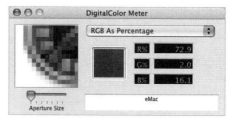

Figure 30 The DigitalColor Meter can tell you the color of any area onscreen—in this case, one of the pixels in its icon.

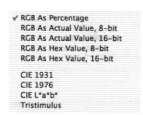

Figure 31 Choose an option to determine the system or units of the color measurement.

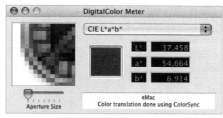

Figure 32 Choosing a different color measurement option from the pop-up menu changes the way the color values appear.

Image

Lock Position	⌘L
Lock X	⌘X
Lock Y	⌘Y
Copy Image	⌘C
Save as TIFF...	⌘S

Figure 33 Use the Image menu to work with the sample image.

Color

Hold Color	⇧⌘H
Copy Color As Text	⇧⌘C
Copy Color As Image	⌥⌘C

Figure 34 Use the Color menu to work with sampled colors.

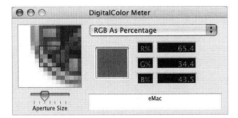

Figure 35 By changing the aperture setting, you can sample more pixels. DigitalColor Meter automatically computes the average.

✔ Tips

- You can use commands under the Image menu (**Figure 33**) to work with the color sample image that appears in DigitalColor Meter's window:

  - ▲ **Lock Position** ((⌃ ⌘L)) prevents the image from moving.

  - ▲ **Lock X** ((⌃ ⌘X)) allows only vertical changes in the color sample.

  - ▲ **Lock Y** ((⌃ ⌘Y)) allows only horizontal change in the color sample area.

  - ▲ **Copy Image** ((⌃ ⌘C)) copies the color sample image to the clipboard.

  - ▲ **Save as TIFF** ((⌃ ⌘S)) saves the color sample image as a TIFF file.

- You can use commands under the Color menu (**Figure 34**) to work with a selected color. (For best results, either use the command's shortcut key or choose Image > Lock Position [**Figure 33**] before using the Color menu's commands.)

  - ▲ **Hold Color** ((Shift ⌃ ⌘H)) saves the color in the sample well until you choose the Hold Color command again.

  - ▲ **Copy Color As Text** ((Shift ⌃ ⌘C)) copies the color information to the clipboard, where it can be pasted into other applications.

  - ▲ **Copy Color As Image** ((Option ⌃ ⌘C)) copies the color information as a color sample to the clipboard, where it can be pasted into other applications.

- You can change the amount of color that is sampled by dragging the Aperture Size slider to the right or left (**Figure 35**). A large aperture size will average the colors within it.

MEASURING COLOR VALUES

Disk Utility

Disk Utility, as the name implies, is a utility for working with disks. Specifically, it can:

◆ Provide general information about a disk or volume.

◆ Verify and repair a disk or volume.

◆ Erase a selected disk or volume.

◆ Divide a disk into several volumes or partitions.

◆ Set up a RAID disk.

◆ Create a blank disk image or a disk image from a file or a disk.

◆ Mount disk images as disks.

◆ Burn a disk image to CD-R or DVD-R.

◆ Restore a disk from a backup image.

In this part of the chapter, I explain how to use Disk Utility's most useful features.

✔ Tips

■ Disk Utility combines the features of Disk Utility and Disk Copy in previous versions of Mac OS X.

■ A *disk* is a storage device. A *volume* is a portion of a disk formatted for storing files.

■ A *disk image* is a single file that contains everything on a disk. You can mount a disk image on your desktop just like any other disk.

■ I tell you more about mounting and unmounting disks in **Chapter 3**.

■ Disk images are often used to distribute software updates or drivers on the Internet.

■ Disk image files often include *.img* or *.dmg* filename extensions.

■ Disk Utility's RAID pane is not covered in this book. To learn more about this feature, enter a search phrase of *RAID* in Mac Help and follow links that appear for specific instructions.

■ Disk Utility's Restore pane is not covered in this book. To learn about creating disk images that can be used to restore a disk, enter a search phrase of *restore* in Mac Help and follow links that appear for specific instructions.

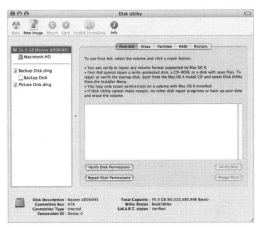

Figure 36 Select the disk or volume you want to work with in Disk Utility's main window. The list includes physical disks and their volumes as well as disk image files you have created and saved on disk.

Figure 37 This window shows information about a disk.

To get information about a disk or volume

1. Open the Disk Utility icon in the Utilities folder (**Figure 1**).

2. In the Disk Utility window that appears, select the disk or volume you want information about. Some information about the item appears at the bottom of the window (**Figure 36**).

3. Click the Info button on the toolbar. A window with additional information appears (**Figure 37**).

To verify or repair a disk or volume or its permissions

1. Open the Disk Utility icon in the Utilities folder (**Figure 1**).

2. In the Disk Utility window that appears, click the First Aid button.

3. Select the disk(s) or volume(s) you want to verify or repair (**Figure 36**).

4. Click the button for the action you want to perform:

   ▲ **Verify Disk Permissions** verifies file permissions on a Mac OS X startup disk or volume.

   ▲ **Repair Disk Permissions** repairs file permissions on a Mac OS X startup volume.

   ▲ **Verify Disk** verifies the directory structure and file integrity of any disk or volume other than the startup disk or volume.

   ▲ **Repair Disk** repairs damage to the directory structure of any volume other than the startup disk, as long as it is not write-protected.

Continued on next page...

GETTING INFO, VERIFYING OR REPAIRING DISKS

Continued from previous page.

5. Wait while your computer checks and/or repairs the selected disk or volume and its permissions. When it's done, it reports its results on the right side of the window (**Figure 38**).

✔ Tips

- Permissions determine how users can access files. If permissions are incorrectly set for a file, it may not be accessible by the users who should be able to use it.

- The startup disk is verified and, if necessary, repaired when you start your computer.

- To verify or repair your startup disk or volume, start your computer from the Mac OS X install disk. When the Installer launches, choose Installer > Disk Utility to run Disk Utility.

- To select more than one disk or volume in step 3, hold down ⌘ while clicking each item.

- Disk Utility's First Aid feature cannot repair all disk problems. For severely damaged disks, you may need to acquire third-party utilities, such as Symantec's Norton Disk Doctor or AlSoft's DiskWarrior.

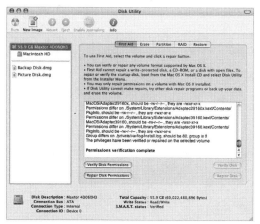

Figure 38 At the end of the verification (or repair) process, Disk Utility's First Aid feature reports results. In this example, Disk Utility has found many errors in the permission on my startup disk.

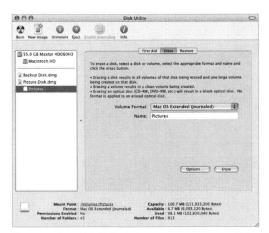

Figure 39 Use Disk Utility's Erase pane to erase a disk or volume.

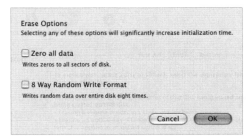

Figure 40 The Erase Options dialog offers two options for securely erasing a disk.

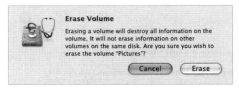

Figure 41 A dialog like this appears to confirm that you really do want to erase the volume or disk.

✖ Caution!

- Erasing a disk or volume permanently removes all data. Do not erase a disk if you think you will need any of the data it contains.

To erase a disk or volume

1. Open the Disk Utility icon in the Utilities folder (**Figure 1**).

2. In the Disk Utility window that appears, click the Erase button.

3. Select the disk or volume you want to erase (**Figure 39**).

4. Set options for the volume:

   ▲ **Volume Format** is the format applied to the volume: Mac OS Extended (Journaled), Mac OS Extended, Mac OS Standard, MS-DOS File System, or UNIX File System.

   ▲ **Name** is the name of the volume.

   ▲ **Mac OS 9 Drivers Installed** installs drivers on the disk so it can be read by computers running Mac OS 9.x. (This option is only available if you select a disk to erase.)

5. To increase security and prevent the disk from being unerased, click the Options button. Then toggle check boxes in the Erase Options dialog (**Figure 40**) for the security options you want to include and click OK:

   ▲ **Zero all data** writes zeros to the entire disk.

   ▲ **8 Way Random Write Format** writes random data over the entire disk eight times.

6. Click Erase.

7. A dialog sheet like the one in **Figure 41** appears. Click Erase.

8. Wait while your computer erases the disk or volume. A progress dialog appears as it works. When it's finished, an icon for the erased disk or volume reappears on the desktop.

Continued on next page...

ERASING DISKS & VOLUMES

Continued from previous page.

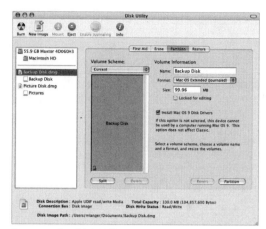

Figure 42 Use Disk Utility's Partition pane to set up partitions on a disk.

✔ Tips

- You cannot erase the startup disk. (And that's a good thing.)

- When you erase a disk, you replace all volumes on the disk with one blank volume. When you erase a volume, you replace that volume with a blank volume.

- To use the disk on a computer started with Mac OS 9, you must turn on the Mac OS 9 Drivers Installed check box in step 4. With this option turned off, you can still use the disk in the Classic environment on a computer started with Mac OS X.

- If you enable either of the Erase Options (**Figure 40**) in step 5, the disk will take considerably longer to erase.

- If you're concerned about unauthorized persons recovering data from files you erase, be sure to check out the new Secure Empty Trash command, which is covered in **Chapter 3**.

Figure 43
The Volume Scheme pop-up menu.

To partition a disk

1. Open the Disk Utility icon in the Utilities folder (**Figure 1**).

2. In the Disk Utility window that appears, click the Partition tab.

3. Select the disk you want to partition (**Figure 42**).

4. Choose an option from the Volume Scheme pop-up menu (**Figure 43**). The area beneath the pop-up menu changes (**Figure 44**).

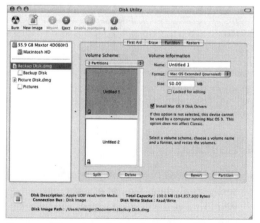

Figure 44 When the volume scheme is set for multiple volumes, you can set options for each one.

Figure 45 If you're sure you want to change the volume scheme, click Partition.

5. In the Volume Scheme area, select a volume. Then set options in the Volume Information area as desired:

   ▲ **Name** is the name of the volume.

   ▲ **Format** is the volume format: Mac OS Extended (Journaled), Mac OS Extended, Mac OS Standard, UNIX File System, or Free Space.

   ▲ **Size** is the amount of disk space allocated to that partition.

   ▲ **Locked for editing** prevents changes to the partition's settings.

   ▲ **Install Mac OS 9 Disk Drivers** enables the disk's partitions to be read by computers running Mac OS 9.x.

6. Repeat step 5 for each partition.

7. Click Partition.

8. A warning dialog like the one in **Figure 45** appears. Click Partition.

9. Wait while your computer erases the disk and creates the new partitions. When it's finished, icons for each formatted partition appear on the desktop.

✖ Caution!

■ As warned in **Figure 45**, saving new volumes will erase all existing volumes, thus erasing data.

✔ Tips

■ If you select Free Space as the format for any partition in step 5, that partition cannot be used to store files.

■ You can also change the partition size in step 5 by dragging the divider between partitions in the Volume Scheme area.

PARTITIONING DISKS

To create a blank disk image file

1. Open the Disk Utility icon in the Utilities folder (**Figure 1**).

2. Choose Images > New > Blank Image (**Figure 46**).

3. In the top half of the New Blank Image dialog that appears (**Figure 47**), enter a name and specify a disk location in which to save the disk image file.

4. Set options in the bottom part of the dialog:

   ▲ **Size** is the size of the disk. Choose an option from the pop-up menu (**Figure 48**). If you choose Custom, use a dialog sheet (**Figure 49**) to set the size.

   ▲ **Encryption** is file encryption to apply to the disk image file. Choose an option from the menu. The selections are none and AES-128.

   ▲ **Format** refers to the type of disk image. Make sure read/write disk image is chosen.

5. Click Create. Disk Utility creates a disk image file to your specifications and mounts it on the desktop (**Figure 50**).

✔ Tips

- The size of a disk image file is determined by the size specified in step 4.

- Once you have created and mounted a blank disk image, you can copy items to it as if it were a regular disk. The items you copy to the disk are automatically copied into the disk image file. Copying files is discussed in **Chapter 2**.

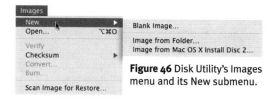

Figure 46 Disk Utility's Images menu and its New submenu.

Figure 47 Use the New Blank Image dialog to set options for a new disk image.

Figure 48
The Size pop-up menu enables you to select from a number of common disk sizes...

Figure 49
...or choose Custom and use this dialog to enter a custom size.

Figure 50
After creating the disk image, Disk Utility mounts it as a disk on your desktop. Here's the disk image created with the settings in **Figure 47**.

CREATING BLANK DISK IMAGE FILES

Figure 51 Start by selecting the folder you want to create a disk image of.

Figure 52 Use the Convert Image dialog to set options for the image file.

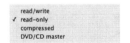

Figure 53 The Image Format pop-up menu offers several options for the type of disk image file.

To create a disk image file from a folder

1. Open the Disk Utility icon in the Utilities folder (**Figure 1**).

2. Choose Images > New > Image from Folder (**Figure 46**).

3. Use the Open dialog that appears (**Figure 51**) to locate, select, and open the folder you want to create a disk image of.

4. In the top half of the Convert Image dialog that appears (**Figure 52**), enter a name and choose a disk location for the image file.

5. In the bottom half of the dialog, set options as desired:
   ▲ **Image Format** (**Figure 53**) refers to the type of disk image.
   ▲ **Encryption** is file encryption to apply to the disk image file. Choose an option from the menu. The selections are none and AES-128.

6. Click Save. Disk Utility creates a disk image file containing the contents of the folder and mounts it on the desktop.

✔ Tips

- The size of a disk image file is determined by the amount of data in the folder and the Image Format option you chose in step 5.

- If you choose read/write from the Image Format pop-up menu (**Figure 53**), you can add files to the mounted disk image disk. Otherwise, you cannot.

CREATING DISK IMAGES FROM FOLDERS

To create a disk image file from another disk

1. Open the Disk Utility icon in the Utilities folder (**Figure 1**).

2. Choose Images > New > Image from *Disk Name* (**Figure 46**).

3. In the top half of the Convert Image dialog that appears (**Figure 52**), enter a name and choose a disk location for the image file.

4. In the bottom half of the dialog, set options as desired:

   ▲ **Image Format** (**Figure 53**) refers to the type of disk image.

   ▲ **Encryption** is file encryption to apply to the disk image file. Choose an option from the menu. The selections are none and AES-128.

5. Click Save. Disk Utility creates a disk image file containing the contents of the disk and mounts it on the desktop.

✔ Tips

■ The size of a disk image file is determined by the amount of data in the original disk and the Image Format option you chose in step 5.

■ If you choose read/write from the Image Format pop-up menu (**Figure 53**), you can add files to the mounted disk image disk. Otherwise, you cannot.

■ You cannot save a disk image file on the same disk you are creating an image of. For example, if you wanted to back up your hard disk to an image file, you must save that image to another disk.

CREATING DISK IMAGES FROM DISKS

Figure 54
A disk image file's icon.

Figure 55 Select the name of the disk image file you want to mount.

Figure 56 Use the Open dialog to locate, select, and open a disk image file.

Figure 57
The disk image's disk icon appears in the list of disks and volumes.

Figure 58 Select the disk you want to unmount.

To mount a disk image

Double-click the disk image file's icon in the Finder (**Figure 54**).

or

1. Open the Disk Utility icon in the Utilities folder (**Figure 1**).

2. Select the name of the disk image you want to mount in the list on the left side of the main window (**Figure 55**).

3. Click the Open button in the toolbar.

or

1. Open the Disk Utility icon in the Utilities folder (**Figure 1**).

2. Choose Images > Open (**Figure 46**).

3. Use the Open dialog that appears (**Figure 56**) to locate, select, and open the disk image file.

The disk image file's disk icon appears on the desktop (**Figure 50**) and, if Disk Utility is open, in the list of disks and volumes (**Figure 57**).

To unmount a disk image

In the Finder, drag the mounted disk icon to the Trash.

or

1. In the Disk Utility main window, select the icon for the disk you want to unmount (**Figure 58**).

2. Click the unmount button in the toolbar.

Although the icon disappears from the desktop, all of its contents remain in the disk image file.

MOUNTING & UNMOUNTING DISK IMAGES

To burn a CD from a disk or disk image

1. Open the Disk Utility icon in the Utilities folder (**Figure 1**).

2. In the main Disk Utility window, select the disk you want to copy to CD (**Figure 55**). The disk can be a physical disk or a disk image.

3. Click the Burn button in the toolbar.

4. A dialog like the one in **Figure 59** appears. Insert a CD-R disc in your drive as instructed and click Burn.

   Wait while Disk Utility writes to the CD. A Progress dialog like the one in **Figure 60** appears as it works. When it is finished, it ejects the disk.

✔ Tips

- You must have a Combo drive, Super-Drive, or compatible CD-ROM writer to create or "burn" CD-ROM discs.

- If a disk image file that you want to burn to CD does not appear in the Disk Utility window, mount it as instructed on the previous page. Then follow these instructions.

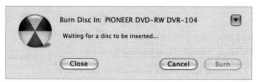

Figure 59 A dialog like this one prompts you to insert a disc.

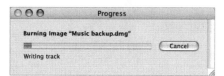

Figure 60 Disk Utility displays a Progress dialog as it creates the disc.

BURNING CDs

Figure 61 If Grab is already running, click its icon in the Dock to make it active.

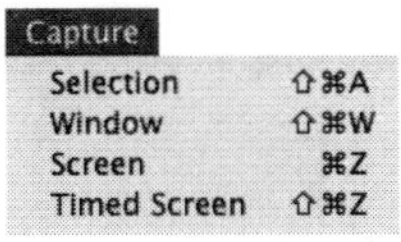

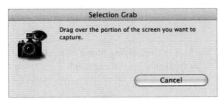

Figure 62
Grab's Capture menu.

Figure 63 The Selection Grab dialog includes instructions for selecting a portion of the screen.

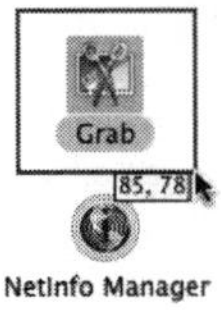

Figure 64
Use the mouse to drag a red rectangle around the portion of the screen you want to capture.

Grab

Grab is an application that can capture screen shots of Mac OS X and its applications. You tell Grab to capture what appears on your screen (or on a portion of it), and it creates a TIFF file. You can then view the TIFF file with Preview or any application capable of opening TIFFs.

✔ Tips

■ You might find screen shots helpful for documenting software—or for writing books like this one!

■ Although Grab is a useful screen shot utility, it isn't the best available for Mac OS X. Snapz Pro X, a shareware program from Ambrosia Software, is far better. If you take a lot of screen shots, be sure to check it out at www.ambrosiasw.com.

To create a screen shot

1. Set up the screen so it shows what you want to capture.

2. Open the Grab icon in the Utilities folder (**Figure 1**).

   or

   If Grab is already running, click its icon on the Dock (**Figure 61**) to make it active.

3. Choose an option from the Capture menu (**Figure 62**) or press its corresponding shortcut key:

   ▲ **Selection** ([Shift] ⌃ ⌘ [A]) enables you to capture a portion of the screen. When you choose this option, the Selection Grab dialog (**Figure 63**) appears. Use the mouse pointer to drag a box around the portion of the screen you want to capture (**Figure 64**). Release the mouse button to capture the screen.

Continued on next page...

CREATING SCREEN SHOTS

Continued from previous page.

▲ **Window** (Shift Ô ⌘ W) enables you to capture a window. When you choose this option, the Window Grab dialog (**Figure 65**) appears. Click the Choose Window button, then click the window you want to capture.

▲ **Screen** (Ô ⌘ Z) enables you to capture the entire screen. When you choose this option, the Screen Grab dialog (**Figure 66**) appears. Click outside the dialog to capture the screen.

▲ **Timed Screen** (Shift Ô ⌘ Z) enables you to capture the entire screen after a ten-second delay. When you choose this option, the Timed Screen Grab dialog (**Figure 67**) appears. Click the Start Timer button, then activate the program you want to capture and arrange onscreen elements as desired. In ten seconds, the screen is captured.

4. Grab makes a camera shutter sound as it captures the screen. The image appears in an untitled document window (**Figure 68**).

5. If you are satisfied with the screen shot, choose File > Save (**Figure 69**) or press Ô ⌘ S and use the Save As dialog sheet that appears to save it as a file on disk.

   or

   If you are not satisfied with the screen shot, choose File > Close (**Figure 69**) or press Ô ⌘ W to close the window. In the Close dialog sheet, click Don't Save.

✔ Tip

■ You can create screen shots without Grab. Press Shift Ô ⌘ 3 to capture the entire screen or Shift Ô ⌘ 4 to capture a portion of the screen. The screen shot is automatically saved on the desktop as a PDF file.

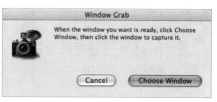

Figure 65 The Window Grab dialog tells you how to capture a window.

Figure 66 The Screen Grab dialog provides instructions for capturing the entire screen.

Figure 67 The Timed Screen Grab dialog includes a button to start the 10-second screen grab timer.

Figure 68
The image you capture—in this case, a single icon in a window—appears in a document window.

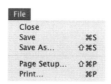

Figure 69
Grab's File menu.

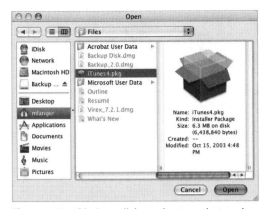

Figure 70 Use this Open dialog to locate, select, and open an Installer document file.

Installer

Installer enables you to install software in Apple Installer document files. In most cases, this program will launch automatically when you open an Installer document. You can, however, launch Installer and use its Open dialog to locate and open an installer document containing software you want to install.

✔ Tip

■ Not all software uses Apple Installer document files. Some software has its own installer or uses the Vise installer.

To install software with Installer

1. Open the Installer icon in the Utilities folder (**Figure 1**).

2. Use the Open dialog that appears (**Figure 70**) to locate and select the Installer document you want to install.

3. Click Open.

4. Follow the instructions that appear onscreen to install the software.

StuffIt Expander

StuffIt Expander is a file compression utility that expands files compressed or encoded with StuffIt (.sit), Zip (.zip), BinHex (.hqx), Tar (.tar), and other schemes. Files distributed over the Internet are commonly compressed or encoded to bundle multiple files into one file and reduce download times.

Figure 71 Drag the icon for the compressed file onto the StuffIt Expander icon.

✔ Tips

■ Developed by Aladdin Systems, Inc., StuffIt is a standard compression scheme for Mac OS computers.

■ StuffIt Expander does not compress files; it only decompresses them. To compress files, you need a program such as StuffIt Deluxe, which is available on the Aladdin Web site, www.aladdinsys.com.

■ Mac OS X 10.3's new Archive command can compress files and create .zip archives. I tell you about the Archive command in **Chapter 4**.

To expand a compressed file

Drag the icon for the compressed file onto the StuffIt Expander icon in the Utilities folder (**Figure 71**). When you release the mouse button, StuffIt Expander launches, expands the file, and quits. The expanded file appears in the same location as the original (or in another location specified in StuffIt Expander's preferences).

✔ Tip

■ When properly configured to work with Internet applications, StuffIt Expander will automatically expand downloaded files as they are received.

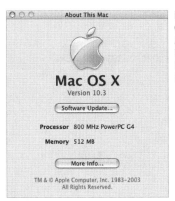

Figure 72 Clicking the More Info button in this window launches System Profiler.

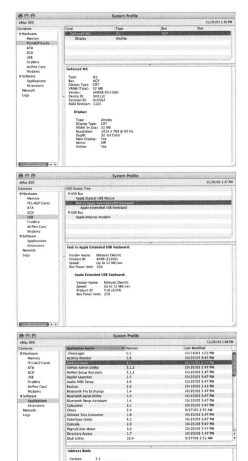

Figures 73, 74, & 75 Three examples of the information System Profiler can provide about your system.

System Profiler

The System Profiler application provides information about your computer's hardware, software, network, and logs. This information can come in handy when you are troubleshooting problems or just need to know more about the hardware and software installed on your computer.

✔ Tips

■ System Profiler was known as Apple System Profiler and had a different interface in previous versions of Mac OS X.

■ Clicking the More Info button in the About this Mac window (**Figure 72**) launches System Profiler.

To view system information

1. Open the System Profiler icon in the Utilities folder (**Figure 1**).

2. In the Contents list of the System Profiler window, click the type of information you want to view (**Figures 73** through **75**).

3. The information appears in the window.

✔ Tips

■ You can click a triangle to the left of an item in any System Profiler window to display or hide detailed information.

■ Clicking an item in the top-right portion of a System Profiler window displays details about that item (**Figures 73** through **75**).

■ You can use the File menu's Save and Print commands to save or print the information that appears in System Profiler. You might find this handy if you need to document your system's current configuration for troubleshooting or backup purposes.

VIEWING SYSTEM INFORMATION

611

Application Services

Some Mac OS X applications provide services that enable you to use content from one application with another. The content can include text, graphics, or movies. For example, the services for Grab are available from within TextEdit (**Figure 76**)—this means you can use Grab to take a screen shot and have the image appear in your TextEdit document.

Although these application services have been available in Mac OS X since its original release, not all applications support it. As a result, the Services submenu, which offers access to application services, often contains dimmed menu commands. This feature of Mac OS X will become more useful as it is adopted by applications.

Figure 76 The services for Grab are supported by TextEdit, enabling you to quickly and easily insert screen shots in a TextEdit document.

To use application services

Display the Services submenu under the application menu and choose the application and command you want.

For example, in **Figure 76**, to take a screen shot of the entire screen for placement in TextEdit, you'd choose TextEdit > Services > Grab > Screen. Grab would launch, take the screen shot, and insert it in your TextEdit document at the insertion point.

Getting Help

Getting Help

Mac OS offers two basic ways to get additional information and answers to questions as you work with your computer:

◆ **Help Tags** identify screen items as you point to them. This help feature is supported by many (but not all) applications.

◆ **Mac Help** uses the Help Viewer application to provide information about using Mac OS and Mac OS X applications. This Help feature, which is accessible through commands on the Help menu, is searchable and includes clickable links to information.

This chapter explains how to get help when you need it.

✔ Tip

■ In previous versions of Mac OS X, searching Mac Help often displayed topics and documents about multiple applications—not just the application you were using. In Mac OS X 10.3, Help has been simplified. It now displays help topics and documents for only one application at a time.

Help Tags

Help Tags identify screen elements that you point to by providing information in small yellow boxes (**Figures 1, 2,** and **3**).

✔ Tips

- Help Tags replace the Balloon Help feature available in Mac OS 9.x and earlier versions of Mac OS.

- Help Tags are especially useful when first starting out with a new software application. Pointing at various interface elements and reading Help Tags is a great way to start learning about how an application works.

To use Help Tags

Point to an item for which you want more information. If a Help Tag is available for the item, it appears after a moment (**Figures 1, 2,** and **3**).

Figure 1 A Help Tag in the Address book main window, ...

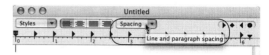

Figure 2 ...in a TextEdit document window, ...

Figure 3 ...and in the Mac Help window.

Mac Help

Mac Help uses the Help Viewer application to display information about Mac OS or a specific application. It includes several features that enable you to find information—and use it—quickly:

◆ **Main Help window** usually provides clickable links to introductory information and a table of contents.

◆ **Search feature** enables you to search for topics containing specific words or phrases.

◆ **Links to related information** enable you to move from one topic to a related topic.

◆ **Links to applications** enable you to open an application referenced by a help topic.

◆ **Links to online information** enable you to get the latest information from Apple's Web site.

✔ Tips

■ Although this feature's generic name is Mac Help, help windows normally display the name of the application that help is displayed for.

■ You can find additional support for Mac OS, as well as Apple hardware and software, on Apple's Support Web site, www.apple.com/support/ or through the AppleCare channel of Sherlock. I tell you about the Internet in **Chapter 11** and about Sherlock in **Chapter 13**.

To open Mac Help

Choose Help > *Application Name* Help
(**Figures 4a, 4b**, and **4c**), or press ⌃⌘?.

or

Click the Help button in a window or dialog
in which it appears.

The main Help window appears (**Figures 5a,
5b**, and **5c**).

To switch from one application's Help to another's

Choose an application from Help Viewer's
Library menu (**Figure 6**). The contents of the
Help window changes to display Help for the
application you chose.

✔ Tips

- The Library menu (**Figure 6**), which is
  new in Mac OS X 10.3, makes it possible
  to open an application's Help without
  opening the application.

- The applications that appear in the
  Library menu (**Figure 6**) vary depending
  on the applications for which you have
  viewed Mac Help.

To browse Mac Help

Click a link in a Help window. The window's
contents change to view information about
the item you clicked (**Figure 7**).

✔ Tip

- Links can be text or graphics. To find out
  if text is a link, point to it. The mouse
  pointer turns into a pointing finger
  (**Figure 7**).

Figures 4a, 4b, & 4c
The Help command on
Help menus for Finder
(top), Address Book
(middle), and TextEdit
(bottom).

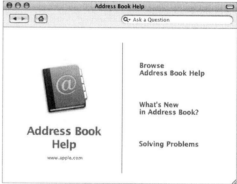

Figures 5a, 5b, & 5c The main Help windows for Finder
(top), Address Book (middle), and TextEdit (bottom).

Figure 6
The Library menu makes it easy to switch from one application's help to another's.

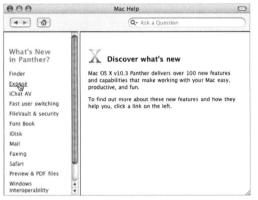

Figure 7 Clicking the What's New in Panther link in Figure 5a displays a split window with a table of contents on one side and information in the other.

Figure 8 Enter a search word or phrase in the field at the top of the Help window.

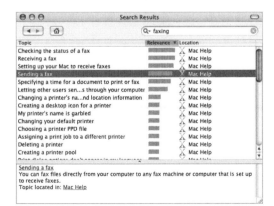

Figure 9 A list of topics matching the search criteria appears.

To search Help

1. Enter a search word, phrase, or question in the entry field at the top of the Help window (**Figure 8**) and press Return.

2. After a moment, a Search Results window appears. Click a topic to display brief information about it in the bottom of the window (**Figure 9**).

3. Double-click a topic in the search results list or click the topic's name in the bottom of the window. The topic's information appears in the window (**Figure 10**).

✔ Tips

- The bars in the Relevance column in the Search Results list (**Figure 9**) indicate how well the topics match your search word, phrase, or question. The bigger the bar, the more relevant the item.

- You can click the Back button (**Figures 9** and **10**) to view previously viewed Help windows.

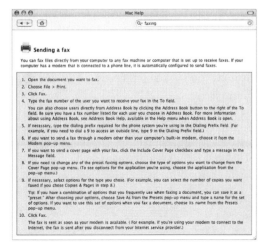

Figure 10 Clicking a link displays information as a Help topic.

Application Help

Many applications include extensive online help. The help features of various applications may look and work differently, so it's impossible to cover them in detail here. Most online help features, however, are easy to use.

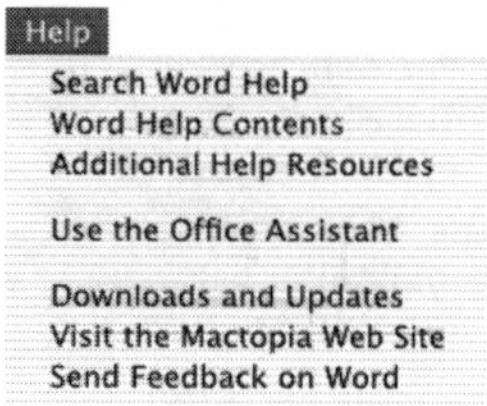

✔ Tips

■ Some applications, such as the Microsoft Office suite of products, include an entire online manual that is searchable and printable.

■ Not all applications include online help. If you can't locate an online help feature for an application, check the documentation that came with the application to see if it has one and how you can access it.

To access an application's online help

Choose a command from the Help menu within that application (**Figure 11**).

or

Click a Help button within a dialog.

Figure 11
The Help menu in Microsoft Word X offers a number of commands for getting onscreen help from within Microsoft Office or on the Microsoft Web site.

Help & Troubleshooting Advice

Here's some advice for getting help with and troubleshooting problems.

◆ **Join a Macintosh user group.** Joining a user group and attending meetings is probably the most cost-effective way to learn about your computer and get help. You can find a users' group near you by consulting the Apple User Group Web site, www.apple.com/usergroups/.

◆ **Visit Apple's Web site.** If you have access to the Web, you can find a wealth of information about your computer online. Start at www.apple.com/support/ and search for the information you need.

◆ **Visit the Web sites for the companies that develop the applications you use most.** A regular visit to these sites can keep you up to date on updates and upgrades to keep your software running smoothly. These sites can also provide technical support for problems you encounter while using the software. Learn the URLs for these sites by consulting the documentation that came with the software.

◆ **Visit Web sites that offer troubleshooting information.** MacFixIt (www.macfixit.com) and MacInTouch (www.macintouch.com) are two excellent resources.

◆ **Read Macintosh magazines.** A number of magazines, each geared toward a different level of user, can help you learn about your computer: *Macworld*, *Mac Addict*, and *Mac Home Journal* are the most popular. Stay away from PC-centric magazines; the majority of the information they provide will not apply to your Macintosh and may confuse you.

Continued on next page...

HELP & TROUBLESHOOTING ADVICE

Continued from previous page.

◆ **Buy a good troubleshooting guide.**
I highly recommend *Mac OS X Disaster Relief* and its Panther-specific revision, *Mac OS X Help Desk, Panther Edition*, a pair of Peachpit Press books by Ted Landau. I'm not recommending these books because Peachpit or Ted asked me to. I'm recommending them because I think they're the best Mac OS X trouble-shooting books around.

Menus & Keyboard Equivalents

Menus & Keyboard Equivalents

This appendix illustrates all of Mac OS X's Finder menus and provides a list of corresponding keyboard equivalents.

To use a keyboard equivalent, hold down the modifier key (usually ⌘) while pressing the keyboard key for the command.

Menus and keyboard commands are discussed in detail in **Chapter 2**.

Apple Menu

Option ⌘ Esc	Force Quit
Shift ⌘ Q	Log Out
Option ⌘ D	Dock > Turn Hiding On/Off

Finder Menu

⌘ ,	Preferences
Shift ⌘ Delete	Empty Trash
⌘ H	Hide Finder
Option ⌘ H	Hide Others
Shift ⌘ Y	Services > New Sticky Note
Shift ⌘ L	Services > Search with Google
Shift ⌘ B	Services > Send File to Bluetooth Device
Shift ⌘ *	Services > Script Editor > Get Result of AppleScript

Finder

About Finder	
Preferences...	⌘,
Empty Trash...	⇧⌘⌫
Secure Empty Trash	
Services	▶
Hide Finder	⌘H
Hide Others	⌥⌘H
Show All	

File Menu

⌘ N	New Finder Window
Shift ⌘ N	New Folder
⌘ O	Open
⌘ W	Close Window
Option ⌘ W	Close All
⌘ I	Get Info
⌘ D	Duplicate
⌘ L	Make Alias
⌘ R	Show Original
⌘ T	Add To Sidebar
Shift ⌘ T	Add To Favorites
⌘ Delete	Move To Trash
⌘ E	Eject
⌘ F	Find

File

New Finder Window	⌘N
New Folder	⇧⌘N
Open	⌘O
Open With	▶
Close Window	⌘W
Get Info	⌘I
Duplicate	⌘D
Make Alias	⌘L
Show Original	⌘R
Add To Sidebar	⌘T
Create Archive of "images"	
Move To Trash	⌘⌫
Eject	⌘E
Burn Disc...	
Find...	⌘F
Color Label:	
✕ ● ● ● ● ● ● ●	

FINDER & FILE MENUS

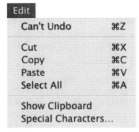

Edit Menu

⌘Z	Undo
⌘X	Cut
⌘C	Copy
⌘V	Paste
⌘A	Select All

View Menu

⌘1	as Icons
⌘2	as List
⌘3	as Columns
Option ⌘T	Show/Hide Toolbar
⌘J	Show/Hide View Options

Go Menu

⌘[	Back
⌘]	Forward
⌘↑	Enclosing Folder
Shift ⌘C	Computer
Shift ⌘H	Home
Shift ⌘K	Network
Shift ⌘I	My iDisk
Shift ⌘A	Applications
Shift ⌘U	Utilities
Shift ⌘G	Go to Folder
⌘K	Connect to Server

Window Menu

⌘⌘M   Minimize Window

Option ⌘⌘M   Minimize All Windows

Window	
Minimize Window	⌘M
Bring All to Front	
images	
✓ Applications	
AppleScript	

Help Menu

⌘⌘?   Mac Help

Help	
Mac Help	⌘?

WINDOW & HELP MENUS

Index

INDEX

INDEX

INDEX

INDEX

windows *(continued)*
  buttons/controls for manipulating, 33
  changing view for, 55
  closing, 132
  creating, 129
  identifying unsaved changes in, 135
  minimizing, 37, 138–139
  moving, 36
  opening/closing, 34
  resizing, 36
  scrolling contents of, 38
  snapping icons to grid in, 31, 88, 92
  sorting contents of, 57
  truncation of file names in, 58
  zooming, 37, 138
Windows File Sharing option, 406

wireless networking, 427. *See also* Bluetooth
Word Format option, 207
word processors, 119, 189
word wrap, 192, 193
World Wide Web, 315. *See also* Web pages; Web sites
worms, 344
wrap, word, 192, 193
Wrap Around check box, 203, 204
Write only (Drop Box) privileges, 416, 417
write privileges, 63
write-protected disks, 63

Y

Yellow Pages channel, Sherlock, 391

Your Apple ID window, 10, 15
Your Internet Connection window, 13
Your Local Area Network window, 13
Your Phone Service window, 14, 16

Z

.Z file extension, 531
zcat command, 531
ZIP compression, 116
Zip disks, 68, 70
.zip file extension, xv, 116, 610
zoom button, 33, 37
Zoom command, 138
Zoom feature, 578